GPSS Primer

GPSS
Primer

Stanley Greenberg

Wiley-Interscience, a Division of John Wiley & Sons, Inc.
New York • London • Sydney • Toronto

To Jean

Preface

GPSS has become the leading computer simulation language because it is widely available and can be applied effectively, yet easily, to a broad range of problems. However, the number of people familiar with GPSS—and their average level of mastery—would probably be much greater if a comprehensive, *easy to understand* explanation of GPSS were available. That is the "mission" of the *GPSS Primer*.

The *GPSS Primer*, like GPSS itself, is suitable for use by nonprogrammers. Its overriding aim is to painlessly impart to the reader a reasonably complete knowledge of GPSS—what it is, how to use it, how it works, and the kinds of problems to which it can be applied. Hopefully, these remarks will encourage the would-be GPSS student to have a go at it. But they serve also to call attention to the fact that this book has a guiding philosophy that was translated into the following objectives:

- Keep the reader oriented at all times with regard to what is being discussed, how it fits into the scheme of things, and what he should know.

- Use concrete examples and step-by-step explanations to convey a clear understanding of, and feel for, the topic at hand.

It is surprising that the need for a basic book on GPSS has gone so long unfilled. Perhaps the closest thing is IBM's *GPSS Education Guide,* a document that is available only to students of IBM's intensive courses in GPSS and which is slanted toward people with a programming background. Otherwise, the only available exposition of GPSS is the manufacturers' manuals which are intended primarily for reference by persons already familiar with GPSS. By contrast, the *GPSS Primer* is designed for persons having no prior knowledge of GPSS or computer simulation techniques and without the benefit of instruction or assistance outside this book.

The *GPSS Primer* is oriented toward GPSS/360, but it also covers GPSS III, Flow Simulator, GPS K, and GPSS V to varying degrees. And it is generally applicable to any version that is based on these five versions. The degree to which the five versions are covered and the way in which their differences are handled are explained in detail in Section 1.2.

The Introduction, utilizing a question-and-answer format, has been placed ahead of Chapter 1 to convey some important facts about GPSS and some general information about this book. You are urged to read it.

This first edition of the *GPSS Primer* may contain minor inaccuracies, especially since periodic revisions to GPSS render certain items obsolete. However, it is emphasized that the value of the *GPSS Primer* lies not in its exposition of programming details but in its ability to *efficiently endow the reader with a reasonably thorough understanding of GPSS,* after which it is a simple matter to validate a few stray details or even to assimilate more advanced material. Thus it is felt that this book can serve as a basically useful text until such time as GPSS is drastically changed or superseded altogether.

The *GPSS Primer* started as a graduate school project whose objective was to provide a palatable explanation of GPSS for computer science students who were befuddled by the available manuals. The project was carried out and subsequently expanded in scope and orientation to the present end product with the encouragement and assistance of Dr. Valdemars Punga,[1] to whom I am most grateful. I would also like to thank Mr. Julian Reitman[2] for his very sound advice with regard to the makeup of the *GPSS Primer*.

Stanley Greenberg

September 1971

---

[1] Professor-in-Charge of the Computer Science Program at the Hartford Graduate Center of Rensselaer Polytechnic Institute.

[2] Chief of System Simulator Group at the Norden Division of the United Aircraft Corporation.

Tables

Illustrations

Contents

GPSS Primer

Introduction

This section is designed as a question-and-answer session that presumably takes place between reader and author. Its purpose is twofold: (1) to tell you a little about GPSS and (2) to tell you about the *GPSS Primer*.

About GPSS

What does "GPSS" stand for?

Believe it or not, this question does not have a single four-word answer. GPSS stands for *General Purpose Simulation System* in GPSS/360 and GPSS V, but it stands for *General Purpose Systems Simulator* in GPSS III. GPS K stands for *General Purpose Simulator K,* and *Flow Simulator* is RCA's name for GPSS.

Are the abovementioned versions of GPSS the only ones available, and how do they compare to one another?

This question is answered fully in Section 1.2, but an abbreviated reply can be given here. There exist several other versions of GPSS; they are all based on either GPSS III or GPSS/360 except for GPSS II which was outmoded by GPSS III. GPSS/360 is an extension of GPSS III, and GPSS V is an extension of GPSS/360. GPS K is comparable to GPSS/360, and Flow Simulator is more or less a cross between GPSS III and GPSS/360.

Why has GPSS become the most prominent computer simulation language?

To put it succinctly, GPSS has received a substantial amount of exposure, and it is a very good simulation tool. To elaborate on the first reason, its development has been pioneered and its use promoted by IBM; this has made the latest versions of it available to a large proportion of computer users and students. In addition, most of the other major computer manufacturers and a number of time sharing services also offer GPSS or soon will. As far as the second reason is concerned, the advantages of GPSS are expounded to some extent in the next few answers (yes, the questions are "rigged") and more fully in the text.

How would you describe GPSS?

GPSS is an application-oriented (rather than machine-oriented) digital computer simulation language which features an elaborate software package that is designed to simplify matters for the user. He translates his problem into a conceptual model which takes the form of a *block diagram* expressed as a GPSS program. And then his program is processed by the GPSS software package.

What is the GPSS software package like?

To oversimplify, it consists of a collection of program segments that reside on an auxiliary storage device. When a user's GPSS program is input, appropriate segments of the package are "called" as needed to (1) verify and deploy the model (defined by the user's program) in the computer's memory section, (2) execute a simulation run, (3) maintain appropriate system statistics, and (4) produce a suitable output.

It seems that the built-in GPSS programs do most of the work for you.

That is the general idea. They handle all of the tedious details such as keeping track of the position and status of every item in the simulated system, accumulating and printing appropriate statistical data, and causing events to occur in proper sequence. As a result, the user's program is uncluttered by the numerous instructions that would be needed to specify these operations in a language such as FORTRAN, and his program tends to "look like" the system being simulated. More important, the user is able to concentrate on the analysis and formulation of his model rather than becoming embroiled in programming details.

Evidently the user has nothing to do except translate his system into a GPSS model. Is that also the "general idea"?

Essentially, yes. He should know something about the inner workings of GPSS if he is to be proficient at building GPSS models. But for the most part, he can confine his attention to the predefined inventory of GPSS *blocks* and the rules for using them to construct models. After the model has been formulated — which is to say that a GPSS program has been written — the GPSS software package takes over.

Just what is involved in translating a system into a GPSS program?

This question cannot be satisfactorily answered at this point because any reply that is very brief — and yet is not a vague generality — must include various terms and concepts associated with simulation models and GPSS. That would tell you nothing and would raise other questions prematurely. Thus it is more prudent to refer you to the first few chapters; they provide an ample appreciation of how one translates a real or postulated system into a GPSS program.

Incidentally, some of the previous responses contain a few terms whose meanings may have eluded you, such as "system statistics" and "blocks." These are also explained in the first few chapters.

About the GPSS Primer

For whom is the GPSS Primer intended?

It is intended for students, programmers, analysts, and others who know little or nothing about GPSS and would like to become partially, substantially, or thoroughly familiar with it. This book should also enable persons who "know a little GPSS" to do much more with it.

How may the GPSS Primer be used?

It can be used as a self-teaching book or as a text for a course in GPSS, computer simulation techniques, computing languages, and so on. Used as a textbook, it should minimize the amount of time spent by the instructor explaining GPSS, thus allowing him to devote more class time to applications of it or to other topics.

What is the role of the GPSS Primer in relation to the manufacturers' manuals?

The *GPSS Primer* is not intended as a complete substitute for the appropriate manuals, but rather as a prelude and supplement to them. After reading the *GPSS Primer,* you will know most of what there is to know about the operation and use of GPSS, and you will be able to build models and write nontrivial programs. But you will have to consult the manual for certain details and for explanations of some of the features not covered here.

Will this book actually enable a novice to write practical GPSS programs?

It will indeed. Someone with no prior knowledge of GPSS should (1) have a good idea of what GPSS is all about and what kinds of problems it can be applied to after reading the first three chapters and, perhaps, skimming a few others; (2) be able to write useful programs by the time he is halfway through this book; (3) possess a good understanding of how GPSS works and be able to write fairly sophisticated programs by the time he has finished it.

This implies that the reader should start at the beginning and progress as far as necessary to attain his desired level of knowledge. Is that how the GPSS Primer is supposed to be used?

For the most part, yes. Someone with no prior knowledge of GPSS should start with Chapter 1 and proceed through the book, chapter by chapter. Depending on his purposes, he may pass over certain material along the way, for instance, details concerning the inner workings of GPSS or sections pertaining to versions of GPSS other than the one in which he is interested. A nonbeginner may start wherever he wishes, and he may use this book for reference purposes. To facilitate its use in that mode, a detailed index, lists of illustrations and tables, and several summary-type appendices have been provided.

How is the GPSS Primer organized?

Chapters 1 and 2 provide a background and introduction to GPSS model building and program writing which, you will find out, are the same thing. Chapters 3 to 7 present some of the basic concepts and components of GPSS in conjunction with illustrative programs. Chapter 8 deals with the underlying logical structure and inner workings of GPSS. Chapters 9 to 14 cover additional concepts and elements and include several more illustrative programs. Chapter 15 summarizes the contents of this book, and it also tells what aspects of GPSS were not covered. Lastly, there are eight appendix sections that should not be overlooked.

In general, the first half of this book (Chapters 1 to 7) can more properly be called a "primer" than can the second half. It is concerned with the basic ingredients of GPSS, the kinds of problems to which it can be applied, and how to use it. The second half of this book (Chapters 8 to 14) deals with some of the subtler aspects and features of GPSS and provides a deeper insight into its structure.

It sounds like illustrative programs have been used as the focus for much of the discussion. What is the advantage of this approach?

This is an important point; thanks for asking. If an actual GPSS program is displayed and explained step by step, the reader can *see* how GPSS programs are formulated, structured, and coded. He can acquire a *feel* for GPSS as he learns about its components and features. This enables him to digest the material as it is presented instead of choking on dozens of precisely defined concepts and terms that remain meaningless until he is able to work with programs and put things into perspective.

How else is the GPSS Primer learner-oriented?

This book is organized in a natural learning sequence; thus a topic is initially presented in a simplified manner that is easily grasped and is then elaborated upon and explained in more rigorous terms. Topics are summarized *after* they have been covered because a detailed synopsis of an unfamiliar topic is seldom meaningful; indeed, it may inhibit comprehension. The writing style is informal and tutorial – almost conversational. The overall effect (or, at least, intention) is to *minimize the total amount of time and effort required to learn GPSS*.

Why do the manuals pose problems for beginners?

The manuals are generally organized so that each chapter is devoted to one aspect of GPSS and covers it fully with precise definitions, rules, exceptions to rules, special cases, and so on. The information is logically organized and is presented in a terse, highly efficient manner. This is fine for the knowledgeable reader who seeks specific information. But a beginner, who requires orientation, perspective, and palpable explanations, finds himself immersed in a multitude of abstractions that cannot be fathomed until he can somehow work his way through enough chapters to unravel the pieces and put them in their proper places. This is obviously a difficult and inefficient way to learn GPSS.

Is that all?

Almost. It should be pointed out that many facts are repeated and points reiterated in order to impress their meaning clearly upon the reader and also to instill a comfortable feeling of familiarity with them. This approach tends to lend a somewhat repetitious and wordy quality to the text which may seem excessive to some nonbeginners. However, I firmly believe that it contributes significantly to the main objective of this book, which is to convey an understanding of GPSS with a minimum expenditure of time and effort by the reader – if I may repeat myself!

CHAPTER 1
Background

The purpose of this chapter is to lay the foundation for a study of GPSS. The development of computer simulation languages is traced with special emphasis on GPSS, naturally enough. Current versions of GPSS are briefly described, and the applicability of the *GPSS Primer* to them is spelled out.

Basic concepts such as *system* and *simulation model* are discussed, primarily as they pertain to GPSS. Simulation models are classified in two ways, again with an eye toward GPSS. Then several typical GPSS applications are described to demonstrate the kinds of problems to which GPSS can be applied and the way in which problems are translated into GPSS simulation models and computer programs.

The last section in this chapter is a summary. The practice of summarizing each chapter is followed throughout this book. The summaries are not always confined to the material in their respective chapters. Besides tying things together and providing a valuable perspective, they sometimes contain new information.

1.1 EVOLUTION OF COMPUTER SIMULATION LANGUAGES

The use of digital computers for simulation and modeling has increased dramatically during the past decade. One of the main reasons for this is the advent and continuing improvement of problem-oriented simulation languages such as GPSS. GPSS is an IBM-developed language which has undergone several revisions since its introduction around 1961. The development of GPSS is discussed further following a thumbnail sketch of the history of computer simulation.

The 1950s and Earlier

Military planning and the development of military systems provided the major impetus for the initial growth of simulation. Aircraft and submarine simulators were first developed in the 1940s, and Monte Carlo analysis came into prominence during the late 1940s in connection with nuclear shielding problems. Game theory and operations research also grew in importance during that period and in the 1950s. All of these areas have gradually become closely tied to digital computers.

Analog computers, which are inherently simulation devices, were relatively popular in the 1950s. The digital computer was also being used for simulation throughout this period although early applications were relatively limited.

Most of the computer languages of the 1950s and 1960s have probably been used for simulation problems to greater or lesser extents. In the late 1950s and early 1960s, general-purpose computational languages such as ALGOL and FORTRAN were probably the most widely used simulation languages. During this period, numerous special-purpose simulation languages were developed to deal with specific areas such as war games and inventory management.

The 1960s — Enter Simulation Languages

As the benefits of digital computer simulation became more widely recognized, the need for better languages increased. The existing languages were too specialized, and they were not easily learned. At the same time, it had become evident that many techniques and logical elements were common to a wide variety of simulation problems. Thus it was that the early 1960s saw the advent of several new general purpose simulation languages. Most were adaptations of FORTRAN (e.g., SIMSCRIPT, DYNAMO, GASP) or ALGOL (e.g., SIMULA). Some were entirely new—for instance, GPS, which soon evolved into GPSS.

What are the advantages of these general purpose *simulation* languages compared to ordinary general-purpose *programming* languages? Perhaps the main advantage is that they incorporate means for controlling the sequence in which events occur. This aspect of simulation models introduces many complexities when an ordinary programming language is being used. There is much room for minor errors which may produce obscure effects that are difficult to detect and eradicate.

Another advantage of simulation languages is that their diagnostic programs can check for logical errors as well as syntax and capacity violations. They usually have built-in provisions for collecting and printing out at least some of the statistical outputs desired from simulation models. And they are usually closer than nonsimulation languages in outward appearance and structure to the actual situation being simulated.

General-purpose simulation languages such as GPSS were developed with the following objectives in mind:

1. To provide a generalized structure for designing simulation models.
2. To provide a rapid way of converting a simulation model into a computer program.
3. To provide a rapid way of making changes in the simulation model that can be readily incorporated into the program.
4. To provide an expeditious way of obtaining useful outputs for analysis.

Perhaps the major disadvantage of most general-purpose simulation languages is that they require a large-scale computer. For example, GPSS/360 is designed for computers with core capacities of 64K or greater, and Flow Simulator is designed for computers of 65K or greater. This is one of the reasons why FORTRAN was the language most often used to write simulation programs in the late 1960s. Another reason is that FORTRAN is very widely used, and programmers naturally tend to go with what they have available and what they know best.

At the present time there are dozens of simulation languages, but most are special-purpose types which are not widely used. Typical of these are ESP, FORSIM, GSP, MILITRAN, MONTECODE, OPS, QUICKSCRIPT, SIMON, SIMPAC, SOL, and WASP. Incidentally, several of these were developed and are used almost exclusively in the United Kingdom.

It is probably correct to say that the major simulation languages in the United States today include GPSS, SIMSCRIPT, SIMULA, and DYNAMO. Of these, GPSS (in its several versions) is the most widely used.

1.2 DEVELOPMENT OF GPSS AND VERSIONS IN USE

One purpose of this section is to give a brief history of GPSS and to acquaint you with the versions presently in use. Another aim is to state which versions of GPSS are covered in the *GPSS Primer* and to explain how we plan to deal with the differences that exist among them.

Evolution of GPSS

GPSS had its origins in some network analysis work that was carried out at the Bell Telephone Laboratories in the late 1950s. Geoffrey Gordon of IBM, J. P. Runyon of Bell Telephone Laboratories, and D. L. Dietmeyer of the University of Wisconsin were instrumental in developing a computer language to perform the desired simulations. Gordon, along with Barbieri and Efron of IBM, further developed and generalized this language. It was called GPS (General Purpose System Simulator), and it was made available late in 1961 to be used on the IBM 704, 709, and 7090. Incidentally, it was sometimes referred to as the "Gordon Simulator" by people who tried to adapt its logical structure or other features to their own particular needs.

GPSS II came on the scene around 1963 as an extension and improvement of GPS, which had begun to be called GPSS. At this time it was strictly an IBM language, not counting the few instances where it may have been adapted to run on other equipment. GPSS II was designed to run on the IBM 7090/94 and 7040/44.

GPSS III became available in 1966, and it was also designed to run on the larger second-generation IBM computers. GPSS III is substantially different from GPSS II; it has more features, runs faster, and is easier to use.

GPSS/360 became available in 1968, and it runs on most models of the IBM 360 which have memory sizes of 64K or larger. GPSS V became available at the end of 1970, and it runs on most models of the IBM 370 series. GPSS V is essentially a refinement and expansion of GPSS/360, which is a refinement and expansion of GPSS III.

Versions of GPSS Currently in Use

GPSS/360 is currently[1] the most widely used version of GPSS, and it is probably the best developed version offered by a hardware manufacturer except, of course, for GPSS V. Its predecessor, GPSS III, was designed to operate on the IBM 7040/44 and 7090/94 computers; it was also adapted to run on some CDC 3600 computers.

Flow Simulator, RCA's version of GPSS, is designed to run on the Spectra 70 computer. It is more or less a cross between GPSS III and GPSS/360, although it incorporates a few features of its own. Despite its different name, Flow Simulator is a bona fide version of GPSS in both its outward appearance and its internal structure.

GPS K is offered by Honeywell and is designed to operate on the Model 1200 or larger central processors of their Series 200 computers. GPS K is very similar to GPSS/360 in both its outward appearance and the features it includes.

GPSS II runs on the Univac 1108 as well as on the IBM 7040/44/90/94 computers. It is not very widely used today because it is substantially less efficient and powerful than the newer versions of GPSS, not to mention that it runs on machines that have become obsolete to a degree.

In addition to IBM, RCA, Honeywell, Univac, and CDC, several other computer manufacturers have recently introduced — or plan to offer — versions of GPSS that are patterned on GPSS III or GPSS/360. It would seem safe to say that a high percentage of the big computers in the United States will be equipped with software to run GPSS during the 1970s. And the appearance of improved versions of GPSS during this period will further contribute to the growing use and usefulness of GPSS.

All of the versions mentioned up to this point are software packages offered by equipment manufacturers to operate on their larger machines. But the most advanced version of GPSS today is one that has been developed under the direction of Julian Reitman at the Norden Division of the United Aircraft Corporation. This version is called *GPSS/360-Norden;* as its name implies, it is an expanded version of GPSS/360.[2] The major improvements incorporated into GPSS/360-Norden relative to GPSS/360 are:

1. The size of a simulation model is not limited to something that can be contained in the computer's core memory. Sections of the model as well as banks of data can be stored on direct access devices and used during the simulation run. This effectively increases the total memory to the point where models of virtually any size can be handled.

2. The output produced during or at the end of a simulation run can be displayed on a CRT unit rather than being limited to printouts. The user can also debug, modify, and monitor his model in an interactive mode by means of the CRT device.

[1] As of mid-1971.
[2] The powerful capabilities of GPSS/360-Norden are available on a national basis through the CSS Time Sharing Service.

These extensions of GPSS/360 greatly enhance its power as a simulation tool.[3] However, their significance can hardly be appreciated by the reader who is not even familiar with "unextended" GPSS and who is not exactly an authority on the concept of "simulation models." In other words, these things will mean much more to you later.

Applicability of GPSS Primer to Various Versions of GPSS

The *GPSS Primer* is designed to provide a clear picture of what GPSS is, how it works, and how to use it effectively. The treatment is by no means superficial; on the other hand, this book does not go into every detailed aspect—nor does it cover every special feature—of GPSS. As a result it possesses an elementary and general quality that makes it at least somewhat applicable to any version of GPSS.

Let us be more specific. Since GPSS/360, GPS K, Flow Simulator, and GPSS III are the most widely used contemporary versions of GPSS, this book has been devoted specifically to them with an emphasis on GPSS/360. The reasons for taking this approach will be given shortly, but first we describe it more fully:

1. In this book *all four versions of GPSS* always mean *GPSS/360, GPS K, Flow Simulator,* and *GPSS III.* For convenience, we do not bother to acknowledge the existence of other versions every time.

2. Every chapter in this book (except this one) is devoted primarily to GPSS/360. For example, the illustrative programs are written in GPSS/360.

3. The next-to-last section in almost every chapter deals with the significant differences between GPSS/360 and the other three versions with respect to the material presented in that particular chapter.

4. Remarks about GPSS III, GPS K, and Flow Simulator may be made at any point where they logically belong, not just in the next-to-last section of each chapter. For example, an effort has been made to point out which GPSS/360 features are not found in GPSS III and Flow Simulator so that users of the latter versions can skip or skim that material.

Now let us explain why this approach was taken. To begin with, why limit this book to GPSS/360, GPS K, GPSS III, and Flow Simulator? Except for GPSS II, all versions of GPSS in use at the present time are extremely similar to the four versions covered here. Since GPSS II differs substantially from these four versions, and since it is somewhat outmoded, it has been omitted.

Why orient this book toward one version, and why is that version GPSS/360? The typical reader is interested in one version and not the other three. He would be inconvenienced and distracted by any attempt to give equal time to all four versions. This suggests that it is best to confine the discussion of GPSS to a single version and to relate the other versions to it elsewhere. The feasibility of this approach is supported by the following facts:

---

[3] GPSS V incorporates some of the capabilities of GPSS/360-Norden, particularly in the area of permitting models whose size exceeds the computer's core capacity.

1. There is one version that is of interest to the majority of readers, namely, GPSS/360. It is the most widely used version of GPSS today, and it is the best version to learn in anticipation of the more advanced versions that will be offered in the coming years.

2. GPSS/360 is, to put it unscientifically, equal to or greater than the other three versions. To be more specific, GPS K is approximately the same as GPSS/360 while Flow Simulator and GPSS III are essentially subsets of it.

So the rationale for orienting the *GPSS Primer* toward GPSS/360 can be boiled down to this:

1. It is advisable to concentrate on a single version as a practical matter.

2. There happens to be one version — GPSS/360 — that is especially well suited to this role.

One consequence of this approach is a tendency to compare the four versions of GPSS. This is not the intention of the author. Another consequence is that GPS K, Flow Simulator, and GPSS III are covered in a somewhat fragmented fashion and not quite so thoroughly as GPSS/360. However, this should not pose any problems to the reader since the manufacturer's manual(s) can be readily consulted to obtain additional details if the need arises.

What about GPSS V? As indicated earlier, GPSS V is basically an extension of GPSS/360, and it was made available by IBM late in 1970. These two facts have made it advisable to handle GPSS V in the following manner in the *GPSS Primer:*

Summarize the differences between GPSS V and GPSS/360 in the appendix — Appendix H, to be exact — and not discuss GPSS V elsewhere in the text.

The GPSS V-oriented reader is advised to read this book with the intention of learning GPSS/360. And then he should read Appendix H to bridge the gap between GPSS/360 and GPSS V.

1.3 MODELING AND COMPUTERIZED SIMULATION

Thus far, we have dealt with nontechnical matters such as the evolution of simulation languages and the orientation of this book. Now we can begin to address ourselves to the subject of computer simulation. This section introduces some fundamental concepts in a general and somewhat theoretical way, and Section 1.4 describes several typical GPSS simulation models.

Systems and Simulation Models

The terms "model" and "system" are basic to any discussion of simulation, but they are only vaguely understood buzz-words to those who have never formally defined a system or built a model. By the same token, it is not obvious to the uninitiated that a computer can be programmed to behave as a simulation model. And, while we are at it, what is meant by the *behavior* of a model?

An effort is made to answer these questions and bring the relevant concepts into reasonably sharp focus in this section and in the remainder of this chapter. However, a really firsthand appreciation of such topics as model building can be gained only by actual experience. The illustrative programs in this book are, in a sense, an attempt to provide some of this experience vicariously.

Let us start off by considering a simple example which illustrates the concepts of *system, model,* and *simulation.* The example concerns a planned tollbooth plaza that must have enough booths to accommodate rush-hour traffic. Based on rough estimates, it is thought that two regular booths and one exact-change booth will suffice for the northbound lanes. (The determination of booths for the southbound lane can be treated as a separate, though similar, problem.)

At this point, the problem can be expressed as follows. What would happen during the peak traffic period if one exact-change and two regular tollbooths were installed across the northbound lanes? If this arrangement is found satisfactory, the problem is solved. If not, it becomes one of determining the suitability of some other combination of regular and exact-change booths.

You may have noticed that we have not talked about finding an *optimum* solution. Instead, we spoke of trying to ascertain whether a proposed solution was acceptable. The former approach is exemplified by analytical models, and the latter approach is taken in simulation. The distinction between the two approaches is explained further in the next section.

Let us temporarily put aside our tollbooth problem in order to define the concept of *system.* Then we can apply this definition to our example.

A system is an assemblage of interrelated objects around which we can conceptually draw a boundary. Having done this, we can identify the links between the system and its external environment. (These links can be envisioned as paths which cross the system boundary.) We can thereafter limit our attention to the objects which lie inside of the boundary and to the activities that take place therein.

A system can be defined in connection with our tollbooth scenario as shown in Figure 1-1. The static objects in the system are tollbooths. The paths that cross the boundary are the vehicles which enter and leave the system. In this problem, we do not care about the vehicles that leave the system, but we are very much interested in those that enter it. In particular, we are interested in the rate at which they arrive and whether they have exact change.

We can define an equivalent *closed* system by inserting within its boundaries a source and sink for vehicles. The source is a device that generates vehicles at the rate at which they arrive during the peak period, and the sink erases them.

Vehicles are created at a specified rate, and a certain percentage of them have exact change. They select the most promising lanes with the restriction that drivers without exact change cannot choose an exact-change booth. They require varying amounts of time to pay their tolls. Then they are of no further interest and are removed from the system.

We succeeded in closing the system boundary—thus making the system completely self-contained—by the simple expedient of incorporating an appropriate generator and destroyer of traffic within it. This strategy can always be applied

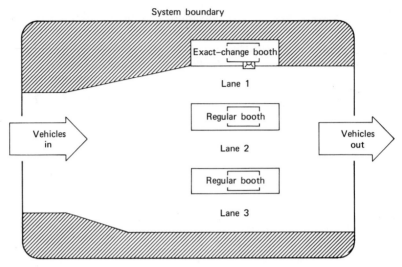

Fig. 1-1. System diagram for toll plaza problem.

to a system that consists of static objects through which units of traffic (or particles) move. As you will see, GPSS involves precisely such systems!

After a system has been defined, the next step is to build a model of it. Unfortunately, the use of the verb "build" suggests a physical object such as a scale model. But we can also *build* (or *construct* or *formulate* or *devise* or *develop*) mathematical or computer models of a real system. For instance, the equation $F = ma$ is a model of the motion of an object in field-free space. We could impart an acceleration to this object and measure the force required. Or we could plug values into the equation of motion to find the force required. This equation is a genuine model of the real system, since it behaves exactly as the real system does. To put it another way, it *simulates* the real system.

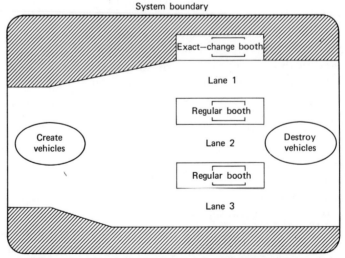

Fig. 1-2. Closed system diagram for toll plaza problem.

It is evident that *model* and *simulation* are closely related concepts. In broad terms, simulation is a technique that involves setting up a model of a real (or potentially real) situation and then performing experiments on that model. The model is amenable to manipulations that would be impossible, too expensive, or too impractical to perform on the system it portrays. The operation of the model can be studied, and from it properties of the actual system can be inferred. These remarks serve as a very general description of simulation models. For our purposes, a more useful definition would be the following:

Simulation is a way of using a computer to produce a reasonable model of a system under study. This model takes the form of a program which contains entities representing the elements of the real system. In executing the program, the computer emulates the behavior of the system. It also keeps track of what happens at various points in the system and accumulates statistics as the run progresses. It produces an output from which the behavior of the model can be deduced.

If you have never worked with computer simulation models, you probably find it difficult to visualize how a computer program can (1) represent a system (such as a toll plaza) and (2) cause a computer to emulate the behavior of this system. It may also be difficult to appreciate the use of the term "statistics" and how one deduces the behavior of a model from them. Most of these things, especially the notion of a computer program as a simulation model, should become clear by the end of Chapter 3 or 4.

Mathematical versus Simulation Models

It is instructive to consider the main similarities and differences between mathematical (or analytical) models and simulation models. Some of the similarities are:

1. Both approaches require a thorough understanding of the process being modeled.
2. Both approaches involve the formulation of an abstract model which represents a concrete situation.
3. The translation of a real situation into either type of model reflects the user's concept of what the key elements of the system are and how they interact.
4. There are many problems that are amenable to either approach.

Some differences between mathematical and simulation models are:

1. The mathematical model yields an analytical solution, whereas the simulation model shows what happens under a particular set of assumptions and does not yield a "solution" in the usual sense of the word.
2. A mathematical model, in order to be soluble, is often so gross a simplification of the actual situation as to yield invalid results. Simulation usually permits a less abstract and relatively more faithful representation of a real system.

Continuous versus Discrete-Event Models

Digital computer simulation models may be either *continuous-change* or *discrete-event* types. Continuous-change models are appropriate when the analyst considers the system he is studying as consisting of a continuous flow of information or material counted in the aggregate rather than as individual items. Such models are naturally suited to analog simulation so long as the dimensions of the problem do not exceed the capabilities of the analog machine. Continuous-change models can be simulated on digital computers by using finite-difference equations which, in the limit, approach the differential equations of continuous flow. Probably the best-known continuous-change digital computer simulation language is *DYNAMO*.

In discrete-event (or discrete-change) models the changes in the state of the system are conceptualized as discrete rather than continuous. These models can be conceived of as network flow systems which are characterized as follows:

1. The system contains components, each of which performs definite and prescribed functions.

2. Items flow through the system from one component to another, requiring the performance of an operation at a component before the item can move on to the next component.

3. Components have finite capacity to process the items; therefore, items may have to wait in line before reaching a particular component.

The computation in this type of simulation consists to a large extent of keeping track of where individual items are at any particular time and moving them along from component to component. The results of a simulation run take the form of statistics which describe the behavior of the simulated system during the run and indicate how many items pass through the system in a given period of simulated time.

Some of the major analytical disciplines associated with discrete-change simulations are queuing, stochastic processes, and frequency distributions. The basic elements in these simulations are the components that comprise the model and the items or units that flow through the model. Prominent discrete-change simulation languages are GPSS, GASP, SIMSCRIPT, SIMULA, and CSL. The foregoing remarks about discrete-change simulation models can be regarded as a conceptual description of GPSS.

1.4 APPLICATIONS OF GPSS AND TYPES OF RESULTS OBTAINED

We have said that GPSS is a discrete-event language that can be used to simulate any system that can be idealized as a network through which particles move. Prior to that we discussed a problem that could be solved using GPSS; namely, the tollbooth plaza. So at this point you should have a partial idea of the kinds of problems to which GPSS can be applied.

The main purpose of this section is to better acquaint you with the kinds of systems that can be simulated with GPSS. Another purpose is to provide some insight into the process by which a problem is translated into a system which is the basis for a GPSS model.

Bank Teller Problem

The Mudville Citizens Bank had experienced excellent growth until recently. Bank officials found that long waiting lines often developed and that the word had gotten around. They considered various ways of alleviating the problem, and two emerged as being worthy of serious consideration. One approach was to add one or two new teller's cages. The other was to have all customers wait in a single line so that the person at the head of the line would always walk over to the first teller who became available.

The "extra tellers" approach was more conventional, but it would be a good deal more expensive. The single line approach was intriguing, but no one was very confident that it would substantially reduce the average customer waiting time. At this point it was suggested that one more teller plus the single-line scheme might be an attractive solution. Bank officials now had four specific alternatives to evaluate:

1. Add one teller's cage.
2. Add two cages.
3. Switch to a single waiting line.
4. Add one teller's cage and switch to a single waiting line.

Fortunately for the president of the Mudville Citizens Bank, his son, Harvey, worked in data processing and knew GPSS. Harvey told his father that he could easily determine which scheme was best, but he first needed some data. This data included a profile of customer arrivals during the busy period and the lengths of time customers took to transact their business at tellers' window. To obtain this information, Harvey's father had some employees inconspicuously loiter around with clipboards and stopwatches for a couple of weeks.

Meanwhile, Harvey familiarized himself with the bank: the number of tellers (three), the location of the door, the floor area, and so on. Then he defined four systems, one corresponding to each alternative. The fourth alternative is depicted as a closed system in Figure 1-3. Note that the units of traffic are customers and that the static items are tellers' cages.

Harvey translated each system into a GPSS model. These models were actually GPSS programs with variables in place of the data he was waiting for. When he received the raw data, he reduced them to a GPSS-compatible form and inserted them into his programs. He then fed his deck into a computer and obtained a printout from which he was able to infer the behavior of each system.

Let us briefly consider what kinds of results Harvey wanted to have printed out for each of his four models. First of all, he wanted a distribution of customer waiting times. Why a *distribution* instead of a simple average? Because the former provides a much better picture of how many people had to wait for how long. Second, he was interested in the utilization of the tellers, that is, the percentage of time that each was busy. This statistic is sometimes very revealing

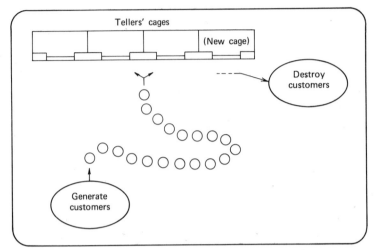

Fig. 1-3. System diagram for fourth bank teller scheme.

as you will see in some of the illustrative programs later on. Harvey was also interested in certain other statistics which we shall not discuss here. The important thing is this: all of the desired statistics were output at the end of the four simulation runs.

The bank teller problem illustrates several important points regarding GPSS models. The analyst defines the system(s) to be simulated, and he obtains valid data from the real world to use in his model(s). He translates each system (if there are more than one) into a GPSS model which ultimately takes the form of a GPSS program. This program, when run on a computer, produces a set of output statistics which, in effect, describe the behavior or operation of the system during the simulated time period.

It should be reiterated that a GPSS program does not perform a system optimization. Rather, it provides the user with a picture of how the postulated system works. To determine which of several systems is optimum, you simulate each of them and compare the results. By the way, this is usually quite easy to do with GPSS for the following reason: If several systems are being evaluated, they are often similar to one another in most respects. Thus it is usually possible to develop a single GPSS model which, with minor changes, can be made to represent all of the systems that are to be simulated.

Distance between Two Random Points

Imagine that we have a square whose sides are of unit length. Now pick two random points, A and B, which lie in this square or on its perimeter. Let d be the distance between points A and B. What is the probability that d will be less than .8?

One way to solve this problem is to pick many pairs of points at random and to measure the distance between them each time. After obtaining many values of d in this way, we could compute the proportion whose magnitude is less than .8. This procedure is admittedly inelegant, but the fact that it can be easily emulated by a GPSS program makes it practicable. Let us see how one would go about it.

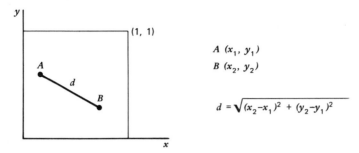

Fig. 1-4.   Distance between random points in a square.

The coordinates of the two points and the distance between them are indicated in Figure 1.4. For any given trial, x_1 may have a value of 0 to 1. The same goes for x_2, y_1, and y_2. This is the key to how our model works. Random values in the range of 0 to 1 would be assigned to each of the four coordinates. Then the distance d would be calculated. If d is less than .8, a counter would be incremented by one. After a thousand trials, the number in the counter could be divided by 1000 to obtain the proportion of trials in which $d < .8$.

The foregoing procedure could be accomplished by a computer in seconds. It may not seem to be amenable to GPSS at first glance because it does not resemble a network through which units of traffic flow. However, it can be easily translated into a GPSS model as shown in Figure 1-5.

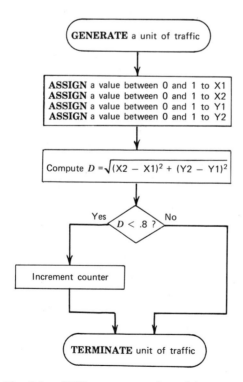

Fig. 1-5.   GPSS-type system for solving random points problem.

Each unit of traffic zips through this simple system, causing the above sequence of operations to occur. After a thousand such passes have been made, the desired answer is stored in the counter in parts per thousand. Two other items bear mentioning in connection with Figure 1-5:

1. The values assigned to X1, X2, Y1, and Y2 are randomly and independently selected during the simulation run.
2. The instructions in boldface capital letters are actual GPSS commands.

This example was presented to demonstrate that problems that do not inherently resemble network flow systems can be so expressed. It also demonstrates the ease with which a stochastic situation can be simulated if the simulation language incorporates a convenient mechanism for assigning random numbers. The GPSS random number mechanism is discussed in Section 2.3.

Is GPSS the best way to solve the distance-between-points problem and others like it? Ordinarily it is not. Problems of this type can often be solved by analytical methods such as probability theory. If an analytical solution is impossible or is beyond the capability of the analyst, a computer program written in a computation-oriented language such as FORTRAN would probably be the next logical choice. However, the ease with which GPSS can be applied to stochastic systems makes it very attractive when you take into account the small amount of time and debugging runs it takes to obtain a working program in GPSS as compared to other languages.

Airport Scheduling Problem

Four airlines submit their desired operating schedules to the officials of the soon-to-be-opened municipal airport. At first glance it appears that there will be only a few minor conflicts and delays during the evening rush hours. But actual arrival and departure times are known to deviate from the scheduled times, and this could aggravate the situation. To determine whether the airlines' proposed schedules will work out all right under the uncertain conditions of real life, airport officials hire a consultant to simulate the system.

The consultant spends several weeks gathering data at other airports and formulating a model of the municipal airport. His model consists of the system shown in Figure 1-6 along with all of the assumptions regarding its operation. Some of the assumptions are:

1. Arriving aircraft have priority over departing aircraft.
2. Aircraft spend four minutes taxiing from the runway to the terminal and vice versa.
3. Landings and takeoffs are spaced at least 2 minutes apart.
4. Each airplane, on arriving at the terminal, waits for its assigned gate; it cannot use another one.
5. Arrivals are usually on time, but they may range from 5 minutes early to 1 hour late.

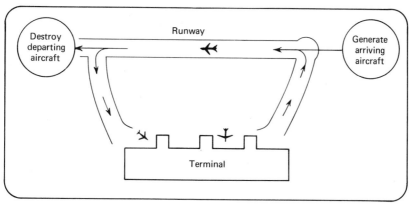

Fig. 1-6. System diagram for airport scheduling problem.

These assumptions as well as other ground rules and empirical data must be incorporated into the logic of the model. For instance, arrivals are simulated by generating airplanes at intervals that correspond to the scheduled interarrival times, plus or minus random deviations. Arriving airplanes must be classified according to their size and intended gate number. Departing airplanes must await their turn for use of the runway, and the first one in line cannot take off if a plane is due to arrive within 2 minutes.

It is evident that this model is considerably more complex than the bank and unit square described previously. The complexity of the airport model lies not in its elements, but in the relationships between them. Note that relationships exist between and among both static and dynamic elements, or entities. Despite its apparent complexity, this problem is not at all difficult to simulate with GPSS.

Supermarket Problem

The operation of a supermarket can be simulated using GPSS. The system boundary corresponds to the walls of the supermarket. Arriving customers are generated by a mechanism located just inside the entrance, and departing customers are likewise destroyed at the exit. The static elements in the system are the cart acquisition and shopping areas and the checkout counters. The dynamic entities are, of course, the customers. This system is illustrated in Figure 1-7.

Several different simulation models can be built around the Figure 1-7 system. The exact nature of the model depends on the logical behavior and activities associated with the elements of the system. To illustrate, let us look at one of the possibilities.

Customers arrive at varying intervals. A certain percentage of them have a large shopping list and are unhappy if no shopping carts are available. In fact, some of them take their business elsewhere. Customers spend varying amounts of time shopping, and then they head for the checkout counter with the shortest waiting line. A certain percentage of customers will qualify for the express

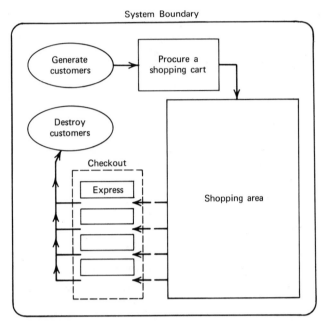

Fig. 1-7.   System diagram for supermarket problem.

checkout because they have six items or less.   The amount of time to add up a customer's purchases and put everything into bags is roughly proportional to the number of items he has bought.   After a customer has passed through the checkout line, he is removed from the system, and his shopping cart becomes available if he had one.

The foregoing scenario can be represented as a GPSS model, and a run can be made to determine how many customers will fail to find carts available.   The output statistics will also reveal how long customers had to wait in checkout queues.   If desired, the number of carts and/or cashiers can be changed, and the run can be repeated.

Other Problems

In addition to tollbooths, airports, banks, and supermarkets, there are many kinds of *commercial enterprises* that can be simulated using GPSS.   The usual objective is to determine what level of service (facilities and personnel) is required to fill the demand or, alternately, to hold customer dissatisfaction to an acceptable level.   Among the systems in this category are barber shops, gas stations, and shipping terminals.

The operation of a *manufacturing department, assembly line* or *job shop* can be simulated using GPSS.   In fact, such problems constitute a classic area of application for GPSS.   The static elements in the system are machines and workers or, alternately, the operations that are performed.   The dynamic elements are the parts, subassemblies, and final products that move through the system.   It is also possible to generate certain items that can be interpreted as machine breakdowns. This is accomplished by the simple expedient of allowing these items to periodically tie up various machines for as long as we want them to be out of commission.

The foregoing remarks suggest the possibility of including more than one traffic generator in a model. This can certainly be done, and it often is.

Another important area to which GPSS has been applied is the operation of *data processing systems*. For example, a central processing unit for a time-sharing system might be simulated to determine how fully it would be utilized. Or it might be desired to determine how rapidly incoming requests would be serviced.

The operation of a *supply depot* or *warehouse* is also very amenable to GPSS simulation. The object is to stock as little merchandise as possible without running out too often. If orders arrive in a random manner, and if the time to replace merchandise varies, it is extremely difficult to determine the optimum inventory levels by analytical methods. By simulating different sets of assumptions, it is possible to gain a rather good idea of what constitutes an acceptable inventory level.

GPSS has also been used to evaluate *transportation systems* and *spare parts policies*. And it has even been used for *capital investment risk analysis*.

1.5 SUMMARY

Digital computer simulation has grown substantially during the past decade, and this trend is expected to continue in the 1970s. The availability of user-oriented languages such as GPSS is a key reason for this growth. GPSS is a discrete-event simulation system which involves the following steps:

1. Define a closed system which includes static and dynamic entities. The latter are generated and terminated *within* the system.
2. Utilize relevant empirical data and assumptions to formulate a model which is essentially the aforementioned system with operating rules.
3. Write a GPSS program which represents this model. Convert the coded program to punched cards.
4. Run the program on a computer to obtain a simulation of the model. Examine the output to infer the behavior of the model.

Simulation models do not yield solutions as such. They behave as the system they have been designed to emulate, and they yield statistical results from which the analyst can determine the consequences of his assumptions.

GPSS can be appropriately applied to a wide variety of problems. It is particularly well suited to queuing problems, but it can be used to simulate any system that can be idealized as a *network through which units of traffic move*. GPSS is often used in preference to other approaches for several reasons:

1. It permits a more faithful replication of the system than, say, an analytical model.
2. It is so easy to write a GPSS program that will run successfully.

3. GPSS includes some built-in features not found in most other computing
   languages, namely a random events mechanism and an automatic output
   option.

Most major computer manufacturers offer GPSS or soon will.   GPSS/360 is
used as the "standard" in this book, but GPS K, Flow Simulator, GPSS III, and
GPSS V are also specifically included.   If you are interested only in GPSS/360 or
GPSS V, you can omit the next-to-last section in most of the succeeding chapters.
In the latter case, you should also read Appendix H.

CHAPTER 2
Introduction to GPSS

In this chapter we begin to look at GPSS itself. Some of its key elements and concepts are introduced, and the process of translating a problem into a GPSS program is discussed further. The general makeup of GPSS programs is described, and some basic coding rules are given. Then the role of random numbers in GPSS is discussed.

As explained in Section 1.2, each chapter is oriented toward GPSS/360, although most of the material applies to all four versions of GPSS. Differences between GPSS/360 and the other three versions are indicated in the next-to-last section in each chapter. Accordingly, Sections 2.1, 2.2, and 2.3 pertain to GPSS/360 without exception, but they contain certain items that do not pertain to GPS K, Flow Simulator, and/or GPSS III. These items, if not noted where they occur, are pointed out in Section 2.4.

2.1 BASIC ELEMENTS AND CONCEPTS

GPSS is a *high-level* digital computer language; that is, a single instruction by the programmer results in the execution of many built-in instructions with which he need not concern himself. Thus he is able to work at the (simplified) *upper level* while most of the complex procedures and routines are handled at the *lower level*. The notion of GPSS levels will be elaborated upon shortly.

After discussing GPSS levels, we talk about some key concepts associated with the upper level such as models, block diagrams, and entities. Then we consider the element of time in relation to GPSS models. To complete this section, we say a few words about the underlying logical structure of GPSS.

GPSS Levels

GPSS can be pictured as having three levels. The upper level consists of that which is "visible" to the user. The middle level encompasses the underlying logical structure of the language. And the lower level pertains to the physical manifestation of a GPSS program in the computer. To put it another way, the upper level consists of the external aspects of GPSS while the middle and lower levels comprise the internal aspects. This division of GPSS into levels is somewhat arbitrary, and it is not an essential GPSS concept.[1] It is primarily an aid to understanding.

GPSS can be characterized as having a very extensive and elaborate internal structure which permits a relatively simple problem-oriented external structure. The phasing relationships, status updating, and bookkeeping functions are built in, so the user is not burdened with these troublesome and time-consuming aspects. He is free to concentrate on applying GPSS to his problem at the upper level.

GPSS can be used effectively by someone who is largely ignorant of its internal aspects. But as a practical matter, any serious effort to learn GPSS requires some cognizance of the internal aspects. For this reason, the *GPSS Primer* devotes a significant amount of attention to the key internal aspects of GPSS.

Figure 2-1 shows the GPSS levels, with the shaded areas indicating the approximate degree of coverage that each level receives in this book. The upper level is fairly well covered with the exception of some of the more specialized and sophisticated features of GPSS. The middle level is covered to a substantial degree, though not quite as fully as the upper level. The lower level is covered in a more limited way with an emphasis on the model as opposed to the internal GPSS programs.

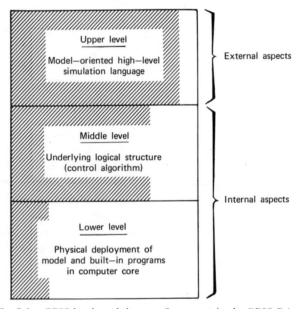

Fig. 2-1. GPSS levels and degree of coverage in the *GPSS Primer.*

Chapters 3 to 7 are almost exclusively concerned with the external aspects of GPSS. Chapter 8 is devoted to its internal aspects. Chapters 9 to 14 deal primarily with the external aspects but relate many of them to the internal aspects.

[1] This concept is not used in the various GPSS manuals.

Block Diagrams and Transactions

It was stated in Chapter 1 that a system which can be idealized as a network through which units of traffic flow can be represented as a GPSS model. A *GPSS model* emulates the characteristics and behavior of the system being investigated. It ultimately takes the form of a computer program in the GPSS language. The translation of a problem into a GPSS model/program is the object of the game.

The terms "model" and "program" are more or less synonymous with the term "block diagram" in GPSS. A block diagram can be visualized as a system flow diagram whose elements are **blocks** that are taken from the standardized repertoire of GPSS blocks, but which represent objects and activities in the system being simulated. These blocks are a fundamental part of GPSS; in fact, a substantial portion of this book is devoted to acquainting you with the inventory of GPSS blocks and their use in block diagrams. *The degree to which the GPSS blocks are covered in this book — and the order in which they are introduced — is roughly proportional to how commonly they are used.*

A block diagram consists of a series of blocks with connecting lines that indicate the flow of traffic (or course of events) through the system. Alternate courses of action that arise in the system are represented by having more than one line leaving a block. One block may have several lines entering it to denote the fact that it is a common step in two or more sequences of events. The choice of paths, where an alternative is offered, may be a statistical event or it may be a logical choice which depends on the state of the system at the time of choice.

A GPSS block diagram is designed to accommodate and control the flow of units of traffic which are called **transactions** (abbreviated to **xacts**). Transactions can be visualized as representing customers in a store, automobiles at a service station, messages in a communication system, and so forth. Transactions are introduced into the model by way of certain blocks at intervals specified by the programmer. They proceed to move through the system in a manner that will be described later.

Each time a transaction enters a block, it causes that block to run through its prescribed series of computations, logical checks, statistical updating, and so on. *The blocks in a GPSS program are essentially dormant except when entered by a transaction.* Thus the transactions, once created, act as the driving force in the simulation. The status of the model does not change if no transactions move through it.

Entities and Attributes

To a beginner, **entities** and **attributes** are two of the most elusive concepts in GPSS. This is not because they are inherently mysterious, but because they cannot be fully appreciated until one has become at least somewhat familiar with GPSS. So the best we can do at this point is to describe these very fundamental GPSS concepts with this admonition: Do not be concerned if you emerge from the following discussion without a concrete understanding of entities and attributes, so long as you have a general idea of what they are.

The term "entity" was introduced in Chapter 1 in connection with some of the closed systems that were discussed. Entities were characterized as static or dynamic elements in a model. This is a valid description as far as it goes, but the concept of a GPSS entity goes beyond this simplistic notion.

Every GPSS model can be thought of as consisting of an assemblage of entities, the number of which depends on (or reflects) the size of the model. Each entity is an abstract element that has associated with it a set of attributes (properties) that describe its makeup and status. Let us look at a couple of specific GPSS entities.

A transaction is an object that can be abstractly described as a unit of traffic. In a given model it may represent an automobile, message, customer, engine part, and so on. At any instant of time, a GPSS model may contain many xacts[2] which can be found at various places (blocks, actually) in the block diagram.

Some of the attributes associated with a xact are its *creation time, priority*, and present *position* in the block diagram. Xacts have many other attributes, most of which would not mean anything to you at this stage. However, it should be evident that the status and properties of a transaction are given by the current values of its attributes.

A **facility** is a "thing" that can be used by only one transaction at a time. So a facility is either *in use* or *not in use;* it can have no other status. A facility might represent a machine tool in one problem and a tollbooth in another. (You will notice that the words "problem," "system," and "model" are often interchangeable in this book.) Thus a facility is merely an abstraction or generalization of an element that appears in various guises in different simulation models.

What kinds of attributes does a facility entity possess? Its two statuses — in use or not in use — are *logical attributes*. If one is true, the other is false. The number of xacts to have occupied the facility and the proportion of time it has been occupied are *numerical attributes*. There are also other facility attributes, but we can see that the status and story of a facility in a model are told by the values of its attributes.

How many types of entities are there? This depends on which version of GPSS you are talking about. Fourteen entity types are defined in GPSS/360 and GPS K, and this convention has been adopted in the *GPSS Primer*.

Transactions and *blocks* are classified as **basic entities** because every GPSS model must have them. The other entities may or may not be included in a given model. Aside from blocks and transactions, *equipment, statistical, computational*, and *savevalue entities* are probably most commonly used. This is only a generalization, and we do not mean to imply that the other entities are less important — far from it. Incidentally, all entities listed in Table 2-1 will be discussed in this book except for groups.

All of the GPSS entities have attributes that describe their status and properties at any given time. We saw some of them in connection with transactions and facilities. Most attributes have numerical values, and some have logical values (true or false).

Many entity attributes are strictly internal and are normally never seen by the

---

[2] For the sake of expedience, the abbreviations "xact" and "xacts" will be used extensively in place of "transaction" and "transactions" from this point forth.

TABLE 2-1. GPSS ENTITIES

Basic entities	Blocks
	Transactions
Equipment entities:	Facilities
	Storages
	Logic switches
Computational entities	Arithmetic variables
	Boolean variables
	Functions
Statistical entities	Queues
	Frequency tables
Reference entities	Savevalues
	Matrix savevalues
Chain entities	User chains
	Groups

programmer. But there are a total of 52 attributes whose values *can* be referenced. Forty are numerical; they are called **standard numerical attributes.** (There are three additional standard numerical attributes that do not pertain to any specific entity.) Twelve are logical; they are called **standard logical attributes.**

As we said, entity attributes are difficult to appreciate until you have become familiar with other parts of GPSS. So we shall not pursue this subject further right now. It will be developed gradually as you become familiar with some of the more tangible aspects of GPSS in the ensuing chapters.

Clock Time and Run Time

We have said that a GPSS block diagram operates by creating transactions and moving them from block to block in a manner that emulates the movement of the units of traffic they represent. Each such movement is an event that is due to occur at some point in time. The internal GPSS program (also called the *GPSS simulator*) maintains a record of the times at which these events are due to occur in their correct time sequence. To accomplish this, it maintains a clock that records the instant of real time that has been reached in the modeled system. This is referred to as the **clock time.** The concept of clock time is basic to discrete-event simulation systems such as GPSS.

All clock times in the simulator are *integer* numbers. The unit of system time represented by a unit of clock time is implied by the user, who enters all time data as multiples of the unit he has selected. He might, for instance, equate a unit of simulator time to 1 second, or to 1 month, or to 1/3 day. The time unit chosen must be adhered to throughout the simulation model.

Thus far we have been talking about *simulated* (or *simulator* or *system* or *real* or *clock*) time, that is, the time being measured in the simulated system. Suppose, for example, that we have a GPSS program in which a clock unit is equated to a minute. If the clock time is 480 at the end of the run, we shall have simulated an 8-hour period.

The *run time* or *simulation time* is simply the *execution time* for the run. When simulation models get to be large and involved, the run time may become a factor. In this case, the programmer may seek ways of making his model more efficient so that it will run faster.

Is the simulation time proportional to the simulated time? Not necessarily, which probably comes as no surprise. The simulation time reflects the number of events and the types of operations performed during the run. It is entirely possible, for instance, that a model with a 10-hour simulated time period could involve fewer events and a shorter run time than a model which has a 10-second simulated time period during which a great many events occur.

Logical Foundation of GPSS

When a simulation run starts, the clock is set to zero, and the model is devoid of transactions. As the run proceeds, xacts are created at one or more places in the block diagram, and they follow appropriate paths through it. In general, if we freeze the model at any instant during the run, we can observe the following:

1. The simulator clock will show the number of clock units that have elapsed since the run began.
2. The status of the model will have changed. In other words, the values of various entity attributes will differ from their initial values. For instance, certain blocks will have been entered by various numbers of xacts.
3. The statistics maintained by the GPSS simulator will reflect the events that have transpired thus far.
4. Each transaction in the system will be at (or associated with) a particular block.
5. Some blocks will have several xacts associated with them; some will "contain" just one xact; and others will have no xacts.
6. One and only one transaction, called the **current transaction,** is being processed (moved through the block diagram) by the simulator.

If only one xact can be *serviced* (or *moved* or *processed*) at any instant, how does the GPSS simulator handle simultaneous events? The answer should be obvious. It handles in a sequential fashion events that, in the real world, may occur simultaneously or sequentially. The exact manner in which it accomplishes this will be explained in due time. The next few paragraphs should shed some light on this subject.

The sequence of events in a GPSS model is dependent on the state of all transactions in the system. The current xact is advanced through as many blocks as possible until an interaction point is reached, that is, until it is either blocked or otherwise delayed by some block. The simulator then selects the next xact to be made current and executes the appropriate functions for the block at which that xact is currently located. This procedure continues until the run is completed.

The **GPSS control algorithm** features a rather complex **scan** designed to respond to a variety of specific state changes as efficiently and automatically as possible. The algorithm operates on two chains of xacts, a **future events chain** and a **current events chain.** When there are no more xacts in the current events chain which can be moved, the simulator clock is updated to the *departure time* of the first transaction in the future events chain. All xacts having this departure time are transferred to the current events chain (first in–first out, within priority class), and the xact at the top of the chain becomes the current xact. In this way, several xacts can be processed while the clock is "frozen," thus making it possible to process events that occur simultaneously.

The scan, clock, and transaction chains are concepts that pertain to the internal workings of GPSS. As indicated earlier, a lot of GPSS programming can be done by someone with relatively little awareness of these internal aspects. Therefore, we will not devote much attention to them until Chapter 8.

2.2 CONSTRUCTING A GPSS MODEL/BLOCK DIAGRAM/PROGRAM

The section heading reflects the fact that the terms "model," "block diagram," and "program" are substantially equivalent in GPSS. This point was made earlier, and it is carried further in this section. The process of translating a problem into a program is described in detail, and the ingredients of which GPSS programs are made are discussed. Then some of the basic GPSS coding rules are given.

Translating a Problem into a GPSS Model

The process of translating a problem into a GPSS program starts with a decision to apply GPSS to the problem at hand. This decision is a highly individual one which depends on the analyst as well as other considerations, as pointed out in Chapter 1.

A system must be defined and analyzed so that its elements and their interactions and functions are clearly understood. The acquisition of relevant empirical data and the preparation of a system flow diagram are usually important parts of this process. The diagram may be a carefully drawn and detailed flow chart, or it may be a roughly drawn sketch that shows the general system configuration. Its format depends on the nature of the problem and the preferences of the analyst.

After the basic configuration of the (closed) system with its operating rules and constraints has been worked out and documented, the next step is to formulate a GPSS model. To do this, the preliminary model must be expressed in terms of GPSS entities. This is where the preliminary flow chart evolves into a block diagram. The latter is a formal flow chart whose elements correspond to – and in fact *are* – GPSS blocks.

An elaborate set of block symbols has been defined by IBM and adopted by other manufacturers for drawing GPSS block diagrams. There is also a simplified set of symbols (the standard flow-charting symbols commonly used by programmers) which can be used to draw GPSS block diagrams.

The next step is to write a GPSS program. It consists of a sequence of instructions that more or less duplicate the elements of the formal block diagram. The main difference is that the block diagram looks like a flow chart and is therefore easier to follow. Also, the block diagram consists of nothing but blocks whereas the program contains various other instructions in addition to the block definitions.

Since a coded GPSS program is basically a nonpictorial representation of a block diagram, the program itself is often referred to as a block diagram. To carry the analogy further, the block-type instructions in a GPSS program are referred to as blocks. Thus the term "block diagram," in the broad sense, denotes the sequence of blocks that comprise a GPSS model, irrespective of their specific representation—diagrammatic or coded.

It is interesting to note that GPSS was originally envisaged as a language that could be programmed simply by drawing a flow diagram in GPSS symbols and then recopying the sequence directly onto a coding form. The evolution of GPSS into a more sophisticated and generalized language and its application to diverse and complex situations have tended to make this approach unfeasible. (Also, as a practical matter, most people who construct computerized models to obtain fast results are inclined to dispense with nonessential steps such as formal block diagrams.) So, in practice, the role of the formal block diagram in GPSS is less prominent than may have once been expected. Its role in this book will be described after we very briefly review the procedure that was outlined for translating a problem into a program:

1. Define and analyze the problem, and collect relevant system data.
2. Draw a preliminary flow chart indicating the structure and operation of the system.
3. Draw a GPSS block diagram.
4. Write (code) the GPSS program.

In practice the first three steps are seldom adhered to as stated. For example, the first two steps are often combined. Or the first three steps may be omitted entirely if the problem is simple enough to be directly expressed as a coded GPSS program. Incidentally, most of the illustrative programs presented in this book are sufficiently straightforward to be handled in the latter manner, but schematic diagrams have been provided anyway.

In situations where a flow diagram is helpful to the programmer, he may draw an informal flow chart but skip the formal block diagram. There are two good reasons for this:

1. The preliminary flow chart may inherently resemble a GPSS block diagram by virtue of the fact that the programmer tends to anticipate the GPSS blocks that will be used.
2. Since the coded program *is* a block diagram, it would be superfluous to draw a formal block diagram.

Hence the formal GPSS block symbols are not used—nor can an honest-to-goodness block diagram be found in schematic form—in this book. For our purposes, a diagram which is more or less a cross between an informal flow chart and a block diagram is preferable because it bridges the gap between the problem statement and the GPSS model and is usually easier to follow than a block diagram. GPSS block diagrams are generally drawn when it is desired to show a GPSS model in a form that is more self-explanatory and to the point than a program listing. You can find the GPSS block symbols in a manual if your curiosity has been aroused. (See the list of references.)

Physical Form and Ingredients of a GPSS Program

GPSS is a high-level digital computer language; that is, a single instruction by the programmer causes the computer to execute a large number of machine-language instructions. To put it another way, one GPSS card usually causes the computer to execute one or more subroutines. Therefore, GPSS programs are usually far more compact than equivalent programs in other languages, such as FORTRAN.

The fact that most of the sequencing, cross-checking, statistical updating, and output format specifications are built into GPSS rather than being specified by the programmer makes it simple to use and minimizes the opportunities for programming errors. It also rids the language of superfluous instructions which tend to obscure the relationship between the coded program and the modeled system. Thus GPSS is a very graphic language in that it tends to look like the model it represents.

Each line on a GPSS coding sheet corresponds to a punched card. So if a program is written which occupies, say, 68 lines of coding, we have a source deck consisting of 68 cards. The terms "source program" and "symbolic program" are synonymous with "source deck," by the way. If we place the appropriate computer control cards before and after a source deck and put this into a computer's card reader, we will get a simulation run.

Generally speaking, a GPSS source deck consists of four types of cards:

Block cards.

Definition cards.

Program control cards (or, simply, control cards).

Comment cards (or remarks cards, or asterisk cards).

These categories represent the usual method of classifying GPSS program cards, but you should recognize that they are somewhat arbitrary. For example, block cards could be regarded as a type of definition card, that is, one which defines a block. Similarly, comment cards could be regarded as a type of control card. Having pointed this out, we shall hereafter use the four categories in this book.

With regard to GPSS cards, note the following:

1. The word "card," used without any qualifying adjective, may refer to any or all of the four types listed above.

2. The terms "block card" and "block" will be used interchangeably.

3. The term "control card" will refer to a *program* control card which is part of the source deck rather than to a *computer* control card which is placed before or after the source deck.

There are 44 different block types in GPSS/360, and they are listed in Appendix A.   Most of them are discussed in the *GPSS Primer,* but some of the less commonly used blocks are not.

There are 10 kinds of *definition cards* in GPSS/360, and they are listed in Appendix B.   All of them are discussed in this book.

There are 44 *control cards* in GPSS/360, and they are listed in Appendix C.   It is important to note that you can get by with only three control cards, namely, SIMULATE, START, and END.   Approximately half of the control cards are discussed in this book.

A *comment card* has an asterisk in column 1, which causes the GPSS simulator to ignore the card as far as the simulation model is concerned.   The comment itself may occupy columns 2 through 72, and it may comprise any letters, digits, or symbols available on the machine, including blanks of course.

Some Basic Coding Rules

For the most part the coding rules given in this section apply to all four versions of GPSS.   However, the various coding sheet (or card) columns that will be specified do not apply to Flow Simulator.

Any standard coding sheet can be used to code a GPSS program, but it is especially convenient to have coding forms divided into fields as shown in Figure 2-2.   Again, each line on a coding sheet corresponds to one punched card.

There is a "standard" coding format to which the vast majority of GPSS cards (except for asterisk cards) conform.   This format can be summarized as follows:

1. Columns 1, 7, and 73 to 80: blank.
2. Columns 2 to 6: location field.
3. Columns 8 to 18: operation field.
4. Columns 19 to 72: operand field.

The location field, when not left blank, is used to specify the label assigned to an entity by the programmer.   This label may be a number or an alphanumeric[3] symbol, but we need not concern ourselves with such details at this stage.

Two of the most commonly used synonyms for *label* are *address* and *tag.*   The terms "label" and "tag" suggest a designation that serves only as an identifier.   The word "address" implies more; it suggests that the entity is identified in terms of its location.   Since this is indeed the case in GPSS, we will usually speak of *entity addresses* rather than *labels* or *tags.*

The *operation field* contains a word or abbreviation that identifies the card type.   This word is indicative of the operation or function of the card, and it must be left-justified; that is, it must begin in column 8.   We saw three of these card type names in Figure 1-5, namely, GENERATE, ASSIGN, and TERMINATE.

The *operand field* consists of a *variable field* followed by a *comments field.*   The variable field starts in column 19 and consists of as few as zero or as many as seven subfields which are separated by commas.   The number of subfields

---

[3] The term "alphanumeric" or "alphameric" refers to a string of characters which consists of any of the 10 digits from 0 through 9 and/or any of the 26 letters of the alphabet.

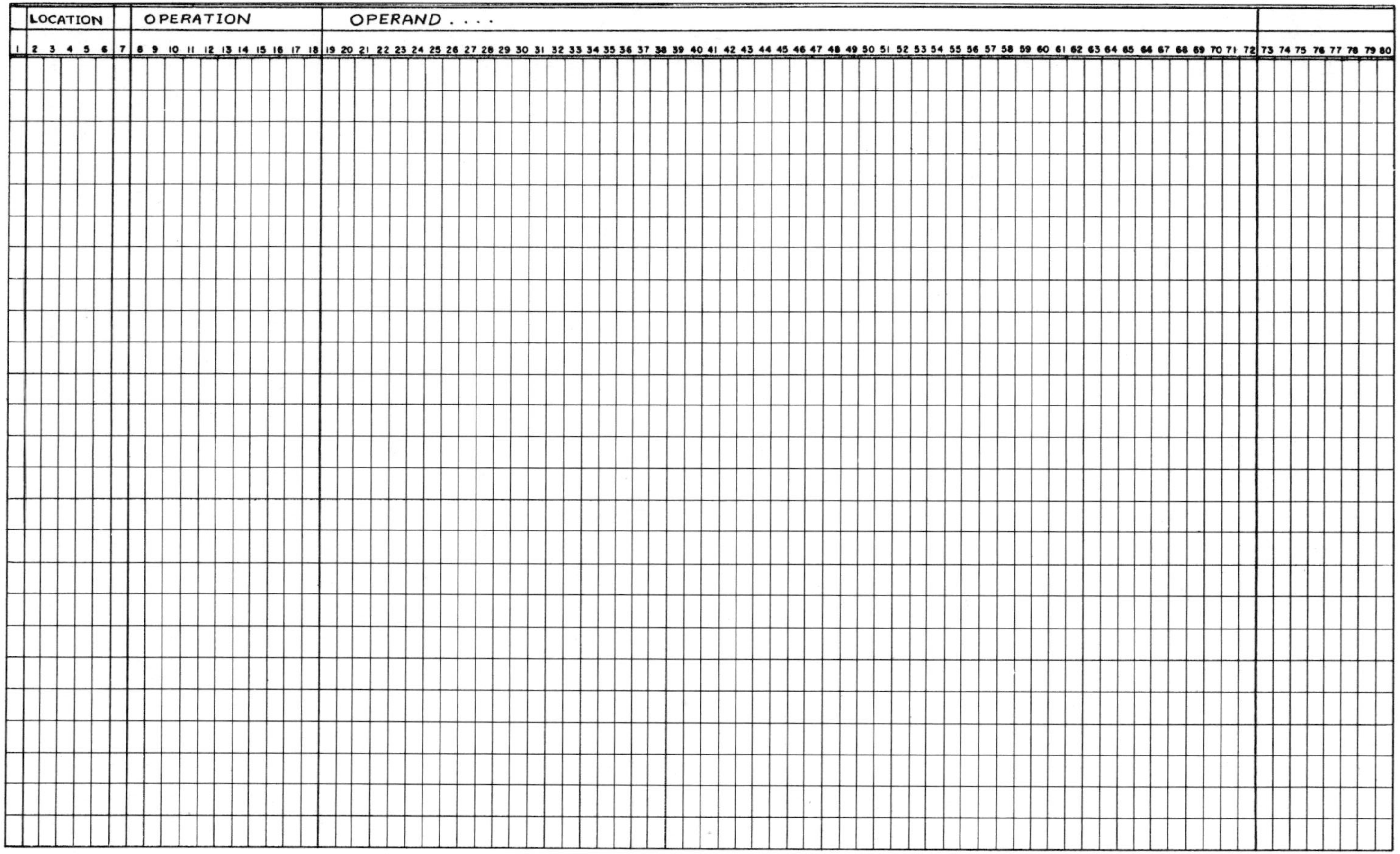

Fig. 2-2. GPSS coding form.

having entries on a given card depends on the card and how many of the available subfields the analyst has chosen to utilize.

The variable field subfields are referred to as $A, B, C, \ldots, G$. Incidentally, the term "subfield" is often shortened to "field" for expedience. For example, we might speak of the *entry* (or *argument*) in *field C* (or in the *C-field*) of the GENERATE block.

No blank characters are permitted among the entries in a card's variable field because the GPSS assembly program[4] interprets the end of the variable field to occur as soon as it encounters a blank character. Thus any information after column 19 which follows a blank is treated as a comment.

If it is desired to make entries in nonadjacent subfields, the correct number of commas must be inserted to indicate the skipped subfields. To illustrate, let us use the START card, for which fields A, B, C, and D are defined.

(a) START   1000,,,1

(b) START   10,,2

(c) START   500

In example (a), fields B and C are blank. This is indicated by the three adjacent commas. Note that there are no blank spaces between the commas. In example (b), fields B and D are blank. Again there are no embedded blanks among the variable field arguments. Note also that there is no comma to denote the blank D-field since it is at the end. In example (c), fields B, C, and D are blank, and no commas are needed since the blank character immediately following the field A entry signifies the end of the variable field.

It is evident that the layout of the operand field may vary greatly from card to card. It may be entirely blank; it may contain zero to seven arguments; the arguments themselves are many and varied; and a narrative comment may or may not be included.

The foregoing description of the location, operation, and operand fields pertains to every card in GPSS except for remarks cards and a handful of definition and control cards. The former were described earlier, and the other cards with nonstandard formats will be clearly indicated when we get to them. Incidentally, blank cards may be inserted in the source deck wherever a skipped line is desired to improve the appearance of the program listing. Blank cards are permitted wherever comment cards are legal.

2.3 THE ROLE OF RANDOM NUMBERS IN GPSS

The element of randomness plays an important part in most GPSS programs. For example, transactions may be introduced into the system at random intervals. Or they may be delayed at some point for random lengths of time. Or a stream of xacts may be split so that X% go to one place while the rest go to another place in the block diagram with the destination of any individual xact

---

[4] The assembly program is one of the programs that comprise the GPSS software package. It interprets and verifies the source program and deploys the model in the computer.

being a matter of chance.   Or random values from a probability distribution may
be required for certain computations.   And so forth.

In GPSS models, stochastic behavior is always simulated by *generating a random
number and then testing its value or converting it to a form that is appropriate for the situation*.   We will soon take a closer look at some of these situations, but first let us
see how random numbers are obtained.

Random Number Generation

GPSS incorporates a *random number generator* which is a subroutine that computes a random number whenever it is called.   An oversimplified description of
this random number generator will now be given.

Each time it is called, it operates on a *seed* number to produce a random
number *RN* as well as the seed that will be used for the next computation.   So
once the initial or base seed has been specified, the ensuing sequence of random
numbers is entirely predetermined.   For this reason, the values of *RN* are
pseudorandom numbers.   They are legitimate random numbers, but they are not
truly the result of chance as they would be if we obtained them by spinning a
number wheel or rolling dice.

Since the random number seed is set to the same value at the start of every
simulation run, the same sequence of random numbers will be generated every
time.   An obvious implication of this is that identical results will be obtained if a
given model is run several times, even if it involves random events.   At first
glance, the fact that random numbers are generated in a duplicable manner
from the same initial seed may seem restrictive.   However, this is not the case.
For one thing, this property enables the user to analyze changes to his model
with the assurance that differences in the results are not due to random effects.
For another thing, GPSS provides several methods for obtaining different
random number sequences if desired.   These methods, as well as the subject of
random number generation, will be elaborated upon when we look at GPSS programs that involve random events.

For the present discussion, we can regard the random number generator as a
black box which produces values of *RN* upon request.   The values of *RN* are
uniformly distributed in the range of 0 to 999 or 0 to .999999, depending on the
type of request made by the GPSS simulator.[5]   Thus *RN* may be either an integer or a decimal fraction, depending on the circumstances.   This is well and
good, but a GPSS model seldom needs uniformly distributed random numbers
between 0 and 1 or between 0 and 1000.   So the trick is to somehow convert *RN*
to the type of random numbers needed in a given situation.   The remainder of
Section 2.3 is concerned with how this is accomplished.

Probability Distributions

It often happens that we want to obtain uniformly distributed random values
which lie in a range other than 0 to 1 or 0 to 999.   For example, we might want

---

[5] By "uniformly distributed" we mean that the next value of *RN* always has an equal probability of
falling anywhere in the specified range.

uniformly distributed integers between 10 and 20, inclusive. In the general case, we might want X to randomly take on values in the range of A to B, inclusive.

If X is a uniformly distributed random variable in the range A to B, and if RN is a uniformly distributed random variable in the range 0 to 1, then RN values can be translated into X values by the following formula:

$$X = A + (RN) \times (B - A)$$

In GPSS, this conversion is handled internally. The user need only specify the range in which X should lie. You will see how this is done in the next chapter. For now it is sufficient to know that values of RN can be readily translated into uniformly distributed values in any specified range.

Now let us see how values of RN can be translated into values of Y, where Y is a random variable which takes on values from an exponential distribution whose mean is m. Then RN and Y are related by the following expression:

$$Y = -m \times ln(RN)$$

This equation indicates that values of RN can be mathematically equated to values of Y. But how is this accomplished in a GPSS program? A detailed answer to this question is deferred until Chapter 4. However, a simplified explanation is as follows. The programmer includes some cards in his deck which define the points on a graph of RN versus Y. Whenever a value of Y is needed during the run, the internal GPSS program generates a value of RN and translates it into a corresponding value of Y, using the input relationship between RN and Y.

The fact that the user can define the relationship between RN and Y is very significant because he can just as well define any kind of distribution he wishes. For instance, Y could be normally distributed, or it could vary in some unusual way which happens to be appropriate for the problem at hand.

Now that we have talked about the random number generator and how to convert values of RN into any type of random variable desired, let us see how the GPSS simulator handles two of the stochastic situations mentioned at the beginning of Section 2.3.

Interarrival Time

The most prominent use of random numbers in GPSS occurs in connection with the **interarrival time** of transactions. The interarrival time (also called the *intercreation interval*) is the number of clock units between the entry of two successive xacts into the system. If xacts enter (or are introduced into) the system at regular intervals, the interarrival time is said to be constant. If xacts enter at irregular intervals, the interarrival time is a random variable.

It should be pointed out that interarrival time is the *inverse* of frequency. For example, if six transactions per minute enter a system, then the frequency is 6 xacts/minute, and the interarrival time is 1/6 minute/xact. To put this example into context with GPSS, imagine that 1 clock unit is equated to 1 second of real time. Then the average interarrival time would be 10 clock units. That is, 1 xact would "arrive" every 10 clock units, or every 10 seconds.

While we are talking about the relationship between interarrival time and frequency, it should be pointed out that if a collection of interarrival times are exponentially distributed, the corresponding frequencies belong to a Poisson distribution. Hence the words "exponential" and "Poisson" are often (but not always correctly) used interchangeably.

How are interarrival times specified in GPSS models? This question will be answered in detail in the chapters that follow, but a simplified answer can be given here. One of the key GPSS blocks is the GENERATE block. This block creates transactions and sends them into the system at intervals specified by the programmer. In conjunction with this block, you specify a *mean interval* which is simply the number of clock units between the creation of xacts. If you specify a *modifier* in addition to the mean value, the internal program computes interarrival times which are randomly distributed about this mean. If you do not specify a modifier, xacts are created at regular intervals.

The foregoing "simplified answer" may not seem so simple since you have no idea of what a GENERATE block looks like. Fear not, because you will soon enough. The point we want to make now is that GPSS provides an easy-to-use mechanism for introducing xacts into a model at uniform or random intervals.

Random Splitting of a Stream of Transactions

It was stated at the beginning of Section 2.3 that random numbers come into play when a stream of transactions is randomly split. To illustrate, imagine that we want 70% of the incoming xacts to go to location AAA with the other 30% going to BBB as shown in Figure 2-3.

When a xact arrives at the decision point, the GPSS program generates a random number. If it falls in the range of 0 to .699999, the xact is sent to AAA. If *RN* lies between .7 and .999999, inclusive, the xact is sent to BBB. Thus the destination of any individual xact is a matter of chance, but in the long run about 70% will go to AAA because 70% of the values of *RN* will be less than .7. And the remaining 30% will go to BBB.

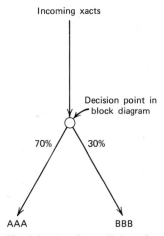

Fig. 2-3.   Random splitting of a stream of transactions.

2.4   DIFFERENCES BETWEEN GPSS/360 AND OTHER VERSIONS

Most of the material covered thus far in Chapter 2 applies to all four versions of GPSS.   However, there are some noteworthy dissimilarities, which are pointed out in this section.   Bear in mind that we do not indicate every minute difference between GPSS/360 and the other versions.   Such details can be looked up in your manufacturer-supplied GPSS manual as the need to know them arises in connection with specific programming questions.

Entities, Card Types, and Attributes

GPSS III and Flow Simulator lack three of the fourteen entity types listed in Table 2-1, namely boolean variables, matrix savevalues, and groups.   As a result, these two versions also lack the block types and other items that pertain to boolean variables, matrix savevalues, and groups.

All four versions of GPSS, as part of their internal logical structure, establish several types of transaction chains:

1. Current events chain.
2. Future events chain.
3. Interrupt chain.   } (Not actually called a "chain" in GPS K.)
4. Matching chain.

These four chains are classified as entities in Flow Simulator but not in the other three versions.   This is not very significant, since referring to these chains as entities does not change anything.

Whereas GPSS/360 and GPS K both include 44 block types, Flow Simulator has 38 and GPSS III has 36.   Five of the "missing" block types in Flow Simulator and GPSS III are associated with group entities.   The complete roster of block types for all four versions can be found in Appendix A.

GPS K utilizes the same 10 definition cards as GPSS/360, but Flow Simulator and GPSS III both lack three of them.   One of the missing cards is associated with boolean variables, and another pertains to matrix savevalues.   The control cards for all four versions of GPSS are listed in Appendix B.

GPS K utilizes 40 control cards, Flow Simulator has 24, and GPSS III has 18. Many of the cards in this category are special-purpose types, and there are a number of cards that are unique to one version of GPSS.   The number of control cards in each version of GPSS is stated with some trepidation because the exact number may depend on the installation and equipment configuration. The GPSS control cards are listed in Appendix C.

GPS K has 43 standard numerical attributes as does GPSS/360.   Forty-one of them are the same, but both versions include two not found in the other.   Flow Simulator has 39 of these attributes while GPSS III has 17.   The GPSS standard numerical attributes are listed in Appendix D.

All four versions utilize the same 12 standard logical attributes.   They are listed in Appendix E.

Coding Format

We said that almost all of the GPSS cards have the same basic format (the so-called standard coding format) except for asterisk cards and a handful of other exceptions. The standard coding format for GPS K and GPSS III is identical to that of GPSS/360, and it is shown in Figure 2-4.

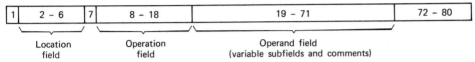

Fig. 2-4. Standard coding format for GPSS/360, GPS K, and GPS III.

The standard Flow Simulator format is similar in the respect that it includes a location, operation, variable, and comments field. But it differs in the fact that these fields are not restricted to specific card (or coding sheet) columns except for the location field which starts in column 1. The coding rules for the standard Flow Simulator format are as follows:

1. The location field must begin in column 1. It may occupy from 1 to 8 columns, depending on the number of characters in the user-supplied tag. Note that Flow Simulator tags may consist of as many as eight alphameric characters whereas GPSS/360, GPS K, and GPSS III addresses are limited to five alphameric characters.

2. The operation field (called the *operational* field in Flow Simulator) must be separated from the location field by at least one blank column, and it is as long as the number of letters in the card name. If there is no entry in the location field, the operation field can start in column 2 or anywhere to the right of column 2.

3. The variable field must be separated from the location field by at least one blank column. As with the other versions of GPSS, the variable field consists of subfields separated by commas and containing no embedded blanks.

4. The comment field must be separated from the variable field by at least one blank column. It extends to column 80.

Although Flow Simulator does not restrict the various fields to specific card columns, a programmer will usually do so in practice for the sake of appearance. For instance, he may start the operation field of every card in his deck in column 10. As a result, the general appearance of a Flow Simulator program is usually similar to that of a GPSS/360 program despite the free format allowed in the former.

Imagine that a Flow Simulator programmer were willing to start his operation field in column 8, start his operand field in column 19, foresake columns 72 to 80, and limit his tags to five characters. Would his deck be accepted by the GPSS/360 assembly program? The answer is no, because his location field must start in column 1. For the same reason, a GPSS/360 program would not be accepted by Flow Simulator.

Two additional points should be made in this connection. If a Flow Simulator program were so trivial as to have no location field entries, it could be made compatible with GPSS/360 and vice versa. The second point is that there are differences among the various GPSS versions in certain card types, above and beyond mere format considerations. These will generally be pointed out as we encounter them in this book.

Remarks cards in all four versions are denoted by an asterisk in column 1. Columns 1 through 72 are printed in the program listing for GPSS/360 and GPSS III; columns 1 through 80 are printed in GPS K and Flow Simulator. In all four versions, the comment may consist of any characters that the machine will print, including blanks.

Random Numbers

All four versions of GPSS have mechanisms that produce pseudorandom numbers as needed during a simulation run. However, these mechanisms are not all alike, and they do not all produce random numbers whose ranges are 0 to 1 or 0 to 1000. The fact that these dissimilarities exist is mentioned just as a point of information; the details are not worth discussing here.

2.5 SUMMARY

GPSS is a discrete-event simulation language that can be studied on three levels. The upper level corresponds to the external aspects, that is, those items that enter directly into the formulation of models. The middle and lower levels correspond, respectively, to the logical operation and physical structure of GPSS, that is, its internal aspects. It is fair to say that the simplified problem-oriented form of the upper level is made possible by the elaborate machine-oriented internal structure of the language.

From the user's point of view, the object of the game is to translate his system into a block diagram through which transactions will move in an appropriate manner. The block diagram can be drawn as a formal flow chart whose elements are GPSS blocks. It is interesting to note that the connecting lines in an ordinary flow chart indicate the order in which operations are performed, but in a GPSS block diagram they also represent the paths followed by transactions.

To construct a block diagram, the analyst defines a closed system whose dynamic elements are represented by transactions and whose static elements are represented by other GPSS entities. He uses blocks, standard numerical and logical attributes, definition and control cards, and so forth, to fashion a model that takes the form of an input deck. This model is read in, verified, allocated, and executed by the built-in GPSS programs, that is, the GPSS software package. System statistics are automatically accumulated and printed out without any such instructions cluttering up the model.

The execution of a simulation run by the GPSS simulator bears little resemblance to the user's view of his model. The internal operations are governed by the GPSS control algorithm which involves the processing of transactions by a scan in conjunction with a clock, transaction chains, and various indicators. The

GPSS simulator keeps track of xacts, performs appropriate computations, calls subroutines, tests statuses, and so on. These internal aspects come under the heading of "how GPSS works," and they are discussed in Chapter 8.

Each version of GPSS offers a specific repertoire of block, control, and definition cards. The user adapts these cards to his needs by making appropriate entries in their location and operand fields. His program is made up entirely of these predefined card types, except for comment cards. GPSS/360 includes 98 card types in its inventory; GPS K includes 94; Flow Simulator includes 72; and GPSS III includes 64.

GPSS is especially well suited to the simulation of systems that have events occurring in a random fashion. In fact, the capabilities of GPSS would be largely wasted if it were applied to systems that did not exhibit stochastic behavior. The element of randomness is provided in a GPSS model by generating a random number and using it in whatever manner is appropriate for the situation. It may be converted to another number, or its value may be tested in order to make a logical decision.

Quite a few GPSS terms have been introduced: *blocks, transactions, card types, location field, operation field, variable field, entities, attributes, GPSS simulator, clock time, transaction chains, block diagram, interarrival time, internal aspects,* and *levels.* If some of these terms fail to arouse a feeling of sheer and utter familiarity, that is to be expected. But they will be used in context with sample GPSS programs in the ensuing chapters, and they will eventually become very familiar to you.

On the subject of GPSS terminology: we have tended to refer to a given object by its various appelations rather than standardizing upon a single term. For example, the words "model," "source program," "symbolic program," "source deck," and "input deck" are more or less synonymous, and we may use any of them at any time — well, almost — rather than settling on one of them. Similarly, the words "address," "label," and "tag" are used interchangeably as are the words "user," "programmer," "analyst," and "reader." We have taken the aforementioned approach because (1) it reminds the reader that there are often several ways to say essentially the same thing and (2) it prevents him from attaching a false air of rigorousness to GPSS terminology. We shall continue to be inconsistent in this way in order to keep you "loose."

CHAPTER 3

Illustrative Program 1

At this point you may have the feeling that we have GPSS quite thoroughly surrounded and should begin to attack it directly. We have discussed its history, its areas of application, its general makeup, its main ingredients, and the process of applying it to a problem. Now it is time to use some specific blocks, entities, and cards to build a model.

A very elementary GPSS program will serve as the focus for our discussion of some of the key components and features of GPSS. This program is explained step by step, and the explanation is interwoven with brief discussions of its components as they are encountered.

3.1 INTRODUCTION TO PROGRAM 1

The system that is simulated by program 1 is briefly described and then translated into a GPSS model. Then we make an initial inspection of program 1 so that some pertinent aspects of GPSS program writing can be brought out. Incidentally, the system that is simulated by program 1 is so trivial that we do not attempt to explain why anyone would bother to simulate it.

Statement of the Problem

Customers arrive at a service desk at intervals of 10 ± 5 minutes. One customer at a time can be accommodated, and the service time per customer is 7 ± 5 minutes. If the service desk is in use when a customer arrives, he waits in line.

We would like to know how long a queue will form. We would also like to obtain a frequency distribution which indicates the time spent in this system by all of the customers who pass through it. For simulation purposes, 500 customers will be serviced before the run is halted.

The GPSS Model

Our system is exceedingly simple. It has one static entity (the service desk) which can be represented in GPSS by a *facility*. The dynamic entities are, of course, the customers; they are represented by *transactions*. We define 1 *clock unit* as being equal to 1 minute of system time.

The interarrival time of xacts varies from 5 to 15 minutes; that is, they are

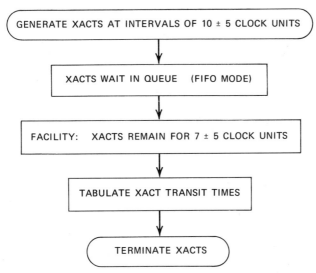

Fig. 3-1. Schematic diagram of GPSS model for program 1.

created at intervals of 10 ± 5 clock units.   After being created, xacts enter a
queue if the facility is not available.   As soon as the facility is free, it is seized by
the xact at the head of the line.   This is the "first in–first out" (FIFO) mode, and
it applies here since all xacts have equal priority.

The seizing transaction remains in the facility for 2 to 12 time units, and then
it releases the facility.   Its *transit time* through the system, measured from the
time it was created, is tabulated, and then it is destroyed.   Xacts proceed from
the facility to their termination in zero clock time.   In other words, they are effectively removed from the system at the moment they leave the facility.

As soon as a xact is destroyed, the xact at the head of the queue seizes the facility.   If no xact is waiting when the facility becomes available, the simulator clock
simply jumps ahead to the time when the next xact is to be created.   This process
continues until 500 xacts have passed through the system and been terminated.

More about GPSS Program Writing

Illustrative program 1 is shown in Figure 3-2.   It is a very short program, occupying only 14 lines.   Thus the source deck consists of 14 cards.

Two comment cards have been placed at the very beginning of the program.
In general, they may be placed almost anywhere in a GPSS deck, ahead of the
START card.   An exception to this rule is encountered in the next chapter, by
the way.   Note that the second card in Figure 3-2 has been inserted as a spacer
for the sake of appearance.   We could have used a completely blank card, since
the GPSS simulator treats them just like comment cards.

As stated in Chapter 2, nearly every GPSS card — the primary exception being
asterisk cards[1] — has an operation field in which its name appears.   All 12 of the
non-asterisk cards in program 1 adhere to this rule.

---

[1] The terms "asterisk card," "comment card," and "remarks card" are used interchangeably.

```
LOCATION  OPERATION  A, B, C, D, ...
*    ILLUSTRATIVE PROGRAM NUMBER 1
*
      SIMULATE
      GENERATE     10,5          CREATE XACTS AT INTERVALS OF 5-15 MINUTES.
      QUEUE        1             ENTER QUEUE NO. 1.
      SEIZE        1             SEIZE FACILITY NO. 1.
      DEPART       1             DEPART QUEUE NO. 1.
      ADVANCE      7,5           REMAIN IN FACILITY 1 FOR 2-12 MINUTES.
      RELEASE      1             RELEASE FACILITY NO. 1.
      TABULATE     5             OBTAIN DISTRIBUTION OF XACT TRANSIT TIMES.
     5TABLE        M1,2,4,20     TABLE DEFINITION CARD
      TERMINATE    1             DESTROY XACT.
      START        500           SIMULATION ENDS WHEN 500 XACTS ARE TERM'D.
      END
```

Fig. 3-2. Illustrative program 1. (See back pocket for a duplicate of this illustration which can be kept in view while reading the chapter.)

Only one of the cards in program 1 has an entry in its location field, and all but two (the SIMULATE and END cards) have entries in their variable fields. Again, we are referring to the non-asterisk cards.

Most of the cards in program 1 have comments in their operand fields. These comments could have been coded as shown in Figure 3-3, but the Figure 3-2 arrangement is more legible.

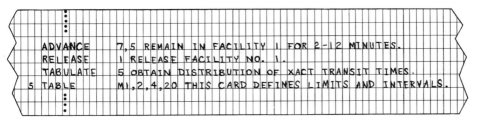

Fig. 3-3.   Alternate coding of comments in program 1.

It was stated in Chapter 2 that a coded GPSS program is analogous to a block diagram through which transactions move. In other words, xacts normally progress from a block to the one that follows it or is below it on a coding sheet. Therefore, you must arrange your blocks in the correct sequence when constructing a program. It should be pointed out that although xacts normally progress from block to block in a sequential fashion, there are a number of GPSS blocks which can be used to send xacts to any point in the block diagram that the programmer desires.

The routing of xacts through block diagrams will be clearly understood after you have examined some sample programs. Note that the paragraph above is concerned with the placement of block cards, but we have said nothing about the placement of control and definition cards. They will be discussed later.

We have now covered most of the fundamental rules of GPSS program writing. This topic is elaborated further, as appropriate, in the sections and chapters that follow. In particular, the coding of individual cards is explained as they are introduced. But for now let us call a halt to the rules and definitions and sink our teeth into an actual GPSS program.

3.2   EXAMINATION OF PROGRAM 1

We shall go through this program, card by card, starting with SIMULATE.

SIMULATE Card

If a simulation run is desired, a SIMULATE card must be included in the input deck. It can be placed anywhere in the deck ahead of the START card, but it is probably wise to place it at or near the front of the deck for the following reasons:

1. So that you will not forget to include it.
2. So that it will not appear in the middle of the block diagram portion of the

program. (This is strictly an aesthetic consideration; it makes no difference to the GPSS program.[2])

If the SIMULATE card is omitted, the program will be checked for errors by the assembly program, but no simulation run will take place. Incidentally, the location and variable fields of the SIMULATE card are always blank.

GENERATE Block

The GENERATE block creates transactions and sends them into the system at regular or random intervals as specified by the programmer. Every GPSS program must include at least one GENERATE block. The GENERATE block may have up to seven subfields specified. The fact that we have specified subfields A and B but not C, D, E, F, or G has no adverse effect. In the absence of those specifications the GENERATE block simply omits certain operations which we do not require in this particular simulation.

Field A of the GENERATE block specifies the average interarrival time or, more precisely, the mean time between the creation of xacts. If field B were blank, xacts would be sent into the system at regular intervals — every 10 clock units. Since field B contains a constant, the simulator interprets it as a *spread modifier* which gives a plus-or-minus value about the field A mean. In program 1, transactions are sent from the GENERATE block to the next sequential block at random intervals ranging from 5 to 15 clock units, inclusive.

As explained in Section 2.3, the computation of each intercreation interval by the GPSS simulator utilizes the built-in random number generator. Although the internal arithmetic involves fractions, the result is always truncated so that *every intercreation interval in GPSS is an integer number of clock units.*

The GENERATE block is the only one in GPSS that is not supposed to be entered by transactions and thus is not activated upon being entered by a transaction. (An error results if a xact attempts to enter a GENERATE block.) The operation of the GENERATE block is keyed to the simulator clock.

The GENERATE block is obviously an important component of GPSS, and it is covered in a more thorough fashion later in this book. Note that we have encountered two of the fourteen GPSS entities in our discussion of the GENERATE block. **Blocks** and **transactions** are called *basic entities* because there can be no GPSS simulation without them.

Queues and Facilities

Four of the next five cards in our program are associated with **queues** and **facilities** which are two more GPSS entities. The QUEUE and DEPART blocks are associated with a queue which we have labeled as *queue 1*. The SEIZE and RELEASE blocks are associated with *facility 1*. Before we return to program 1, let us discuss QUEUE, DEPART, SEIZE, and RELEASE blocks themselves.

---

[2] "GPSS program" is more or less synonymous with "GPSS simulator." These terms pertain to the built-in GPSS program as opposed to the user's *model* or *source program* which he naturally regards as being a "GPSS program."

Field A of QUEUE and DEPART blocks specifies the address of a queue. As far as the programmer is concerned, this address can be regarded as the label, tag, or number of the queue; take your choice. The field A argument may take any of several forms. It may be an *index number* (any number from 1 to 150 when running on a 128K computer), or it may be a *symbolic address*. A symbolic address consists of three, four, or five alphameric characters of which the first three must be letters of the alphabet. The fourth and fifth characters, if used, may be letters or digits, but no nonalphameric symbols such as blanks or /;#$.*, are permitted. Symbolic addressing is discussed further in the next chapter.

Field B of the QUEUE and DEPART blocks specifies the number of transactions to be added to and removed, respectively, from the queue each time a xact enters these blocks. It may not be clear why anyone would want to increment the contents of a queue by any number other than 1, but let us not worry about that now. If field B is left blank, the simulator automatically adds 1 unit to the queue whenever a xact enters the QUEUE block, and it subtracts 1 unit whenever a xact enters the DEPART block. Incidentally, fields C to G are not defined for the QUEUE and DEPART blocks.

QUEUE and DEPART blocks with the address *j* in field A comprise a set which corresponds to queue *j*. The QUEUE block must logically precede the DEPART block in a program, and every QUEUE block must have a corresponding DEPART block. QUEUE and DEPART blocks never refuse entry to xacts, and they are zero-delay blocks. The entry of a xact into a QUEUE block causes a series of queue statistics to be incremented and updated. The entry of a xact into a DEPART block causes certain queue statistics to be decremented and updated.

It should be understood that xacts may form queues at various places in a GPSS model, but QUEUE/DEPART blocks need not be used wherever queues occur. These blocks are used only where it is desired to gather queue statistics. They have no effect on entering xacts, and they play no part in the formulation of waiting lines. One point should be reiterated: A transaction is considered to enter a queue when it enters a QUEUE block, and it does not leave that queue until it enters the corresponding DEPART block.

The SEIZE and RELEASE blocks comprise a set which corresponds to a facility, and that facility is specified in field A. Fields B to G are not defined for SEIZE and RELEASE blocks.

A facility can contain or be seized by one xact at a time. In our illustrative program, a xact may enter the SEIZE block only if facility 1 is empty. Otherwise it is blocked by the SEIZE block until facility 1 is vacated. When a xact enters the SEIZE block, the status of the facility is changed from "not in use" to "in use," and various facility statistics are updated. The facility will remain in use until the xact that seized it enters the corresponding RELEASE block.

The RELEASE block never refuses entry to a transaction. This is in contrast to the SEIZE block which refuses entry to xacts until a certain condition is met, namely "facility not in use."

To recapitulate: Upon leaving the GENERATE block, a transaction enters the QUEUE block, that is, it enters queue 1. The appropriate statistics for queue 1 are incremented, and the xact attempts to enter the SEIZE block. If facility 1 is empty, the xact enters the SEIZE block and thus enters facility 1. At this point the xact has entered the facility but has not left the queue. However, it spends zero time in the SEIZE block and immediately enters the DEPART block which signals its departure from the queue. It is important to recognize that the xact progresses from the GENERATE block to the DEPART block in zero clock time if it finds facility 1 empty. Thus the xact leaves the queue and enters the facility in the same clock instant, and this is what we want.

ADVANCE Block

We have noted the important fact that a transaction will move through the system in zero clock time until it encounters a block that blocks or delays it. The ADVANCE block is the *only* GPSS block that can delay a xact for a *specified* period of time. The field A argument of the ADVANCE block specifies the mean number of time units for which a xact will be delayed. The field B argument is a modifier just as in the GENERATE block. The ADVANCE block in program 1 will delay xacts for anywhere from 2 to 12 clock units, selecting a number within this range at random each time a xact enters it.

When a xact enters the ADVANCE block, a delay time is immediately computed in accordance with fields A and B. (Incidentally, fields C to G are not defined for ADVANCE blocks.) That time is added to the current clock time to obtain the clock time when the xact should be passed to the next sequential block.

This typifies the way in which the GPSS program works. It maintains a record of the clock times when future events are scheduled to occur, and it scans the future events chain in order to execute events in their correct time sequence. For instance, while a xact is being held in the ADVANCE block, a new xact may be sent from the GENERATE block into the QUEUE block, being blocked at the SEIZE block until the former xact releases facility 1.

After a transaction leaves the ADVANCE block in program 1, it enters the RELEASE block, thus releasing (or exiting from) facility 1. It then enters the TABULATE block which, like the RELEASE block, never refuses entry to a xact.

Frequency Tables

There are many instances when it is desirable to have a certain statistic printed out in the form of a **frequency table.** To obtain such a table, the user must include a TABULATE block and a TABLE definition card in his program.

The TABULATE block is part of the block diagram, and like any GPSS block (except for GENERATE) it is activated when it is entered by a transaction. When activated, the TABULATE block causes an appropriate entry to be made in the table which is defined by the TABLE card.

Field A of the TABULATE block specifies the address of the corresponding TABLE card. An index number has been used in program 1, but a symbolic address could have been used. The field A address not only identifies the corresponding TABLE card—it is also the address of the table entity with which the TABULATE and TABLE cards are associated. Incidentally, field B of the

BLOCK DIAGRAM

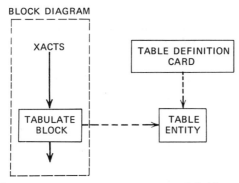

Fig. 3-4. Relationship between TABULATE block, TABLE definition card, and TABLE entity.

TABULATE block is defined, but it is not used in this instance. No other sub-fields can be used in the TABULATE block.

The TABULATE block should be placed at the point in the block diagram where it is desired to make entries in the table. The TABLE card may be placed just about anywhere since it is not part of the block diagram and is, therefore, "invisible" to xacts.

The table address, as specified in field A of the TABULATE card, appears in the location field of the TABLE card. It can lie anywhere within columns 2 to 6. Subfield A of the TABLE card contains the *argument* (or *quantity*, or *statistic*, if you prefer) to be tabulated. M1 is the SNA which stands for the transit time of a transaction through the system, measured from the instant it was created. In program 1, M1 is the number of clock units from the time a xact leaves the GENERATE block until it enters the TABULATE block.

Subfields B, C, and D of the TABLE card are used to specify the configuration of the table. Field B specifies the upper limit of the lowest interval being tabulated. Field C gives the width of the intervals in the frequency table. And field D gives the number of intervals or classes. The resulting table, as defined in program 1, is depicted in Figure 3-5.

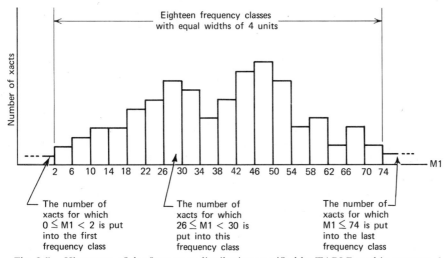

Fig. 3-5. Histogram of the frequency distribution specified by TABLE card in program 1.

Every xact which enters the TABULATE block in program 1 has a value of M1 associated with it. (M1 is one of the SNAs that are associated with transaction entities.) This value will fall into one of the 20 frequency classes in table 1, and an entry will be made in that particular class. Since an entry is made in the table each time a xact enters the TABULATE block, the total number of entries in table 1 will be 500.

The first and last frequency classes in a table, unlike the interior intervals, are not limited in width to the figure specified in field C of the TABLE card. This important point is illustrated in Figure 3-5. The lowest class is credited with an entry whenever M1 is less than 2. And the upper class has its entry count upped whenever a xact has M1 equal to 74 or any higher value. GPSS frequency tables are open-ended so they can accommodate argument values that exceed the range anticipated by the analyst.

Control of Simulation Run Length

Xacts are removed from the system immediately upon entering a TERMINATE block. Field A specifies how many units are to be deducted from the *termination count* each time a xact enters the TERMINATE block. Thus the "1" in field A of our TERMINATE block means that the termination count is decremented by 1 each time a xact enters this block. A "2" in field A would cause the termination count to be decremented by 2 each time a xact entered the TERMINATE block. A zero or blank in field A would cause nothing to happen to the termination count, but entering transactions would be wiped out just the same. In this program, a zero in the field A of the TERMINATE block would cause the simulation model to run indefinitely, as we shall see shortly. Fields B to G are not defined for the TERMINATE block.

The START card indicates to the simulator that the run may proceed, and it is always the next to the last card in a GPSS program. Field A specifies the *run termination count,* and it is decremented by the number specified in field A of the TERMINATE block each time a transaction enters that block. When it has been decremented to zero or less, the run will terminate. Thus the combination of the TERMINATE block and START card controls our simulation run so that it will cease upon the termination of 500 xacts. There may very well be xacts in the facility and/or queue at the time the run halts.

The START card has fields A, B, C, and D defined, but we did not need the last three in our problem, and it was perfectly all right to leave them unspecified.

The END card specifies the end of the input deck. It returns control to the system supervisor. If we wanted to stack several programs and run them in sequence, we would use a JOB card instead of an END card for all but the last (bottom) program in our total deck. The location and variable fields of the END card are always blank.

3.3   OUTPUT FROM PROGRAM 1

If we place the proper computer control cards before and after our 14-card program and feed the deck into a computer, we obtain a printout which consists of the following:

1. Miscellaneous phrases and "gibberish" related to the handling and processing of our model by various segments of the GPSS software package.

2. A *symbolic listing* and an *input listing* of our program.

3. An *output* consisting of:

    a. Relative and absolute clock times.
    b. Block counts.
    c. Statistics for facility 1.
    d. Statistics for queue 1.
    e. A frequency table called "table 5."

Item 1 will not be discussed, since this portion of the printout is usually ignored—if not discarded—by the user. It is items 2 and 3 that we are interested in, and they will be examined in the ensuing discussion. The printout for program 1 has been scissored so that it will fit more neatly into the three illustrations that accompany the following discussion.

The symbolic and input listings are shown in Figure 3-6. The former shows our program just as it was coded with the addition of block numbers on the left and card numbers on the right. The latter is essentially a stripped rendition of the symbolic program with the variable field arguments spaced out in definite fields.

The input listing shows the model after it has been interpreted by the assembly program in preparation for a simulation run. To appreciate the significance of the input listing, it is necessary to have at least a rudimentary understanding of what entity addressing is all about. So let us look into this matter before we move ahead to the output, that is, the *results* portion of the printout.

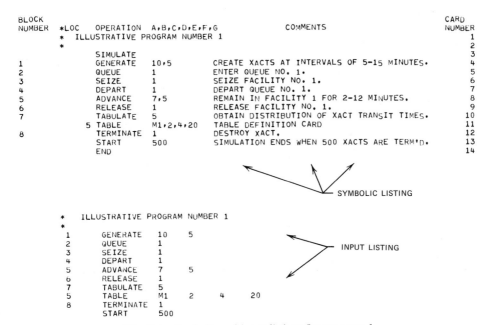

```
BLOCK                                                                          CARD
NUMBER  *LOC    OPERATION  A,B,C,D,E,F,G                 COMMENTS              NUMBER
          *   ILLUSTRATIVE PROGRAM NUMBER 1                                      1
          *                                                                      2
                SIMULATE                                                         3
    1           GENERATE    10,5          CREATE XACTS AT INTERVALS OF 5-15 MINUTES.  4
    2           QUEUE       1             ENTER QUEUE NO. 1.                      5
    3           SEIZE       1             SEIZE FACILITY NO. 1.                   6
    4           DEPART      1             DEPART QUEUE NO. 1.                     7
    5           ADVANCE     7,5           REMAIN IN FACILITY 1 FOR 2-12 MINUTES.  8
    6           RELEASE     1             RELEASE FACILITY NO. 1.                 9
    7           TABULATE    5             OBTAIN DISTRIBUTION OF XACT TRANSIT TIMES.  10
          5 TABLE         M1,2,4,20       TABLE DEFINITION CARD                  11
    8           TERMINATE   1             DESTROY XACT.                          12
                START       500           SIMULATION ENDS WHEN 500 XACTS ARE TERM'D.  13
                END                                                              14
```

SYMBOLIC LISTING

```
          *   ILLUSTRATIVE PROGRAM NUMBER 1
          *
    1           GENERATE    10     5
    2           QUEUE       1
    3           SEIZE       1
    4           DEPART      1
    5           ADVANCE     7      5
    6           RELEASE     1
    7           TABULATE    5
    5           TABLE       M1     2     4     20
    8           TERMINATE   1
                START       500
```

INPUT LISTING

Fig. 3-6. Symbolic and input listings for program 1.

Entity Addresses

When a GPSS program is fed into a computer for the purpose of carrying out a simulation run, the assembly program takes a large area of the computer core and partitions it into sections—one for each entity type. Thus there is a section for blocks, one for transactions, one for queues, and so on. Sections are allocated for every GPSS entity type regardless of whether or not they happen to be specified in the model being run.[3]

The amount of blocks, xacts, facilities, and so on, that are allocated depends on the version of GPSS being used and the memory size of the computer. For example, GPSS/360 normally allows a model to contain up to 35 facilities on a 64K machine and up to 150 facilities on a 128K machine. Similarly, there are maximum quantities of each entity type that may be included in a given model.[3]

If you assign a numeric address (i.e., an index number) to an entity, the assembly program will use it as is, as long as it does not exceed the maximum quantity for that entity type. If you assign a symbolic address to an entity, the assembly program will convert it to a numeric address. If you assign no address to an entity (as is the case with most blocks and all xacts), the assembly program will supply a numeric address. The significance of this address is explained by the following examples:

1. Queue 10 resides at location 10 of the *queues section* of the core.
2. Block 133 resides at location 133 of the *blocks section* of the core.
3. Facility 1 resides at location 1 of the *facilities section* of the core.

Now let us summarize some basic facts about entity addressing that are pertinent to program 1:

1. Each entity associated with a GPSS program (model) must be assigned a core location or address before the run may proceed.
2. Blocks, facilities, queues, tables, and transactions are entities; hence each is assigned an address.
3. Since blocks, facilities, queues, and tables are permanent entities (for the duration of the run), their addresses can be specified as numbers that are known to the programmer; we see them in the input listing.
4. Since xacts are transient entities, so to speak, each one is assigned a location when it is created which it occupies until it is destroyed. We do not see nor care about these addresses under normal circumstances.
5. For most purposes, it is less confusing and thus desirable to regard addresses as labels or tags. For example, "block 3" is less awkward than "the block at location 3 in the block entity section of the computer core." This concession to phraseology is perfectly all right, so long as we do not forget that the label of an entity is also its address.

Now let us look at the input listing in Figure 3-6. It shows how our model has

---

[3] Provisions for overriding the standard allocation of the core among various entity types are briefly discussed in Section 8.4.

been deployed in the computer's core by the GPSS assembly program.   Each block has been assigned a numerical address which is indicated to its left.   The queue, facility, and table have the addresses that we assigned to them, but all other entity addresses were assigned by the assembly program.

Note that the ADVANCE block occupies location 5 in the *blocks* section of the core while the table occupies location 5 in the *tables* section of the core.   Note, too, that comments have been deleted from block, definition, and control cards, and the variable field arguments have been placed into rigidly defined fields. Also, the SIMULATE and END cards have been deleted.

Clock Times; Block Counts; Facility and Queue Statistics

Figure 3-7 shows part of the results of our run.   Since we included no instructions that would reset the system clock, the relative and absolute clock times are equal.   (The significance of *relative* and *absolute* clock time will become clear in later chapters.)

The next thing shown in Figure 3-7 is a list of *block counts*.   Since all the current counts are zero, we know that there were no transactions in the system at the time that the five hundredth xact was terminated, that is, when the run ended. The total counts confirm this fact; each block in the model was entered by exactly 500 transactions during the run.   Keep in mind that this is a simple situation. In most models, various blocks are bypassed, and the total block (entry) counts will not all be the same.

The facility statistics are given next.   They are interpreted as follows:

1. The facility was in use during 69.2% of the simulation run time, that is, 3573 clock units.

2. Five hundred transactions entered the facility during the run.

3. The average transaction spent 7.147 clock units in the facility.   Recall that

```
        RELATIVE CLOCK          5163  ABSOLUTE CLOCK          5163
        BLOCK COUNTS
        BLOCK CURRENT      TOTAL
           1        0        500
           2        0        500
           3        0        500
           4        0        500
           5        0        500
           6        0        500
           7        0        500
           8        0        500
```

FACILITY	AVERAGE UTILIZATION	NUMBER ENTRIES	AVERAGE TIME/TRAN	SEIZING TRANS. NO.	PREEMPTING TRANS. NO.
1	.692	500	7.147		

QUEUE	MAXIMUM CONTENTS	AVERAGE CONTENTS	TOTAL ENTRIES	ZERO ENTRIES	PERCENT ZEROS	AVERAGE TIME/TRANS	$AVERAGE TIME/TRANS
1	2	.114	500	350	69.9	1.181	3.939

$AVERAGE TIME/TRANS = AVERAGE TIME/TRANS EXCLUDING ZERO ENTRIES

Fig. 3-7.   Program 1 output statistics—clock, blocks, facility, and queue.

we specified a range of 2 to 12 clock units in the ADVANCE block, and 7.0 is the exact mean value.

4. If the facility were being seized or preempted when the run ended, the number of the seizing or preempting transaction would appear as part of the facility statistics.

The queue statistics are given next. They are interpreted as follows:

1. The maximum contents were 2. In other words, there were never more than two xacts waiting in line at any time during the run. This makes sense when you consider that the service intervals in the facility tend to be a good deal shorter than the interarrival times in this model.

2. On the average, the queue had one xact in it during 11.4% of the simulated time period. Thus the total number of "xact-minutes" spent in queue 1 was .114 of 5163, namely, 589. (The average contents of a queue may very well exceed 1.0 in a given run.)

3. Five hundred xacts entered the queue during the run.

4. Three hundred and fifty of the entering xacts did not have to wait in line at all, since the facility was not in use at the moment they entered the queue.

5. Of the entering xacts 69.9% were "zero entries."

6. The average transaction spent only 1.181 clock units waiting in line; this average includes those that had no wait at all.

7. The last queue statistic gives the average waiting time for only those xacts that were forced to wait in line; it excludes zero entries.

Table Statistics

Table 5 is shown in Figure 3-8. Looking at the summary statistics above the table, we see that the average transit time through the system was 8.329 units. This is equal to the average time in the facility plus the average time in the queue. The standard deviation about the mean is also given. The total number of clock units spent by all transactions passing through the system is given as 4165.0, and this figure is obviously the product of 8.329 and 500.

The table itself lists the frequency classes in the left-hand column. The observed frequencies are interpreted as follows:

1. Thirty-four xacts (customers) had transit times of 2 minutes or less.

2. One hundred and forty-one xacts had transit times of 3 to 6 minutes.

3. One hundred and eighty xacts had transit times of 7 to 10 minutes.

4. One hundred and sixteen xacts had transit times of 11 to 14 minutes.

5. Eighteen xacts had transit times of 15 to 18 minutes.

6. Eleven xacts had transit times of 19 to 22 minutes.

7. No xacts had transit times of 23 or more minutes.

The total of the observed frequencies is 500, of course. Note that the transit time ranges are stated in whole numbers since the values of M1 are always in-

```
TABLE   5
ENTRIES  IN  TABLE              MEAN  ARGUMENT              STANDARD  DEVIATION
            500                        8.329                              3.980

            UPPER         OBSERVED        PER CENT       CUMULATIVE
            LIMIT        FREQUENCY        OF TOTAL       PERCENTAGE
              2              34             6.79             6.7
              6             141            28.19            34.9
             10             180            35.99            70.9
             14             116            23.19            94.1
             18              18             3.59            97.7
             22              11             2.19           100.0
REMAINING  FREQUENCIES  ARE  ALL  ZERO
```

```
                    SUM OF  ARGUMENTS
                         4165.000              NON-WEIGHTED

        CUMULATIVE          MULTIPLE        DEVIATION
        REMAINDER          OF  MEAN         FROM  MEAN
            93.1              .240            -1.590
            65.0              .720             -.585
            29.0             1.200              .419
             5.8             1.680             1.424
             2.2             2.160             2.429
              .0             2.641             3.434
```

```
                              END
```

```
Y O U R   JOB STATISTICS --       19 CARDS READ --        101 LINES PRINTED --


    0 CARDS PUNCHED  --      0.31 MINUTES EXECUTION TIME
```

Fig. 3-8.   Program 1 output statistics — table.

tegers.   Note also that just the first six frequency classes were printed out although our TABLE card specified 20 intervals.   There would be no point in printing out 14 lines of zeroes.

The meaning of the third, fourth, and fifth columns should be self-evident, but the last two columns should perhaps be explained.   The *multiple of mean* figures are equal to the upper limit of the frequency class divided by the mean argument.   For example, $.240 = 2/8.329$.   The *deviation from mean* figures are equal to the difference between the frequency class upper limit and the mean argument, divided by the standard deviation.   For example, $-1.590 = (2 - 8.329)/3.980$.

The significance of some of the table statistics may be lost on the nonstatistically-oriented reader.   However, all of them are provided automatically anyway, so you need only pay attention to the portions that are meaningful to you.

Following the table are some selected phrases clipped from the printout.   The fact that 19 cards were read tells you that five computer control cards were used, since our symbolic program consisted of 14 cards.   The execution time for this run bears no relationship to the simulation clock, as explained in Section 2.1.

Interpretation of Results

The system described at the beginning of Chapter 3 was translated into a GPSS program, and the output from this program contained the answers to the questions that were originally posed. The first question pertained to the maximum queue length that would occur: it was 2. The second request was for a distribution of transit times: it was given by table 5.

It is important to remember that the results are based on stochastic events; hence they should not be interpreted literally. For instance, a different random number sequence might have resulted in a maximum queue length of 1 or, perhaps, 3. Therefore, the correct interpretation of this statistic is not simply that the maximum queue length is 2. Rather, it is that the maximum queue length is *approximately* 2, that is, it is a small number.

In cases where you want to minimize the dependence of the results on the random number sequence, it is often advisable to increase the simulation run length and thus obtain a better sample.

It should be pointed out that the process of checking an input deck for errors, deploying the model in the computer, and readying the GPSS simulator for a run accounts for a significant portion of the execution time. Our model could have been run for 5000 instead of 500 terminations with much less than a ten-fold increase in running time.

3.4   DIFFERENCES BETWEEN GPSS/360 AND OTHER VERSIONS

The GPSS model represented by program 1 could just as easily be constructed using the other three versions. The results obtained would not be numerically identical, however, for the simple reason that the four versions use different random number sequences.

If program 1 had been written in GPS K, it would look precisely like the one shown in Figure 3-2. Moreover, everything else in this chapter applies to GPS K in a general sense. However, there are a few detailed differences with respect to entity addressing, the most important of which is the following. If a given entity type is assigned a symbolic address, all other entities of that type must also have symbolic addresses: the same goes for numeric addresses. Thus a model may contain facilities with all symbolic addresses and queues with all numeric addresses, but it may not contain some facilities with symbolic labels and other facilities with index numbers.

If program 1 had been written in GPSS III, it would look just like the one in Figure 3-2 except for one detail. The SIMULATE card in GPSS III must have an asterisk in column 1, and it must be one of the first two cards in the deck. It can be preceded by a single comment card, if desired, but no other type of card. By the way, GPSS/360 accepts the SIMULATE card with or without the asterisk, but it must be the first or second card in the deck if it has the asterisk.

GPSS III differs from GPSS/360 in another respect that is more important but is not apparent from looking at program 1. Whereas any GPSS/360 entity may have a symbolic address, only blocks may have symbolic addresses in GPSS III, and all other entities must have numeric labels. Therefore, the use of index numbers for the queue and facility entities in program 1 is optional in GPSS/360 but mandatory in GPSS III.

Flow Simulator differs from GPSS/360 in two ways that show up in connection with program 1. First, Flow Simulator does not include a SIMULATE card. The technique for suppressing a Flow Simulator run is to omit the START card. Second, Flow Simulator requires all tags to be symbolic. However, there are provisions for equating symbolic tags to index numbers.

Figure 3-9 shows how program 1 might look if it were written in Flow Simulator. All comments have been omitted so that we can concentrate on the model itself. Comparing this figure to Figure 3-2, we see that the symbolic tags WAITING, SERVDESK, and TIME have been used in place of the index numbers *1*, *1*, and *5*, respectively. The two EQUATE cards are entirely unnec- essary and have been included only to show how they work. If, for some reason, we wanted the table to be tagged with the number *5*, we could equate its symbolic tag to *5* as has been done by the first EQUATE card. Similarly, the queue tag could be equated to the number *1*, as is done by the second EQUATE card.

The coding of the EQUATE card (a Flow Simulator control card) is apparent from Figure 3-9. The symbolic tag goes in the location field; the desired index number goes into field A; and a key letter that denotes the entity type goes in field B. The EQUATE card can be used in more complex modes than this, but they will not be mentioned here. Again, there was no real reason for equating the symbolic tags to numbers in program 1 except to show how it is done, but this capability can be very useful in certain situations.

Fig. 3-9.   Program 1 in Flow Simulator.

3.5   SUMMARY

The purpose of program 1, in a nutshell, was to simulate and obtain statistics
about a simple situation in which people arrive at a service desk every 10 ± 5
minutes and spend 7 ± 5 minutes being serviced.   At minimum, a GPSS model
to accomplish this must include a transaction generator and a facility.   But what
about the queue?   The only reason for using a queue entity in a GPSS program
is to obtain statistics about a waiting line which you expect to occur.   The waiting
line will form irrespective of the presence or absence of a queue entity in the program.

Program 1 introduced you to eight block types, three control cards (not
including the EQUATE card in Flow Simulator), and one definition card.   It
also introduced you to five of the 14 GPSS entities, namely *blocks, transactions,
queues, facilities,* and *tables.*

All of the blocks in program 1 were zero-delay blocks except for the GENER-
ATE and ADVANCE blocks.   A zero-delay block is one which a xact leaves at
the same clock instant at which it entered it.   None of the blocks in program 1
ever refuse entry to xacts except for the GENERATE and SEIZE block.   If a
xact attempts to enter the GENERATE block, an error results.   All of the blocks
in program 1 are essentially dormant until they are entered by a xact except for
the GENERATE block whose operation is keyed to the simulator clock.

We saw how a typical GPSS program is organized, and we covered some more
coding rules.   We saw how easy it is to have the simulator produce uniformly distributed random numbers by specifying a mean and modifier in fields A and B
of the GENERATE and ADVANCE blocks.   We saw how the TERMINATE
and START cards control the run length via the run termination count.

We saw that a QUEUE and a DEPART block represent a queue; a SEIZE and
a RELEASE block represent a facility; a TABULATE block and a TABLE definition card represent a frequency table.   We interposed the SEIZE block
between the QUEUE and DEPART blocks so that xacts would be counted as
remaining in the queue until they entered the facility.   Similarly, we put the AD-
VANCE block after the SEIZE block and ahead of the RELEASE block so that
xacts would be counted as remaining in the facility until the delay interval was
over.

We saw that a definition card was required for the table entity but not for the
queue and facility.   The presence of QUEUE/DEPART and SEIZE/RELEASE
blocks was adequate to define the latter entities.   The queue and facility
addresses were specified in the variable fields of these four blocks, whereas the
table address was specified in two places—the variable field of the TABULATE
block and the location field of the TABLE card.

A number of basic points emerged with respect to entity addressing.   All four
versions "prefer" symbolic block addresses but allow numeric addresses as long
as they agree with those assigned by the assembly program.   The addresses of all
other entity types are as follows:

1. Either numeric or symbolic in GPSS/360 and GPS K.

2. Always symbolic in Flow Simulator unless equated to numeric by the programmer.

3. Always numeric in GPSS III.

Numeric addresses may be assigned in any arbitrary order, but they must lie within the allowable limits for the respective entity types. These limits correspond to the numbers of entity locations allocated in the core. This is discussed further in Section 8.4.

Our program contained no instructions to print or write, nor did it contain any format specifications. Just the fact that it ran ensured that the printout would include a symbolic listing, an input listing, clock times, and block counts. The fact that our program contained a facility, a queue, and a table automatically ensured the printout of statistics for those entities. This automatic output feature is called the *standard output option*. There is another output option called the *output editor* which allows the programmer to exercise complete control over what will be printed out. This is taken up in Chapter 13.

CHAPTER 4
Illustrative Program 2

As in the preceding chapter, we relate our discussion to a sample — and simple — program. Some new entities and cards are introduced, and symbolic addressing, standard numerical attributes, and random number generation are elaborated upon.

4.1 INTRODUCTION TO PROGRAM 2

The situation that is simulated by program 2 is sufficiently straightforward to be translated into a GPSS model without a preliminary system definition. Consequently the problem is stated almost as if it were in the form of a GPSS model.

Statement of the Problem

The interarrival times of customers are distributed exponentially about a mean of 45 seconds. Customers attempt to enter a service area which can accommodate up to three customers simultaneously. The service times for customers range from 70 to 130 seconds. An arriving customer must wait in line if all three compartments in the service area are occupied. (Note that the service area is, in effect, three facilities in parallel; in GPSS, this sort of entity is called a **storage.**)

Upon leaving the storage, 40% of the customers, on the average, pass through a facility called FACIL while the other customers leave the system directly. We would like to know how long it takes customers to travel through this system and how long the waiting lines tend to be.

The GPSS Model

Figure 4-1 contains a schematic diagram of the GPSS model. Although it is not a block diagram in the strict sense, it is quite suggestive of one so far as its elements and connecting lines are concerned. An actual block diagram would (for instance) show QUEUE, SEIZE, DEPART, and RELEASE blocks where Figure 4-1 shows QUEUE and FACILITY boxes. In other words, every box in a block diagram corresponds to a block, whereas some of the boxes in our flow chart are analogous to entities. This point has been made to further clarify the subject of

block diagrams versus other types of flow diagrams—not that it is such an important matter.

Figure 4-1 indicates that program 2 will contain one GENERATE block and
two TERMINATE blocks. Two queues may form, one in front of the storage
and the other in front of the facility. The path of transactions through the block
diagram splits after the storage with 40% going to the facility and the remaining
60% leaving the system directly.

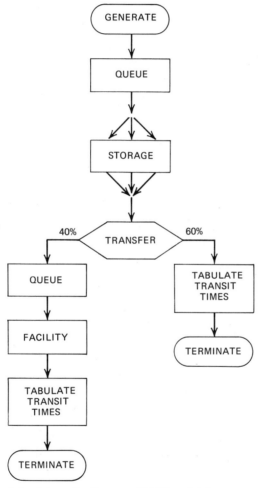

Fig. 4-1. Schematic diagram of GPSS model for program 2.

A Look at Illustrative Program 2

Program 2 is shown in Figure 4-2. The symbolic listing has been used because
it is more compact than the hand-coded version and also because the computer
has provided block and card numbers that will facilitate references to the
program. Some key coding sheet columns are indicated in parentheses.

```
BLOCK                                                                        CARD
NUMBER   *LOC    OPERATION   A,B,C,D,E,F,G              COMMENTS             NUMBER
         *                                                                    1
         *     ILLUSTRATIVE PROGRAM NUMBER 2                                  2
         *                                                                    3
               SIMULATE        ┌(Column 19}                                   4
         EXPON FUNCTION     RN1,C24      EXPONENTIAL PROBABILITY DISTRIBUTION  5
         0,0/.1,.104/.2,.222/.3,.355/.4,.509/.5,.69/.6,.915/.7,1.2/.75,1.38/  6
         .8,1.6/.84,1.83/.88,2.12/.9,2.3/.92,2.52/.94,2.81/.95,2.99/.96,3.2/  7
         .97,3.5/.98,3.9/.99,4.6/.995,5.3/.998,6.2/.999,7/.9997,8             8
 1               GENERATE    45,FN$EXPON AVERAGE INTERARRIVAL TIME IS 45 SECONDS.  9
 2               QUEUE       1           ENTER QUEUE NO. 1                    10
 3               ENTER       1           ENTER STORAGE NUMBER 1               11
               1 STORAGE     3           STORAGE NO. 1 CAN ACCOMMODATE 3 XACTS.  12
 4               DEPART      1           DEPART FROM QUEUE NO. 1              13
 5               ADVANCE     100,30      REMAIN IN STORAGE 1 FOR 70-130 SECONDS  14
 6               LEAVE       1           LEAVE STORAGE NO. 1                  15
 7               TRANSFER    .40,OUT,LINE 40 PERCENT OF XACTS GO TO QUEUE NO. 2  16
 8           OUT TABULATE    3           OBTAIN DISTRIBUTION OF XACT TRANSIT TIMES  17
 9               TERMINATE               DESTROY XACT                        18
10          LINE QUEUE       2           ENTER QUEUE NO. 2                    19
11               SEIZE       FACIL       SEIZE FACILITY NAMED FACIL          20
12               DEPART      2           DEPART FROM QUEUE NO. 2              21
13               ADVANCE     25,FN$EXPON AVG SERVICE TIME IN FACILITY IS 25 SECONDS  22
14               RELEASE     FACIL       RELEASE FACILITY                    23
15               TABULATE    4           OBTAIN DISTRIBUTION OF XACT TRANSIT TIMES  24
16               TERMINATE               DESTROY XACT                        25
               1 QTABLE      1,10,10,10  TABULATE WAITING TIMES IN QUEUE NO. 1  26
               2 QTABLE      2,0,5,15    TABULATE WAITING TIMES IN QUEUE NO. 2  27
               3 TABLE       M1,80,20,10 TABLE DEFINITION CARD               28
               4 TABLE       M1,80,20,10 TABLE DEFINITION CARD               29
17               GENERATE    5000        RELEASE A XACT AFTER 5000 SECONDS   30
18               TERMINATE   1           DESTROY ABOVE XACT; DECR'M'T RUN TERM. COUNT  31
                 START       1           SIMULATION ENDS AFTER 5000 SECONDS  32
                 END                                                         33
         {Column 8}                  {Column 19}
```

Fig. 4-2. Illustrative program 2 — symbolic listing. (See back pocket for a duplicate of this illustration which can be kept in view while reading the chapter.)

Program 2 consists of 33 cards of which the first three are asterisk cards. From the block numbers (assigned by the assembly program) we can see that there are 18 blocks in our model.

4.2 SOME FEATURES FOUND IN PROGRAM 2

Cards 5 to 9 embody several features which are new or merit further explanation. For example, cards 5 to 8 correspond to a function entity; these have not been previously discussed. Card 5 has a symbolic address in its location field, and it calls for random numbers in subfield A. Card 9 combines a standard numerical attribute with a symbolic address in subfield B. In all, there are four topics that we should bone up on before proceeding through program 2: symbolic addressing, standard numerical attributes, random number generation, and function entities. The first three have already been covered to some extent, and they will now be developed further.

Symbolic Addressing

As stated in the preceding chapter, all GPSS/360, GPS K, and Flow Simulator entities can be assigned *symbolic addresses*. A symbolic address in GPSS/360 and GPS K may consist of three, four, or five alphameric characters, but the first three must be alphabetic. A symbolic address in Flow Simulator may consist of one to eight alphameric characters with the first one alphabetic. (To avoid pos-

sible confusion with SNAs, the first three characters should be alphabetic.)
There are four examples of symbolic addressing in Figure 4-2:

1. The function has been labeled "EXPON."
2. The facility has been labeled "FACIL."
3. The first TABULATE block has been labeled "OUT."
4. The second QUEUE block has been labeled "LINE."

Note the distinction between the *queue entity* (whose address is specified as "2")
and the QUEUE *block* (whose address is specified as "LINE") associated with
queue 2.   The queue is an entity that has an address, while the block is also an
entity that has its own address.

Symbolic addressing is primarily for the benefit of the programmer.   It allows
him to identify various entities in a meaningful way rather than simply using an
index number.   When a source program is fed into the computer, the GPSS assembly program assigns numeric addresses to all entities with symbolic addresses, and the simulation is carried out using the former.

If any of the entities in a program have symbolic addresses, the printout
includes a *cross-reference dictionary* which immediately follows the symbolic listing
and precedes the input listing.   It lists the user-assigned symbolic addresses and
corresponding assembler-assigned numeric addresses.   The cross-reference dictionary and input listing for program 2 are shown in Figure 4-3.

Standard Numerical Attributes

By way of review, there are 43 standard numerical attributes (SNAs) in
GPSS/360, and they are listed in Table D-1.   Every one pertains to a specific entity type except for three that are classified as *systemwide attributes.*   A standard
numerical attribute, when referenced, assumes a *numerical* value which is nearly
always an integer.   The only SNA we have encountered thus far is the transit
time, denoted by M1.

A SNA usually consists of one or two mnemonic characters followed by an entity address.   (M1 happens to be an exception.)   If the address is numeric, the
SNA is coded and interpreted as shown by the following examples:

FN3 = value of function 3
F6   = status of facility 6 (0 if available, 1 if not)
Q6   = current contents of (number of xacts in) queue 6

If the entity address is symbolic, it must be preceded by a dollar sign as per the
following examples:

FN$EXPON = value of the function whose address is EXPON
F$FACIL   = status of the facility whose address is FACIL
Q$AAA3   = current contents of the queue whose address is AAA3

Perhaps the most common reason for using SNAs is to make the operation of
certain blocks dependent on the properties of other parts of the model.   To put
it another way, SNAs provide dynamic access to the current status of various

parts of the model. This can be better appreciated with the help of an example:

    ADVANCE   Q4

When a xact enters this block, it will be delayed for a number of clock units equal to the current number of xacts in queue 4. Thus the delay times for xacts are not specified beforehand. They are computed (or obtained, if you prefer) every time a xact enters the ADVANCE block shown above.

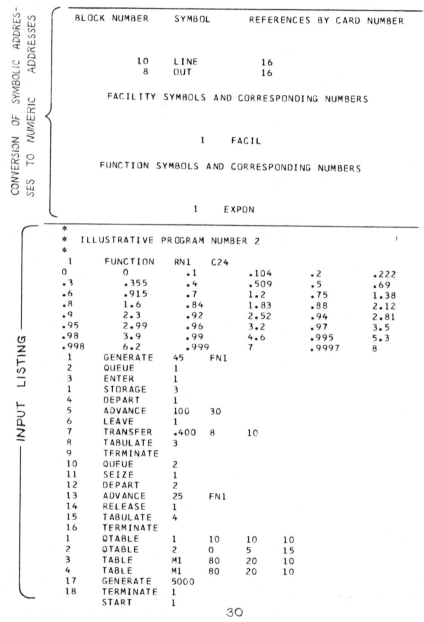

Fig. 4-3. Cross-reference dictionary and input listing for program 2.

There are three SNAs in program 2: RN1, FN$EXPON, and M1. RN1, when referenced, gives a random number. This will be explained in the next section. M1, as you know, gives the transit time of the current transaction. This leaves us with FN$EXPON which, you will notice, is used as the field B argument of blocks 1 (GENERATE) and 13 (ADVANCE).

When the intercreation interval for the next xact is to be computed by the GENERATE block, it references the function. A value is computed and returned to field B, whereupon it is multiplied by the value in field A to obtain the desired intercreation interval. The ADVANCE block works much the same way, except that it references the function when a xact enters it. A value of the function is computed, returned to subfield B, and multiplied by subfield A to obtain a delay time for the xact which had entered the ADVANCE block.

As an important "aside," it should be pointed out that both the GENERATE and ADVANCE blocks operate as follows:

1. If the field B argument is a constant or any SNA except FNj, it is interpreted as a plus-or-minus value about the field A mean.
2. If the field B argument is FNj, its value is multiplied by the field A mean.

Random Number Generation

As explained in Section 2.3, all four versions of GPSS have built-in random number generators that produce random numbers upon request. Let us now see what kinds of random numbers are produced in response to the types of requests that may be made.

The requests to which the random number generator responds fall into one of two categories—*directly specified* or *implied*. A directly specified request is made by using the standard numerical attribute RNx as an argument in a card's variable field. An implied request is made when the situation implies the need for a random number, but when RNx does not appear.

Whenever a card with RNx in its variable field is activated or referenced—blocks are activated and definition cards are referenced—a value for RNx is supplied by the random number generator. In GPSS/360, it is as follows:

1. $0 \leq RNx \leq .999999$ if RNx is a function argument.
2. $0 \leq RNx \leq 999$ in all other instances.

Implicit requests for random numbers occur in situations such as this:

```
ADVANCE        100,30
```

Whenever a transaction enters this ADVANCE block, a delay time of 70 to 130 clock units must be computed. It is gotten by having the random number generator supply a number which is translated into an integer in the range 70 to 130. The request for a random number is *implied* in this situation, since RNx does not appear in the variable field of the requesting block.

Random numbers that are produced in response to an implied request may be used in one of two ways:

1. To obtain a random integer (e.g., ADVANCE block).
2. To make a decision (e.g., TRANSFER block).

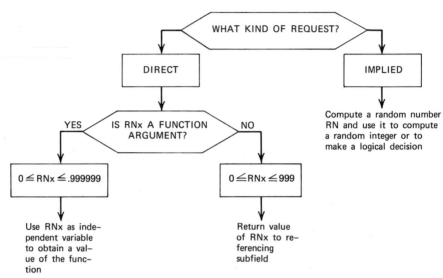

Fig. 4-4.   Operation of the GPSS/360 random number generator (a conceptual diagram).

The operation of the random number generator is summarized in Figure 4-4. This diagram does not necessarily depict the exact logical operations that take place, but it will help you visualize what happens.   Although the specific numbers in Figure 4-4 pertain to GPSS/360, the general sequence of events is typical of all four versions of GPSS.   It should be pointed out that the "x" in RNx may stand for 1 through 8 in GPSS/360 and Flow Simulator, but it must be 1 in GPS K and GPSS III.   The ability to specify different values of x is a convenience in certain situations.   But this is a fine point that need not be considered here.

Functions

There are many instances when it is desirable to have the value of a block argument dependent on the value of some other quantity.   This suggests that we would like to be able to have certain block arguments computed via a functional relationship.   Such relationships can be incorporated into a GPSS model by using **function** entities.   Functions are one of the two types of *computational entities* provided in GPSS.   **Variables** are the other type, and they are discussed in Chapter 6.

A function entity is incorporated into a GPSS program by using a FUNCTION definition card plus one or more *function follower* cards.   There are no block types associated with functions, so xacts do not directly affect functions. Functions are activated only when they are referenced by the standard numerical attribute FNj.

There are five basic types of functions in GPSS.   They are listed below, along with their code letters:

Continuous numerical-valued: C

Discrete numerical-valued: D

List numerical-valued: L

Discrete attribute-valued: E

List attribute-valued: M

A FUNCTION definition card is coded as follows:

1. Function address in the location field.
2. The word "FUNCTION" in the operation field.
3. Argument of the function; that is, the independent variable, in subfield A.
4. A function type code letter (C, D, L, E, or M), immediately followed by a number which specifies the number of coordinate pairs, in subfield B.

A function follower card is coded as follows:

1. Pairs of coordinates are listed sequentially in columns 1 to 72. They are listed in the order $X_1,Y_1/X_2,Y_2/X_3,Y_3/$ . . . , where X is the independent variable.
2. The first X value on every function follower card must start in column 1. Blank spaces are only allowed after the last slash on a card, and no slash appears after the last Y value on the last card.

The FUNCTION and function follower cards which pertain to a given function may not have any remarks cards interspersed among them. This is an exception to the general rule that remarks cards and blank cards may be inserted anywhere in the input deck. Another exception to the coding rules outlined in Section 2.2 is the format of the function follower cards. These cards do not adhere to the standard format, that is, location, operation, and operand fields.

Generally speaking, a GPSS function operates as follows:

1. It remains passive until it is referenced via FNj, where j is the function address or tag.
2. Upon being referenced, a function assigns an appropriate value to its argument. In some cases, this value must itself be computed in a complicated manner. For instance, the argument of a function could be another function, or it could be a random number which must be generated.
3. Using the relationship defined via the function follower cards, the function then obtains (or computes) a value for the dependent variable.
4. This value (of the dependent variable) is returned to the referencing block subfield. It becomes, in effect, the value of FNj. It is always an integer except when FNj appears in subfield B of the GENERATE or ADVANCE blocks or subfield C of the ASSIGN block.

Now let us restrict the present discussion to C-type functions. These functions which can be represented as a continuous[1] graph of X versus Y, where:

1. X denotes the independent variable and Y denotes the dependent variable.
2. For each value of X there is a unique value of Y.

[1] In mathematics, the word "continuous" implies a smooth curve with no breaks or angular features. But in this context we use the term "continuous" to connote an unbroken line that consists of the series of segments that join the points specified on the function follower cards.

3. The coordinates specified on function follower cards are successive points on the curve of the function. The values of X must be monotonically increasing, but values of Y may trend either way. See Figure 4-5.

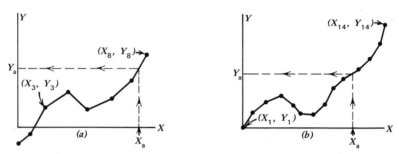

Fig. 4-5. Typical continuous numerical-valued GPSS functions. (*a*) C7 in subfield B of FUNC-TION definition card; (*b*) C14 in subfield B of FUNCTION definition card.

The diagram shows two examples of how a continuous function is defined by a series of points (X,Y-pairs). It also shows how a value X_a of the function argument is translated into a value Y_a by linear interpolation. Remember that Y corresponds to FNj, and X is the value of the field A argument in the FUNC-TION card.

The C-type (continuous numerical-valued) functions can be subdivided into two categories—those whose argument is RNx and those whose argument is any other SNA.

It should be obvious that a function whose argument is RNx will take on random values. For example, if the argument of function 17 is RN1, then the values of FN17 will be stochastic. The remainder of this discussion will deal with C-type functions whose argument is RNx.

As explained in Section 2.3, it is possible to construct a functional relationship between exponentially and uniformly distributed random numbers. To do this with a function entity, the exponentially distributed numbers have a mean value of 1.0, and they are the dependent variable. The uniformly distributed numbers (denoted by RNx) lie in the range 0 to 1, and they are the independent variable.

The use of GPSS functions to obtain random numbers from various types of probability distributions will be demonstrated in several of the illustrative pro-grams to follow, and it is also explained in detail in Appendix G. But for our immediate purposes (to understand program 2), it is sufficient to know the fol-lowing:

1. The GENERATE block sends transactions into the system at random in-tervals of time which are taken from an exponential distribution with a mean of 45.

2. To compute an intercreation interval, the GENERATE block multiplies the field A mean value by the field B function modifier. The use of a function rather than a constant in field B automatically causes this mode of computa-tion by the GENERATE block.

3. To obtain a value for its field B argument, the GENERATE block references the function whose address is EXPON. When referenced, the function will compute a random number from the exponential distribution whose mean is 1.0.

4. To do this, the function first calculates a random number RN1 whose value lies in the interval 0 to 1. It then uses the functional relationship defined by the function follower cards to compute a corresponding random number. This "corresponding" number is from the exponential distribution whose mean is 1.0, and it becomes the value of FN$EXPON. (The next time it is referenced, the function will calculate another value of RN1, and FN$EXPON will take on another value from the exponential distribution whose mean is 1.0.)

5. The GENERATE block receives the freshly computed value of FN$EXPON and multiplies it by 45 to obtain an intercreation interval. If the product is not an integer, the fractional portion is simply truncated.

6. Keep in mind that the actual process of computing an intercreation interval for each new transaction takes a fraction of a second of actual computer running time and zero simulator clock time.

7. Field A of the FUNCTION card specifies one of eight *seeds* from which uniform random numbers will be generated.

8. Field B of the FUNCTION card conveys the fact that our distribution is continuous and has been specified via 24 pairs of coordinates.

4.3 EXAMINATION OF PROGRAM 2

Now that the groundwork has been laid, we can progress fairly quickly through the Figure 4-2 program. We have already covered the first nine cards in program 1 and are now at the point where xacts enter queue 1 after leaving the GENERATE block. They then attempt to enter storage 1.

Blocks 3 to 6 (Cards 11 to 15)

If the storage is not completely full, the xact is able to enter the ENTER block. It then proceeds to enter the DEPART block, thus departing from queue 1. It then enters the ADVANCE block where it remains for 70 to 130 clock units.

If the storage is in full use, xacts are blocked by the ENTER block, and a queue forms. As soon as a xact leaves the storage by virtue of entering the LEAVE block, the xact at the head of the line can be admitted to the storage. The ENTER/LEAVE blocks pertain to a storage entity in the same way that the SEIZE/RELEASE blocks pertain to a facility entity. However, a storage also has a definition card associated with it, namely, the STORAGE card.

The STORAGE definition card for storage 1 appears after the ENTER block in program 2. Since it is a definition card, it could have been placed anywhere between the last function follower card and the START card. The address of the storage is indicated in the location field of the STORAGE card (as well as in field A of the ENTER/LEAVE blocks). The field A argument of the STORAGE card specifies the storage capacity.

In models containing more than one storage entity, a single STORAGE card can be used to define several storages, if desired, by using the following format:

1. Blank location field.

2. Sequence of storage addresses and capacities in the variable field.

A storage address must be preceded by the letter "S" and separated from its capacity by a comma. The addresses and capacities of different storages must be separated by slashes. Storage addresses should be in ascending order. For example:

STORAGE   S1,3/S3,5/S4,100/S10,50

A range of storages which all have the same capacity can be denoted as shown in this example:

STORAGE   S3-S10,20/S12,6/S15-S18,50

Transfer Block (Card 16)

The TRANSFER block is the most commonly used means for diverting transactions to nonsequential blocks in a GPSS block diagram. It can function in any of nine different modes in all four versions of GPSS. The mode is specified in field A, and the other subfields are used to specify appropriate arguments for whatever mode is being used.

Three of the nine TRANSFER block modes will now be described by means of examples:

(a) TRANSFER   ,AAA
(b) TRANSFER   .2,AAA,BBB
(c) TRANSFER   BOTH,AAA,BBB

Example (a) illustrates the *unconditional* or *blank* transfer mode. Every xact that enters this block will be sent to the block whose address is AAA.

Example (b) illustrates the *fractional* or *decimal point* mode. Entering xacts will be sent to block AAA or block BBB on a random basis. The probability of going to block BBB is .2, while that of going to block AAA is .8. Thus the field A argument specifies the proportion of entering xacts that will be sent to the field C address, with the other xacts going to the field B address.

Example (c) illustrates the BOTH selection mode. Entering xacts will be sent to block AAA or block BBB. The B-field block is tried first. If it refuses entry to the xact, the C-field block is tried. If it also refuses entry, the xact remains in the TRANSFER block and repeats this sequence of trials each time the clock is updated until it finds an exit.

Program 2 uses the fractional selection mode. Of the entering xacts 40% are sent to the block whose address is LINE, and the remaining 60% are sent to OUT; the destination of any individual xact is a matter of chance. To put this another way, xacts entering block 7 in our model have a .4 probability of going to block 10 and a .6 probability of going to block 8.

When operating in the decimal point mode, a TRANSFER block makes implied requests to the random number generator in order to make a decision about where to send each entering xact. You may recognize the operation of the TRANSFER block in this mode to be the "random splitting of a stream of transactions," discussed in Section 2.3.

Blocks 8 to 16 (Cards 17 to 29)

Those transactions which proceed to OUT have their transit times tabulated in table 3 and are then removed from the system. Notice that field A of the TER-MINATE block is blank, so there is no effect on the run termination count.

Those xacts which proceed to LINE enter queue 2 to await entry into the facility named FACIL. Following the familiar QUEUE-SEIZE-DEPART sequence, transactions are delayed in the facility for random lengths of time which are exponentially distributed with a mean of 25 seconds. They are then released from this facility. They proceed to block 15 to have their transit times tabulated. Note that the transit times in table 4 will include time spent in queue 2 and the facility whereas the times in table 3 will not.

After the TABLE definition cards we find two QTABLE definition cards. These cards will cause the waiting times of transactions in queues 1 and 2 to be recorded and printed out in a frequency table. No TABULATE block is required since a QTABLE card corresponds to the queue whose index number is specified in field A of the QTABLE card. Subfields B, C, and D of the QTABLE card have the same meaning as they do for the TABLE card.

Notice that a QTABLE card specifies two different entity addresses. Field A specifies the queue address, and the location field specifies the table address. No two tables may have the same address, even if one is a QTABLE and the other is not. Thus the following definition cards could not appear in the same model:

```
1   QTABLE      1,10,10,10
1   TABLE       M1,80,20,10
```

Control of Simulation Run Length (Cards 30 to 32)

Now we come to the last new feature of program 2 — the use of the GEN-ERATE-TERMINATE-START cards to control the simulation run length in terms of clock time rather than number of transactions terminated. Up to this point, no provision has been made to control the simulation run, since TERMI-NATE blocks with a blank in field A do not decrement the run termination count. Instead, our run will be controlled by a "timer" as follows:

1. Five thousand time units after the program starts, one xact will be sent from the second **GENERATE** block to the **TERMINATE** 1 block.

2. The run termination count will be decremented by 1.

3. Since there is a 1 in field A of the START card, the run termination count will go from 1 to 0, and this is the condition that causes the run to stop.

If the START card contained a 5 in field A, this procedure would occur 5 times, and the run time would be 25,000 clock units.

4.4   STANDARD STATISTICAL OUTPUT

The output from program 2 is printed out following the symbolic listing, cross-reference dictionary, and input listing.   As usual, the clock times and block counts appear first, followed by the other statistics.   Since program 2 contains a

RELATIVE CLOCK   5000   ABSOLUTE CLOCK   5000
BLOCK COUNTS

BLOCK	CURRENT	TOTAL	BLOCK	CURRENT	TOTAL	BLOCK
1	0	115	11	0	46	
2	0	115	12	0	46	
3	0	115	13	1	46	
4	0	115	14	0	45	
5	0	115	15	0	45	
6	0	115	16	0	45	
7	0	115	17	0	1	
8	0	69	18	0	1	
9	0	69				
10	0	46				

FACILITY	AVERAGE UTILIZATION	NUMBER ENTRIES	AVERAGE TIME/TRAN	SEIZING TRANS. NO.
FACIL	.187	46	20.347	9

STORAGE	CAPACITY	AVERAGE CONTENTS	AVERAGE UTILIZATION	ENTRIES
1	3	2.422	.807	115

	AVERAGE TIME/TRAN	CURRENT CONTENTS	MAXIMUM CONTENTS	
	105.313		3	

QUEUE	MAXIMUM CONTENTS	AVERAGE CONTENTS	TOTAL ENTRIES	ZERO ENTRIES	PERCENT ZEROS
1	5	.536	115	54	46.9
2	1	.036	46	38	82.6

$AVERAGE TIME/TRANS = AVERAGE TIME/TRANS EXCLUDING ZERO ENTRIES

AVERAGE TIME/TRANS	$AVERAGE TIME/TRANS	TABLE NUMBER	CURRENT CONTENTS
23.313	43.950	1	
4.000	23.000	2	

Fig. 4-6.   Program 2 output statistics—clock, blocks, facility, storage, and queues.

facility, a storage, two queues, and four tables, statistics for these eight entities will automatically be printed out.

Clock, Block, Facility, Storage, and Queue Statistics

All of the output statistics except for the tables are shown in Figure 4-6. The relative and absolute clock times are 5000, which is exactly how long we wanted the simulation run to last. The block counts indicate that 115 transactions entered the TRANSFER block; 69 of them (60%) went to OUT, and 46 of them (40%) went to LINE.

The facility statistics reveal that FACIL was occupied during only 18.7% of the total simulated time period. Xact 9 was seizing it at the time that the run ended.

The facility statistics require no explanation. The storage statistics are not difficult to interpret. The *average contents* are computed by summing all of the clock units spent in the storage by xacts and dividing by 5000. The *average utilization* is obtained by dividing the average contents by the storage capacity. The other storage statistics require no explanation.

Statistics for both queues are shown at the bottom of Figure 4-6. It is obvious that xacts spent very little time in queue 2. Its maximum contents were 1, and the percentage of zero waiting times was 82.6. Note that the queue statistics tell us that tables 1 and 2 are Qtables.

Tables

Four tables were requested in program 2, and they are shown in Figures 4-7 and 4-8. The table printouts are shown in their entirety except for the "Deviation from Mean" columns which have been omitted due to space limitations.

Tables 1 and 2 are concerned with the waiting times of transactions in queues 1 and 2. Looking at table 1, we can make the following observations:

1. One hundred and fifteen xacts entered queue 1.
2. The average xact spent 23.313 seconds in queue 1.
3. The total number of clock units spent in queue 1 by all xacts was 2681.
4. Sixty-four out of 115 xacts spent 10 or fewer clock units in queue 1.
5. Four out of 115 xacts spent 91 or more clock units in queue 1. Their average waiting time was 118.25 seconds.

Whereas all ten of the specified frequency classes in table 1 had entries, only 7 of the fifteen specified frequency classes in table 2 had entries. Another interesting aspect of table 2 is that the first frequency class contains the number of zero entries, that is, 38.

Table 3 shows the distribution of transit times of transactions which left the system without entering facility FACIL. These xacts spent 125.971 seconds in the system, on the average. Most of them spent between 81 and 140 seconds in the system.

Table 4 shows the distribution of transit times of those xacts which traveled through queue 1, storage 1, queue 2, and facility FACIL. These xacts spent 158.355 seconds in the system, on the average. Most of them spent between 101 and 200 seconds in the system.

TABLE 1
ENTRIES IN TABLE 115
MEAN ARGUMENT 23.313
STANDARD DEVIATION 32.062
SUM OF ARGUMENTS 2681.000

UPPER LIMIT	OBSERVED FREQUENCY	PER CENT OF TOTAL	CUMULATIVE PERCENTAGE	CUMULATIVE REMAINDER	MULTIPLE OF MEAN
10	64	55.65	55.6	44.3	.428
20	7	6.08	61.7	38.2	.857
30	9	7.82	69.5	30.4	1.286
40	6	5.21	74.7	25.2	1.715
50	5	4.34	79.1	20.8	2.144
60	7	6.08	85.2	14.7	2.573
70	5	4.34	89.5	10.4	3.002
80	5	4.34	93.9	6.0	3.431
90	3	2.60	96.5	3.4	3.860
OVERFLOW	4	3.47	100.0	.0	

AVERAGE VALUE OF OVERFLOW 118.25

TABLE 2
ENTRIES IN TABLE 46
MEAN ARGUMENT 4.000
STANDARD DEVIATION 11.375
SUM OF ARGUMENTS 184.000

UPPER LIMIT	OBSERVED FREQUENCY	PER CENT OF TOTAL	CUMULATIVE PERCENTAGE	CUMULATIVE REMAINDER	MULTIPLE OF MEAN
0	38	82.60	82.6	17.3	-.000
5	1	2.17	84.7	15.2	1.250
10	1	2.17	86.9	13.0	2.500
15	1	2.17	89.1	10.8	3.750
20	0	.00	89.1	10.8	5.000
25	3	6.52	95.6	4.3	6.250
30	0	.00	95.6	4.3	7.500
35	1	2.17	97.8	2.1	8.750
40	0	.00	97.8	2.1	10.000
45	0	.00	97.8	2.1	11.250
50	0	.00	97.8	2.1	12.500
55	0	.00	97.8	2.1	13.750
60	1	2.17	100.0	.0	15.000

REMAINING FREQUENCIES ARE ALL ZERO

Fig. 4-7. Program 2 output statistics—tables 1 and 2.

TABLE 3
ENTRIES IN TABLE 69   MEAN ARGUMENT 125.971   STANDARD DEVIATION 38.562   SUM OF ARGUMENTS 8692.000

UPPER LIMIT	OBSERVED FREQUENCY	PER CENT OF TOTAL	CUMULATIVE PERCENTAGE	CUMULATIVE REMAINDER	MULTIPLE OF MEAN
80	5	7.24	7.2	92.7	.635
100	14	20.28	27.5	72.4	.793
120	20	28.98	56.5	43.4	.952
140	11	15.94	72.4	27.5	1.111
160	6	8.69	81.1	18.8	1.270
180	5	7.24	88.4	11.5	1.428
200	5	7.24	95.6	4.3	1.587
220	2	2.89	98.5	1.4	1.746
240	0	.00	98.5	1.4	1.905
OVERFLOW	1	1.44	100.0	.0	

AVERAGE VALUE OF OVERFLOW 262.00

TABLE 4
ENTRIES IN TABLE 45   MEAN ARGUMENT 158.355   STANDARD DEVIATION 39.687   SUM OF ARGUMENTS 7126.000

UPPER LIMIT	OBSERVED FREQUENCY	PER CENT OF TOTAL	CUMULATIVE PERCENTAGE	CUMULATIVE REMAINDER	MULTIPLE OF MEAN
80	0	.00	.0	100.0	.505
100	1	2.22	2.2	97.7	.631
120	8	17.77	19.9	80.0	.757
140	8	17.77	37.7	62.2	.884
160	9	19.99	57.7	42.2	1.010
180	7	15.55	73.3	26.6	1.136
200	6	13.33	86.6	13.3	1.262
220	2	4.44	91.1	8.8	1.389
240	2	4.44	95.5	4.4	1.515
OVERFLOW	2	4.44	100.0	.0	

AVERAGE VALUE OF OVERFLOW 249.00

Fig. 4-8. Program 2 output statistics — tables 3 and 4.

4.5   DIFFERENCES BETWEEN GPSS/360 AND OTHER VERSIONS

To refresh your memory, we point out the relevant differences that were brought out in Section 3.4. Then we note the additional differences connected with program 2 and the material in Sections 4.1 through 4.4.

GPS K

Program 2, as shown in Figure 4.2, would be acceptable to the GPS K simulator. However, GPS K has a built-in exponential function that enables the user to do the following:

1. Omit function EXPON from his model.
2. Instead, specify the letters "EF" in subfield B of the GENERATE or ADVANCE block.

The details of random number generation are different in GPS K than in GPSS/360, but the general approach sketched in Figure 4-4 applies.

Flow Simulator

If program 2 were written in Flow Simulator, it would do the following:

1. Lack the SIMULATE card.
2. Have symbolic tags for all entities.
3. Have location field entries starting in column 1.

All of these items were pointed out in Section 3.4. Except for minor details, everything else in this chapter applies to Flow Simulator as well as to GPSS/360.

GPSS III

If program 2 were written in GPSS III, it would do the following:

1. Have an asterisk in column 1 of the SIMULATE card.
2. Utilize index numbers rather than symbolic addresses for the function and facility entities.

In addition to these differences, GPSS III utilizes a fixed format for the function follower cards. Each card (except for the last one) must have six pairs of (X,Y) coordinates in 12 six-column fields. X_1 would be coded in columns 1 to 6; Y_1 goes into columns 7 to 12; X_2 goes into columns 13 to 18; Y_6 goes into columns 67 to 72. Similarly, (X_7, Y_7) through (X_{12}, Y_{12}) are coded in columns 1 to 72 of the second function follower card, and so on.

Whereas GPSS III accepts only the fixed format just described, the other three versions accept function follower cards using either the fixed or free format. The only proviso is that any set of function follower cards which define a particular function cannot intermix formats.

GPSS III does not permit multiple storage definitions on a single STORAGE card. The format for defining one storage entity is as described for GPSS/360.

4.6 SUMMARY

Program 2 introduced you to three new blocks: ENTER, LEAVE, and TRANSFER. It also introduced you to two new entities: *functions* and *storages*. Program 2 consisted of 3 comment cards, 18 blocks, 3 control cards, and 9 definition cards, for a total of 33 cards in our source deck.

We saw how the user can define a function via FUNCTION definition and follower cards and how he can reference that function by using the standard numerical attribute FNj. A GPSS function is a user-defined relationship between two variables. The independent variable is specified in field A of the FUNCTION definition card, and the dependent variable is FNj.

No block types are associated with functions, and they are therefore an adjunct to the block diagram rather than a part of it. A continuous numerical-valued function may have RNj as its argument, in which case it takes on random values. If the function follower cards define a relation between RNj and an exponential distribution, then the values of the function belong to an exponential probability distribution.

Program 2 utilized three SNAs, namely, RNx, FNj, and M1. RNx represents a random number from 0 to .999999 whose seed x is specified by the user as an integer between 1 and 8, inclusive. Incidentally, FNj and M1 are the most frequently used SNAs in GPSS.

Random number generation was discussed further. Random numbers may be requested directly via RNx, or they may be requested by implication, so to speak. If directly requested, they lie between 0 and 1 or between 0 and 1000, depending on where RNx appears. If implied, they are used to compute a needed value or to make a decision.

We saw how the TRANSFER block can be used to transfer transactions to nonsequential blocks. TRANSFER blocks can operate in several different modes, and three of them were defined. The decimal mode, used in program 2, involves a random choice for individual transactions on the basis of a probability which is specified by the user.

The ENTER and LEAVE blocks are used for storages just as the SEIZE and RELEASE blocks are used for facilities. The inclusion of these blocks automatically results in the printout of storage statistics.

We saw that a program may contain more than one GENERATE and TERMINATE block, so long as the block diagram is logical. The GENERATE/TERMINATE/START blocks can be used to control the simulation run length in terms of clock units elapsed rather than number of xacts terminated.

CHAPTER 5
Illustrative Program 3

At this juncture we are still demonstrating basic concepts rather than trying to solve practical problems. So once again a trivial model is used to introduce some new card types and features.

5.1 INTRODUCTION TO PROGRAM 3

Problem Statement and GPSS Model

Since it is so simple, the situation that is simulated by program 3 can be represented as a GPSS model without a preliminary system definition. It is shown in Figure 5-1, and the problem statement is as follows:

Transactions enter the system with random interarrival times distributed exponentially about a mean of 15 minutes. They pass through three queues and facilities which are arranged in series. It is desired to monitor their progress through the system by tabulating their transit times after leaving each facility. The simulation ends when the two hundredth transaction has left the last facility in the series.

A Look at Illustrative Program 3

Program 3 is shown in Figure 5-2. Cards 1 to 9 should be familiar. Note that, for no particular reason except variety, we have assigned a numerical label to the exponential function rather than the symbolic address that was used in program 2.

Card 10 is a new block type which corresponds to a new entity. Looking down the Figure 5-2 listing, you will also notice some other new card types as well as some unusual block arguments, such as *10. It is evident that there are several new ingredients to be found in program 3. So let us become acquainted with some of them before continuing our perusal of the program.

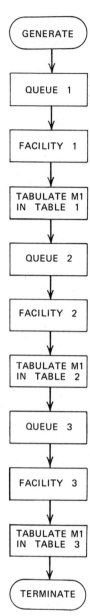

Fig. 5-1. Schematic diagram of GPSS model for program 3.

5.2   SOME FEATURES FOUND IN PROGRAM 3

Savevalues

A SAVEVALUE block corresponds to a **savevalue** entity.   A savevalue is merely a location in which a numerical value (always an integer) is stored for future reference.

BLOCK NUMBER	*LOC	OPERATION	A,B,C,D,E,F,G	COMMENTS	CARD NUMBER
		*			1
		*	ILLUSTRATIVE PROGRAM NUMBER 3		2
		*			3
		SIMULATE			4
		1 FUNCTION	RN5,C24	EXPONENTIAL PROBABILITY DISTRIBUTION	5
		0,0/.1,.104/.2,.222/.3,.355/.4,.509/.5,.69/.6,.915/.7,1.2/.75,1.38/			6
		.8,1.6/.84,1.83/.88,2.12/.9,2.3/.92,2.52/.94,2.81/.95,2.99/.96,3.2/			7
		.97,3.5/.98,3.9/.99,4.6/.995,5.3/.998,6.2/.999,7/.9997,8			8
1		GENERATE	15,FN1	AVERAGE INTERARRIVAL TIME IS 15 MINUTES	9
2		SAVEVALUE	1,3	VALUE OF SAVEVALUE 1 IS 3	10
3		ASSIGN	3,X1	ASSIGN VALUE OF SAVEVALUE 1 TO PARAMETER 3	11
4	AGAIN	ASSIGN	10+,1	INCREMENT VALUE OF PARAMETER 10 BY 1	12
5		QUEUE	*10	ENTER QUEUE WHOSE INDEX NO. IS IN PAR. 10	13
6		SEIZE	*10	SEIZE FACILITY WHOSE INDEX NO. IS IN P10	14
7		DEPART	*10	DEPART FROM QUEUE NO. *10	15
8		ADVANCE	10,FN1	REMAIN IN FACILITY FOR 10 MINUTES, ON AVG.	16
9		RELEASE	*10	RELEASE FACILITY NO. *10	17
10		TABULATE	*10	TABULATE TRANSIT TIME THRU SYSTEM THUS FAR	18
11		LOOP	3,AGAIN	GO TO AGAIN IF P3 NOT YET DECREMENTED TO 0	19
		1 TABLE	M1,10,10,10	TABLE DEFINITION CARD	20
		2 TABLE	M1,10,10,10	TABLE DEFINITION CARD	21
		3 TABLE	M1,10,10,10	TABLE DEFINITION CARD	22
12		TERMINATE	1	DESTROY XACT; DECREMENT RUN TERM. CT. BY 1	23
		START	200	SIMULATION ENDS AFTER 200 XACTS DESTROYED	24
		END			25

Fig. 5-2. Illustrative program 3—symbolic listing. (See back pocket for a duplicate of this illustration which can be kept in view while reading the chapter.)

Field A of the SAVEVALUE block specifies the address of a savevalue entity. Field B specifies the quantity to be stored in the savevalue location specified in field A.   Field C of a SAVEVALUE block may contain the character "H" if a *halfword* savevalue is desired.   If there is no entry in field C, a *fullword* savevalue is assumed by the GPSS program.

The field A argument of a SAVEVALUE block may be followed by a plus sign (+), minus sign (−), or nothing to denote addition, subtraction, or replacement, respectively.   These options are illustrated below:

SAVEVALUE	1+,3	Add 3 to the current contents of savevalue 1.
SAVEVALUE	1−,3	Subtract 3 from the current contents of savevalue 1.
SAVEVALUE	1,3	Replace the current contents of savevalue 1 with the constant 3.

Savevalues are normally set to zero at the outset of a run; that is, the GPSS simulator places a zero in every savevalue location initially.   There are ways to override this automatic feature (that is, to initialize savevalues with nonzero values), but they will not be discussed now.

A model may include several SAVEVALUE blocks which all correspond to the same savevalue entity.   For example, imagine that the following blocks are located at various points in a block diagram:

```
SAVEVALUE     TOTAL,5

SAVEVALUE     TOTAL−,3

SAVEVALUE     TOTAL,FN5
```

Whenever a xact enters any of these three blocks, the number being stored in the savevalue labeled TOTAL will be altered.   If a xact enters the first SAVEVALUE block, the savevalue will be set to 5.   If a xact enters the second SAVEVALUE block, the contents of the savevalue will be reduced by 3.   If a xact enters the third SAVEVALUE block, the savevalue will be set to the currently computed value of function 5.

It is also possible for a single SAVEVALUE block to correspond to more than one savevalue entity.   For example, consider this block:

```
SAVEVALUE     FN3,10
```

When a xact enters this block, function 3 is referenced, and it computes an integer value.   Since this value is returned to field A of a SAVEVALUE block, it is interpreted by the simulator as the address of a savevalue entity.   The number 10 (in field B) is stored in that savevalue.   Since FN3 could presumably take on many different values, this SAVEVALUE block might put the number 10 into many different savevalue locations in the course of a simulation run.

GPSS/360 includes both halfword and fullword savevalues, as indicated earlier.   As the terms suggest, a fullword savevalue can store a larger number than a halfword savevalue.   The current value of fullword savevalue j can be referenced via the SNA, Xj.   The current value of halfword savevalue j can be referenced via the SNA, XHj.

Whereas a savevalue is used to store a single number, a **matrix savevalue** can be used to store an array of numbers. Matrix savevalues are discussed in Chapter 14.

Transaction Parameters and Assign Block

In order to understand the function of the ASSIGN blocks in program 3, it is necessary to know what is meant by *transaction parameters.* Of the many transaction attributes, only six can be referenced directly by means of standard numerical and logical attributes. The SNAs are Pj, M1, MPj, and PR; the SLAs are M and NM. Only M1 has been used so far, and now we look at Pj. The other four attributes are covered later on.

Every transaction, when created by a GENERATE block, normally has 12 parameters associated with it. These parameters can be used to store numerical values (integers only) which describe or correspond to the xact. For example, the time to be spent by a xact in a facility could be stored in parameter 5 and subsequently referenced via the SNA, P5.

Field F of the GENERATE block can be used to specify up to 100 parameters for every xact created by that block; 12 parameters are assumed if it is blank. Field G can be used to specify halfword or fullword parameters; the former are assumed if it is left blank. Let us look at an example:

```
GENERATE      100,,,,,50
```

Xacts would emerge from this block at intervals of 100 clock units, and each xact would have 50 halfword parameters associated with it.

Upon leaving a GENERATE block, transactions have zeroes in all of their parameters. There are various means for entering nonzero values during the run, of which the ASSIGN block is the principal one. Before this block is described, it should be stressed that *Pj gives the value of parameter j of the xact that happens to be "in process" (current) when the value of Pj is sought.*

Field A of the ASSIGN block specifies which parameter (of the entering xact) is to be altered, and field B specifies the quantity that will be used to alter it. Field A of the ASSIGN block is analogous to field A of the SAVEVALUE block in that its argument may be suffixed by +, −, or nothing to denote addition, subtraction, or replacement.

Field C can be used to specify the address of a function which modifies the B-field argument. If this is done, the value assigned to (or added to or subtracted from) the parameter is the product of the contents of field B and the untruncated value of the field C modifier. For example:

```
ASSIGN      3,X5,2
```

The contents of savevalue 5 (an integer) would be multiplied by the currently computed value of function 2 (not necessarily an integer), and the product would be truncated and placed in parameter 3. Note that this works exactly like fields A and B of the ADVANCE and GENERATE blocks when a function modifier is used. The only difference is that "FN" must be specified in those blocks' B-fields, but it is not needed in the ASSIGN block's C-field.

This raises a subtle but basic point. The ASSIGN block C-field entry is interpreted as the *address of a function.* Thus 2 denotes *function 2,* and the GPSS simulator evaluates this function directly to obtain a value which multiplies the field B value. But *FN2* in field C would be treated as follows. The GPSS simulator would evaluate function 2 in order to obtain the *address of some other function,* which would in turn be evaluated to obtain a value that multiplied the field B value. In other words, function 2 is used as the modifier if field C contains a 2, but some other function is used as the modifier if field C contains *FN2.*

To state it more generally, if field C of the ASSIGN block contains a constant *k*, the function whose index number is *k* is evaluated to obtain the modifier. If field C contains SNAj, then the value of that SNA is taken to be *k*, and function *k* is evaluated to obtain the modifier.

A similar "principle" applies to field A of the ASSIGN block, but with respect to parameters rather than functions. If *P3* were entered instead of *3*, the affected parameter would not be parameter 3; it would be the parameter *whose number was given by parameter 3.* Thus parameter 3 of the entering xact would be examined, and its contents would be interpreted as the number of the parameter to be assigned a value — the value specified in fields B and C.

Indirect Addressing

Indirect addressing (or *indirect specification*) is a technique for using transaction parameters to specify entity addresses. The use of indirect addressing enables a single block entity to reference or correspond to more than one function entity, or queue entity, or savevalue entity, and so on. These statements can be better appreciated by looking at some examples.

QUEUE   *10   When a xact enters this block, it enters the queue whose index number is contained in parameter 10 of that xact. The queue address is indirectly specified; it is not singularly defined by the programmer before the run starts. Note that in this particular example, the SNA, P10, could have been used in place of *10.

SAVEVALUE   *4,5   When a xact enters this block, the number 5 is placed in the savevalue whose index number is contained in parameter 4 of that xact. Again it happens that *4 and P4 are interchangeable in this particular example.

ADVANCE   FN*3   When a xact enters this block, its delay time is computed by referencing the function whose index number is contained in parameter 3 of that xact. Note that P3 could not be used in place of *3 in this example. The general rule, which you may have surmised, is:

If *n is used as a variable field argument, it could as well be written as Pn. But if *n is used as the address portion of a standard numerical attribute, it cannot be written as Pn. For example, X*5 could not be written as XP5.

How would you interpret this block?

ASSIGN   X15,P*5

Savevalue 15 contains the number of the parameter into which the field B quantity will be put. The field B quantity is interpreted as the value of the parameter whose number is specified in parameter 5 of the entering xact. To clarify this, let us assume that a xact enters this ASSIGN block with P5 = 10 and P10 = 45. Let us also assume that X15 = 8. P∗5 is the value of parameter 10, namely 45. Thus the number 45 would be put into parameter 8.

Indirect addressing is a powerful feature. It permits a more compact and efficient program, and it allows the user to design more sophisticated models.

5.3   EXAMINATION OF PROGRAM 3

We had progressed as far as card 9 before pausing to discuss savevalues, parameters, and indirect addressing. So let us now start with card 10 which is block 2.

Blocks 2 to 4 (Cards 10 to 12)

The meanings of these blocks are adequately explained by the accompanying comments. (See Figure 5-2.)

The observant reader may wonder why cards 10 and 11 were used instead of a single card, namely, **ASSIGN   3,3**. The reason is that GPSS provides a convenient means for making multiple runs with different savevalues but not with different ASSIGN block values. So the arrangement used in program 3 is more flexible than the single ASSIGN card suggested above; however, we will not utilize this capability here.

When a xact first enters the ASSIGN block whose address is AGAIN, its parameter 10 is incremented from 0 to 1. If the same xact were to later reenter this ASSIGN block, its parameter 10 would be incremented from 1 to 2. If it eventually entered this block a third time, it would have P10 incremented to 3. As you will see, this is just what happens.

Blocks 5 to 10 (Cards 13 to 18)

Blocks 5, 6, 7, 9, and 10 utilize indirect addressing. As you know, the notation ∗10 stands for the *value* of parameter 10 of the *entering* transaction. As you also know, we could have used P10 instead of ∗10 in blocks 5, 6, 7, 9, and 10. Now let us consider the effect of indirect addressing in program 3.

If a xact passes through blocks 5 to 10 with P10 = 1, it is treated (by the simulator) as passing through queue 1 and facility 1. It also has its transit time tabulated in table 1. If the same xact passes through blocks 5 to 10 with P10 = 2, it is treated as passing through queue 2 and facility 2, and its transit time is entered in table 2. This is not difficult to visualize if there is only one xact in the system. But you may have an uneasy feeling about what happens when many xacts with different values of P10 occupy blocks 5 to 10 simultaneously. This will be explained soon.

Loop Block (Card 19)

When a xact enters a LOOP block, it may be sent to either the next sequential block or to the block whose address is in field B of the LOOP block. Let us see how this works in program 3.

The LOOP block works in conjunction with the first ASSIGN block to send each xact through the same path a specified number of times. Field A of the LOOP block specifies which xact parameter is to be used as a counter, and field B is interpreted as the next block to which the xact proceeds if the value of the specified parameter is *not* zero *after* passing through the LOOP block. If it *is* zero, the xact passes to the next sequential block.

It is instructive to consider what would happen if the positions of blocks 2 and 3 were reversed in program 3. Imagine that the first xact in the simulation run enters the ASSIGN   3,X1 block. Parameter 3 will be assigned the current contents of savevalue 1, namely zero. This xact will next enter the SAVEVALUE   1,3 block, causing X1 to change from zero to 3. But this will have no effect on P3 which was assigned a zero because X1 was zero *at the time it was referenced.*

To continue, our xact, with P3 = 0, will proceed through the block diagram until it reaches the LOOP block. The LOOP block will attempt to decrement P3 by 1, but P3 is already zero. This will cause an error in the run.

Effect of Blocks 2 to 11

Now let us return to the *real* program 3. Blocks 2 to 11 are exactly equivalent to the 18 blocks sandwiched between GENERATE and TERMINATE in Figure 5-3. Incidentally, Figure 5-3 is a true block diagram, contrary to our "promise" in Section 2.2 not to include any in this book. However, this breach of promise is mollified by the fact that Figure 5-3 does not utilize any of the formal GPSS block symbols.

The movement of xacts through the Figure 5-3 block diagram is very easily visualized. It should be kept in mind as we go back to the Figure 5-2 block diagram and follow the progress of one transaction through it.

The xact initially has P3 = 3 and P10 = 1 as it enters queue 1. It eventually releases facility 1, makes an entry in table 1, and enters the LOOP block for the first time. The value of P3 is decremented to 2, and the xact goes to the "AGAIN block" where P10 is incremented from 1 to 2.

The xact enters queue 2 and facility 2. It makes an entry in table 2 and enters the LOOP block for the second time. P3 is decremented to 1, and the xact goes to the AGAIN block where P10 is incremented from 2 to 3.

The xact enters queue 3 and facility 3. It makes an entry in table 3 and enters the LOOP block for the third time. P3 is decremented to 0, and the xact is therefore sent to the next sequential block which is TERMINATE.

The use of indirect addressing in conjunction with the LOOP block gives the impression that the xacts in our model travel a circular path. This is true as far as their movement through the blocks is concerned, but it is not true of their pas-

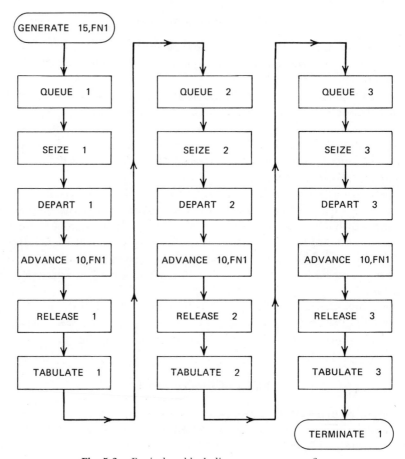

Fig. 5-3. Equivalent block diagram to program 3.

sage through the model which is actually a *serial arrangement of entities* as per Figure 5-1. The GPSS program allocates three queues, three facilities, and three tables in the computer core for our model just as it would do for the Figure 5-3 block diagram.

It is easy enough to follow the movement of one transaction through the Figure 5-2 block diagram. But what about a *stream* of xacts? Again, the answer is to think of Figure 5-2 as if it were Figure 5-3. For example, if we could look inside of our model at some clock instant, we might find three xacts in the AD-VANCE block (block 8). But the GPSS simulator would have each one in a particular facility, scheduled to make an entry in the correct table. Similarly, we might see many xacts waiting at the SEIZE block (block 6). But each would be in one of three queues and in a definite position within that queue as far as the GPSS simulator is concerned.

The real advantage of indirect addressing lies in the fact that it permits dynamic selection of the entities through which transactions pass during a run. The fact that it causes our coded program to lose its resemblance to the system flow chart (if there is one) poses no problem for the experienced user.

Closeout (Cards 20 to 25)

Each table must have its own definition card. A TABLE card cannot utilize indirect addressing because *xacts do not enter or activate definition cards — just block cards.*

The TERMINATE block and START card control the run length so that it will end after the two hundredth xact has been destroyed.

5.4 STANDARD STATISTICAL OUTPUT

The symbolic listing was shown in Figure 5-2, and the input listing will not be shown. Again, these listings are part of the *printout,* but they are not considered part of the *output.*

Clock, Block, Facility, Savevalue, and Queue Statistics

Figure 5-4 shows the *standard statistical output* associated with the above entities. In this particular model, we are not really concerned with the time spent in

```
RELATIVE CLOCK        2970   ABSOLUTE CLOCK            2970
BLOCK COUNTS
BLOCK  CURRENT    TOTAL    BLOCK  CURRENT    TOTAL
  1       0        214       11      0        605
  2       0        214       12      0        200
  3       0        214
  4       0        619
  5      12        619
  6       0        607
  7       0        607
  8       2        607
  9       0        605
 10       0        605
```

FACILITY	AVERAGE UTILIZATION	NUMBER ENTRIES	AVERAGE TIME/TRAN	SEIZING TRANS. NO.
1	.778	204	11.333	6
2	.627	203	9.177	12
3	.650	200	9.659	

```
CONTENTS OF FULLWORD SAVEVALUES (NON-ZERO)
SAVEVALUE  NR,        VALUE      NR,        VALUE
            1           3
```

QUEUE	MAXIMUM CONTENTS	AVERAGE CONTENTS	TOTAL ENTRIES	ZERO ENTRIES	PERCENT ZEROS
1	13	3.799	214	41	19.1
2	11	1.184	203	88	43.3
3	7	1.042	202	75	37.1

$AVERAGE TIME/TRANS = AVERAGE TIME/TRANS EXCLUDING ZERO ENTRIES

AVERAGE TIME/TRANS	$AVERAGE TIME/TRANS	TABLE NUMBER	CURRENT CONTENTS
52.728	65.225		13
17.334	30.599		
15.331	24.385		2

Fig. 5-4. Program 3 output statistics — clock, blocks, facilities, savevalue, and queues.

queues, queue lengths, and so on.   We are more interested in the movement and position of xacts in the block diagram.

From the block counts we see that, when the program ended, there were 12 transactions in the QUEUE block.   From the queue statistics, we can see that ten of those transactions were in queue 1, and two were in queue 3.   From the facility statistics, we can see that transactions were in facilities 1 and 2 when the run ended.   The fact that facility 3 was empty is easy to explain; the two hundredth transaction left facility 3 and was terminated before another transaction could seize that facility.

Tables

Figure 5-5 shows the three tables which were requested in program 3.   The sum of arguments, cumulative remainders, multiples of mean, and deviation from mean have been deleted.   From the mean arguments we can deduce that, on the average, transactions left facility 1 after 65 minutes, facility 2 after 91.3 minutes, and facility 3 after 115.7 minutes (measured from the time they entered the system).

5.5   DIFFERENCES BETWEEN GPSS/360 AND OTHER VERSIONS

The differences that have been noted in Sections 3.4 and 4.5 will not be reiterated with respect to this chapter.   For example, you already know that RN5 is legal in GPSS/360 and Flow Simulator but not in GPS K and GPSS III.   So we shall not mention it here — except as an example of what we do not mention here.

GPS K

GPS K makes no distinction between halfword and fullword savevalues.   As a result, field C of the SAVEVALUE block is not defined, and Xj is the only SNA associated with savevalues.

GPS K has two sizes of parameters, and it permits varying numbers of parameters per transaction, but it implements these options in an entirely different way than GPSS/360.   Fields F and G of the GENERATE block are undefined in GPS K.   To specify nonstandard numbers of — or large-size — parameters, a CONTROL card must be used.   (See Section 8.4.)   The standard number of parameters per xact ranges from 5 to 25, depending on the size of the computer being used.   (See Table 8-2.)

Flow Simulator

Flow Simulator includes and defines halfword and fullword savevalues and parameters in exactly the same way as GPSS/360.   However, field F of the GENERATE block can be used to specify up to 127 parameters per xact rather than 100.   If field F is blank, field G is ignored by the GPSS simulator, and 12 halfword parameters are associated with every transaction.

```
TABLE    1
ENTRIES IN TABLE          MEAN ARGUMENT            STANDARD DEVIATION
        203                  64.935                        52.562

        UPPER        OBSERVED        PER CENT        CUMULATIVE
        LIMIT        FREQUENCY       OF TOTAL        PERCENTAGE
        10              32            15.76            15.7
        20              25            12.31            28.0
        30              21            10.34            38.4
        40               6             2.95            41.3
        50              10             4.92            46.3
        60              10             4.92            51.2
        70              11             5.41            56.6
        80              13             6.40            63.0
        90              13             6.40            69.4
     OVERFLOW           62            30.54           100.0
AVERAGE VALUE OF OVERFLOW             129.90


TABLE    2
ENTRIES IN TABLE          MEAN ARGUMENT            STANDARD DEVIATION
        202                  91.262                        60.625

        UPPER        OBSERVED        PER CENT        CUMULATIVE
        LIMIT        FREQUENCY       OF TOTAL        PERCENTAGE
        10               8             3.96             3.9
        20              17             8.41            12.3
        30              18             8.91            21.2
        40              16             7.92            29.2
        50               7             3.46            32.6
        60              14             6.93            39.6
        70              10             4.95            44.5
        80               9             4.45            49.0
        90               8             3.96            52.9
     OVERFLOW           95            47.02           100.0
AVERAGE VALUE OF OVERFLOW             147.03


TABLE    3
ENTRIES IN TABLE          MEAN ARGUMENT            STANDARD DEVIATION
        200                 115.669                        70.812

        UPPER        OBSERVED        PER CENT        CUMULATIVE
        LIMIT        FREQUENCY       OF TOTAL        PERCENTAGE
        10               1              .49              .4
        20               6             2.99             3.4
        30              11             5.49             8.9
        40              12             5.99            14.9
        50              19             9.49            24.4
        60              10             4.99            29.4
        70              12             5.99            35.4
        80               7             3.49            38.9
        90               8             3.99            42.9
     OVERFLOW          114            56.99           100.0
AVERAGE VALUE OF OVERFLOW             165.85
```

Fig. 5-5. Program 3 output statistics—tables 1, 2, and 3.

GPSS III

GPSS III makes no distinction between halfword and fullword savevalues and parameters. Accordingly, field C of the SAVEVALUE block and field G of the GENERATE block are not utilized. Xj is the only legal SNA for savevalues.

As in GPSS/360, GPSS III transactions may have up to 100 parameters with the number being specified in field F of the GENERATE block. A blank F-field results in 12 parameters.

5.6 SUMMARY

Program 3 utilized three new blocks: SAVEVALUE, ASSIGN, and LOOP. These blocks never refuse entry to transactions, and they are zero-delay blocks. The SAVEVALUE block operates on (is associated with) savevalue entities, and the ASSIGN and LOOP blocks operate on xacts.

A SAVEVALUE block assigns a numerical value to—or modifies the value of—a savevalue entity when entered by a xact. This value can subsequently be referenced by using Xj or XHj for a fullword or halfword savevalue, respectively. (GPS K and GPSS III do not distinguish between fullword and halfword savevalues; consequently these versions include Xj but not XHj.)

The ASSIGN block is used to assign a numerical value to—or modify the value of—a specified parameter of an entering transaction. Each xact has 12 parameters which the programmer may use, but he may specify up to 100 (127 in Flow Simulator) by using field F of the GENERATE block.

Savevalues must be used in order to transmit parameter values from one transaction to another. This is an important point, and it should be clearly understood; so let us consider an example that illustrates it. Imagine that xact 1 has $P5 = 5$ and that we want to put this value into parameter 8 of xact 2. If xact 2 enters the block ASSIGN   8,P5, the value of P5 of *xact 2* will be assigned to parameter 8 of the *same transaction*. This is because xact 2, having just entered the ASSIGN block, is the *current transaction*, and so all parameter references pertain to it.

Now imagine that xact 1 had previously entered the SAVEVALUE   1,P5 block, thus causing the value of its fifth parameter to be stored in savevalue 1. If xact 2 subsequently enters the block ASSIGN   8,X1, its eighth parameter will be assigned the value of X1, which is the value of parameter 5 of xact 1, namely, 5. End of example.

The LOOP block is used to send a transaction through the same portion of a model a specified number of times. If a xact enters a LOOP block with a field A parameter value of n, and the parameter is not altered anywhere, the xact will enter the LOOP block n times and be sent to the field B address $n - 1$ times.

The concept of indirect addressing was introduced. It was used in program 3 to reduce the number of cards in our source deck. We saw how a single block card could be made to pertain to several of a particular entity type, such as several queues or several facilities. Incidentally, indirect addressing cannot be used in the GENERATE block because it utilizes the parameters of entering xacts, and xacts cannot enter the GENERATE block.

The significance of the following symbols should be clearly understood: *n, Pn, and P*n. The first two denote the value of parameter n of the current xact. But P*n has a completely different meaning; it stands for the value of the parameter whose number is given by (or stored in) parameter n.

The standard numerical attribute Kn has not been mentioned until now. It is one of the three systemwide attributes, and it stands for the (integer) constant whose value is n. The use of this SNA is optional, since the constant may be used by itself without the prefix "K." Why explain Kn here? We chose this place because K*n is also equivalent to *n and Pn.

Let us take stock of the ways in which entities can be addressed. Addresses may be either *static* (rigidly specified at the outset of a run) or *dynamic* (assigned during the run). Symbolic labels and index numbers are static, whereas SNAs and indirect addresses are dynamic. Static addresses are assigned by the user and may be symbolic or numeric. Dynamically assigned addresses are always numeric.

CHAPTER 6
Miscellaneous Card Types

Whereas the last three chapters have centered around illustrative programs, this chapter does not. Now that you are able to visualize a GPSS program, it is expedient to introduce a number of new card types without using a sample program. However, most of the cards covered in this chapter are used in illustrative programs in the chapters that follow. So we are only temporarily departing from the approach used in Chapters 3 through 5.

The following block cards are covered in this chapter: INDEX, COUNT, SELECT, LOGIC, GATE, and TEST. The following definition cards are covered: VARIABLE, FVARIABLE, BVARIABLE, and INITIAL. The following control cards are covered: RESET, CLEAR, and JOB.

In the process of discussing some of these cards, three more entities are introduced: **logic switches, arithmetic variables,** and **boolean variables.** The use of *standard logical attributes* is also demonstrated for the first time.

6.1 THE INDEX, COUNT, AND SELECT BLOCKS

The INDEX block is included in all four versions of GPSS. The SELECT block is not in GPSS III, and the COUNT block is not in GPSS III or Flow Simulator.

The INDEX, COUNT, and SELECT blocks all place a value in a parameter of entering xacts. They never refuse entry to xacts, and they are zero-delay blocks.

INDEX Block

The INDEX block is used to change the value of parameter 1 of entering xacts. It is coded as follows:

Operation field: INDEX.

Variable subfield A: a parameter number.

Variable subfield B: a numerical value.

When a xact enters an INDEX block, the value specified in field B is added to the current value of the parameter specified in field A, and the sum is placed in parameter 1 of the entering xact. Let us look at some examples:

(a) **INDEX 4,3**   Set P1 equal to the sum of 3 plus whatever is currently in P4.

(b) **INDEX 1,1**   Set P1 equal to the sum of 1 plus whatever is currently in P1.

(c) **INDEX   ∗2,X13**   Set P1 equal to the sum of whatever is currently in savevalue 13 plus the current contents of the parameter whose number is in P2.

It should be evident that the INDEX block is related to the ASSIGN block. For example, (b) has the following equivalent representation:

    ASSIGN   1+,K1

Example (a) could be represented by two ASSIGN blocks:

    ASSIGN   1,P4

    ASSIGN   1+,3

The advantage of the INDEX block is that it is neater and faster than equivalent ASSIGN block representations.

Transactions are never refused entry to an INDEX block, and they always pass to the next sequential block in zero clock time. Incidentally, the field A and B entries may be any SNA except in GPSS III which permits only constants.

COUNT Block

The COUNT block is available only in GPSS/360 and GPS K. It is used to determine how many items meet a specified condition and to place the count in a parameter of the entering xact. For example, we might want to know how many halfword savevalues contain 10 or less at a particular time. We would cause a xact to enter the COUNT block at that time to have the desired count recorded in one of its parameters.

Subfields A, B, C, D, and E are defined for the COUNT block. In addition, a mnemonic *operator* (conditional or logical) must be specified starting in column 14.

Field A of the COUNT block is used to specify the parameter number in which the count will be placed. Indirect addressing can be used; for example, the entry "∗6" in field A of the COUNT block is interpreted as follows: Place the count in the parameter whose number is given by parameter 6 of the entering xact.

Fields B and C of the COUNT block specify the lower and upper limits, respectively, of the range of the specified entity that is to be tested. The meaning of this statement will become clear when we look at some examples.

Before we discuss the purpose of fields D and E, it is necessary to take note of the operators which appear in the operation field, starting in column 14. There are ten logical and six conditional operators which may be used, and they are shown in Table 6-1. If a COUNT block utilizes a *logical* operator, fields D and E must be *blank*. If a *conditional* operator is used, fields D and E must *both* have entries.

Field D of the COUNT block contains an SNA which will be compared against the SNA in field E. There is an important difference between the form of the SNAs in fields D and E. The D-field SNA takes the usual form; that is, it consists of a mnemonic abbreviation followed by a numeric or symbolic address. But the E-field SNA consists of the mnemonic abbreviation alone. This is because the

TABLE 6-1. AUXILIARY OPERATORS FOR COUNT AND SELECT BLOCKS

Logical Operators[a]

U	Facility in use (seized or preempted)
NU	Facility not in use (hence available)
I	Facility interrupted (preempted)
NI	Facility not interrupted (hence either seized or available)

SE	Storage empty
SNE	Storage not empty
SF	Storage full
SNF	Storage not full

LR	Logic switch reset
LS	Logic switch set

Conditional Operators[b]

L	Less than
LE	Less than or equal to
E	Equal to
NE	Not equal to
GE	Greater than or equal to
G	Greater than

Special Operators (SELECT Block Only)

MIN	Minimum
MAX	MAXIMUM

---

[a] The logical operators are standard logical attributes (SLAs).

[b] The interpretation of the conditional operators can be summarized as follows: Let "CO" denote any one of the six conditional operators. Then the specified condition is satisfied if

[value of E-field SNA] CO [value of D-field SNA]

index numbers specified in fields B and C serve as the entity addresses of the E-field SNA. This is now illustrated with two examples.

(a) COUNT E   3,1,4,X$SCORE,X

(b) COUNT LR   P2,7,12

Example (a) uses a conditional operator and thus has entries in fields D and E. When a xact enters this COUNT block, fullword savevalues 1 through 4 are tested. The quantity of them which are found to contain a value equal to the value of savevalue SCORE is placed into parameter 3 of the entering xact. Note that the field E entry is an SNA without an appended address. Any SNA can be specified in field E except MX and MH.

Example (b) uses a logical operator, so that fields D and E are blank. When a xact enters the COUNT block, logic switches 7 through 12 are tested. If n of them are found to be in the reset condition, the number n is placed in the parameter whose number is given by parameter 2 of the entering xact. (Logic switches will be discussed shortly.)

SELECT Block

The SELECT block is quite similar to the COUNT block except that, instead of counting the number of entities that meet a specified condition, it selects the first entity that meets the condition. Fields A through F are defined for the SELECT block.

Like the COUNT block, the SELECT block must have one of the Table 6-1 mnemonics in its operation field following the word "SELECT." Note that the operators "MAX" and "MIN" may be used in conjunction with the SELECT block but not the COUNT block. In GPSS/360 and GPS K, the mnemonic operator starts in column 14, immediately following the last letter of SELECT. In Flow Simulator, a blank column separates the two operation field entries.

Since subfields A through E are identical to those of the COUNT block, they will be described very briefly here. Field A specifies the number of the parameter which will store the index number of the selected entity. Fields B and C specify the lower and upper limits, respectively, of the range of the specified entity type to be tested. Field D contains an SNA which is to be compared against the field E SNA. The field E entry consists of a mnemonic with no appended address, since its range of addresses is specified in fields B and C.

The foregoing paragraph is sketchy on the assumption that you read the more explicit description of subfields A through E in the preceding section. In any event, the meaning of these subfields will soon be clarified with some examples. But first we shall point out the relationship between the Table 6-1 operators and fields D and E. Second, we shall explain field F. And then come the examples.

If one of the ten *logical* operators is used with the SELECT block, fields D and E should not be used. If either MAX or MIN is used, field D should be blank. If one of the six *conditional* operators is used, fields D and E should be used.

Field F of the SELECT block is used to specify an alternate block address to which the entering xact will be sent if no field E entity in the field B, C range meets the specified condition. If field F is blank, the xact always proceeds to the next sequential block.

The operation of the SELECT block can be better understood with the help of several examples:

(a) SELECT SE   10,3,3,,,OTHER
(b) SELECT MIN   5,X5,X6,,FC
(c) SELECT L   1,1,4,FN3,Q,ALT3

Example (a) uses a logical operator, so fields D and E are blank. When a xact enters the SELECT block, storage 3 (and only storage 3) is tested to determine whether it is empty. If it is empty, the number 3 is placed in parameter 10 of the entering xact, and this xact proceeds to the next sequential block. If storage 3 is not empty, nothing is put into parameter 10, and the entering xact proceeds to the block whose address is OTHER.

Example (b) uses one of the two operators which call for field D to be blank. Note that the field B and C values are given by the contents of fullword savevalues 5 and 6. Let us denote the contents of these savevalues as i and j, respectively. Note also that the field E argument stands for the number of en-

tries for a facility.[1] When a xact enters this SELECT block, the number of entries for every facility whose index numbers lie in the range i to j, inclusive, is
examined. The index number of the facility with the minimum number of entries (thus far in the run) is placed in parameter 5 of the entering xact. Then
that xact proceeds to the next sequential block.

Example (c) uses a conditional operator, so that fields D and E have entries.
When a xact enters this SELECT block, the current length of queue 1 is compared with a computed value of function 3. If Q1 is less than FN3, the number
1 is put into parameter 1 of the entering xact, and it proceeds to the next sequential block. If the test is not met by Q1, the SELECT block tries Q2, and so on. If
it turns out that none of the four queues has fewer xacts in it than the value of
FN3, nothing is put into parameter 1, and the entering xact is sent to the block
whose address is ALT3.

6.2 LOGIC SWITCHES: LOGIC AND GATE BLOCKS

Facilities, storages, and logic switches are the three *equipment entities* in GPSS.
The first two have already been covered, and they are reasonably straightforward. The logic switch entity is now introduced and, if anything, it is simpler
than the other two equipment entities.

A logic switch has only two properties that matter—its address and its status.
Its status is either *set* (S) or *reset* (R). The status of all logic switches is normally R
at the beginning of a run.

LOGIC Block

The status of a logic switch is controlled by one or more LOGIC blocks.   Field
A of the LOGIC block specifies the address of a logic switch, and no other sub-
fields are defined. Column 14 must contain one of these three letters: S, R, or I.
The operation of the LOGIC block is best explained by using several examples:

LOGIC S 20 When a xact enters this block, logic switch 20 is set; if it was
      previously set, it remains set.

LOGIC R XYZ When a xact enters this block, logic switch XYZ is reset, or it
      remains reset, as the case may be.

LOGIC I 20 When a xact enters this block, logic switch 20 is inverted. If it
      was S, it becomes R, and vice versa.

A LOGIC block never refuses entry to a xact, and it has no effect upon entering xacts. Indeed, the logic switch itself would be useless if it were not for the
GATE block which will be explained next.

GATE Block

A GATE block is used to monitor the status of a facility, storage, logic, switch,
or transaction matching condition (to be discussed in Chapter 9). Depending on

[1] See Table D-1.

the current status of whatever it is monitoring (or testing), the GATE block may block xacts, send them to a specified location, or pass them to the next sequential block.

The coding and operation of the GATE block are as follows:

1. The word "GATE" in the operation field.

2. A standard logical attribute, starting in column 13. There are 12 SLAs, and they are listed in Table 6-2. (The SLAs that pertain to "preempting facilities" and "matching transactions" will be understood when these topics are covered in Chapters 11 and 9, respectively.)

3. Field A specifies the address of the facility, storage, or logic switch to be tested.

4. If field B is blank (conditional entry mode), the GATE block refuses entry to the xact until the SLA is true. In other words, the xact is blocked if the SLA is false, and it passes to the next sequential block if the SLA is true.

5. If field B contains the address of an alternate block (unconditional entry mode), the GATE block will never refuse entry to xacts. If the SLA is true (i.e., the condition is met), the xact passes to the next sequential block. If it is false (i.e., the condition is not satisfied), the xact is sent to the field B address.

The preceding rules will have more meaning if we look at several examples:

GATE SF   16   If storage 16 is full, xact passes to next block. If storage 16 is not full, xact is blocked, and test is repeated later.

TABLE 6-2. GATE BLOCK AUXILIARY OPERATORS

Facility Logical Attributes[a]

NU	Facility not in use (neither seized nor preempted)
U	Facility in use
NI	Facility not being preempted
I	Facility being preempted

Storage Logical Attributes[a]

SE	Storage empty
SNE	Storage not empty
SF	Storage full
SNF	Storage not full

Logic Switch Logical Attributes[a]

LS	Logic switch set
LR	Logic switch reset

Transaction Logical Attributes

M	A xact is in a matching condition.
NM	No xact is in a matching condition.

[a] The particular entity for which the SLA is tested is the one whose address is specified in Field A of the Gate block.

GATE LR   14,BETA   If logic switch 14 is reset, xact passes to next block.   If
   logic switch 14 is set, send xact to address BETA.

GATE NU   FACIL   If facility FACIL is not in use, xact passes to next block.   If
   FACIL is in use, xact is blocked.

It is instructive to see how GATE and LOGIC blocks can be used in place of
SEIZE/DEPART blocks to act as a facility:

Scheme A		Scheme B	
QUEUE	1	QUEUE	1
SEIZE	1	GATE LR	1
DEPART	1	DEPART	1
ADVANCE	10	LOGIC S	1
RELEASE	1	ADVANCE	10
		LOGIC R	1

Schemes A and B are equivalent except that no facility statistics will be printed
out with Scheme B.   In a GPSS run, all logic switches are initially reset.   So the
first xact through Scheme B will pass through the first four blocks in zero clock
time, and it will set logic switch 1.   Any xacts attempting to enter the second
block will thus be impeded by the GATE block until the first xact resets logic
switch 1 in the last block.   Then one xact will enter the second, third, fourth, and
fifth blocks, and the process repeats.

6.3   THE TEST BLOCK

The TEST block specifies a condition that is to be met when a xact enters it.   If
this condition is met, the xact passes to the next sequential block without delay.
If it is not satisfied, the xact may be blocked if subfield C is blank, or sent to the
address in subfield C.   The format for a TEST block is as follows:

Columns 8 to 11: the word "TEST."

Columns 13 to 14: one of the following mnemonics: L, LE, E, NE, G, GE.

Subfield A: first SNA.

Subfield B: second SNA.

Subfield C: address of next block if relation is false.

The operation of the TEST block can be explained with several examples:

TEST E   Q6,K10   The condition tested is Q6 = 10.   If there are 10 xacts in
   queue 6 when a xact enters the TEST block, it will immediately proceed to
   the next sequential block.   If this condition is not met, the xact is denied
   entry to the TEST block until such time as Q6 = 10.

TEST GE   X21,P7,AAA   The condition tested is that the value of savevalue 21
   is greater than or equal to the value of parameter 7 of the xact entering the
   TEST block.   If this relation is true, the xact proceeds to the next sequential

block. If it is not true, the xact is sent directly to location AAA where it may or may not be admitted into the block at that location.

TEST NE FN8,50 If FN8 is not equal to 50 when the xact enters the TEST block, it proceeds to the next sequential block. If FN8 = 50, the xact is blocked by the TEST block.

The TEST block is similar to the GATE block in that it may block a xact, pass it to the next sequential block, or send it to another location, depending on whether a certain condition is satisfied. Also, the TEST and GATE blocks do not alter any xact attributes. But the TEST block controls the flow of xacts as a function of whether certain numerical relations are true, whereas the GATE block action depends on the truth or falsity of various SLAs.

6.4 VARIABLES

Two types of variable entities are defined in GPSS/360: *arithmetic* and *boolean*. An arithmetic variable is included in a model by using a VARIABLE or FVARIABLE definition card. A boolean variable is included in a model by using a BVARIABLE definition card.

When referenced via the standard numerical attribute Vj, an arithmetic variable computes the value of an algebraic expression and returns it to the referencing subfield. When referenced via BVj, a boolean variable evaluates a logical expression and returns either a 1 or 0 to the referencing subfield, depending on the truth or falsity of the expression. No block types are associated with variables, so a variable is computed only when it is referenced via an appropriate SNA.

All three variable definition cards adhere to the following format:

1. Mandatory address in the location field.
2. The word "VARIABLE," "FVARIABLE," or "BVARIABLE" in the operation field.
3. A *variable definition statement* in the variable field.

There are two kinds of arithmetic variables—*ordinary* and *floating-point*. The VARIABLE card is used for the former, and the FVARIABLE card is used for the latter. Hereafter we shall refer to an ordinary arithmetic variable as an "arithmetic variable." And we shall refer to a floating-point arithmetic variable as a "floating-point variable."

Arithmetic Variables

The variable definition statement is an algebraic combination of SNAs which is defined by the user. In defining a variable statement, the following algebraic operators may be used:

+ Denotes algebraic addition.
− Denotes algebraic subtraction.

* Denotes algebraic multiplication.

/ Denotes algebraic division.

@ Denotes modulo division (quotient is discarded and remainder, considered positive, is result).

( ) Parentheses, used for multiplication or grouping.

Any number of combinations of the operations above may be specified in columns 19 to 71, inclusive. There must be no blanks within a variable definition statement, since the simulator interprets a blank as the end of the variable field. If a variable definition statement is too long to fit into columns 19 to 71, it should be split into two or more VARIABLE cards with each one referencing (in effect incorporating) the variable before it via the SNA, Vj.

Variable statements are evaluated from left to right but according to the following hierchary. Parenthetical quantities are evaluated first, starting with the innermost parentheses. Multiplication, division, and modulo division are on the same level, and they take precedence over addition and subtraction. Note that there is no provision for exponentiation; a quantity must be written out as a chain of multiplications to achieve the effect of raising it to a power. Note also that multiplications can be denoted without using the asterisk by using parentheses as in ordinary algebra. Unsigned quantities are considered positive, and division by zero yields zero rather than an error message.

Arithmetic variables are evaluated in an integer mode; that is, decimal fractions are truncated *whenever* they appear. Thus all quantities that comprise the variable definition statement are evaluated and truncated *before* any algebraic operations take place. Any intermediate noninteger results obtained during the algebraic operations are immediately truncated. The final result is always an integer which may be positive or negative.

Let us look at two examples of arithmetic variables:

13   VARIABLE   P10+25

AAA   VARIABLE   P12+V27/27∗K50

Whenever variable 13 is referenced via V13, its value is computed as the value of parameter 10 of the current xact plus 25. Whenever variable AAA is referenced via V$AAA, its value is computed as P12 plus V27/V27 times 50. P12 is the value of parameter 12 of the current transaction. V27 is the value of variable 27 which must also be referenced. If V27 is less than 1.0, it becomes zero due to the truncation of decimal fractions at all stages of the computation. So if $V27 < 1.0$, then $V27/V27 = 0/0 = 0$, and $V\$AAA = P12$. But if $V27 \geq 1.0$, then $V27/V27 = 1$, and $V\$AAA = P12 + 50$.

Floating-Point Variables

The floating-point variable, specified by using an FVARIABLE card, is similar to the arithmetic variable in all respects except that (1) elements are *not* truncated *before or during the computation* of the value of the user-defined algebraic expression in the variable field, but the *final value* is truncated; (2) modulo division is not permitted.

The same SNA, namely Vj, is used to reference both arithmetic and floating-point variables. So a floating-point variable may not have the same address as an arithmetic variable in the same model.

Some examples are now given to illustrate the operation of floating-point and arithmetic variables.   You will note that they may yield unexpected results if the programmer is not fully aware of how they work.

1	FVARIABLE	1/5	$V1 = 0$
2	FVARIABLE	100(V1)	$V2 = 19$
3	FVARIABLE	10(11/5)	$V3 = 36$
4	VARIABLE	10(11/3)	$V4 = 30$
5	FVARIABLE	1/2+1/2	$V5 = 1$
6	VARIABLE	1/2+1/2	$V6 = 0$

Variable 2 references V1 and does not immediately truncate the decimal value of 1/5. This value is not .2 as you might expect; it is .1999 since that is the floating-point representation of 1/5. The product of 100 and .1999 is 19.99 which is truncated to 19.

Variable 3 is computed as follows:

$$V3 = 10 \times 3.67 = 36.7 = 36$$

Variable 4 truncates the 3.67 factor to 3, and then it multiplies this by 10 to obtain 30.

Boolean Variables

Boolean variables are analogous to arithmetic and floating-point variables in that a variable definition statement is evaluated whenever a boolean variable is referenced via the SNA, BVj.   But boolean variables differ in two important respects:

1. The variable definition statement expresses a *logical condition* that is to be tested rather than an algebraic relation that is to be computed.

2. The value of a boolean variable is always 1 or 0, depending on whether or not the logical condition is met.

A boolean variable definition statement consists of some combination of SNAs and operators.   Three types of operators may be used: *logical, conditional,* and *boolean.* These operators are shown in Table 6-3.

The use of the various operators to formulate boolean variable statements is illustrated by the following examples:

1   BVARIABLE   F5   If facility 5 is being either seized or preempted, $BV1 = 1$.
   Otherwise $BV1 = 0$.

2   BVARIABLE   LR4   If logic switch 4 is reset, $BV2 = 1$.   Otherwise $BV2 = 0$.

3   BVARIABLE   Q$WAIT'GE'10   If the current contents of the queue labeled WAIT are equal to 10 or more, $BV3 = 1$.   Otherwise $BV3 = 0$.

4   BVARIABLE   (V1'L'100)+SNF5   If either V1 is less than 100 *or* storage 5 is not full, $BV4 = 1$.   If neither of these conditions is met, $BV4 = 0$.

TABLE 6-3.   BOOLEAN VARIABLE OPERATORS

Logical Operators

FUn or Fn	1 if facility n is seized or preempted
FNUn	1 if facility n is available
FIn	1 if facility n is being preempted
FNIn	1 if facility n is not being preempted
SFn	1 if storage n is full
SNFn	1 if storage n is not full
SEn	1 if storage n is empty
SNEn	1 if storage n is not empty
LRn	1 if logic switch n is reset
LSn	1 if logic switch n is set

Conditional Operators

'G'	Greater than
'L'	Less than
'E'	Equal to
'NE'	Not equal to
'LE'	Less than or equal to
'GE'	Greater than or equal to

Boolean Operators

+	Logical "or" (1 if either or both)
*	Logical "and" (1 if both)

6.5   THE INITIAL CARD

The INITIAL card is a definition card that is inserted at the beginning of a program for the following purposes:

1. To place nonzero values in selected savevalue locations.
2. To place nonzero values in various cells of selected matrix savevalues.
3. To set logic switches.

The INITIAL card enables the programmer to avoid the wasteful use of SAVEVALUE, MSAVEVALUE, or LOGIC blocks to load constants into a model or initially set logic switches. For example, 10 savevalues could be assigned values by causing a xact to pass through 10 SAVEVALUE blocks. But one or two INITIAL cards can accomplish the same thing more simply and in fewer milliseconds of running time.

An INITIAL card must have a blank location field, and it must be placed at the beginning of any program in which it is used.

Initialization of Savevalues

The use of the INITIAL card to assign integer values (positive or negative) to savevalue locations can best be explained with some examples.

INITIAL   X28,401   Place the value 401 into fullword savevalue 28.

INITIAL   X1,40/X3,−11/X4−X8,50000   Place the value 40 into fullword savevalue 1.   Place the value −11 into fullword savevalue 3.   Place the value
   50,000 into fullword savevalue locations 4, 5, 6, 7, and 8.

INITIAL   X1,17/X2−X5,20/XH1−XH5,50   Place the value 17 into fullword savevalue 1.   Place the value 20 into fullword savevalues 2, 3, 4, and 5.   Place the
   value 50 into halfword savevalues 1, 2, 3, 4, and 5.

When two or more savevalues (fullword or halfword) are specified in the variable field of an INITIAL card, they must be in ascending order.   For instance,
X2 could not appear to the left of X1.   The entries in the variable field cannot
have any blanks among them since the GPSS program ignores all characters to
the right of a blank.

Initialization of Logic Switches

The use of the INITIAL card to set logic switches will be demonstrated with
some examples.

INITIAL   LS10   Set logic switch 10.

INITIAL   LS1/LS5−LS8   Set logic switches 1, 5, 6, 7, and 8.

INITIAL   XH4,12/LS3−LS4   Place the value 12 into halfword savevalue 4, and
   set logic switches 3 and 4.

When two or more logic switches are specified in the variable field of an INI-
TIAL card, they must be in ascending order.   For instance, the sequence
LS5−LS2 is illegal.   It is permissible to initialize savevalues and logic switches on
the same card.   It does not matter which comes first—logic switches, fullword
savevalues, or halfword savevalues.   But the items within each category must be
in ascending order.

Initialization of Matrix Savevalues

Matrix savevalues are not discussed until Chapter 14, so you will have to
overlook the fact that this section is somewhat out of place.

There are fullword as well as halfword matrix savevalues, and the contents of
their cells are referenced by the following standard numerical attributes:

MXj(m,n) is the value in row m, column n of fullword matrix savevalue j.

MHj(m,n) is the value in row m, column n of halfword matrix savevalue j.

Now let us see how the INITIAL card is used to assign values to matrix
savevalue locations.

INITIAL   MX5(2,4),−33   Place the value −33 into row 2, column 4 of fullword
   matrix savevalue 5.

INITIAL   MH1−MH3(1−4,1),10/MX1−MX3(1,5),−10   Place the value 10 into
   column 1 in rows 1 to 4 of halfword matrix savevalues 1, 2, and 3.   Place the
   value −10 into row 1, column 5 of fullword matrix savevalues 1, 2, and 3.

INITIAL   MX2(1,1),5/LS1−LS4/XH3−XH5,50   Place the value 5 into row 1, column 1 of fullword matrix savevalue 2. Set logic switches 1 through 4. Place the value 50 into halfword savevalues 3 through 5.

When two or more matrix savevalues (fullword or halfword) are specified in the variable field of an INITIAL card, they must be in ascending order. It is possible to initialize any combination of savevalues, matrix savevalues, and logic switches with the same INITIAL card. But the items within each category must be in ascending order.

6.6 THE RESET, CLEAR, AND JOB CARDS

The presence of an END card at the end of a source deck causes the GPSS simulator to return control to the system supervisor after the run is concluded. A RESET, CLEAR, or JOB card can be used in place of an END card if the user wants to obtain another run without relinquishing control to the system supervisor. But the last request for a run must be punctuated with an END card.

How the RESET, CLEAR, and JOB Cards are Used

The use of RESET, CLEAR, and JOB cards is illustrated in Figure 6-1. The rectangular column represents a stack of input cards which will yield four runs. The first three runs involve essentially the same model, and the fourth run may involve a completely different model.

The cards within the "run 1" bracket could be any of the illustrative programs we have covered. The only difference is that instead of the END card, a RESET card has been used here. The RESET card will soon be discussed in detail, but for now it is sufficient to say that it wipes out the accumulated system statistics in preparation for the next run.

The RESET card may be followed by one or more definition cards which specify certain entity attributes for the next run. For example, one or more INITIAL cards may be used, or various functions may be redefined, or storage capacities may be altered, and so forth.

The second run will then be executed using essentially the same model as the first run. However, the second run (in Figure 6-1) will end after 1500 terminations rather than 1000.

The CLEAR card will soon be discussed in detail, but for now it can be thought of as clearing the model of all statistics and transactions. The CLEAR card may also be followed by various definition cards if desired.

The third run (in Figure 6-1) will be made using essentially the same model as in the first two runs. It will end after 1000 terminations have occurred.

The JOB card will also be discussed in awhile, but for now we can say that it wipes out the entire model—block diagram and all. The JOB card is followed by a complete input deck such as any of the illustrative programs. After the new model has been read into the computer, the fourth and final run (in Figure 6-1) is made.

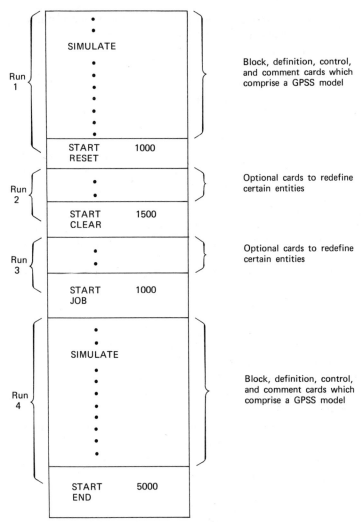

Fig. 6-1. Use of RESET, CLEAR, and JOB cards.

RESET Card

The RESET card always has a blank location field. Its operand field may or may not be blank, depending on which of these two modes it is used in:

1. Regular mode (blank operand field), where its effect applies to every block, facility, queue, storage, table, and user chain entity in the system. (User chains are covered in Chapter 12.)

2. Selective mode (one or more of the following mnemonics in the operand field: Fj, Qj, Sj, TBj, and CHj), where the entities specified in the variable field are excluded from the reset operation.

The use of the *selective reset operation* is explained after we summarize the main effects of the RESET card upon various GPSS entities.

1. Blocks
   Status (current contents): unaffected.
   Entry count (total entries): set to zero.

2. Facilities
   Status (in use or not in use): unaffected.
   Cumulative time integral (total number of clock units spent by all xacts in facility): set to zero.
   Entry count: set equal to contents of facility at end of previous run.

3. Storages
   Status (number of xacts currently in storage): unaffected.
   Cumulative time integral (total number of clock units spent by all xacts in storage): set to zero.
   Entry count: set equal to contents of storage at end of previous run; same as status.
   Maximum contents: set equal to new entry count; same as status.

4. Queues
   Status (current contents): unaffected.
   Cumulative time integral (total number of clock units spent by all xacts in queue): set to zero.
   Entry count: set equal to contents of queue at end of previous run; same as status.
   Maximum contents: set equal to new entry count; same as status.
   Number of zero delay entries: set to zero.

5. Frequency Tables
   Frequency counts, sums, and averages: set to zero.

6. User Chains
   Status (number of xacts currently on chain): unaffected.
   Cumulative time integral (total number of clock units spent by all xacts on chain): set to zero.

No other entity types are affected by the reset operation. For example, xacts are left as they were when the previous run ended. (Remember that transactions are a type of entity!) Savevalues are not zeroed, and logic switches are not reset. The absolute clock time and the random number seed are not affected, but the relative clock time (C1) is set to zero.

The selective reset option is very straightforward; it merely involves the specification of entities that will be exempt from the reset operations just enumerated. The rules for specifying these entities are amply illustrated by the following pair of examples:

```
RESET    Q4–Q8,Q10,F1–F5,S7,TB1–TB3
RESET    CH5,TB4–TB6,F3,Q6–Q10
```

All entities of the same type must be contiguous; that is, intermixing of entity types is not permitted. And entity addresses must be listed in ascending order. Thus the following formats would be illegal in GPSS/360:

```
RESET    Q1,Q8–Q10,Q6
RESET    Q1,F3–F8,Q3
```

CLEAR Card

Whereas the RESET card affects six entity types, the CLEAR card affects eleven. It sets to zero everything that the RESET card sets to zero. In addition, it does the following:

1. Sets the absolute clock to zero.
2. Sets all savevalues and matrix savevalues to zero.
3. Resets all logic switches.
4. Eliminates all xacts from the model including incipient xacts in the GEN-ERATE block.
5. Sets all accumulated as well as current counts and statistics to zero.

To put it simply, the CLEAR card wipes out everything but the block diagram itself. It returns the model to its initial state in all respects except for the random number seed.

Like the RESET card, the CLEAR card always has a blank location field, and it can be used in a selective mode if desired. However, the only entities that can be excluded from the clear operation are savevalues. The *selective clear option* is illustrated by the following examples:

```
CLEAR    X1-X10, XH1-XH5
CLEAR    X3,X8
```

It is not permissible to intermix X's and XH's, and the savevalue addresses must be listed in ascending numerical order. Thus the following formats are illegal:

```
CLEAR    X4,X1–X2
CLEAR    XH3,X7,XH5
```

JOB Card

The JOB card performs all the functions of the CLEAR card, and it also removes all blocks, functions, variables, tables, and storages. In other words, a JOB card wipes the slate clean like an END card, but it does not return control to the system supervisor. It is used when there are a series of different GPSS programs to be run, one after the other, with a single set of computer control cards for the total deck.

6.7 DIFFERENCES BETWEEN GPSS/360 AND OTHER VERSIONS

GPS K

The INDEX, COUNT, SELECT, LOGIC, GATE, and TEST blocks are the same in GPS K as in GPSS/360 except for the following minor detail: GPS K utilizes FNU, FU, FNI, and FI as COUNT and SELECT block operators whereas GPSS/360 utilizes NU, U, NI, and I, respectively.

GPS K incorporates arithmetic, floating-point, and boolean variables which are exactly as described for GPSS/360 except for one minor detail: GPS K permits an additional logical operator in boolean variable statements, namely BVn. This makes it possible to express a complex logical statement on multiple BVARIABLE cards, where one includes the other(s).

The INITIAL card is used just like the one in GPSS/360, and so are the RESET and CLEAR cards. However, the selective CLEAR option differs from that of GPSS/360 in two respects:

1. XHj should not be used since GPS K does not include halfword savevalues. However, GPS K will accept XHj and interpret it as Xj.
2. GPS K allows the mnemonic MXj in the variable field of the CLEAR card. It is thus possible to exclude one or more matrix savevalues from the clear operation; for example:

CLEAR   X1–X10,MX1,MX3–MX4

GPS K does not have a JOB card. Instead, a MODEL card is used which serves the same purpose. In addition, columns 19 to 70 of a MODEL card can be used to write a title which will appear on every page of output until the next MODEL card is encountered.

Flow Simulator

The INDEX, SELECT, LOGIC, GATE, and TEST blocks are the same in Flow Simulator as in GPSS/360. The COUNT block is not offered in Flow Simulator. Flow Simulator incorporates arithmetic variables, and they are defined by a VARIABLE card as in GPSS/360. However, Flow Simulator does not offer floating-point variables or boolean variables, defined by FVARIABLE and BVARIABLE cards, respectively.

The INITIAL card is the same in Flow Simulator as in GPSS/360 except that matrix savevalues are never initialized because they do not exist in Flow Simulator.

The RESET, CLEAR, and JOB cards are the same in Flow Simulator as in GPSS/360. However, Flow Simulator allows intermixing of entity types when using the selective reset and clear options, whereas GPSS/360 does not. Thus the following cards are legal in Flow Simulator:

RESET   Q4–Q7,F1,Q10,F4–F8,TB2
CLEAR   XH1,X20–X25,XH20–XH29

GPSS III

The INDEX, LOGIC, GATE, and TEST blocks are the same in GPSS III as in GPSS/360. The COUNT and SELECT blocks are not included in GPSS III.

GPSS III includes arithmetic variables but no floating-point or boolean variables, hence no FVARIABLE and BVARIABLE cards. The variable definition statement in a VARIABLE card differs from its GPSS/360 counterpart in two respects:

1. Parenthetical expressions cannot be used.
2. The symbol for modulo division is (rather than @.

The INITIAL card has a much more limited function in GPSS III than in GPSS/360. It can only be used to enter a constant in a single (fullword) savevalue.

The RESET, CLEAR, and JOB cards serve the same purposes in GPSS III as in GPSS/360, but they differ in several respects:

1. There is no selective reset option; thus the variable field of the RESET card is always blank.
2. There is no selective clear option; thus the variable field of the CLEAR card is always blank.
3. The JOB card must have a dollar sign ($) in column 1.

6.8   SUMMARY

Six block types, four definition cards, three control cards, and three entities were discussed. All of them are offered in GPSS/360 and GPS K, but some are omitted from Flow Simulator and GPSS III.

The INDEX, COUNT, SELECT, and LOGIC blocks never refuse entry to transactions; thus they are zero-delay blocks. The GATE and TEST blocks do not refuse entry to xacts if used in the unconditional entry mode. But they may block xacts if used in the conditional entry mode.

The INDEX block modifies a transaction attribute; namely, the value of parameter 1. The COUNT and SELECT blocks do the same, but not necessarily to parameter 1. The number of entities which meet a specified condition can be recorded in a xact parameter by passing the xact through a COUNT block. The index number of the first entity which meets a specified condition can be recorded in a xact parameter by passing the xact through a SELECT block.

Logic switches are simple entities that may be either reset or set. The LOGIC block is used to control the status of logic switches. GATE LR and GATE LS blocks are used to control the flow of xacts as a function of the states of logic switches. The GATE block may also utilize ten other standard logical attributes.

The TEST block is similar to the GATE block in what it may do to entering xacts. It may or may not delay them, and it may or may not send them to a nonsequential block. The main difference between the TEST and GATE blocks is that the former tests a numerical relationship while the latter tests the truth of SLAs.

Arithmetic and boolean variables, along with functions, comprise the three computational entities in GPSS. No block types are associated with these entities. They compute values only when referenced via the following SNAs: Vj, BVj, FNj.

Arithmetic variables are FORTRAN-like algebraic combinations of SNAs. Ordinary arithmetic variables are defined by a VARIABLE card, and floating-point variables are defined by an FVARIABLE card. Boolean variables are logical combinations of SNAs whose truth or falsity is tested. They are defined by a BVARIABLE card.

The INITIAL card affords a convenient and efficient means for loading constants into savevalues and matrix savevalues at the beginning of a model. It also allows the user to set logic switches which are normally reset at the start of a run. The INITIAL card is also very useful when it follows RESET or CLEAR cards.

By using RESET or CLEAR cards with their selective options, and by redefining various entities, you can arrange for a model to run several times in succession with certain specified aspects being varied. This makes it possible — in fact, easy — to see how a model behaves when certain assumptions and inputs are varied.

It is perhaps worth noting that the VARIABLE, FVARIABLE, BVARIABLE, INITIAL, selective RESET, and selective CLEAR cards do not have their variable fields divided into the usual A, B, C, . . . subfields.

CHAPTER 7

Illustrative Program 4

In this chapter we study a GPSS program that is more interesting and sophisticated than the first three. All of the card types used in program 4 are familiar except for one, which will be explained when we get to it. There are some new wrinkles among the familiar cards, and they are explained as we proceed through the program. For the most part, however, we concentrate on the model per se, since it deals with a significant problem and incorporates some useful programming techniques.

7.1 THE PROBLEM AND THE MODEL

The problem concerns a multiplexor channel which links four terminals with a central processing unit. Inquiries "arrive" at the terminals at random intervals, and messages flow back and forth through the channel, one at a time. It should be obvious that a system of this type can be represented by a GPSS block diagram.

The problem that is taken up in this chapter is hypothetical and does not purport to depict the true operating characteristics of computer terminals, channels, and CPUs. However, it is representative of an important class of problems to which GPSS is very well suited.

Statement of the Problem

The problem is defined in Figure 7-1. It involves a system that is quite simple in its outward configuration. But its operating characteristics are a bit more involved, as you will see.

Two types of messages are processed by the system. Of them, 80% are classified as *data entries,* and 20% are *inquiries.* Inquiries are assumed to always be 50 characters in length while data entries are 30, 50, or 80 characters long. Any type of message may emanate from any of the four terminals, but the terminals are not all equally busy.

Messages arrive at the four stations in a random fashion, and they wait to be serviced. The stations are repeatedly polled by the multiplexor channel in accordance with some predefined pattern. For instance, the polling pattern might be 1-2-3-4, 4-2-4-1-3-4-3-2, or any order we specify. The time required to poll a station is 500 milliseconds.

If a message is found to be waiting at a particular station, polling is suspended

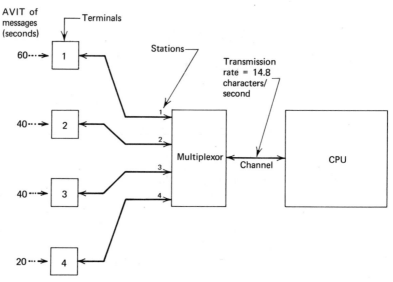

Fig. 7-1. Definition of problem for program 4.

Two types of messages
   Inquiries (20%): 50 characters long
   Data entries (80%):
      10% are 30 characters long
      70% are 50 characters long
      20% are 80 characters long

Length of responses
   To all inquiries: 50 characters long
   To all data entries: 20 characters long

Time Spent in CPU
   Inquiries: 700 to 1300 milliseconds
   Data entries: 1 millisecond/character

while it is serviced. Polling is not resumed until that message has been processed and a reply received at the terminal. Then the next station is polled. No attempt is made to ascertain whether a second message was waiting at the previously polled station. So if two or more messages are waiting at a station, only the first one will be serviced when that station is polled. The next message must wait until the next time it is polled.

Messages arrive more frequently at station 4 than at the other three stations, and they arrive least frequently at station 1. Therefore, any polling mechanism which goes from station to station looking for messages should tend to favor station 4 and pay less attention to station 1. One of the primary objectives of our simulation will be to find the optimum polling pattern; it is defined as the one which results in the minimum *average response time*. In this problem, the latter is taken as the interval of time between the arrival of a message at the multiplexor and the receipt of a response at the terminal.

Each simulation run will show the behavior of the system with a different polling scheme. By examining the statistics generated in each run, we can ascertain which polling schemes tend to give minimum response times at all four terminals. We may not find the absolute optimum arrangement, but we can be confident that we will at least come very close if we make a reasonable number of runs which simulate a representative period of time.

Our simulation model can be designed to also accomplish other objectives. For example, we might want to try polling times other than 500 milliseconds. If we found the response time to be very sensitive to the polling time, we might consider going to faster equipment.

Again, the equipment-oriented reader is cautioned against paying too much attention to the assumed message lengths, transmission rates, polling time, hardware configuration, and so on. It is the *class of problem* and the *formulation of a GPSS model* that are paramount here.

The GPSS Model

It is convenient to envisage the required model as having two separate parts which interact at certain points. One part simulates the arrival, transmission, and processing of messages and responses. The other part consists of the polling mechanism.

Figure 7-2 schematically depicts the GPSS model that was devised for this problem. The diagram does not conform to the standard flow-charting format, nor is it a GPSS block diagram. Its format was dictated strictly by the nature of the model it portrays.

The Figure 7-2 diagram represents one approach to modeling the stated problem. It is by no means the only way of applying GPSS to the problem. For example, we could have used separate GENERATE blocks to create message transactions at each of the four terminals. Instead we have elected to create all of the message xacts at one place and then allot them to the four terminals. Either approach is acceptable as long as it results in the arrival of messages at the stations at the frequencies specified in the problem description.

By inverting the interarrival times in Figure 7-1, we find that the following numbers of messages originate at the various terminals in an average 60-second interval

1.0 message at terminal 1.

1.5 messages at terminals 2 and 3.

3.0 messages at terminal 4.

So of all the messages which arrive during a given interval of time, 14.3% originate at terminal 1, 21.4% originate at terminal 2, 21.4% originate at terminal 3, and 42.9% originate at terminal 4.

Now that we have developed a basis for distributing messages among the various terminals, we can focus our attention on one station which is denoted by j in Figure 7-2. Each message is represented by a transaction, as you have no doubt surmised. As soon as a message xact is created, its type (inquiry or data entry), terminal number, and length (number of characters) are assigned to parameters 1, 2, and 3, respectively. This xact is sent to station j where it waits to

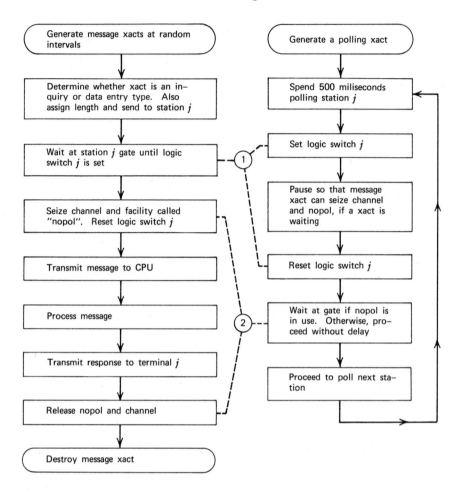

Fig. 7-2. Schematic diagram of GPSS model for program 4.

seize the channel. As long as logic switch j is reset, it is blocked at this point by a gate.[1]

When logic switch j is set, the message xact can seize the channel. As soon as it seizes the channel, it resets logic switch j so the xact behind it (if there is one) cannot enter the channel. It is then transmitted to the CPU where it is processed. A reply is transmitted back through the channel to the terminal, and the channel is freed.

---

[1] We are using the word "gate" because it is more descriptive than "GATE block," which would be more correct. We do not mean to imply the existence of a *gate entity;* there is no such "animal" in GPSS.

While many message xacts are being generated and subsequently destroyed, there is *only one polling xact which is never destroyed.* It is created at the beginning of the run, and it goes from station to station in accordance with the user-defined polling pattern. The polling xact governs the servicing of message xacts, but its own movement is also affected by the message xacts as indicated in Figure 7-2. Let us see how this works.

At the start of the run, the polling xact goes to station j and spends 500 milliseconds polling it. (Meanwhile, a message xact may or may not arrive at station j.) The polling xact next sets logic switch j, and then it pauses. (Remember that logic switches are always initially reset.) If a message xact is waiting at gate j, it will take this opportunity to seize the channel as well as facility NOPOL, and it will reset logic switch j. Then the polling xact proceeds to its gate where it is blocked because NOPOL is in use. Later on, when the message xact releases NOPOL, the polling xact passes through its gate and proceeds to the next station in the polling pattern.

If the polling xact finds no message xact waiting at station j, it resets logic switch j to block the next message xact that may arrive. Then it passes immediately through its gate, since NOPOL is not in use, and it proceeds to the next station.

It should be evident that our GPSS model will contain two GENERATE blocks, four logic switches, two facilities, and five gates. Four of the gates are associated with the logic switches, and one is associated with the NOPOL facility.

7.2   INTRODUCTION TO PROGRAM 4

First we stand back and look at the whole program, and then we examine some of the definition cards that precede the actual block diagram. The latter are discussed in Sections 7.3 and 7.4.

Overview of Program 4

Illustrative program 4 is shown in Figures 7-3 and 7-4 as a facsimile of the symbolic listing. Notice that the symbolic program is divided into four sections to facilitate the discussion. These sections are clearly labeled by comment cards. This division of program 4 into sections is purely superficial; the GPSS simulator "sees" the model without the comments and artificial separations.

As you can see, the symbolic listing is well endowed with explanatory comments. This allows us to concentrate on new aspects and highlights of the program without having to say something about every card.

Section 1: D-Type Functions

GPSS functions were discussed in Section 4.2, and the initial part of that discussion pertained to discrete numerical-valued (D-type) functions as well as to the other types (i.e., C, L, E, and M). However, only C-type functions have been demonstrated up to now.

Program 4 contains one C-type function, three D-type functions, and one L-type function. The C-type function is the familiar exponential function. The D-type functions are covered here, and the L-type function is covered next. Incidentally, attribute-valued functions (E and M) are not covered in this book.

Function TYPE is a simple discrete numerical-valued function which, when referenced, takes on the value 1 or 2, depending on the value computed for the independent variable RN1. The operation of this function can be summarized as follows:

If $0 \leq RN1 \leq .8$, FN\$TYPE = 1.

If $.8 < RN1 < 1.0$, FN\$TYPE = 2.

Function TERM operates as follows:

If $0 \leq RN1 \leq .143$, FN\$TERM = 1.

```
* SIMULATION OF MULTIPLEXOR CHANNEL WITH FOUR TERMINALS

* SECTION 1 (DEFINITION OF FUNCTIONS)

        SIMULATE
        INITIAL     XH1,500       SET HALFWORD SAVEVALUE # 1 = 500.
 EXPON FUNCTION      RN1,C24       CUMULATIVE EXPONENTIAL DISTRIBUTION
0,0/.1,.104/.2,.222/.3,.355/.4,.509/.5,.69/.6,.915/.7,1.2/.75,1.38/
.8,1.6/.84,1.83/.88,2.12/.9,2.3/.92,2.52/.94,2.81/.95,2.99/.96,3.2/
.97,3.5/.98,3.9/.99,4.6/.995,5.3/.998,6.2/.999,7/.9997,8

  TYPE FUNCTION      RN1,D2        SPECIFIES IF MESSAGE IS TYPE 1 OR 2
.8,1/1.0,2
  TERM FUNCTION      RN1,D4        APPORTIONS MESSAGES TO TERMINALS
.143,1/.357,2/.571,3/1.0,4
 LNGTH FUNCTION      RN1,D3        NO. OF CHARACTERS IN DATA ENTRIES
.1,30/.8,50/1.0,80
  POLL FUNCTION      P1,L14        SPECIFIES STATION FOR POLLING XACT
,1/,4/,3/,4/,2/,4/,3/,1/,4/,2/,4/,3/,4/,2

* SECTION 2 (PORTION OF BLOCK DIAGRAM INVOLVING MESSAGE XACTS)

        GENERATE     8571,FN$EXPON,,,1   CREATE MESS. XACTS WITH PR. 1
        ASSIGN       1,FN$TYPE     P1 CARRIES MESSAGE TYPE, 1 OR 2.
        ASSIGN       2,FN$TERM     P2 CARRIES TERM. NO., 1,2,3, OR 4.
        TEST E       P1,1,ALT      IF P1=1, XACT IS A DATA MESSAGE AND
*                                  GOES TO NEXT BLOCK.  OTHERWISE IT IS
*                                  AN INQUIRY AND IS SENT TO ALT.
        ASSIGN       3,FN$LNGTH    P3 = 30, 50, OR 80 FOR DATA XACTS.
 WAIT QUEUE          *2            XACTS WAIT AT STATION GIVEN BY P2.
      GATE LS        *2            HOLD MESSAGE AT ITS STATION UNTIL LO.
*                                  SW. SPECIFIED IN P2 IS SET.
        DEPART       *2            XACTS DEPART QUEUE GIVEN BY P2.
        LOGIC R      *2            MESSAGE XACT RESETS ITS LOGIC SWITCH.
        SEIZE        CHANL         MESSAGE XACT SEIZES CHANNEL.
        SEIZE        NOPOL         MESSAGE XACT SEIZES NOPOL.
        ADVANCE      V$TRANS       NO. OF MILLISEC. FROM STATION TO CPU.
 TRANS VARIABLE      P3*10000/48   (NO. OF CHAR.) X (NO. OF MS. PER CHAR.)
        RELEASE      CHANL         VACATE CHANNEL AND ENTER CPU.
        TEST E       P1,1,INQ      IF P1 NOT EQUAL TO 1, MESSAGE IS AN
*                                  INQUIRY, SO SEND XACT TO INQ.
        ADVANCE      P3            NO. OF MS. IN CPU = NO. OF DATA CHAR.
        ASSIGN       3,K20         SET P3 = 20 FOR DATA XACTS.
  OUT SEIZE          CHANL         XACT SEIZES CHANNEL TO RETURN TO TERM.
        ADVANCE      V$TRANS       NO. OF MILLISEC. FROM CPU TO STATION.
        RELEASE      CHANL         VACATE CHANNEL.
```

Fig. 7-3. Replica of symbolic listing of program 4.

```
          TABULATE    *2              TABULATE M1 FOR XACTS AT EACH TERMINAL.
        1 TABLE       M1,50000,50000,30
        2 TABLE       M1,50000,50000,30
        3 TABLE       M1,50000,50000,30
        4 TABLE       M1,50000,50000,30

          RELEASE     NOPOL           MESSAGE XACT RELEASES NOPOL.
          TERMINATE   1               DESTROY MESSAGE XACTS.

    ALT ASSIGN        3,50            INQUIRIES ARE 50 CHARACTERS LONG.
        TRANSFER      ,WAIT           INQUIRY XACTS GO TO JOIN DATA XACTS
*                                     WAITING AT STATIONS.
    INQ ADVANCE       1000,300        TIME IN CPU FOR INQUIRY XACTS.
        TRANSFER      ,OUT            GO SEIZE CHANNEL OUTBOUND FROM CPU.

* SECTION 3 (PORTION OF BLOCK DIAGRAM INVOLVING POLLING XACT)

          GENERATE    ,,,1            CREATE ONE XACT WITH PRIORITY ZERO.
    INIT ASSIGN       1,14            SET P1 = 14.
    STEP ASSIGN       2,FN$POLL       PUT NO. OF NEXT STATION INTO P2.
          ADVANCE     XH1             NO. OF MILLISEC. TO POLL STATION.
          LOGIC S     P2              SET LOGIC SWITCH 1,2,3, OR 4.
          BUFFER                      POLLING XACT PAUSES WHILE GPSS SCAN
*                                     MOVES FIRST MESSAGE XACT AT STATION
*                                     (I.E., GATE) P2, IF THERE ARE ANY.
          LOGIC R     P2              RESET LOGIC SWITCH 1,2,3, OR 4.
          GATE NU     NOPOL           POLLING XACT BLOCKED IF NOPOL IN USE.
          LOOP        1,STEP          DECREMENT P1 BY 1 AND GO TO STEP IF
*                                     P1 IS NOT 0.  ELSE GO TO NEXT BLOCK.
          TRANSFER    ,INIT           AFTER COMPLETING POLLING PATTERN,
*                                     INITIALIZE P1 AGAIN AND REENTER LOOP
*                                     TO REPEAT POLLING SEQUENCE.

* SECTION 4 (QTABLE DEFINITION CARDS, SPECIFICATION OF RUN LENGTH,
*            AND REQUEST FOR SECOND RUN)

        5    QTABLE      1,50000,50000,30
        6    QTABLE      2,50000,50000,30
        7    QTABLE      3,50000,50000,30
        8    QTABLE      4,50000,50000,30

          START       200             RUN ENDS WHEN 200 MESSAGE XACTS HAVE
*                                     BEEN DESTROYED.
          CLEAR       XH1             CLEAR MODEL OF ALL XACTS AND STATIS-
*                                     TICS, BUT LEAVE XH1 = 500.

    POLL FUNCTION    P1,L14      REDEFINE POLL FUNCTION.
    ,4/,4/,1/,2/,3/,4/,4/,1/,2/,3/,4/,4/,2/,3

          START       200
          END
```

Fig. 7-4.   Replica of symbolic listing of program 4 (*continued*).

If $.143 < RN1 \leq .357$, FN\$TERM = 2.

If $.357 < RN1 \leq .571$, FN\$TERM = 3.

If $.571 < RN1 < 1.0$, FN\$TERM = 4.

Since the values of RN1 are uniformly distributed between 0 and 1, it is evident that RN1 will most often fall in the fourth interval; thus FN\$TERM will most often be equal to 4.

Function LNGTH operates as follows:

If $0 \leq RN1 \leq .1$, FN\$LNGTH = 30.

If $.1 < RN1 \leq .8$, FN\$LNGTH = 50.

If $.8 < RN1 < 1.0$, FN\$LNGTH = 80.

Function LNGTH will be equal to 50 seven times out of ten since RN1 will lie between .1 and .8 that often.

Section 1: L-Type Functions

Function POLL is a list numerical-valued function. L-type functions are used when the independent variable takes on values that belong to a string of consecutive integers, starting with 1. So the values of X in the function follower cards are always 1, 2, 3,. . . . Let us look at an example:

```
10 FUNCTION      S5,L10
1,3/2,7/3,11/4,20/5,30/6,60/7,30/8,22/9,16/10,12
```

S5 stands for the *current contents of storage* 5. If S5 = 4 when function 10 is referenced, then FN10 = 20. If S5 = 8, then FN10 = 22. If S5 = 1, then FN10 = 3. And so on. It is important to note that S5 can only take on integer values between 1 and 10, inclusive, but it can take them on in *any* order. In other words, the independent variable of an L-type function need not be equal to $i + 1$ if it was previously equal to i.

Since the X-coordinates of an L-type function always run from 1 to n (where n follows L in field B of the FUNCTION card), the GPSS simulator does not bother to examine the X arguments in the function follower cards. It obtains the value of the function argument (S5 in our example), and then it goes directly to the corresponding value of Y. So if the value of the argument is i, then the function immediately becomes equal to Y_i.

Since the GPSS program ignores the X values anyway, they can be omitted from the function follower cards for L-type functions. This is why no X values appear in the function follower card for function POLL in program no. 4. The operation of this function should be evident at this point:

If P1 = 1, FN$POLL = 1.
If P1 = 2, FN$POLL = 4.
If P1 = 3, FN$POLL = 3.
And so forth. . . .

7.3   SECTION 2 OF PROGRAM 4

Section 2 contains the major portion of the block diagram. It includes the terminals, stations, channel, CPU, and messages. For ease of reference, this part of program 4 has been reproduced in Figure 7-5.

Entry of Message Transactions

Since an average of seven messages arrive every 60 seconds, the average interarrival time is 60/7 = 8.571 seconds per xact. Since we are equating one clock unit to a millisecond, the average interarrival time is 8571 clock units or milliseconds. This explains field A of the GENERATE block.

```
*  SECTION 2 (PORTION OF BLOCK DIAGRAM INVOLVING MESSAGE XACTS)

           GENERATE      8571,FN$EXPON,,,1   CREATE MESS. XACTS WITH PR. 1.
           ASSIGN        1,FN$TYPE     P1 CARRIES MESSAGE TYPE, 1 OR 2.
           ASSIGN        2,FN$TERM     P2 CARRIES TERMINAL NO., 1,2,3, OR 4.
           TEST E        P1,1,ALT      IF P1=1, XACT IS A DATA MESSAGE AND
*                                      GOES TO NEXT BLOCK.   OTHERWISE IT IS
*                                      AN INQUIRY AND IS SENT TO ALT.
           ASSIGN        3,FN$LNGTH    P3 = 30, 50, OR 80 FOR DATA XACTS.
      WAIT QUEUE         *2            XACTS WAIT AT STATION GIVEN BY P2.
           GATE LS       *2            HOLD MESSAGE AT ITS STATION UNTIL
*                                      LOG. SW. SPECIFIED IN P2 IS SET.
           DEPART        *2            XACTS DEPART QUEUE GIVEN BY P2.
           LOGIC R       *2            MESSAGE XACT RESETS ITS LOGIC SWITCH.
           SEIZE         CHANL         MESSAGE XACT SEIZES CHANNEL.
           SEIZE         NOPOL         MESSAGE XACT SEIZES NOPOL.
           ADVANCE       V$TRANS       NO. OF MILLISEC. FROM STATION TO CPU.
     TRANS VARIABLE      P3*10000/48   (NO. OF CHAR.) X (NO. OF MS. PER CHAR.)
           RELEASE       CHANL         VACATE CHANNEL AND ENTER CPU.

           TEST E        P1,1,INQ      IF P1 IS NOT EQUAL TO 1, MESSAGE IS
*                                      AN INQUIRY, SO SEND XACT TO INQ.
           ADVANCE       P3            NO. OF MS. IN CPU = NO. OF DATA CHAR.
           ASSIGN        3,K20         SET P3 = 20 FOR DATA XACTS.

       OUT SEIZE         CHANL         XACT SEIZES CHANNEL TO RETURN TO TERM.
           ADVANCE       V$TRANS       NO. OF MILLISEC. FROM CPU TO STATION.
           RELEASE       CHANL         VACATE CHANNEL.

           TABULATE      *2            TABULATE M1 FOR XACTS AT EACH TERMINAL.
         1 TABLE         M1,50000,50000,30
         2 TABLE         M1,50000,50000,30
         3 TABLE         M1,50000,50000,30
         4 TABLE         M1,50000,50000,30

           RELEASE       NOPOL         MESSAGE XACT RELEASES NOPOL.
           TERMINATE     1             DESTROY MESSAGE XACTS.

       ALT ASSIGN        3,50          INQUIRIES ARE 50 CHARACTERS LONG.
           TRANSFER      ,WAIT         INQUIRY XACTS GO TO JOIN DATA XACTS
*                                      WAITING AT STATIONS.
       INQ ADVANCE       1000,300      TIME IN CPU FOR INQUIRY XACTS.
           TRANSFER      ,OUT          GO SEIZE CHANNEL OUTBOUND FROM CPU.
```

Fig. 7-5.   Section 2 of program 4.

Field E of the GENERATE block has been used to assign a priority of 1 to each message xact when it is created. If field E of the GENERATE block is left blank (as in previous illustrative programs), xacts have a zero priority. The reason for assigning a nonzero priority in this instance will become apparent later.

As soon as they are created, xacts are assigned a type (1 or 2) and a terminal number (1, 2, 3, or 4). Type 1 xacts are data entries, and type 2 xacts are inquiries. Xacts are than assigned a length. Note that type 2 xacts are temporarily diverted to ALT by the TEST block to have their lengths assigned.

After having a type, terminal, and length assigned, all transactions enter the QUEUE block labeled WAIT. The QUEUE/DEPART blocks have been inserted so that queue statistics will be printed out for each terminal, or station. These blocks do not affect the logical behavior of the model, as you know.

A transaction may not depart from its queue until the logic switch corresponding to its station has been set. The GATE LS block refuses entry until this condition is met. As soon as a xact is admitted to the channel, it resets its station's logic switch, thus blocking any xacts behind it from entering the channel.

Facilities CHANL and NOPOL

Having reset a logic switch, a message xact seizes two facilities simultaneously: CHANL and NOPOL. In general, a transaction may seize any number of facilities at various times, and it may release them in any order. Note that we are talking about xacts seizing facilities rather than occupying them. This is a subtle distinction, but it should by all means be understood; so let us dwell on it for a moment.

It is less restrictive and also more accurate to regard the seizing of a facility as an action that alters the status of the facility rather than as the entrance of a xact into some sort of enclosure (or channel, or booth, or whatever). In other words, you should think in terms of a *facility being seized* instead of a transaction being *in* a facility. For example, message xacts in program 4 seize NOPOL and later release it. During the time that a xact is seizing NOPOL, it is not considered to be in this facility.

When a xact gets past the LOGIC R block in Section 2 of program 4, it will always find the channel free. Thus the **SEIZE   CHANL** block will never refuse entry to any xacts. So what purpose does it serve? It was inserted in order to obtain facility statistics that will indicate the utilization of the channel. Yes, we can think of xacts as being *in* facility CHANL, but this is incidental. The point is that a facility may be used as a place which xacts enter, but it is primarily an entity whose *status* is affected one way or the other.

ADVANCE Blocks and Variables

When a xact enters the first of the three ADVANCE blocks, it references the variable called TRANS. This variable is computed using the value of P3 of the xact which just entered the ADVANCE block, that is, the current transaction. The formula for V$TRANS was obtained as follows:

Transmission rate = 14.8 characters/second = 1/14.8 seconds/character
= 1000/14.8 milliseconds/character
= 10000/148 milliseconds/character

The time spent in the CPU is given by the second ADVANCE block. There are two "second ADVANCE blocks," one for data entries and one (labeled INQ) for inquiries. After leaving the CPU, a message xact represents a *reply* rather than a message. The transmission time for the reply is given by the third AD-VANCE block.

Upon arriving back at their originating terminals, message xacts are destroyed. However, before that happens, they release CHANL, have their transit times tabulated, and release NOPOL.

7.4   SECTION 3 OF PROGRAM 4

Section 3 contains the portion of the block diagram through which the polling transaction cycles. This portion of program 4 has been reproduced in Figure 7-6.

```
*  SECTION 3 (PORTION OF BLOCK DIAGRAM INVOLVING POLLING XACT)

         GENERATE    ,,,1          CREATE ONE XACT WITH PRIORITY ZERO.
    INIT ASSIGN     1,14          SET P1 = 14.
    STEP ASSIGN     2,FN$POLL     PUT NO. OF NEXT STATION INTO P2.
         ADVANCE     XH1           NO. OF MILLISEC. TO POLL STATION.
         LOGIC S     P2            SET LOGIC SWITCH 1,2,3, OR 4.

         BUFFER                    POLLING XACT PAUSES WHILE GPSS SCAN
*                                  MOVES FIRST MESSAGE XACT AT STATION
*                                  (I.E., GATE) P2, IF THERE ARE ANY.

         LOGIC R     P2            RESET LOGIC SWITCH 1,2,3, OR 4.
         GATE NU     NOPOL         POLLING XACT BLOCKED IF NOPOL IN USE.

         LOOP        1,STEP        DECREMENT P1 BY 1 AND GO TO STEP IF
*                                  P1 IS NOT 0.  ELSE GO TO NEXT BLOCK.

         TRANSFER    ,INIT         AFTER COMPLETING POLLING PATTERN,
*                                  INITIALIZE P1 AGAIN AND REENTER LOOP
*                                  TO REPEAT POLLING SEQUENCE.
```

Fig. 7-6.   Section 3 of program 4.

A single polling xact is created at the beginning of the run with priority zero. On its first pass through the system, it has P1 = 14 and P2 = 2 since FN$POLL = 2 when P1 = 14. The polling xact, after a delay of 500 milliseconds, sets logic switch 2. This is how station 2 is polled. At this point, we want to momentarily freeze the polling xact and allow a message xact at station 2 to pass the gate and enter the channel. This is where the BUFFER block comes in.

The normal mode of operation of the *GPSS control algorithm* is to move the current xact through the block diagram until it is blocked, delayed, or destroyed. Only then does the simulator attempt to process another xact. If it were not for the BUFFER block, the polling xact would be processed in the usual way. To be specific, here is what would happen.

After leaving the ADVANCE block, the polling xact would set logic switch P2, reset logic switch P2, and attempt to enter the GATE block. Since message xacts would have no opportunity to pass through the **GATE LS** *2 block, they would never seize NOPOL. So the polling xact would "sail" through the **GATE NU NOPOL** block and finally come to rest in the ADVANCE block. Five hundred clock units later, it would repeat the circuit, and message xacts would continue to queue up at the four stations.

The BUFFER block is one of the only two blocks in GPSS that causes the GPSS simulator to stop moving a xact and to look for a higher priority xact to process. But an xact which enters the BUFFER block will always be moved again at the *same* clock time. The operation of the BUFFER block is intimately connected with the internal operation of the GPSS simulator, particularly the scan and the current events chain. Therefore a fuller explanation of it will be deferred until the next chapter.

Getting back to section 3 of our program, the polling xact sets logic switch P2 and then enters the BUFFER block. It pauses there momentarily while the GPSS scan checks whether there are any higher priority xacts that can be moved at that clock time. Since logic switch P2 was just reset, any message xact at gate P2 is not blocked. Since message xacts have a higher priority than the polling xact, a waiting message xact will be processed before the movement of the

polling xact (which is also waiting at this point) is resumed. The message xact
sets logic switch P2 and seizes facilities LINE and NOPOL before it comes to rest
in an ADVANCE block.

Having processed the message xact as far as it can, the GPSS scan resumes
moving the polling xact. But now NOPOL is in use, and the polling xact is
stopped by the GATE NU block until the message xact has been destroyed. If
this has not been clear to you, go back and review Section 7.2 where the model is
described.

7.5 SECTION 4 OF PROGRAM 4

Section 4 contains four QTABLE definition cards which pertain to both runs
because they are not redefined after the CLEAR card. Section 4 also contains
the control and definition cards that cause two consecutive simulation runs to be
made using different polling patterns. This portion of program 4 has been
reproduced in Figure 7-7.

Simulation Run Length

Since this is just an illustrative program and not the "real thing," both runs end
after only 200 messages have been processed. Of course this makes for a rather
small sample, and the results could be misleading. In a real life situation, we
would specify a termination count of perhaps several thousand.

Use of CLEAR Card to Obtain Second Run

It was suggested earlier that a number of runs would be desirable in order to
experiment with different polling schemes and, perhaps, polling times other
than 500 milliseconds. Figure 7-7 shows how we would obtain one additional
run. The effect of the CLEAR card with the selective clear option was described
in Section 6.6 and requires no explanation here.

Function POLL has been redefined for the second run. Functions can always

```
*  SECTION 4 (QTABLE DEFINITION CARDS, SPECIFICATION OF RUN LENGTH,
*            AND REQUEST FOR SECOND RUN)

      5 QTABLE      1,50000,50000,30
      6 QTABLE      2,50000,50000,30
      7 QTABLE      3,50000,50000,30
      8 QTABLE      4,50000,50000,30

        START       200            RUN ENDS WHEN 200 MESSAGE XACTS
*                                  HAVE BEEN DESTROYED.
        CLEAR       XH1            CLEAR MODEL OF ALL XACTS AND STA-
*                                  TISTICS, BUT LEAVE XH1 = 500.

   POLL FUNCTION    P1,L14         REDEFINE POLL FUNCTION.
 ,4/,4/,1/,2/,3/,4/,4/,1/,2/,3/,4/,4/,2/,3

        START       200
        END
```

Fig. 7-7. Section 4 of program 4.

be redefined after RESET or CLEAR cards, but they must replace functions that were included in the previous run.   The new function need not be of the same type as the one it replaces.

The second run will differ from the first not only with regard to the polling sequence used—it may also start with a different random number seed.   The CLEAR card does not initialize the random number seed, so the second run starts out with the value that existed at the end of the first run.   One obvious effect is that the pattern of message arrivals, which is governed by function EXPON, could be different in the second run.   Since we are processing only 200 messages in each run, the effects of different random number sequences could be significant.   Thus any major differences in the results of the two runs may not be clearly attributable to different polling schemes.

7.6   STANDARD STATISTICAL OUTPUT

Two sets of output statistics result from program 4, one for each run.   The printout will not be shown as it was for the first three illustrative programs because it would occupy quite a few pages and also because it contains nothing that you have not already seen as far as its general makeup is concerned.

What the Output Consists Of

Table 7-1 lists all of the items that appear in the printout in their order of appearance.   The portion pertaining to the first run is exactly what you would expect if there were no other runs.   It consists of the symbolic listing, cross-reference tables, input listing, and statistical output.

The portion pertaining to the second run does not include the symbolic listing or cross-reference tables.   (Why should it?)   It does not include the input listing either, except for the cards which request and define the second run.   This segment of the input listing is followed by the complete standard statistical output for the second run.

Simulation Results

The results of the two runs, extracted from the statistical outputs, are summarized in Table 7-2.   Let us examine them.

Both runs halted as soon as the reply to the two hundredth message had been received.   Run 1 lasted for about 1% more clock units than run 2, but 13% more message xacts were generated in run 2.   This clearly illustrates the kinds of differences that can result from using different initial random number seeds and then taking a small sample.

It is interesting to note that 284 terminals were polled in run 1 as compared with only 211 in run 2.   This means that the polling transaction found no messages in 84 out of 284 attempts in run 1, but it "failed" only 11 times in run 2.   Somehow the timing was much better in the second run.   That is, the polling xact almost always went to stations that had at least one message waiting to be serviced.   Can we conclude that the second polling scheme is better than the

TABLE 7-1. CONTENTS OF THE PRINTOUT FROM PROGRAM 4

Run 1
- • Symbolic listing in its entirety
- • Cross-reference tables for blocks, facilities, variable, and functions
- • Input listing, up to and including the first START card
- • Statistical output, including:
  - Clock times (relative and absolute)
  - Block counts (current and total)
  - Facility statistics (for CHANL and NOPOL)
  - Queue statistics (for queues 1, 2, 3, 4)
  - Table statistics (for tables 1 through 8)

Run 2
- • Input listing, consisting of:
  - CLEAR   XH1
  - 5 FUNCTION   P1   L14
  - (Contents of function follower cards for redefined function, in fixed field format)
  - START   200
- • Statistical output, consisting of:
  - Clock times (relative and absolute)
  - Block counts (current and total)
  - Facility statistics (for CHANL and NOPOL)
  - Queue statistics (for queues 1, 2, 3, and 4)
  - Table statistics (for tables 1 through 8)

first? Probably not. Since we took such a small sample, the results are largely a matter of chance.

The queue contents at the end of run 1 were very close to their maximum levels during the run, and the maximum and final queue contents were identical in run 2. This suggests that the waiting lines were on the increase when the runs ended and that they would probably have continued to lengthen if more time had elapsed. Moreover, the channel utilization was about 95% in both runs, which leaves little, if any, excess capacity. These statistics tell us that the system is probably inadequate to handle the volume of arriving messages regardless of which polling scheme is used!

The queue waiting times are very long—10 to 15 minutes, on the average. The time spent in a queue greatly outweighs the processing time for the average message. Thus the system response time consists almost entirely of waiting time. This is another indication that our system is being overrun with too high a level of message traffic.

Commentary on Simulation Results

Our original objective was to find a more or less optimum polling scheme. Since program 4 was academic, we specified only two runs and only 200 terminations per run. We did not expect one polling scheme to prove clearly superior to the other due to the small sample size.

Upon examining the results, we saw that the influence of the random number sequence was indeed pronounced. For example, 13% more message xacts were generated in run 2 in 1% fewer clock units. So it seemed that the results, like the

TABLE 7-2.   SUMMARY OF PROGRAM 4 OUTPUT

		Run 1	Run 2
Clock time at end of run		3,421,847	3,458,591
Number of messages generated ①	Data	314 (81%)	344 (79%)
	Inquiry	74 (19%)	93 (21%)
	Total	388	437
Number of messages that arrived at various terminals ②	Terminal 1	62 (16%)	65 (15%)
	Terminal 2	75 (19%)	92 (21%)
	Terminal 3	84 (22%)	85 (19%)
	Terminal 4	167 (43%)	195 (45%)
	Total	388	388
No. of terminals polled during run ①		284	211
Maximum length of waiting lines ③	Queue 1	34	36
	Queue 2	33	50
	Queue 3	46	41
	Queue 4	79	110
Number of messages waiting at terminals at end of run ④	Queue 1	34	36
	Queue 2	32	50
	Queue 3	44	41
	Queue 4	78	110
	Total	188	237
Utilization of channel ⑤		.945	.954
Average waiting time at terminal for messages, in milliseconds ⑥	Queue 1	782,127	932,124
	Queue 2	813,666	865,852
	Queue 3	1,002,826	717,455
	Queue 4	771,743	878,375
Average response time for various terminals, in milliseconds ⑦	Terminal 1	798,933	949,008
	Terminal 2	828,879	882,214
	Terminal 3	1,019,248	735,073
	Terminal 4	788,576	894,857

① Deduced from block counts.
② Queue statistics: total entries.
③ Queue statistics: maximum contents.
④ Queue statistics: current contents.
⑤ Facility statistics: utilization of CHANL.
⑥ Qtable statistics: mean argument.
⑦ Table statistics: mean argument.

model itself, would only be of academic interest.

However, we discovered that the terminal-channel-CPU system was inadequate to handle the assumed rate of message arrivals, polling schemes notwithstanding.   This important revelation was not expected, and it came despite the "budget-length" simulation runs.   If we were playing for keeps, we would put aside the polling scheme evaluation for a while and investigate methods of increasing the overall system capacity.

This illustrates the kind of thing that often happens in simulation work. And it points up the desirability of obtaining a complete set of system statistics which may reveal unanticipated trends.

7.7   DIFFERENCES BETWEEN GPSS/360 AND OTHER VERSIONS

We shall run through program 4 and point out all of the major differences between GPSS/360 and the other three versions. All of these differences have come to light in previous chapters, so this will serve largely as a review.

GPS K

INITIAL card: GPS K does not include halfword savevalues, but the symbol XHj is accepted and is interpreted as Xj.

The exponential function could be omitted completely. The letters "EF" would be used in the B-field of the GENERATE block instead of FN$EXPON.

Flow Simulator

SIMULATE card: Flow Simulator does not include the SIMULATE card. The presence of the START card causes a run to occur.

GPSS III

SIMULATE card: this card must have an asterisk in column 1.

INITIAL card: GPSS III does not include halfword savevalues, and so the symbol XHj is illegal. Only fullword savevalues are permitted.

The functions, facilities, and variables could not have symbolic addresses; they must have numerical labels in GPSS III. The free-format function follower cards could not be used in GPSS III; fixed format cards must be used.

CLEAR card: the selective clear option is lacking in GPSS III. To start off the second run with savevalue 1 containing 500, we would have to follow the CLEAR card with an INITIAL   X1,500 card.

7.8   SUMMARY

Illustrative program 4 represented a big step forward from the trivial programs presented previously. It did not use many new features, but it simulated a fairly interesting system, and it utilized relatively sophisticated logic and programming techniques. If, perchance, you did not completely understand program 4, and if your objective is to really learn GPSS, the following steps are recommended:

1. Finish reading this summary.
2. Go back and reread Section 7.1, especially the description of the GPSS model. Examine Figure 7-2 carefully.

3. Slowly work your way through program 4 (Figures 7-3 and 7-4), paying close attention to the explanatory comments in the operand field.

4. Then reread this summary.

The alert reader will notice that this procedure is, in effect, a closed cycle, and he will not allow himself to become entrapped in Chapter 7. Now, let us proceed with the summary.

GPSS includes three types of numerical-valued functions (C, D, and L), and they all appeared in program 4. Numerical-valued functions are characterized by the fact that, when referenced, they always compute and return a numerical value for FNj.

GPSS also provides two types of attribute-valued functions (E and M) which are not explained in this book. They are similar in most respects to the numerical-valued functions with the basic difference being this: When an attribute-valued function is referenced, FNj assumes the value of an SNA rather than a constant. The SNA is then evaluated to obtain a numerical value for FNj.

The concept of a facility entity was expanded from "something that can contain one transaction at a time" to the following:

1. A mechanism for providing output statistics about a particular part of a model.

2. A device whose status can be used to control the flow of xacts elsewhere in the model via GATE blocks.

The BUFFER block was described as one of the only two block types in GPSS that can halt the movement of a transaction through the block diagram before it reaches a normal stopping point or is destroyed. The manner in which xacts are manipulated by the GPSS simulator is explained in the next chapter. And the two block types that are exceptions to the normal mode of operation are also thoroughly described.

Program 4 incorporated some interesting programming techniques. The source program was organized in four sections for the sake of clarity. This had no effect on how it was interpreted by the GPSS program which saw it as a single, continuous model.

The polling transaction was used as a mechanism for controlling the operation of the rest of the model. The *control* section of the model (if we can call it that) was synchronized with the *controlled* part of the model by means of a facility, logic switches, and gates.

CHAPTER 8
Internal Aspects of GPSS

Up to this point, we have dealt primarily with the *external* aspects of GPSS; that is, those aspects that pertain to the model, block diagram, source program, and simulation results. We have said relatively little about the *internal* aspects except for brief discussions of the middle level in Section 2.1 and the lower level in Section 3.3. As you know, the middle level pertains to the underlying logical structure of the language, especially the GPSS control algorithm. The lower level pertains to the physical configuration of the GPSS simulator and the user's model in the computer's core.

In this chapter we look inside of GPSS. We examine the middle level, particularly the control algorithm, which is explained in some detail. The BUFFER and PRIORITY blocks are described, and a simple program segment is dissected to demonstrate the operation of the GPSS simulator with and without the BUFFER block.

We also examine the lower level, but in a more general way. The core can be crudely visualized as being divided into two parts—one occupied by the built-in GPSS program and the other occupied by the user's model. We consider only the latter in this chapter and, in fact, in this book.

Our excursion into the inner workings of GPSS, at least on the middle level, is confined to this chapter. Subsequent chapters contain a number of remarks and discussions that will reinforce and expand your comprehension of the underlying logical structure of GPSS.

8.1 THE GPSS CONTROL ALGORITHM

We said earlier that the GPSS simulator processes events *one at a time* and in a *sequential* fashion despite the fact that the events in the simulated system may occur simultaneously as well as serially. This means keeping track of everything that is supposed to happen in the system and making sure that all events occur at the right time and in the right order. It also requires some sort of system for monitoring status changes and propogating their effects to other elements in the model. How is this accomplished? The mechanism used in GPSS, the so-called *GPSS control algorithm*, will now be described.

The GPSS Clock and Scan

In order to provide the correct time sequence, the program maintains a *clock* that records the instant of *real time* that has been reached in the modeled system. The flow of time as handled by the simulator clock is, in a sense, the reference axis or independent variable during a simulation run. The latter analogy would be strictly true if the clock were updated at regular intervals and the scan were designed to search for events which coincided with the new clock time. But this is not an efficient approach since events generally occur unevenly in time in a simulation. It is more efficient to have the clock jump ahead to the time of the next most imminent event. This is the method used in GPSS, and as a result the clock is not really an independent variable in a simulation run.

After the *scan* has serviced all of the transactions that were scheduled to be moved at a particular clock time, the following sequence of events occurs:

1. Update the clock to the most imminent *block departure time* (BDT) in the *future events chain*. This is the clock time at which the first xact in the future events chain is due to be processed.

2. Move the first xact from the future events chain into the *current events chain*, placing it behind the xacts with the same priority which are already there from a previous clock time (if there *are* any).

3. Scan the next xact in the future events chain. If its BDT coincides with the present clock time, merge it into the current events chain as described in step 2.

4. Move all other xacts with the present BDT from the future chain events chain into the current events chain the same way.

5. Having completed step 4, scan each xact in the current events chain in sequence. Ignore those that are on *inactive status*. Process those that are on *active status*, moving each xact through as many blocks in the block diagram as possible before processing the next one.

6. The scan may make several passes through the current events chain. When no more can be done with the xacts remaining in the current events chain, the clock is updated to the BDT of the *first xact* in the future events chain.

This sequence of events is shown schematically in Figure 8-1. Note that there are two scans—the *overall GPSS scan* and the *current events chain scan*. This distinction will often not be made in this book since there is no danger of a misleading ambiguity.

It is evident that the scan is the heart of a GPSS simulation. It examines all potential events, updates the clock, processes xacts, and checks for status changes and other conditions. This being the case, it is important to organize the scan in such a way as to minimize the required amount of computing time. The uneven clock update intervals and the distinction between active and inactive xacts are two examples of how the efficiency of the scan is enhanced.

The use of transaction chains also contributes to the efficiency of the scan by providing an orderly search pattern of eligible xacts instead of having to check every xact and status indicator in an unsystematic way at every clock update. The xacts in a chain are not physically moved into contiguous locations in the core of the computer. Each xact contains, among its basic bytes, the locations of the xacts which precede and follow it in the current or future events chain. That is how xacts in a chain are linked, and it is much more efficient than shifting them around in the core. More about this later.

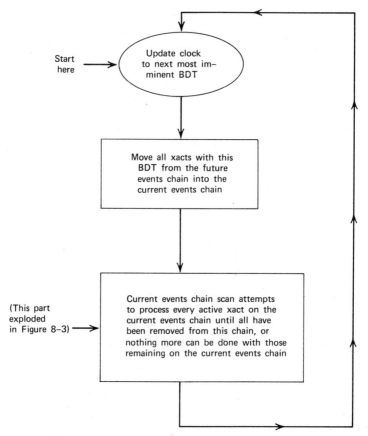

Fig. 8-1. Operation of the overall GPSS scan.

Transaction Chains

If a GPSS run is frozen at any instant, every transaction in the model will be in at least one of five chains:

1. Current events.
2. Future events.
3. User (associated with LINK, UNLINK blocks).
4. Interrupt (associated with PREEMPT, RETURN blocks).
5. Match (associated with MATCH, ASSEMBLE, and GATHER blocks).

The current and future events chains are present (internally) in every GPSS simulation. But the user, interrupt, and match chains are only established for models which contain the block types in parentheses. Whereas the current and future events chains are an integral part of the control algorithm, the other transaction chains are an adjunct to it, in a manner of speaking. These other chains are not discussed in this chapter, but they are covered in subsequent chapters.

The future events chain contains those transactions whose scheduled departure times are greater than the current clock time.   Such transactions are placed in the future events chain in ascending order of event time.   Thus the transaction whose scheduled event time is closest to the current clock time is first, while the transaction whose scheduled event time is farthest in the future is at the rear. No distinctions are made in this chain on the basis of priority.   The following types of transactions may be found in the future events chain:

1. Transactions that have been delayed in ADVANCE blocks.
2. Incipient transactions in GENERATE blocks.
3. Dummy transactions that are internally utilized when there are tables operating in the RT mode or when jobtapes are used.

The current events chain contains those xacts whose scheduled event times are equal to or less than the current value of the clock.   In other words, it contains transactions that are scheduled to move at the current clock time or were scheduled to move at a prior clock time but have been blocked.   The current events chain has xacts in descending order of priority (i.e., the highest priority transactions first), and within each priority class, in the sequence in which they were placed in the chain.   Thus the last priority 2 transaction to be merged into the chain is placed after the priority 2 xacts that are already in the chain, but it is ahead of all priority 1 and priority 0 transactions.

Figure 8-2 shows a current events chain that might exist during the running of a hypothetical simulation model.   We can see, for example, that xact 9 was merged into this chain before xact 8.   This assumes that neither of the xacts in question entered a PRIORITY block — to be explained in Section 8.2.   Incidentally, xact 9 may have been merged into the current events chain at an earlier clock time than xact 8, or both may have been put on the current events chain during the same clock instant.

The diagram at the top of Figure 8-2 depicts the current events chain as viewed on the middle level, that is, logically.   But xacts 5 and 11 (for instance) are not physically contiguous in the core as they are in the current events chain. Instead, xact 5 is located between xacts 4 and 6, while xact 11 is located between xacts 10 and 12 in the core.   In other words, the xacts *are* contiguous on the *lower* level; they are situated in straight numerical order in the core.

If xacts are in 1-2-3-4 . . . order in the core, how is the current events chain formed?   Each xact contains, among its inaccessible attributes, the numbers (addresses) of the xacts that precede and follow it in the current events chain. The current events chain scan uses these attributes as *pointers* to the next xact in the chain so that it services xacts as if they were lined up in the manner suggested by the Figure 8-2 diagram.   The *linkages* for those xacts are indicated in the table beneath the diagram.   The scan would pick up the number 4 as the address of the first xact in the current events chain, and it would thereafter utilize the pointers to proceed from one xact to the next in accordance with their order in the current events chain.

As you would expect, the same method is used to link xacts on the future events chain.   Every xact includes, among its inaccessible attributes, the addresses of the xacts that precede and follow it in the future events chain.

There are two types of status indicators which play a vital role in the operation

Middle level

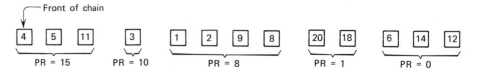

Front of chain

| 4 | 5 | 11 | | 3 | | 1 | 2 | 9 | 8 | | 20 | 18 | | 6 | 14 | 12 |

PR = 15   PR = 10   PR = 8   PR = 1   PR = 0

Lower Level

Xact Address	Address of Preceding Xact on C.E.C.	Address of Following Xact on C.E.C.	Xact Address	Address of Preceding Xact on C.E.C.	Address of Following Xact on C.E.C.
1	3	2	9	2	8
2	1	9	11	5	3
3	11	1	12	14	4
4	12	5	14	6	12
5	4	11	18	20	6
6	18	14	20	8	18
8	9	20			

Fig. 8-2. Organization of a hypothetical current events chain.

of the current events chain scan. There is a *status change flag* which may be *set* (*on*) or *not set* (*off*). There are certain times when the scan will check the status change flag; for instance, after it has finished moving a transaction. If the status change flag is set, the scan transfers directly to the beginning of the current events chain. It resets the flag to off, and then it proceeds to work its way down the chain from the beginning.

Whereas there is one status change flag associated with the current events chain, each transaction has a *scan status indicator*. If it is *set* (*on*), the transaction is on *inactive status*, and it is ignored by the current events chain scan. If the scan status indicator is *off*, the transaction is on *active status*, and the scan will attempt to move it when it gets to it.

The operation of the current events chain scan is shown in Figure 8-3. The effects of the BUFFER and PRIORITY blocks are not accounted for in this diagram to prevent unnecessary confusion. Incidentally, the block labeled "Move xact as far as possible . . . " could be exploded into a very complicated flow diagram that would involve some things that have not yet been covered; so we shall not attempt to show or describe it here. Instead, the movement of xacts by the current events chain scan will be explained piecemeal, as appropriate, and you need not be concerned that you may be missing some vital knowledge.

Every inactive transaction in the current events chain is on a *delay chain*. There are eleven types of delay chains; four are associated with facilities, five with storages, and two with logic switches:

Facilities: In use, Not in use, Interrupted, Not interrupted.

Storages: Full, Not full, Empty, Not empty, To be entered.

Logic Switches: Set, Reset.

A delay chain is merely a list of transactions that cannot be moved until a par-

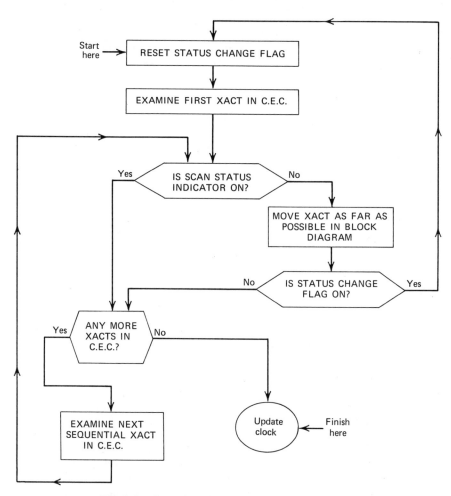

Fig. 8-3. Operation of the current events chain scan.

ticular change of status occurs in a particular item of equipment. For example, transactions that are blocked by a SEIZE block because of the unavailability of a facility would be put into a "facility in use" chain. Later, when the facility becomes available, all of the transactions in this delay chain would be switched to active status.

To take another example, transactions may be blocked by a GATE SF block. They would be put into a "storage not full" delay chain. Later, when the storage becomes full, they will be switched to active status. It should be pointed out that if a transaction becomes a member of a delay chain, it still retains its place in the current events chain. Membership in a delay chain merely implies inactive status in the current events chain.

It should be evident that delay chains are useful in reducing running time since the scan does not attempt to process transactions blocked by equipment until the blocking condition changes. However, no such chains exist for transactions which are blocked by a TEST, GATE M, GATE NM, TRANSFER ALL, or TRANSFER BOTH block. In these cases, the transactions remain in active status in the current events chain, and the scan will try to advance them each time it encounters them. Such blocked transactions can, therefore, materially slow down a GPSS run, so the aforementioned blocks should be used with discretion.

An Example of How the Current Events Chain Works

At this point, it would be beneficial to look at an example. We shall follow the actions of the current events scan on a "play-by-play" basis. Consider the hypothetical current events chain shown in Figure 8-4. Assume that our hypothetical

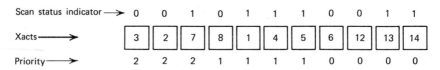

Scan status indicator → 0   0   1   0   1   1   1   0   0   1   1

Xacts → | 3 | 2 | 7 | 8 | 1 | 4 | 5 | 6 | 12 | 13 | 14 |

Priority → 2   2   2   1   1   1   1   0   0   0   0

STATUS OF TRANSACTIONS WHEN CURRENT EVENTS CHAIN SCAN BEGINS
TO OPERATE ON THIS CHAIN

Xact 6 is seizing facility 15, ready to release it.

Xacts 7, 13, and 14 are waiting to seize facility 15, hence are in a delay chain.

Xacts 1, 4, and 5 are in a different delay chain associated with some other equipment entity elsewhere in the model.

Xacts 3, 2, 8, and 12 are at various blocks in the model, ready to be moved; that is, they are not presently blocked or otherwise rendered inactive.

Fig. 8-4.   Another hypothetical current events chain.

program contains no BUFFER, PRIORITY, LINK, PREEMPT, or RETURN blocks. (Or, alternately, assume that these transactions do not enter any of these blocks when they are being moved through the block diagram at this particular clock time.) Assume that transactions 7, 13, and 14 are awaiting entry into facility 15. Thus they are in the "in use" delay chain for facility 15. Assume that transaction 6 is scheduled to vacate facility 15 at the present clock time. Assume that transactions 1, 4, and 5 are in some other delay chain. Assume that the current events chain scan is about to begin, and the status change flag is on..

The scan immediately resets the status change flag to off, and it picks up xact 3. Transaction 3 is moved as far as possible in the block diagram. Its movement through various zero delay blocks will not cause its position in the current events chain to shift. When it has moved as far as it can in the block diagram, it may do the following:

1. Remain in the current events chain in a delay chain.
2. Remain in the current events chain on active status, but blocked by a condition for which no delay chain exists.
3. Be merged into the future events chain or some other chain.
4. Be removed from the system.

After it surrenders a transaction, the scan always checks the status change flag. If it is still off, the scan proceeds to process the next sequential active transaction. In our example, this is transaction 2. After processing transaction 2 and again checking the status change flag, the scan bypasses transaction 7 and picks up transaction 8 and then transaction 6.

Remember that transaction 6 was occupying facility 15. As soon as transaction 6 enters the **RELEASE   15** block, three things happen:

1. The various statistics associated with facility 15 are appropriately incremented or otherwise calculated.

2. Transactions 7, 13, and 14 have their scan status indicators set to off; they are thus removed from their delay chain.

3. The status change flag is set on.

The scan continues to process transaction 6 until it can be moved no further. Then the scan checks the status flag and "sees" that it is set. So the scan reverts back to the very beginning of the current events chain and immediately resets the status flag to off. At this point, our hypothetical current events chain might look as shown in Figure 8-5. Note that transactions 3, 8, and 6 are no longer in

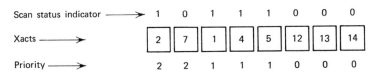

STATUS OF TRANSACTIONS WHEN CURRENT EVENTS CHAIN SCAN REVERTS
BACK TO FRONT OF CHAIN AFTER HAVING PROCESSED XACT 6

Xacts 3, 8, and 6 are no longer in the current events chain.
Xact 2 has been processed and is now inactive.
Xacts 7, 13, and 14 are now active since facility 15 is not, at this instant, in use.
Xacts 1, 4, and 5 are still inactive.
Xacts 12, 13, and 14 have not yet been reached by the current events chain scan.

Fig. 8-5. Hypothetical current events chain, a little later.

the current events chain. They have either been merged into some other chain or removed from the system. Note also that transaction 2 is now in a delay chain, but transactions 7, 13, and 14 are no longer in a delay chain.

The scan bypasses transaction 2 and begins to move transaction 7. Transaction 7 seizes facility 15, and so transactions 13 and 14 revert back to inactive status, and the status change flag is set to one. Assuming that xact 7 has entered a positive time ADVANCE block, it is merged into the future events chain. Since the status change flag is set, the scan reverts to the beginning of the current events chain. It resets the status change flag and bypasses every transaction except for xact 12 which is still active at this clock time.

After moving transaction 12 as far as it can go, and after checking that the status change flag is off, the current events chain scan returns control to the overall scan. The clock is updated to the block departure time of the first xact in the future events chain, and the cycle is repeated.

The Three "Images" of a Transaction

A transaction that is sitting in the current events chain may, at the same time, be moving through the block diagram and having some of its attributes modified. This is easy to visualize if you think of a transaction as having three representations:

1. A unit of traffic in the block diagram (upper level — conceptual representation).
2. A member of a transaction chain (middle level — logical representation).
3. A group of "words" in the transactions section of the computer core (lower level — physical or electronic representation).

When a transaction is created, it occupies a small portion of the computer core whose location is given by the number (address) of the xact. For instance, transaction 3 is deployed in location 3 of the transaction entities section of core, and it occupies that location (plus an auxiliary location) until it is destroyed. In other words, *the physical image of a xact never moves* although the xact may be moved all over the place in the middle and upper levels. Changes to the status and attributes of the xact are accomplished by altering appropriate bits and bytes among the words that comprise it in the core.

We have already seen that a string of xacts in a transaction chain are not necessarily contiguous in the core. By the same token, a waiting line of xacts in a model are not necessarily located one behind the other in the core or in the current events chain.

8.2   THE BUFFER AND PRIORITY BLOCKS

BUFFER Block

As we saw in program 4, the BUFFER block is useful when we would like to pause or go back and try to move a previously blocked transaction before the current xact has been moved as far as it can go at the present clock time. The BUFFER block never refuses entry to xacts, and they always proceed to the next sequential block after leaving it. The BUFFER block temporarily interrupts the movement of a xact, but it always allows that xact to proceed to the next block at the same clock time. Thus the BUFFER block is a zero-delay block. Incidentally, its variable field is always blank.

If a transaction enters a BUFFER block, the scan ceases to move that xact through the block diagram. It immediately reverts to the beginning of the current events chain and attempts to process xacts in the usual manner. When it gets to the xact which "stalled" in the BUFFER block, it simply picks it up and attempts to move it from that point in the block diagram. If a transaction which enters a BUFFER block happens to be at the front of the current events chain, the BUFFER block serves no purpose.

The effect of the BUFFER block can perhaps be better appreciated by referring to the Figure 8-3 box which says "Move xact as far as possible in block diagram." If the xact being moved enters a BUFFER block, the current events chain scan immediately reverts to the beginning of the current events chain. It does not bother with the status change flag at all. We could easily add a line to Figure 8-3 to show this, if we wished.

PRIORITY Block

When a transaction enters a PRIORITY block, several things happen:

1. Its priority is changed to the value specified in field A of the PRIORITY block. This value may range from 0 to 127, inclusive. It may be less than, equal to, or greater than the priority of the incoming transaction.
2. The status change flag is set on.
3. The transaction which entered the PRIORITY block is moved to the end of its new priority class within the current events chain.

The scan will continue to move the transaction through the block diagram as though nothing had happened except that it may now have a new priority. Then the scan will find the status change flag set, and it will revert to the beginning of the current events chain.

If a PRIORITY block has the word "BUFFER" coded in field B, it operates as follows:

1. The priority of the entering transaction is set equal to the value in field A of the PRIORITY block.
2. The entering transaction is moved to the rear of its new priority class in the current events chain.
3. The scan immediately reverts back to the beginning of the current events chain as if the transaction had entered a BUFFER block.

The BUFFER and PRIORITY blocks are very handy in certain situations. But their use is limited and should usually be avoided by inexperienced programmers.

8.3 AN EXAMPLE OF HOW THE CONTROL ALGORITHM WORKS

The purpose of this section is twofold:

1. To present a blow-by-blow description of the operation of the GPSS clock, scan, current events chain, and future events chain.
2. To show how the BUFFER block can be used to alter the sequence in which transactions are processed.

We observe the events in a simple program in order to see how xacts are processed by the GPSS simulator. This program is examined in two versions—first without a BUFFER block and then with one.

For sake of expedience, the following abbreviations are used:

BDT   Block departure time.
CEC   Current events chain.
FEC   Future events chain.
SSI   Scan status indicator.
T   Absolute and relative clock time.
Xact j Transaction number j.

Notice that the status change flag is not mentioned in the foregoing list. That is because it will not be mentioned in the ensuing discussion. Its role has been thoroughly explained, and so we will take it for granted rather than taking the trouble to note when it gets set and reset.

Sample Program Segment

We consider the program segment shown in Figure 8-6. Let us now follow the events that occur in this block diagram in chronological order, starting at the beginning. We assume that the ADVANCE block assigns delay times of 17, 12, 16, and 21 clock units, respectively, to the first four xacts that enter it. These figures are hypothetical, but they are entirely plausible.

T = 0. An *incipient transaction* is created by the GENERATE block. Its BDT is 20. It is placed in the FEC.

T = 20. Xact 1 is moved into the CEC. The CEC scan then begins to move xact 1. As soon as xact 1 gains entry to the ASSIGN block (thus vacating the GENERATE block), a new incipient xact is created by the GENERATE block and is merged into the FEC with a BDT of 40. The scan then continues to move xact 1 until it reaches the ADVANCE block. Its delay time is computed to be 17, so it is merged into the FEC with a BDT of 37, ahead of xact 2 which has a later BDT.

Since there are no more xacts in the CEC, the clock is updated to the time of the next imminent event.

T = 37. Xact 1 is put into the CEC and is picked up by the scan. It moves through the RELEASE, LOOP, QUEUE, SEIZE, and DEPART blocks. (This is the external view of what happens to xact 1.) At each of these blocks, the appropriate subroutines and status changes are executed. When xact 1 enters the AD-VANCE block (for the second time), a delay time of 12 is computed, so its BDT is 49. Xact 1 is then merged into the FEC behind (incipient) xact 2.

T = 40. Xact 2 is placed into the CEC, and it is then picked up by the CEC scan and moved as far as the QUEUE block. It cannot enter the SEIZE block since facility 5 is presently in an unavailable status. The SSI of xact 2 is set to 1 to denote inactive status. Xact 2 is thus in a delay chain in the CEC. As soon as xact 2 entered the ASSIGN block, incipient xact 3 was created and merged into the FEC with a BDT of 60. Keep in mind that no clock time elapsed while all of

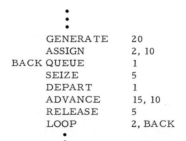

```
                    ⋮
           GENERATE      20
           ASSIGN        2, 10
      BACK QUEUE         1
           SEIZE         5
           DEPART        1
           ADVANCE       15, 10
           RELEASE       5
           LOOP          2, BACK
                    ⋮
```

Fig. 8-6. Sample program segment.

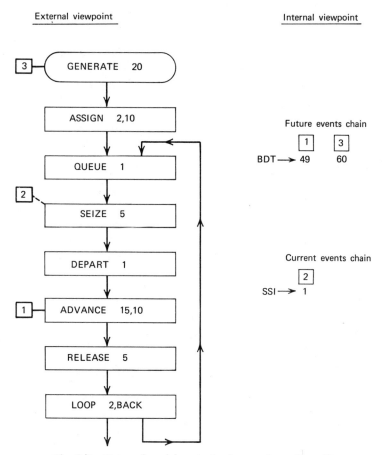

Fig. 8-7.   Status of model as clock advances from 40 to 49.

these things happened.   The situation at this point is summarized in Figure 8-7.

T = 49.   Xact 1 is moved from the FEC to the rear of the CEC.   The scan then starts at the beginning of the CEC, but it bypasses xact 2 since its SSI contains a 1. The scan next comes to xact 1 which is on active status.   Xact 1 is once again moved through the RELEASE, LOOP, QUEUE, SEIZE, and DEPART blocks. When xact 1 entered the RELEASE block, it freed facility 5, so the SSI of xact 2 (waiting for facility 5) was set to zero.   But when xact 1 entered the SEIZE block, thus regaining facility 5, the SSI of xact 2 was reset to 1.

When xact 1 enters the ADVANCE block, its delay time is computed to be 16. So its BDT is 65, and it is merged into the FEC.   At this point, the status of the model is exactly as depicted in Figure 8-7, except that xact 1, with a BDT of 65, is now behind xact 3 in the FEC.

T = 60.   Xact 3 is placed into the CEC behind xact 2.   It is moved to the QUEUE block but cannot enter the SEIZE block.   So it is placed on inactive status.   Meanwhile, incipient xact 4 was created and placed into the FEC with a BDT of 80.   At this point the chains are as follows:

Current Events Chain	Future Events Chain
Xact 2 (inactive)	Xact 1 (BDT = 65)
Xact 3 (inactive)	Xact 4 (BDT = 80)

T = 65.   Xact 1 is placed at the end of the CEC.   The scan bypasses xacts 2 and 3 and moves xact 1 around the loop until it again enters the ADVANCE block.

It is clear that transaction 1 will continuously occupy facility 5 while incoming transactions accumulate in queue 1.   When transaction 1 finally leaves the loop after ten cycles of it, transaction 2 will enter facility 5.   Transaction 2 will then occupy facility 5 continuously until it leaves the loop.

Intuitively, it may seem that xact 1 should have been blocked by the xacts in the queue when it came back around the loop.   Indeed, that is probably what the programmer would want to happen.   This is a good example of the difference between the external and internal views of the program.   The waiting xacts in queue 1 were not "in the way of" xact 1 as far as the GPSS simulator is concerned.   Xact 1 was being processed, and it would not be discarded by the CEC scan until:

1. Its arrival at a blocking condition (unavailable facility, "closed" gate, etc.).
2. Its arrival at a TERMINATE, ASSEMBLE, GATHER, or MATCH block.
3. Its arrival at a positive time ADVANCE block.
4. Its arrival at a BUFFER block or a PRIORITY block with BUFFER option.

So transactions are not *directly* or *physically* blocked by other transactions. They can be blocked only by encountering one of the conditions above.   Of course some of these conditions are *caused* by other transactions.

Sample Program Segment with BUFFER Block

What if we want transactions to go to the rear of the line (i.e., queue 1) after leaving facility 5?   This can be accomplished by inserting a BUFFER block as shown in Figure 8-8.

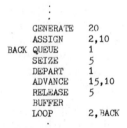

```
        ⋮
     GENERATE   20
     ASSIGN     2,10
BACK QUEUE      1
     SEIZE      5
     DEPART     1
     ADVANCE    15,10
     RELEASE    5
     BUFFER
     LOOP       2,BACK
        ⋮
```

Fig. 8-8.   Sample program segment with buffer block.

Let us start by examining the situation just at the point where the clock is updated to T = 49.   (See Figure 8-7.)   This is the point where xact 1 is in the FEC and is ready to release facility 5 for the second time.   Xact 2 is waiting in queue 1, and xact 3 has not yet entered the system.

T = 49.   Xact 1 is put into the CEC behind xact 2.   Since xact 2 is in a delay chain, the scan picks up xact 1 and begins to move it.   When xact 1 enters the RELEASE block, the SSI of xact 2 is reset to 0, and the availability of facility 5 is noted in the proper core location.   (This is the same as the previous case, so far.)

When xact 1 enters the BUFFER block, the scan returns to the beginning of the CEC.   It picks up xact 2 which is *now* active.   It moves xact 2 into the ADVANCE block where its delay time is computed to be 16.   Xact 2 is then merged into the FEC with a BDT of 65.   (When xact 2 entered the SEIZE block, facility 5 became unavailable to other xacts.)

The scan next picks up xact 1, since it is second in the CEC.   Xact 1 is moved through the LOOP and QUEUE blocks at which point it is impeded.   The SSI of xact 1 is set to 1, and the CEC finds no more xacts to move.   So the clock is updated to the time of the most imminent event.   The status of the model at this juncture is shown in Figure 8-9.

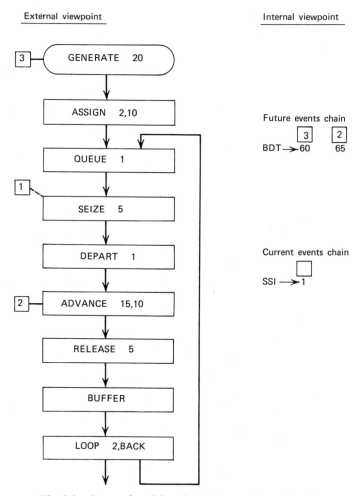

Fig. 8-9.   Status of model as clock advances from 49 to 60.

T = 60. Xact 3 is put into the CEC behind xact 1. The scan moves xact 3 through the QUEUE block, and its SSI is set to 1. Now xacts 1 and 3 are in a delay chain in the CEC.

Incipient xact 4 is created and placed in the FEC with a BDT of 80. At this point, the chains are as follows:

Current Events Chain	Future Events Chain
Xact 1 (delay status)	Xact 2 (BDT = 65)
Xact 3 (delay status)	Xact 4 (BDT = 80)

T = 65. Xact 2 is moved from the front of the FEC to the rear of the CEC. The scan bypasses xacts 1 and 3 and begins to move xact 2 which was in the AD-VANCE block.

As soon as xact 2 enters the RELEASE block, the SSIs of xacts 1 and 3 are set to zero. As soon as xact 2 enters the BUFFER block, the scan reverts to the begin-ning of the CEC. Since xact 1 is now active, it is picked up by the scan and moved into the SEIZE block. This causes the SSI of xact 3 to be set to one.

Xact 1 is moved into the ADVANCE block where a delay time of 21 is computed. Xact 1 is merged into the FEC with a BDT of 86. The scan ignores xact 3 which is back on inactive status, and it picks up xact 2 which is waiting in the BUFFER block.

Xact 2 goes through the LOOP and QUEUE blocks but is refused entry by the SEIZE block. Its SSI is set to 1, and no more can be accomplished by the current events chain scan at T = 65. The status of the model at this point is shown in Figure 8-10.

The pattern should be clear. The use of the BUFFER block has produced the desired effect in this case, that is, a FIFO mode of facility seizing. Do not conclude that the BUFFER block should be used whenever the FIFO mode is desired! It just happened to be appropriate in this situation. Recall that the FIFO mode was obtained in programs 1, 2, and 3 without using a BUFFER block.

8.4 DEPLOYMENT OF A MODEL IN THE CORE

This section has several purposes:

1. To provide a feel for the way in which a GPSS model, as defined by an input deck, is deployed inside the computer.
2. To indicate how many of each entity type may be included in a model.
3. To convey a simplified but enlightening picture of how a single entity in a model is represented as a collection of computer words in the core.
4. To provide further insight into the significance of entity addresses.

Overall Arrangement of Core

To begin with, let us clarify what is meant by the term "core." The primary storage (or memory) in most computer CPUs in recent years has consisted of a

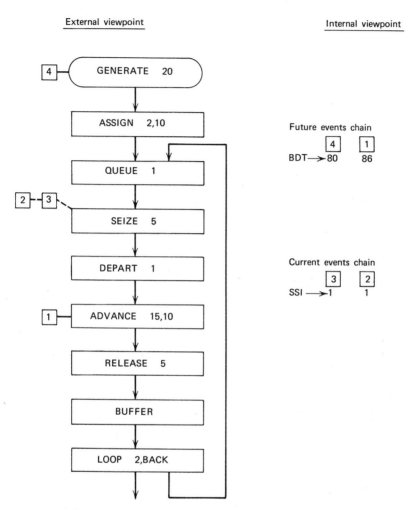

Fig. 8-10. Status of model as clock advances from 65 to 80.

matrix of thousands of tiny doughnut-shaped cores, each representing one *bit*. Thus the primary storage area has come to be called, simply, the *core*. Although some of the latest computers (notably the IBM 370) do not utilize core-type memories, the use of the word "core" in the aforementioned context lingers on because it is a handy and widely understood piece of terminology. So, with due apologies for the slight technical inaccuracy involved, we shall refer to the primary storage area as the core. And now let us consider the status of the computer just before a GPSS source deck is fed into the card reader.

The GPSS software package consists of a collection of (roughly a dozen) program modules, each of which performs a particular function. It is normally deployed on an auxiliary storage device such as a disk. It resides there so that it can be quickly brought into the core by the system supervisor when a GPSS deck is to be processed. Let us imagine that this is about to happen; that is, the computer has just finished a job, and it is about to read in the next input deck which is a GPSS program. Here is what happens:

1. The leading control cards tell the system supervisor that this job involves
   GPSS, and so the GPSS control module is gotten from the auxiliary storage
   device and loaded into the core, whereupon it assumes control. It resides
   in the core for the duration of the run, fetching other GPSS program
   modules from the auxiliary storage device as they are needed to carry out
   the assembly, simulation, and output phases. Incidentally, any module
   being executed during the run may itself call other modules.

2. The first program module brought into the core by the control module is
   the *assembly program*. Its basic task is to read the input deck, check the
   model for errors, and deploy it in the core. It takes a large chunk of the
   core and subdivides it into sections for all of the GPSS entity types as well as
   a *common* area. This procedure is automatic and takes no heed of the particular set of entities that are specified in the user's model unless the input
   deck contains special control cards which request a nonstandard partitioning of the core. The configuration of the core at this point is illustrated
   in Figure 8-11 which is *not* drawn to scale.

3. After the core has been thus configured, the assembly program assigns
   locations to the various entities in the model. For instance, if the model
   contains two facilities whose index numbers are 5 and 8, they will occupy
   locations 5 and 8 in the facilities section of the core. Entities with symbolic
   addresses are assigned the lowest available numerical addresses within their
   respective sections.

4. If the assembly program succeeds in deploying the model in the core, and if
   it encounters no serious errors in the input deck, the simulation run may
   proceed. It is performed by other program modules which, in their
   proper sequence, replace the assembly program in the core. These program modules comprise the so-called *GPSS simulator*.

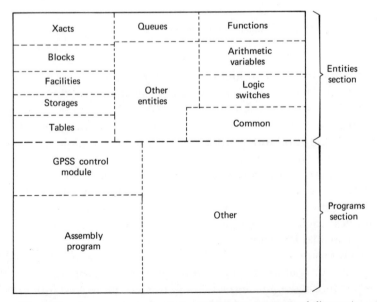

Fig. 8-11. Arrangement of core for a GPSS run (conceptual diagram).

To give you a rough idea of how much of the core capacity is taken up by what, about 25% of a 64K memory is normally allocated to the various entity sections while more than half of the core contains the GPSS program segments. Of course there is room for many more entities in a larger machine since the GPSS program modules do not require proportionally more storage.

A consideration of the various routines which comprise the overall GPSS program is beyond the scope of this book. The remainder of this section is concerned with the *entities portion of the core*, that is, the section where the model is deployed.

Entities Section of the Core

The entities section of the core is partitioned into 16 sections in GPSS/360—one for every entity type. The two extra sections (there are *14* entity types) are due to the allocation of separate sections for halfword and fullword savevalues and matrix savevalues.

The facilities section is configured to contain 35 facilities in a 64K machine, 150 in a 128K machine, and 300 in a 256K machine. Similarly, the queues section accommodates 70, 150, or 300 queues, depending on the size of the computer's memory. We could go on to list the capacity of each entity section as a function of the memory size. This has been done for all four versions of GPSS in Tables 8-1 and 8-2.

TABLE 8-1.   STANDARD ALLOCATION OF ENTITIES IN GPSS/360, FLOW SIMULATOR, AND GPSS III

	Normal Maximum Number of Entities					
	GPSS/360			Flow Simulator		GPSS III
Entity Type	64K	128K	256K[a]	65K	131K	
Blocks	120	500	1000	120	750	500
Transactions	200	600	1200	200	600	750
Facilities	35	150	300	35	200	200
Storages	35	150	300	35	200	200
Logic switches	200	400	1000	200	400	500
Tables	15	30	100	15	30	50
Groups	5	10	25	0	0	0
Queues	70	150	300	70	400	200
Arithmetic variables	20	50	200	15	30	100
Boolean variables	5	10	25	0	0	0
User chains	20	40	100	20	40	50
Savevalues (fullword)	100	400	1000	0	400	500
Savevalues (halfword)	50	200	500	100	1000	0
Matrix savevalues (fullword)	5	10	25	0	0	0
Matrix savevalues (halfword)	5	10	25	0	0	0
Functions	20	50	200	20	50	100

[a] And larger.

TABLE 8-2.   STANDARD ALLOCATION OF ENTITIES IN GPS K

Entity Type	Normal Maximum Number of Entities							
	65K	81K	93K	114K	131K	163K	196K	229K
Blocks	150	300	450	600	750	900	1000	1000
Transactions	150	300	450	550	600	700	750	750
Xact parameters	5	6	7	8	10	12	15	18
Facilities	25	30	35	40	50	100	150	200
Storages	25	30	35	40	60	100	150	200
Logic switches	25	30	35	40	75	100	150	200
Tables	10	15	20	25	30	50	75	100
Groups	5	10	15	20	30	50	75	100
Queues	25	30	35	40	75	100	150	200
Arithmetic variables	25	30	35	40	50	75	100	200
Boolean Variables	25	30	35	40	50	75	100	200
User chains	5	10	15	20	30	50	75	100
Savevalues	50	60	70	80	100	150	200	300
Matrix savevalues	5	10	15	20	25	50	75	100
Functions	25	30	35	40	50	75	100	200

The figures in these two tables represent the maximum numbers of entities allowed in a model.   For instance, a GPSS/360 model run on a 128K machine cannot contain more than 40 user chains, 30 tables, and so on.   However, there are provisions for apportioning the entities section of core differently if you want to include, say, more queues and facilities at the expense of boolean variables and groups.

To specify a nonstandard core configuration, the REALLOCATE card is provided in GPSS/360 and Flow Simulator, and the CONTROL card may be used in GPS K and GPSS III.   The use of these cards will not be explained, but two points will be made:

1. In their absence, the standard allocation of entities is made in accordance with Tables 8-1 and 8-2.
2. Since various entity types require different amounts of storage, you cannot simply request, say, 40 transactions in place of 40 savevalues.   *You must be aware of the number of computer words required by each entity type in order to use the reallocate feature.*

It was pointed out in Section 5.5 that, in GPS K, neither the number of parameters per transaction nor the parameter size is specified in the GENER-ATE card.   Instead, the CONTROL card is used if the analyst wants a different number of parameters than those indicated in Table 8-2.   The CONTROL card is also used to specify bigger parameters.

Entity Addressing

The user may assign numerical addresses to entities in any order he pleases. For example, he may specify savevalues 30, 11, 22, 3, and 4 — in that order.   The only restriction is that all such index numbers must lie within the allowable maximum for the entity type and machine size.

If the user assigns symbolic addresses, the assembly program assigns numerical addresses. These addresses normally correspond to the lowest available slots in the respective entity sections. For example, suppose that a model specifies the following facilities: FACIL, DESK, 1, 5, and 6. FACIL and DESK would be equated with 2 and 3, respectively, and locations 1, 2, 3, 5, and 6 of the facilities section would thus be used during this run.

Transactions are always created and allocated during a run and not before. The first xact is assigned location 1, the second xact is assigned location 2, and so on, until a xact is destroyed. Then the next xact will be assigned that location. This is because newly created xacts are always assigned the lowest available location in the transactions section of the core.

Entity Words

For the sake of concreteness, the following discussion pertains to GPSS/360 and a 64K machine. However, the principles are readily generalized to other versions and machines.

From Table 8-1 we see that the facilities section is normally configured to accommodate 35 facilities. This section consists of 980 bytes, and each facility is allocated 28 bytes (or 10 words). Facilities are contiguous within this section; that is, the 10 words for facility location 1 are next to the words comprising facility location 2, and so on.

If our model contains no facilities, the 35 facility locations will be allocated at the beginning of the run as usual, but they will never be used during the run. If our model happens to contain two facilities which are labeled as 9 and 33, then locations 9 and 33 of the facilities section will be referenced during the run. If our model contains a block such as **SEIZE   81**, we will have an error condition.

Now let us take a closer look at the 28 bytes which comprise *any one facility*. They are grouped into 6 halfwords (2 bytes each) and 4 fullwords (4 bytes each). These 10 words are denoted by F1, F2, F3, . . ., F10. Each one contains a specific piece of information about the facility. For example, F1 contains the number of the xact currently seizing the facility; F2 contains the number of the xact currently preempting the facility; F3 contains the cumulative time integral of facility usage; and so forth.

GPSS/360 facilities are always allocated 28 bytes *apiece*. The only difference from one memory size to another is in the *total number* of facilities.

The fullword savevalues section of a 64K core comprises 400 bytes. At 4 bytes per word, there are 100 savevalues. Similarly, the queues section comprises 70 queues, each of which occupies 32 bytes. We could go on and do this for all of the other entity types except for one thing: certain entity types occupy varying amounts of core. Let us see what this means.

The number of bytes associated with a facility or savevalue is known at the outset of a run; it never changes. But the number of bytes associated with tables, functions, variables, transactions, and so on, cannot be predetermined. To handle this, a common storage area is allocated along with the entity "blocks."

To understand how it works, let us consider how tables and transactions are stored in the core of a 64K computer.

The *tables block* consists of 720 bytes comprising 15 tables of 48 bytes each. The 48 bytes per table is a basic or minimum storage requirement for any table. To this must be added 4 bytes per frequency class. Those bytes are stored contiguously in the common block, and their address is stored in the eighth word among the *basic* 48 bytes. In this way any number of frequency classes can be defined (or redefined after a RESET or CLEAR card) without affecting the arrangement in the core, outside of *common*.

Each transaction, upon creation, is allotted 16 bytes, and the *transactions block* holds 200 transactions in a 64K computer. (Thus there may be as many as 200 transactions in the model at any instant.) When a transaction is active, it requires 20 additional bytes, and these are located in the common block. Four additional bytes are required for every fullword parameter used, and these too are located in the common block.

8.5   SUMMARY

This chapter does not contain a section devoted to the differences between GPSS/360 and other versions for two reasons:

1. The description of the control algorithm as well as the BUFFER and PRIORITY blocks applies to all four versions of GPSS.
2. The description of entity allocations in the core is applicable to all four versions in its general aspects. Tables 8-1 and 8-2 summarize the only detailed differences that need be mentioned in an introductory book such as this.

Lower Level

Before a GPSS simulation run can start, the computer's core is partitioned into two main sections. One contains the programs and subroutines that comprise the GPSS simulator. The other contains entity sections plus a common area and is configured (i.e., allocated or partitioned) in a standard way unless special control cards have been used to reallocate the available core differently among various entity types.

The user's model is deployed in the entities section and common area by the assembly program. After the run begins, transaction entities are established and erased, as appropriate. If indirect addressing is used, other entities may also be established in the core during the run, but they are not destroyed until a JOB or END card is encountered.

Middle Level

After the run starts, the GPSS program (or simulator) takes over, and the control algorithm is executed until the run is over. The controlling mechanism is the GPSS scan (overall and current events chain) which works in conjunction with the simulator clock, transaction chains, and various indicators. The scan updates the clock to the next BDT, transfers xacts from the future events chain to the current events chain, and attempts to process every active xact in the current events chain.

The scan, at any time, is attempting to move only one transaction, and that is called the current transaction. It moves this xact as far as it can go during the current instant of clock time before proceeding to another xact which is also due to move at that instant. The only exception to this mode of operation is when a xact is moved into a BUFFER block or a PRIORITY block with the BUFFER option. In that case, the scan quits moving the current xact and returns to the beginning of the current events chain to pick up the first active xact it encounters.

You should be aware of the manner in which the scan moves the current xact through the block diagram. The xact does not progress through the blocks in a continuous manner. Rather, it is jumped from block to block, and it waits at each block for a tiny fraction of a second while the block-type subroutine is executed. If the block is a type that can refuse entry to xacts, a test must be made before the current xact is allowed to "enter" that block. This paragraph has the following implications:

1. Various things happen in the model (e.g., indicators are changed, statistics are updated) *during* the time that a transaction is being moved by the current events chain scan.

2. The movement of the current xact can be characterized as a series of discrete events; it is not a smooth process.

3. The current events chain scan holds onto the current xact for several milliseconds of *simulation* (running) time, but for zero *simulated* (clock) time.

If the current events chain scan finds that a transaction is blocked on the basis of the status of an equipment entity, the xact is placed in a delay chain. The xact retains its position in the currents events chain, but it is bypassed by the scan as long as it remains inactive. If a transaction is blocked by a condition for which no delay chain exists, the scan attempts to move it every time it encounters it in the current events chain.

General Nature of Entities

We are now in a position to picture GPSS entities—at least those that have been introduced thus far—on all three levels. Transactions are dynamic entities and all the others are static entities; this is the upper level viewpoint. After all, transactions move through the block diagram while all of the other entities are stationary objects.

On the middle level, the so-called static entities do not really enter the picture except insofar as they are affected by, or affect, the movement of transactions. Transactions themselves may be shifted *from* one chain to another, and if they enter a PRIORITY block, be shifted *within* the current events chain. A transaction may be motionless on the middle level while it is moving through the block diagram on the upper level. The converse is also true; that is, a xact may be moved from one chain to another while it sits at one block.

On the lower level, all entities are always stationary; they never move around inside the computer's core. Their relationship to one another, their membership in chains, their position in the block diagram, and so forth are all denoted by the contents of the computer words of which they are composed. These words contain the entity attributes among which are various pointers, indicators, and numerical values. The lower level is dynamic in the sense that various bits and bytes are continually being altered as the run proceeds.

You should now have at least an inkling of how a GPSS model, which looks so unlike a typical lower level (machine language) computer program, is able to give rise to a simulation run by the computer. A useful exercise is to imagine that you were starting with the internal aspects and were attempting to invent the upper level.

CHAPTER 9
Transactions and Assembly Sets

Now that you know GPSS inside as well as out, you are probably anxious to apply your newly acquired insight to an illustrative program. However, there are some loose ends to be tied up first as far as transactions are concerned. And there is another chunk of information that should be conveyed—also having to do with transactions—namely *assembly sets*. The payoff will come in Chapter 10 where we examine two illustrative programs that incorporate some of the elements discussed in this chapter.

Transactions, as you probably realize, are the bloodstream of a GPSS model. They permeate it and affect its components. Conversely, xacts are affected in many different ways: nearly half of all the GPSS blocks do something to xacts. So while a substantial amount of our time has already been devoted to xacts, there is quite a bit more ground to cover.

Transactions are reviewed to some extent, and the operation and use of the GENERATE block are fully explained. (It has only been discussed piecemeal so far.) Then the bulk of this chapter is devoted to assembly sets and the blocks associated with them.

9.1 REVIEW OF TRANSACTIONS

Transactions are one of the two *basic* entities in GPSS; blocks are the other. Each time a xact enters a block, it causes that block to perform its prescribed functions. In this sense, xacts are the driving force in a GPSS model—there can be no change in the status of the system unless xacts move through it.

What Can Happen to Transactions

Aside from those blocks which create or destroy xacts, GPSS blocks always do the following things to xacts that attempt to enter them:

1. Pass them to the next sequential block, or send them to a nonsequential block.
2. Allow them to pass through at the same clock time at which they entered, or delay them for a specified length of time, or refuse entry until a particular condition is met.
3. Modify one of the transaction attributes, or leave them unchanged.

The notion that each xact has three sides to its "personality" is helpful to one's understanding of GPSS. A xact may be sitting motionless in the current events chain while being moved through the block diagram. On the other hand, it may be removed from one chain and linked to another while residing at some place in the block diagram. And through it all, a xact is never shifted about physically in the computer.

Transaction Attributes

There are many attributes associated with a xact, but most of them cannot be referenced by the user. For example, there are no SNAs for the BDT of a xact or the number of the xact which follows it in the future events chain. These transaction attributes are contained among the words that comprise the xact in the computer.

There are several xact attributes to which the programmer has access via four SNAs and two SLAs. The SNAs are M1, MPj, Pj, and PR; the SLAs are M and NM. The SLAs are discussed later in this chapter, and the SNAs are discussed now.

MPj and M1 are not stored attributes; they must be computed at the time they are referenced. These two SNAs are computed as the difference between the current absolute clock time and either the *mark time* or a *parameter time* (to be explained later).

A xact may have up to 100 parameters (127 in Flow Simulator). Pj is used to obtain the *contents of parameter j of the current transaction*. Initially, all parameters have a value of zero, but there are various blocks which can be used to alter parameter values, most notably the ASSIGN block.

PR is used to obtain the priority of the current xact. Xacts are created with zero priority unless specified otherwise. The priority of a xact can be changed only by having it enter a PRIORITY block. Priorities of up to X may be assigned to xacts, where X is equal to: 127 in GPSS/360 and Flow Simulator, 31 in GPS K, and 7 in GPSS III.

9.2 THE GENERATE AND MARK BLOCKS

GENERATE Block: General Comments

The GENERATE block creates xacts and sends them into the system at constant or variable intervals specified by the user. All xacts move to the next sequential block after exiting from the GENERATE block. If the next block after GENERATE is one which sometimes refuses entry to xacts, the actual intercreation interval may sometimes exceed that specified by the user. (This will be explained soon.) Thus it is recommended that GENERATE blocks always be followed by blocks that never refuse entry to xacts—unless the user is willing to have the creation of xacts affected by a blocking condition.

Transactions may not enter a GENERATE block. This is no problem if the GENERATE block appears at the beginning of a model. But if it lies "inside" the block diagram, xacts from previous blocks must either be terminated ahead of or diverted around it.   The TRANSFER block is an obvious way to accomplish the latter.   Indirect addressing ($*n$, SNA $*n$) is illegal in all fields, since xacts never enter the GENERATE block.

GENERATE Block: Intercreation Interval

The mean time between the creation of xacts is specified in field A.   The interpretation of the field A argument is best explained with the aid of an example:

    GENERATE   47

At the start of the simulation (i.e., $T = 0$), one xact is created.   Physically speaking, four basic words are allocated at the location 1 in the transactions area of the core.   This xact is merged into the future events chain with a BDT of 47. Externally speaking, xact 1 sits in the GENERATE block as an incipient xact until $T = 47$.

At $T = 47$, xact 1 is merged into the current events chain, and it attempts to enter the next sequential block after the GENERATE block.   Now that it has become a "visible" xact in the block diagram, it is allocated some additional words in the common area.

If xact 1 is able to enter the next sequential block, the GENERATE block creates xact 2, and it is merged into the future events chain with a BDT of 94. The important thing here is that *the successor incipient xact is not created until after the newly visible xact succeeds in entering the next block* after the GENERATE block. So if a xact is blocked when its time comes to enter the block diagram, a successor incipient xact will not be created internally.   Only when the former xact enters the next block will a successor incipient xact be created, and then it will be merged into the future events chain to await its appearance in the block diagram.

To avoid getting *actual* interarrival times that are occasionally greater than those specified in fields A and B of the GENERATE block, the next block should be one that never refuses entry to xacts.   A useful trick is to use an ADVANCE block with a zero in field A.

The field B argument can be a *spread modifier* (denoted by a constant-type SNA such as Kn or Xj) or a *function modifier* (denoted by FNj).   A spread modifier, in conjunction with the field A mean, specifies a range within which random integer values are computed and assigned to each incipient xact when it is initially created.   A spread modifier cannot be larger than the mean since negative intercreation times are illegal.   A function modifier obtains a value by referencing a function defined in the program.   This value (usually a decimal fraction) is multiplied by the field A mean, and the product is truncated to obtain an intercreation interval which is an integer.

The field C argument specifies an *initialization* (or *offset*) *interval* whose interpretation can be explained with the following example:

    GENERATE   49,20,150

The first xact will be released after 150 clock units have elapsed.   Thereafter, xacts will be sent into the system at intervals of 29 to 69 clock units.

GENERATE Block: Fields D to G

Field D specifies a *creation limit.* If it is blank, the GENERATE block will create transactions at appropriate intervals until the run ends. If a number m is specified in field D, no successor to the mth xact will be created. Let us look at an example:

```
GENERATE    31,,,X8
```

Fields B and C are omitted, so there is no variation in the mean intercreation interval, and the offset interval does not differ from the intercreation interval. The number of xacts created by this block is given by savevalue 8, the value of which must have been specified earlier in the program.

It is possible to use only field D; for instance:

```
GENERATE    ,,,10
```

Ten xacts would be created at the very beginning of the run and sent to the next sequential block, one after the other. All 10 xacts would travel as far as possible at $T = 0$. Thereafter, no more xacts would be created by this block.

Field E specifies a *priority level.* Newly created xacts have a priority of zero unless another value is specified in this field. Priorities up to 127 may be specified.

Field F specifies the *number of parameters* that will be assigned to each xact. Up to 100 parameters may be assigned. But if field F is blank, 12 parameters are assigned to each xact. When a xact leaves the GENERATE block, all of its parameters contain zero.

Field G may contain either an F or H, or it may be blank. The F specifies fullword parameters, and the H specifies halfword parameters. If neither is specified, the halfword assignment will be made.

MARK Block, Mark Time, and Transit Time

When a xact first enters the block diagram, the absolute clock time is stored as one of its attributes. This is called the *mark time,* and it cannot be directly referenced by the programmer. However, there are two SNAs whose values are based upon the mark time: M1 and MPn. We shall look at how these work after a brief description of the MARK block.

The MARK block can operate in either of two modes:

1. If field A is blank or zero, the transaction's mark time is changed to the current absolute clock time, that is, the clock time when it entered the MARK block.

2. If field A specifies a parameter number, that parameter is marked with the current value of the absolute clock, and the mark time is unaffected.

M1 is the transit time of a xact, and it is computed (when referenced) as the difference between the current absolute clock time and the mark time. So if a xact has *not* entered a MARK block with a *blank* A-field, its transit time will be the amount of clock time elapsed *since it entered the system.* If it *has* entered such a

MARK block, M1 will give the number of clock units elapsed *since it entered (or left) the MARK block.* A xact is never refused entry to a MARK block, and it passes through it in zero clock time.

MPn is the so-called *parameter transit time* of a xact. It is computed as the difference between the current absolute clock time and the value of parameter n of the current xact. MPn can never exceed M1, of course.

An Example of How the MARK Block Works

The effect of the MARK block can be better appreciated by considering an example. The relevant cards from a hypothetical program are shown in Figure 9-1.

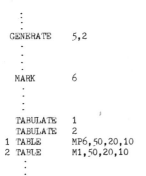

```
          :
          :
      GENERATE     5,2
          .
          :
          :
      MARK         6
          .
          :
          :
      TABULATE     1
      TABULATE     2
  1   TABLE        MP6,50,20,10
  2   TABLE        M1,50,20,10
          :
          :
```

Fig. 9-1.   Excerpts from a hypothetical program.

Assume xact 100 leaves the GENERATE block when the absolute clock reads 500. Thus its mark time is 500.

Assume that xact 100 enters the MARK block at $T = 575$. Parameter 6 is assigned the value 575.

Assume that xact 100 enters the TABULATE blocks at $T = 700$. The value of MP6 entered in table 1 is $700 - 575 = 125$. The value of M1 entered in table 2 is $700 - 500 = 200$.

9.3   ASSEMBLY SETS

Aside from the GENERATE block, the SPLIT block is the only block type that can create transactions. Whereas the former is keyed to the simulator clock, the SPLIT block creates copy xacts whenever it is entered by a transaction. The *parent* and its *offspring* comprise an *assembly set.* There are certain blocks that allow us to make the movement of xacts dependent on other members of their assembly sets. These block types are covered in this section.

SPLIT Block

The SPLIT block never refuses entry to a transaction, and it is a zero-delay block. The number of *copies* to be made when a *parent* xact enters the SPLIT block is specified by the field A argument, which may be any SNA. All of the specified copies are created as soon as a xact enters the SPLIT block. The parent xact then attempts to enter the next sequential block, and all of the copy xacts attempt to enter the block specified in field B. That could be the next sequential block if the user so specifies. There is no restriction upon the number of times that a xact may enter SPLIT blocks, and it is permissible to split copy xacts. Thus copy xacts may enter SPLIT blocks and act as parent transactions.

Fields A and B of the SPLIT block must contain arguments, but the use of fields C and D is optional. Field C is used to designate a transaction parameter which is used for *serial numbering* of the xacts involved. This can be explained easily with an example:

        SPLIT   5,NEXT,10

When a xact enters this block, five copy xacts are created. All of these copies have the same number of parameters as the parent xact, and all of those parameters will contain the same values as the corresponding parameters of the parent xact—except for parameter 10. If the parent xact had $P10 = k$ before entering our SPLIT block, it would emerge with $P10 = k+1$ and proceed to the next sequential block. The copy xacts would have P10 equal to $k+2$, $k+3$, $k+4$, $k+5$, and $k+6$, respectively, and they would proceed to the block whose address is NEXT.

Field D specifies the number of parameters to be assigned to each copy xact. If field D is blank, the number of parameters assigned will be the same as that of the parent xact, and all values of the parent's parameters will be placed in the corresponding parameters of each copy except for the parameter specified in field C. If field D contains an SNA (whose value may be 0 to 100), the copies will have that many parameters and those parameters will have the same values as the corresponding parameters of the parent. Incidentally, the copy xacts have the same priority and mark time as the parent.

Consider a xact which is created by a GENERATE block and eventually enters a SPLIT block. The parent xact plus its offspring constitute an assembly set. If any members of that assembly set subsequently enter a SPLIT block, their offspring are considered to also be members of the original assembly set. Thus a xact is a member of *one and only one* assembly set, but any number of xacts may comprise a given assembly set.

It follows that each xact created by a GENERATE block constitutes an independent assembly set, where the "set" may comprise one or more xacts. A xact which is created by a GENERATE block and never enters a SPLIT block can be regarded as a degenerate or trivial assembly set. The significance of assembly sets will become apparent when we discuss the ASSEMBLE, MATCH, and GATHER blocks.

ASSEMBLE Block

The ASSEMBLE block is used to recombine a specified number of members of an assembly set. This number, called the *assembly count,* is specified in field A.

No other subfields are defined for the ASSEMBLE block. The function of the ASSEMBLE block will be more clearly understood if we use an example:

        ASSEMBLE   5

Imagine that a simulation run has just started. The first xact to enter this block will be detained until four more xacts that are members of its assembly set arrive. The latter four xacts are destroyed when they enter the ASSEMBLE block. When the fifth member of the assembly set enters the ASSEMBLE block, the original xact is permitted to proceed to the next sequential block. At this point it is finished with the ASSEMBLE block, regardless of whether or not it succeeds in entering the next block. So much for this example.

The effect of the ASSEMBLE block is to join a specified number of xacts together into a single xact which has the characteristics of the initial member of the assembly set to have entered it. ASSEMBLE blocks never refuse entry to xacts. Now let us take a closer look at how the ASSEMBLE block works.

When a xact arrives at an ASSEMBLE block, the block checks to see if any other members of its assembly set are waiting there. If *not,* this xact is held as the first member of its assembly set, and the assembly count is decremented by 1. If *so,* this xact is destroyed, and the assembly count for its assembly set is decremented by 1. When the assembly count has been decremented to zero, the first member of the assembly set to have entered is sent to the next sequential block.

Several things should be obvious (or at least understandable) in view of the preceding paragraph. Only one subset of an assembly set may be in the assembly process at one ASSEMBLE block at any particular time. However, several subsets of the same assembly set can be simultaneously in the process of assembly at several different ASSEMBLE blocks. Several subsets of the same assembly set can be assembled at the same ASSEMBLE block during successive intervals of time. It is also possible for several different (independent) assembly sets to be simultaneously in the process of assembly at the same ASSEMBLE block. Incidentally, the members of an assembly set need never be assembled; they may be terminated individually and at different times; or they may not be terminated at all, depending upon the program.

GATHER Block

The GATHER block is used to accumulate a specified number of xacts belonging to the same assembly set at some point in the block diagram. When the number of xacts specified in field A have gathered, they are all allowed to pass to the next sequential block after the GATHER block. Thus the GATHER block is quite similar to the ASSEMBLE block, except that it does not destroy any xacts.

Field A, which is the only subfield defined for the GATHER block, contains the *gather count.* When there are enough xacts from the same assembly set at the GATHER block to reduce the gather count to zero, all of these xacts are let go.

As with ASSEMBLY blocks, only one subset of any given assembly set may be in the gathering process at a GATHER block at a given time. Several subsets of the same assembly set can be gathering in different GATHER blocks at the same time. Subsets of the same assembly set may be gathered in the same GATHER block at successive intervals of time. Several different assembly sets may be simultaneously gathered in the same GATHER block.

MATCH Block

The MATCH block is the third type of block that can be used to synchronize the progress of xacts from the same assembly set. Field A is the only subfield defined for the MATCH block, and it contains the address of another MATCH block in the model, called the *conjugate* MATCH block. To help explain the function of the MATCH block, we will use an example:

.

.

.

BOLTS MATCH   NUTS

.

.

.

NUTS MATCH   BOLTS

.

.

.

When a xact enters the MATCH block labeled BOLTS, a test is made to determine whether a member of its assembly set is waiting at the block labeled NUTS. If so, both xacts are allowed to pass to the next sequential blocks following their respective MATCH blocks. The xact which just entered BOLTS continues to move as far as possible in the block diagram. And then, at the same clock instant, the xact which had previously entered NUTS leaves that block and proceeds to be moved as far as possible.

If, when a transaction arrives at BOLTS, no members of its assembly set are at NUTS, it is detained there. If several members of the same assembly set arrive at BOLTS, and none have yet arrived at NUTS, the xacts at BOLTS wait in line, so to speak. When a member of their assembly set arrives at NUTS, the first one to have arrived at BOLTS is freed.

MATCH blocks are generally used in conjugate pairs as in the preceding example. But a MATCH block, by referencing its own address in field A, can be its own conjugate. In this case, it would behave just like a GATHER block with a 2 in field A.

Comparison of MATCH, GATHER, and ASSEMBLE Blocks

It is instructive to make a comparison between the MATCH block on one hand, and the ASSEMBLE and GATHER blocks on the other hand. First, let us list some of the key similarities:

1. All three blocks have the function of synchronizing the movement of members of the same assembly set through the block diagram.
2. Only field A may contain an argument.

3. These blocks never refuse entry to xacts.

4. These blocks can simultaneously assemble, gather, or match (as the case may be) groups of transactions belonging to different assembly sets.

The major differences are:

1. Whereas ASSEMBLY and GATHER blocks operate singly, MATCH blocks are generally used in conjugate pairs.

2. Whereas ASSEMBLY and GATHER blocks collect as many xacts as the user specifies, MATCH blocks always synchronize two transactions.

9.4   MATCHING CHAIN AND GATE M/NM BLOCKS

The existence of the matching chain in models containing ASSEMBLE, GATHER, and/or MATCH blocks was alluded to in Section 8.1. It is discussed in this section, but not in excruciating detail.

The GATE block was discussed in Section 6.2. You will recall that there are 12 SLAs that may be used as auxiliary operators, and two of them (M and NM) pertain to transactions that are or are not in a *matching condition*. The other 10 SLAs pertain to equipment entities. The GATE M and GATE NM blocks are explained in this section.

Matching Chain

One of the nonaddressable attributes of every xact is the number of the next xact in its assembly set. If a xact is the only member of its assembly set, its own number is used. If there are ten xacts in an assembly set, the first points to the second, which points to the third, and so on; and the tenth xact points to the first. Thus all the members of an assembly set are linked together in a closed chain, so to speak. But this chain is not regarded as one of the GPSS transaction chains.

The first member of an assembly set to arrive at an ASSEMBLE block is removed from the current events chain and placed in *interrupt status* on the *matching chain*. It remains in this status until enough additional members of its assembly set have arrived to satisfy the field A assemble count. When the count has been reduced to zero, the transaction in question is returned to the current events chain.

Similarly, the first member of an assembly set to enter a GATHER block is shifted into the matching chain. Succeeding members of its assembly set are likewise put on interrupt status when they enter the GATHER block. They are chained to the initial xact in a one-way FIFO chain.

When the gather count has been reduced to zero, all of these xacts are merged into the current events chain as the last xacts in their respective priority classes and in the order in which they entered the GATHER block. Note that the members of a given assembly set may acquire different priorities as they take various routes through the block diagram.

If a transaction arrives at a MATCH block and finds no member of its assembly set waiting at the conjugate MATCH block, it is placed on the matching chain. When the match is accomplished, it is removed from the matching chain and merged into the current events chain at the rear of its priority class.

Why have we been speaking of a matching *chain* rather than matching *chains*? All xacts that are in the process of being assembled, gathered, or matched have their (nonaddressable) *match indicators* turned *on*. All such xacts are regarded as members of the matching chain despite the fact that they may belong to different assembly sets and not be linked to one another in any direct manner. It is evident that the concept of the matching chain is purely a matter of definition; to be sure, the notion of a matching chain is absent from GPS K.

Gating on Match Conditions

Let us first review the GATE block format and modes of usage, but *in connection with the operators M and NM*.

Subfield A contains the address of an ASSEMBLE, GATHER, or MATCH block. Subfield B may optionally contain the address of the next block if the SLA is false. The GATE block never refuses entry to xacts if there is an address in field B; this is the *unconditional entry mode*. But if field B is blank, it blocks xacts until the SLA becomes true; this is the *conditional entry mode*.

It should be mentioned that xacts which are blocked by a GATE M or GATE NM block are not put into any kind of delay chain. So the current events chain scan attempts to move them every time it works its way through the current events chain. Thus indiscriminant use of GATE M/NM blocks can materially lengthen the running time of a model.

As mentioned in the preceding section, a xact is in a matching condition if its matching indicator has been turned on (set to *one*, actually). Members of assembly sets find themselves in a matching condition under the following circumstances:

1. A transaction which is being assembled in an ASSEMBLE block is in a matching condition. This xact would have to be the initial member of its set or subset to have entered the ASSEMBLE block, of course.

2. All the xacts being gathered in a GATHER block are in a matching condition.

3. A transaction which is in a MATCH block awaiting the entry of another member of its assembly set into the conjugate match block is in a matching condition.

The flow of xacts can be controlled by using GATE blocks which test for the existence (or lack) of specified matching conditions. This will be explained by means of an example.

An Example of Gating on Match Conditions

Figure 9-2 shows some blocks that have been excerpted from a hypothetical model to demonstrate the use of GATE M and GATE NM blocks.

The ASSEMBLE, MATCH, and GATHER blocks require no explanation, especially since explanatory comments are given in the operand field.

The first GATE block operates as follows. When a transaction attempts to gain entry, the GATE block subroutine checks to see if any *members of the current*

```
        :
        :
AAA ASSEMBLE   8              ASSEMBLE 8 XACTS INTO 1 XACT.
        :
        :
    GATE M     CCC            FIRST GATE BLOCK.....
        :
        :
BBB MATCH      DDD            MATCH XACT WITH XACT AT BLOCK DDD.
        :
        :
CCC GATHER     4              GATHER 4 XACTS, THEN RELEASE THEM.
        :
        :
    GATE NM    BBB,ALT        SECOND GATE BLOCK.....
        :
        :
DDD MATCH      BBB            MATCH XACT WITH XACT AT BLOCK BBB.
        :
        :
    GATE M     AAA            THIRD GATE BLOCK.....
        :
        :
ALT QUEUE      10
        :
        :
```

Fig. 9-2.   Excerpts from a hypothetical program.

xact's assembly set are in the gathering process at block CCC; that is, on the matching chain and also in block CCC.

If any such xacts are found, the SLA (M) is true, and the current xact is admitted to the GATE block whereupon it immediately proceeds to the next sequential block. If no such xacts are being gathered at block CCC, the SLA is false, and the current xact is refused entry into the GATE block until the match condition (M) is satisfied.

The second GATE block operates as follows. It allows xacts to enter unconditionally, since an alternate exit is specified in field B. When a xact enters this block, the GATE block subroutine checks to see if a member of the current xact's assembly set is in block BBB awaiting a match at block DDD.

If such a xact is found, then the SLA (NM) is false, and the current xact is sent to ALT. If no such member of the current transaction's assembly set is waiting in block BBB, then the SLA is true, and the current xact passes to the next sequential block. Notice that the second GATE block looks for xacts that are (1) in the same assembly set as the current xact, (2) in block BBB, and (3) on the matching chain. If it finds any, NM is false; otherwise, NM is true.

The third GATE block, like the first, operates in a conditional entry mode. When a xact arrives, it checks whether a member of that xact's assembly set is on the matching chain and in block AAA. If one is found, the SLA (M) is true, and the current xact enters the GATE block and proceeds to the next sequential block. If no such xact is found, the SLA is false, and the current xact is blocked.

9.5   DIFFERENCES BETWEEN GPSS/360 AND OTHER VERSIONS

The differences that are pointed out in this section are mainly of a superficial nature. There are very few significant differences between GPSS/360 and the other versions as far as the material in this chapter is concerned.

GPS K

Fields A, B, and D of the GENERATE block are identical to their respective counterparts in GPSS/360. But fields C and E differ, and fields F and G are not defined. (It has already been pointed out that GPS K does not handle the amount and size of parameters in the same way as the other three versions, namely, fields F and G of the GENERATE block. Instead, the CONTROL card is used for this purpose.) Now let us look at fields C and E, in that order.

As in GPSS/360, field C of the GENERATE block specifies an offset interval for the first transaction created during the run. But this interval is not used alone; it is added to the intercreation time computed from fields A and B. To illustrate how this works, we will use the same example that was used for GPSS/360 in Section 9.2:

```
GENERATE     49,20,150
```

Assume that the absolute clock time is zero and that an intercreation interval of 50 is computed from the A-field and B-field entries. The first xact will be sent from this block when the absolute clock reads 200. (200 = 50 + 150) In GPSS/360, the first xact would emerge from this block at 150 on the absolute clock.

GPS K permits priority assignments of 0 to 31, inclusive. So field E of the GENERATE block cannot contain a value greater than 31.

Field D of the SPLIT block (specifies the number of parameters for newly created xacts) is not defined in GPS K for the same reason that field F of the GENERATE block is not defined.

The MATCH block in GPS K may refer to an ASSEMBLE or GATHER block as well as a conjugate MATCH block. For example, a transaction that arrives at a MATCH block would be allowed to proceed if a member of its assembly set were being assembled in the block named in field A of the just-entered MATCH block.

The MARK, GATHER, ASSEMBLE, GATE M, and GATE NM blocks are just as described for GPSS/360. Likewise, the discussions of transaction attributes and assembly sets apply perfectly to GPS K.

GPS K differs from GPSS/360 in its interpretation of interrupt status. Transactions that are put on the matching chain in GPSS/360 would simply be considered to be on interrupt status in GPS K. The mechanism is not basically different, but the term "matching chain" is not used in GPS K.

Flow Simulator

Everything discussed in this chapter for GPSS/360 is applicable to Flow Simulator except for one detail: The C-field of the GENERATE block operates as described for GPS K.

GPSS III

All fields of the GENERATE block except for E and G are the same as in GPSS/360. The maximum value allowed in field E is 7 since transaction priorities only range from 0 to 7 in GPSS III. Field G is blank since GPSS III does not distinguish between halfword and fullword parameters.

Everything else in this chapter that applies to GPSS/360 also applies to GPSS III.

9.6 SUMMARY

This section is divided into two parts. First we summarize the material in this chapter. Then we take inventory of the block types we have encountered that "do something" to transactions.

Chapter 9 Summary

There are four standard numerical attributes (Pn, PR, M1, and MPn) and two standard logical attributes (M, NM) associated with transactions. In addition, there are many nonreferencable attributes such as the mark time, block departure time, and number of the next assembly set member.

The only block types that can create and send xacts into a block diagram are GENERATE and SPLIT. The operation of the GENERATE block is keyed to the simulator clock, but it can be affected by the blockage of xacts trying to leave it. Every xact created by a GENERATE block represents a potential assembly set, and so every transaction in a GPSS model belongs to an assembly set consisting, at minimum, of itself.

The SPLIT block creates copy transactions which are indistinguishable from the parent xact unless field C specifies a serializing parameter. SPLIT blocks are used to create assembly sets that can be synchronized and controlled on the basis of their set membership by means of ASSEMBLE, GATHER, MATCH, GATE M, and GATE NM blocks.

The ASSEMBLE block is used to collect a specified number of transactions from an assembly set and to permit only the first xact that entered to proceed intact. This block perfectly represents a situation such as the assembly into one unit of several parts that arrive at various times.

The GATHER block is used to collect a specified number of transactions from an assembly set and to permit all of them to proceed to the next sequential block after the specified number have been gathered.

MATCH blocks are used to synchronize the progress of two members of an assembly set which may be at different parts of the block diagram.

GATE M and GATE NM blocks are used to control the movement of a xact on the basis of whether another member of its assembly set is or is not in a matching condition at the block specified in field A. M is true if another member of the assembly set of the xact currently being processed at a GATE block is in a matching condition at the field A block. NM is true if no other member of its assembly set is in a matching condition at the field A block.

A transaction that is waiting in an ASSEMBLE, GATHER, or MATCH block is in a matching condition. More specifically, its match indicator is set, and it is in interrupt status on the matching chain.

Assembly sets are very useful, and they are further discussed in Chapter 10.

Inventory of Transaction-Oriented Blocks

Roughly half of all GPSS blocks are oriented towards transactions as opposed to other entities. We have already covered about 90% of the transaction-oriented block types, and they will be reviewed for the sake of perspective. We list them and comment on what they do to xacts.

ADVANCE   Never refuses entry. Holds xact for user-specified time period. Xacts proceed to next sequential block.

ASSEMBLE   Never refuses entry. Holds xacts for unspecified length of time. Destroys some xacts. Xacts proceed to next sequential block.

ASSIGN   Never refuses entry. Zero-delay block. Modifies a xact parameter. Xacts proceed to next sequential block.

BUFFER   Never refuses entry. Zero-delay block. Arrests movement of xact temporarily. Xacts proceed to next sequential block.

COUNT   Never refuses entry. Zero-delay block. Modifies a xact parameter. Xacts proceed to next sequential block.

GATE   Never refuses entry in unconditional entry mode. May refuse entry in conditional mode. Xacts proceed to next sequential block except when SLA is false in unconditional entry mode.

GATHER   Never refuses entry. Holds xacts for unspecified length of time. Xacts proceed to next sequential block.

GENERATE   Cannot be entered by xacts. Creates xacts which proceed to next sequential block.

INDEX   Never refuses entry. Zero-delay block. Modifies a xact parameter. Xacts proceed to next sequential block.

LOOP   Never refuses entry. Zero-delay block. Modifies a xact parameter. Xacts proceed to next sequential block only when loop count is reduced to zero.

MARK   Never refuses entry. Zero-delay block. Updates mark time or modifies a xact parameter. Xacts proceed to next sequential block.

MATCH   Never refuses entry. Holds xacts for unspecified length of time when no match can be made. Xacts proceed to next sequential block.

PRIORITY   Never refuses entry. Zero-delay block. Modifies xact priority. Xacts proceed to next sequential block.

SELECT   Never refuses entry. Zero-delay block. Modifies a xact parameter. Xacts proceed to a nonsequential block only if search fails and alternate exit is specified.

SPLIT   Never refuses entry. Zero-delay block. Creates copy xacts. May modify a xact parameter. Parent proceeds to next sequential block. Copies proceed to specified block.

TERMINATE   Never refuses entry. Zero-delay block. Destroys xacts; they proceed no farther.

TEST   Never refuses entry in unconditional entry mode. May refuse entry in conditional mode. Xacts proceed to next sequential block except when condition is not met in unconditional entry mode.

TRANSFER   Never refuses entry. May be zero-delay or may hold xact for unspecified length of time, depending on its mode. Xacts usually proceed to nonsequential blocks.

Illustrative Programs 5 and 6

Two illustrative programs are presented which make use of the block types introduced in the preceding chapter. Illustrative program 5 simulates a simple-minded supply depot operation. Illustrative program 6 simulates a job shop in which three subassemblies are fabricated separately before finally being assembled together. Warehouse and job shop situations, incidentally, represent classic areas of application for GPSS.

The material in this chapter entails no differences between GPSS/360 and the other versions that have not already been brought out. Consequently, there is no section devoted to "differences" in this chapter.

10.1 SUPPLY DEPOT PROBLEM: ILLUSTRATIVE PROGRAM 5

Operation of the Supply Depot

A small and not very efficient supply depot is staffed by a clerk and a stock handler. Orders come into the depot every 4.5 to 7.5 minutes. An incoming order must wait until all previous orders have been fully processed. When its time comes, an order is handled as follows:

1. The clerk accepts the order and takes between 1 and 7 minutes to complete the paperwork, including making up an invoice.
2. While the clerk is handling the paperwork, his cohort takes a copy of the order, fetches the required item from the stockroom, and brings it back to the desk. It takes him 2.5 to 7.5 minutes to do this.
3. The invoice is attached to the item ordered. Only then can the next order be processed.

As mentioned before, this supply depot is not very cleverly run. For example, the clerk may have to wait idly while the stock handler is finishing his job or vice versa. Also, there is no provision for saving time if an item is found to be out of stock.

It is obvious that there is room for improvement in this particular supply depot. It would be interesting to devise a more efficient arrangement and compare it with the present arrangement. This is done in Chapter 11.

Illustrative Program 5

The translation of our supply depot into a GPSS model is extremely simple. So we dispense with flow charts and schematic diagrams and proceed directly to the coded program. It is shown in Figure 10-1.

All of the card types used in program 5 should be familiar. In addition, a large number of explanatory comments have been included in the symbolic program. Therefore, no explanation of this program is given here, since you need only peruse Figure 10-1 to understand how it works.

Simulation Results

Program 5 yields two sets of output statistics, both of which consist of the following:

1. Absolute and relative clock times.
2. Block counts.
3. Facility statistics for DEPOT.
4. Table 1.

```
* SIMULATION OF SUPPLY DEPOT OPERATION

* 2 CLOCK UNITS EQUAL 1 MINUTE OF SYSTEM TIME.

        SIMULATE
        GENERATE     12,3        ORDERS ARRIVE EVERY 4.5-7.5 MINUTES.
        ADVANCE      0           ENSURES CORRECT INTERARRIVAL TIME OF
*                                ORDERS BY ACCOMMODATING BLOCKED XACTS
        SEIZE        DEPOT       TIE UP DEPOT WITH 1 ORDER AT A TIME.
        SPLIT        1,CLERK     CREATE 1 COPY XACT; IT GOES TO CLERK.

* THE PARENT XACT REPRESENTS THE ITEM WHICH WAS ORDERED.  THE COPY
* XACT REPRESENTS THE ACCOMPANYING PAPERWORK.

        ADVANCE      10,5        ITEM IS FETCHED IN 2.5-7.5 MINUTES.
ITEM    MATCH        PAPER       ITEM WAITS UNTIL PAPERWORK IS READY.
        RELEASE      DEPOT       FREE DEPOT TO PROCESS NEXT ORDER.

        TABULATE     1           TABULATE TRANSIT TIMES IN TABLE 1.
   1    TABLE        M1,2,2,20

        TERMINATE                DESTROY PARENT XACT.

CLERK   ADVANCE      8,6         PAPERWORK COMPLETED IN 1 TO 7 MINUTES
PAPER   MATCH        ITEM        PAPERWORK WAITS UNTIL ITEM IS READY.
        TERMINATE                DESTROY COPY XACT.

* USE "TIMER" TO MAKE SIMULATION RUN LENGTH EQUAL TO 8 HOURS.

        GENERATE     960         GENERATE AN XACT AFTER 480 MINUTES.
        TERMINATE    1           DESTROY TIMER XACT.
        START        1           RUN TERMINATION COUNT IS 1.

* RESET SYSTEM STATISTICS BUT DO NOT ERASE ANY XACTS THAT MAY BE
* PRESENT, AND REPEAT SIMULATION RUN FOR ANOTHER 8 HOUR PERIOD.

        RESET
        START        1

        END
```

Fig. 10-1.   Illustrative program 5.

TABLE 10-1. SUMMARY OF PROGRAM 5 OUTPUT

	First Day	Second Day
Absolute clock	960	1920
Relative clock	960	960
Facility statistics		
Average utilization	.949	.903
Number of entries	79	79
Average time/xact	11.544	10.974
Table statistics		
Number of entries	78	78
Mean argument	15.935	13.282
Standard deviation	4.378	3.449

The key clock, facility, and table statistics are summarized in Table 10-1. Let us see what these statistics, along with the undisplayed block counts, indicate.

On the first day, 79 orders arrived. Of these, 78 were processed, and one was in the works at the end of the day. The depot was in use 94.9% of the time, or 7.6 out of 8 hours. The average elapsed time from the arrival of an order until it was disposed of was 7.97 minutes—half the mean argument of table 1, since 2 clock units equal 1 minute.

On the second day, 78 orders arrived. The left-over order from the first day was finished, and then 77 more orders were processed. When time ran out, one order was being processed. The average utilization was 90.3%, and the average elapsed time for orders was 6.64 minutes.

The results indicate that the supply depot is utilized to a high degree and could not accommodate much of an increase in the incoming order rate. However, we do not know how much idle time is spent by the clerk and the stock handler due to the stipulation that they must start processing each order *in unison*. We could have found out by treating each as a separate GPSS facility, but as long as one cannot start before the other, it would not matter anyway. However, we shall represent the clerk and stock handler as individual facilities in illustrative program 7 in the next chapter, and they will not be required to start processing each order in unison.

Efficient Acquisition of Statistics over an Extended Time Period

Since we only simulated two days' worth of events, our results are quite susceptible to the particular sequence of random numbers that was generated during the simulation. In other words, we have a rather poor sample, in a statistical sense. It would be better to simulate a period of several weeks rather than a couple of days. This is easily accomplished by inserting as many pairs of RESET and START cards as we wish.

Perhaps the main drawback to this approach is that we would obtain a large amount of statistical output data that would have to be sifted, sorted, summed, and averaged. One way to avoid this is to use the output editor feature described in Chapter 13.   Another, and perhaps better, approach is to insert a few additional instructions which suppress unwanted outputs and make the program compute the desired overall averages.   A method for doing this is now given.

Figure 10-2 shows program 5 with some additions that will accomplish our stated objective.   These additions are:

1. Five SAVEVALUE blocks inserted between GENERATE   960 and TERMINATE   1.
2. Two VARIABLE cards.
3. "NP" in field B of the first START card.

```
* SIMULATION OF SUPPLY DEPOT OPERATION

          SIMULATE                  ⌐
          GENERATE      12,3        |
          ADVANCE       0           |
          SEIZE         DEPOT       |
          SPLIT         1,CLERK     |
          ADVANCE       10,5        |
     ITEM MATCH         PAPER       ⟩      Comments Deleted
          RELEASE       DEPOT       |
          TABULATE      1           |
        1 TABLE         M1,2,2,20   |
          TERMINATE                 |
    CLERK ADVANCE       8,6         |
    PAPER MATCH         ITEM        |
          TERMINATE                 ⌐
```

```
* USE "TIMER" TO MAKE SIMULATION RUN LENGTH EQUAL TO 8 HOURS.
* USE TIMER XACT TO ENTER CERTAIN STATISTICS INTO SAVEVALUES
* WHOSE CONTENTS WILL BE UNAFFECTED BY THE RESET CARD.

          GENERATE      960         CREATE TIMER XACT EVERY 8 HOURS.
          SAVEVALUE     1+,1        ADD 1 TO PREVIOUS CONTENTS OF X1.
          SAVEVALUE     2+,TB1      ADD MEAN ARGUMENT OF TABLE 1 TO X2.
          SAVEVALUE     3+,FR$DEPOT ADD AVG. UTILIZATION OF FACILITY
*                                     DEPOT TO X3.
          SAVEVALUE     4,V4        SET X4 EQUAL TO VARIABLE 4 RESULT.
          SAVEVALUE     5,V5        SET X5 EQUAL TO VARIABLE 5 RESULT.
          TERMINATE     1           DESTROY TIMER XACT AT THE SAME
*                                     CLOCK TIME AS IT WAS CREATED.
        4 VARIABLE      X2/X1       V4 IS EQUAL TO THE SUM OF TABLE 1
*                                     MEAN ARGUMENTS THUS FAR, DIVIDED BY
*                                     THE NUMBER OF RUNS.   THUS V4 GIVES
*                                     AVG. MEAN ARGUMENT OF TABLE 1.
        5 VARIABLE      X3/X1       V5 IS EQUAL TO THE SUM OF AVG. UTIL.
*                                     OF THE FACILITY THUS FAR, DIVIDED BY
*                                     THE NUMBER OF RUNS.   THUS V5 GIVES
*                                     THE AVG. UTILIZATION OF FACILITY DEPOT.
          START         1,NP        SUPPRESS PRINTOUT OF STATISTICS AFTER
*                                     FIRST RUN.
```

```
* RESET SYSTEM STATISTICS, BUT DO NOT ERASE ANY XACTS THAT MAY BE
* PRESENT, AND DO NOT INITIALIZE SAVEVALUES.   THEN SIMULATE ANOTHER
* 8 HOUR PERIOD.

          RESET
          START         1

          END
```

Fig. 10-2.   Illustrative program 5, modified.

The effects of these additions can probably be deduced from the comments in Figure 10-2. However, there are some aspects worth pointing out, so let us now follow the progress of the *timer transaction* which is created at the end of the first run, when the absolute and relative clocks read 960.

The timer transaction goes from the GENERATE block to the TERMINATE block in zero clock time, passing through five SAVEVALUE blocks enroute. It first sets savevalue 1 equal to 1. It then adds the mean argument of table 1 (which is the average transit time in half-minutes for the first run) to savevalue 2. Since savevalues only store integers, the value of TB1 will be truncated and stored as 15 instead of 15.935. The loss of the fractional part could be avoided by defining a floating-point variable which multiplies TB1 by 1000, and storing its value in savevalue 2.

When the timer xact enters the third SAVEVALUE block, the average utilization in parts per thousand is added to savevalue 3. This value is 949.

When the fourth SAVEVALUE block is entered, the value of variable 4 is computed and put into savevalue 4. At this point, it is V4 = 15/1 = 15. Similarly, when the fifth SAVEVALUE block is entered, the value of V5 (= 949/1 = 949) is put into savevalue 5.

The "NP" in field B of the START block causes the printout of statistics for the just-ended run to be deleted. It does not in any way affect the gathering of statistics; it merely prevents their being printed out. The operation of the START card is fully explained in Chapter 13.

The RESET card causes most of the accumulated system statistics to be erased, but it does not affect the savevalues. So the values put into the five savevalues at T = 960 will remain unchanged until T = 1920, when the second timer xact is created at the end of the second run.

At the end of the second run, savevalue 1 has its value incremented to 2. Savevalue 2 is incremented to 28, and savevalue 3 is incremented to 1852. (Check the Table 10-1 statistics, and remember that the mean argument of table 1 is truncated when added to savevalue 2.)

Savevalue 4 is set equal to 28/2 = 14, and savevalue 5 is set equal to 1852/2 = 926. Since the second START card has its B-field blank, these savevalue contents will be printed out along with the other statistics for run 2.

To simulate an *n*-day period, we would use *n-1* START cards with "NP" in field B; the *n*th START card would not have the "NP." Regardless of how many days are simulated, the following will be true:

1. Statistics will appear for only the last run.
2. X1 will give the number of days simulated.
3. X4 will give the average transit time for all orders processed during the *n*-day period.
4. X5 will give the average daily utilization of the depot.

The value of X4 is simply divided by 2 to obtain the number of minutes per order, and X5 is divided by 10 to obtain the average utilization in per cent. Of course, we could have incorporated these operations into variables 4 and 5, respectively, if we had thought of it.

10.2 JOB SHOP PROBLEM

The job shop problem will be simulated by program 5. It involves a much larger system than the supply depot, but it is just as easily translated into a GPSS model.

General Description of the Problem

A manufacturing operation is being established to produce *whatsits*. The shop foreman has tentatively scheduled the construction of whatsits to commence at 5-hour intervals. But for various reasons he knows that this interval will fluctuate by ±100 minutes. Since whatsits are made at such a slow rate, this shop has three shifts and operates around the clock.

The primary objective of the simulation is to determine whether a 200 to 400 minute interval between the start of whatsits will result in an efficient utilization of men and machines. We will let the foreman decide what constitutes an acceptable level of efficiency. Our concern is with the simulation that will tell him how the shop operates as a function of the mean starting interval.

In addition to the primary objective, the simulation is also intended to reveal how the job shop functions in general. Do long queues form? Are certain key tasks completed within an acceptably short period of time? Are the men and machines overworked or underworked?

The GPSS Model

The operation of the job shop will be described in terms of the model that was devised to simulate it. This model is diagrammed in Figure 10-3. This diagram is somewhat similar in format to a GPSS block diagram, but some liberties have been taken in the interest of clarity. The words in parentheses correspond to block addresses in program 6.

The manufacture of a whatsit begins every 200 to 400 minutes. The parent xact represents the main subassembly, hereafter referred to as *sub-1*. This xact is split to create two other subassemblies which will be referred to as *sub-2* and *sub-3*. Note that the parent xact has $P1 = 1$, and the copy xacts have $P1 = 2$ and $P1 = 3$, respectively, after emerging from the SPLIT block.

Sub-1 is fabricated on line 1, and this process takes between 120 and 300 minutes. The wide variation is due mainly to the fact that there are several different models of whatsits. And, of course, the shop personnel do not perform a given task in exactly the same number of minutes every time.

With $P1 = 2$, sub-2 is fabricated on line 2. After a period of time which varies between 100 and 200 minutes, it must be brought together with sub-3 to line up certain critical dimensions. This operation takes 10 minutes. Then sub-2 spends 10 to 30 minutes more in line 2.

With $P1 = 3$, sub-3 is fabricated on line 3. After a period of time which varies between 55 and 95 minutes, it is brought together with sub-2. Following this 10-minute operation, it spends 25 to 45 more minutes in line 3. In Figure 10-3, the 10-minute interval is combined with the 35 ± 10-minute interval for sub-3, just as it is combined with the 20 ± 10-minute interval for sub-2.

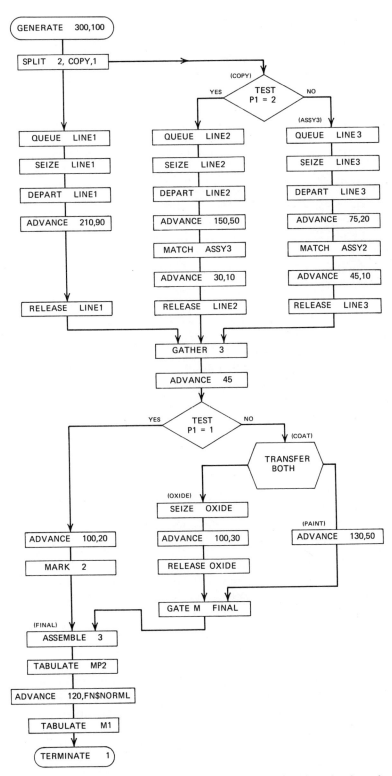

Fig. 10-3. Schematic diagram of GPSS model for program 6. (See back pocket for a duplicate of this illustration which can be kept in view while reading the chapter.)

After all three subassemblies have been fabricated, they are temporarily mated in order to perform certain operations which consume 45 minutes. After that, it is necessary to do some finish work on sub-1 and to apply protective coatings to sub-2 and sub-3.

The finish work on sub-1 takes from 80 to 120 minutes. When this work is done, the current clock time is put into P2 of the parent xact, and it goes to the ASSEMBLE block to wait for the two copies.

Sub-2 receives an oxide coating, and sub-3 is painted. The two copy xacts are sent to OXIDE and PAINT by the **TRANSFER   BOTH** block. Note that at this point in the block diagram, it does not matter which of the two copy xacts represent sub-2 or and sub-3. After all, the only difference between these xacts is that one has P1 = 2 while the other has P1 = 3. As long as the value of P1 is not used, they are indistinguishable as units of traffic.

The GATE block is used to ensure that the two copy xacts do not enter the AS-SEMBLE block until the parent xact has arrived there. Thus the parent xact will always be the one to emerge from the ASSEMBLE block.

The parameter transit time of the parent xact is tallied when it leaves the AS-SEMBLE block. The resulting frequency table indicates how much time sub-1 spends waiting for the other two subassemblies. This particular waiting time is significant in the manufacture of whatsits, but we cannot say why.

The final assembly and inspection phase takes 2 hours on the average. These times are normally distributed with a standard deviation of 20 minutes. The last step is to tally the number of minutes it takes to obtain a completed whatsit, measured from the moment it was scheduled to begin to be fabricated.

Once again we are working with a fictitious situation which is unrealistic in certain respects. And once again the reader is reminded that the validity of the problem is secondary to its translation into a GPSS model.

10.3   ILLUSTRATIVE PROGRAM 6

The GPSS program that was written to simulate the production of whatsits is shown in Figures 10-4 and 10-5. It has been divided into six sections so that it will be easier to follow. These sections more or less correspond to logically separable portions of the block diagram. Bear in mind that this division of the program into six sections is purely superficial. The GPSS simulator sees one continuous program (i.e., one model) without comments or separations.

Section 1

The INITIAL card is used to place 300 and 100 into savevalues 1 and 2, respectively. This allows us to assign different values to fields A and B of the GENERATE block via X1 and X2 if we choose to make a series of runs to try different starting intervals.

The continuous numerical-valued function NORML is used to generate normally distributed random numbers in the range of -4.265 to $+4.265$. The 46 coordinate pairs represent points on the *cumulative standard normal distribution*

```
* SIMULATION OF JOB SHOP TO MANUFACTURE WHATSITS

* SECTION 1    (PRELIMINARIES)

        SIMULATE
        INITIAL    X1,300/X2,100
 NORML FUNCTION    RN1,046         CUMULATIVE STD. NORMAL DISTRIBUTION
0.0,-4.265/0.00001,-4.265/0.0001,-3.719/0.001,-3.090/0.005,-2.576/
0.01,-2.236/0.02,-2.054/0.025,-1.960/0.03,-1.881/0.04,-1.751/
0.05,-1.645/0.06,-1.555/0.07,-1.476/0.08,-1.405/0.09,-1.341/0.1,-1.282/
0.15,-1.036/0.2,-0.842/0.25,-0.674/0.3,-0.524/0.35,-0.385/0.4,-0.253/
0.45,-0.126/0.5,0.0/0.55,0.126/0.6,0.253/0.65,0.385/0.7,0.524/
0.75,0.674/0.8,0.842/0.85,1.036/0.9,1.282/0.91,1.341/0.92,1.405/
0.93,1.476/0.94,1.555/0.95,1.645/0.96,1.751/0.97,1.881/0.975,1.960/
0.98,2.354/0.99,2.326/0.995,2.576/0.999,3.090/0.9999,3.719/.99999,4.265

        GENERATE    X1,X2,,,,5,H   CREATE EMBRYONIC WHATSITS.
        SPLIT       2,COPY,1       CREATE 2 COPY XACTS; SERIALIZE P1.

* SECTION 2    (FABRICATION OF MAIN SUBASSEMBLY)
        QUEUE       LINE1          PARENT XACT (SUB-1) WAITS FOR LINE 1.
        SEIZE       LINE1
        DEPART      LINE1
        ADVANCE     210,90         120 TO 300 MINUTES TO MAKE SUB-1
        RELEASE     LINE1
        TRANSFER    ,UNITE

* SECTION 3    (FABRICATION OF OTHER TWO SUBASSEMBLIES)

 COPY  TEST E      P1,K2,ASSY3    SUB-2 HAS P1=2 AND PROCEEDS TO NEXT
 *                                BLOCK.  SUB-3 GOES TO ASSY3 BLOCK.
        QUEUE       LINE2          SUB-2 WAITS FOR LINE 2.
        SEIZE       LINE2
        DEPART      LINE2
        ADVANCE     150,50         100 TO 200 MINUTES ELAPSE.
 SUB2  MATCH       SUB3           MUST CHECK DIMENSIONS WITH SUB-3.
        ADVANCE     30,10          20 TO 40 MORE MINUTES IN LINE 2.
        RELEASE     LINE2
        TRANSFER    ,UNITE

 ASSY3 QUEUE       LINE3          SUB-3 WAITS FOR LINE 3.
        SEIZE       LINE3
        DEPART      LINE3
        ADVANCE     75,20          55 TO 95 MINUTES ELAPSE.
 SUB3  MATCH       SUB2           MUST CHECK DIMENSIONS WITH SUB-2.
        ADVANCE     45,10          35 TO 55 MORE MINUTES IN LINE 3.
        RELEASE     LINE3

* SECTION 4    (TEMPORARILY MATE 3 SUBASSEMBLIES.)

 UNITE GATHER      3
        ADVANCE     45
        TEST E      P1,1,COAT      SUB-2 AND SUB-3 GO TO COAT.
```

Fig. 10-4.   Illustrative program 6.

curve.   The standard normal distribution is defined as having a mean (μ) of zero and a standard deviation (σ) of one.   A complete explanation of how FN$NORML is constructed is given in Appendix G.

A value of FN$NORML can be interpreted as *the number of standard deviations above or below the mean*.   This fact enables us to translate values of FN$NORML (which are normally distributed with $\mu = 0$ and $\sigma = 1$) into values which belong to a "nonstandard" normal distribution.   A GPSS variable is used to do this as you will see when section 6 of program 6 is discussed.

Since we will not require many xact parameters in this program, and since relatively small numbers will be put into the parameters we do use, five halfword

```
* SECTION 5   (3 SUBASSEMBLIES SEPARATED FOR FINISHING OPERATIONS)

        ADVANCE    100,20      SUB-1 FINISHED IN 80 TO 120 MINUTES.
        MARK       2           PUT CURRENT CLOCK TIME INTO P2.
        TRANSFER   ,FINAL

  COAT  TRANSFER   BOTH,OXIDE,PAINT

  OXIDE SEIZE      OXIDE
        ADVANCE    100,30      SUB-2 FINISHED IN 70 TO 130 MINUTES.
        RELEASE    OXIDE
        TRANSFER   ,HOLD

  PAINT ADVANCE    130,50      SUB-3 FINISHED IN 80 TO 180 MINUTES.

  HOLD  GATE M     FINAL       HOLD SUB-2 AND SUB-3 UNTIL SUB-1 HAS
  *                            ARRIVED AT "FINAL".

* SECTION 6   (FINAL ASSEMBLY AND INSPECTION)

  FINAL ASSEMBLE   3           SUB-1 XACT WILL ALWAYS ARRIVE BEFORE
  *                            SUB-2 AND SUB-3 XACTS, SO LAST 2 XACTS
  *                            WILL ALWAYS BE DESTROYED HERE.
        TABULATE   WAIT        TALLY TIME SPENT BY SUB-1 WAITING IN
  *                            ASSEMBLE BLOCK.
        ADVANCE    V1
        TABULATE   TIME        TALLY TRANSIT TIMES, FROM BEGINNING TO
  *                            END.
        TERMINATE  1

  WAIT  TABLE      MP2,0,10,10
  TIME  TABLE      M1,400,50,15
      1 VARIABLE   20*FN$NORML+120    V1 CONVERTS A RANDOM NO. FROM
  *                            THE STANDARD NORMAL DISTRIBU-
  *                            TION TO ONE FROM THE NORMAL DISTRIBU-
  *                            TION WHOSE MEAN IS 120 AND WHOSE STD.
  *                            DEVIATION IS 20.

        START      50
        END
```

Fig. 10-5. Illustrative program 6 (*continued*).

parameters have been specified in the GENERATE block to conserve core capacity. The saving in core space is trivial (in fact pointless) in this instance, but this sort of frugality can pay off handsomely in large models. Incidentally, the "H" in field G is unnecessary.

The parent xact and the two offspring created by the SPLIT block constitute an assembly set. Each member of this set is linked to the next member as shown in Figure 10-6.

There are no means for distinguishing between parent and copy xacts inside the computer. Once a copy is created, it is just another member of the assembly set to which it is linked. It is in no way subordinate to the parent xact. We could certainly have used a copy xact to denote the main assembly. The only reason that we distinguish between parent and copy xacts in discussing program 6 is that it helps us to follow the progress of items through the block diagram.

Sections 2 to 4

For convenience, sections 2 to 4 of program 6 have been repeated in Figure 10-7. In section 2, the parent xact denotes sub-1. It is fabricated in line 1, and then it waits (if necessary) to be mated with the other two subassemblies.

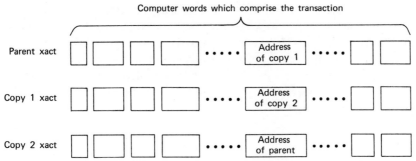

Fig. 10-6.   Linkages between assembly set members in job shop model.

In section 3, the other two subassemblies are fabricated in lines 2 and 3, respectively. Their progress is synchronized at the MATCH blocks. After they are fabricated, they go to be mated with each other and with sub-1.

The three assembly lines have been represented as facilities so that each of them can accommodate only one subassembly at a time. (They are, admittedly, unusual assembly lines.) Since they are vacated at different times, the subassemblies for the next whatsit may capture them (i.e., begin to be fabricated) at different times.

In section 4, the three subassemblies are mated for 45 minutes. Note that the **ADVANCE**   45 block is not preceded by a SEIZE block. If it were, the three xacts representing the three subassemblies would enter the ADVANCE block at

```
* SECTION 2    (FABRICATION OF MAIN SUBASSEMBLY)
          QUEUE       LINE1        PARENT XACT (SUB-1) WAITS FOR LINE 1.
          SEIZE       LINE1
          DEPART      LINE1
          ADVANCE     210,90       120 TO 300 MINUTES TO MAKE SUB-1
          RELEASE     LINE1
          TRANSFER    ,UNITE

* SECTION 3    (FABRICATION OF OTHER TWO SUBASSEMBLIES)

COPY    TEST E      P1,K2,ASSY3    SUB-2 HAS P1=2 AND PROCEEDS TO NEXT
                                   BLOCK.   SUB-3 GOES TO ASSY3 BLOCK.
          QUEUE       LINE2        SUB-2 WAITS FOR LINE 2.
          SEIZE       LINE2
          DEPART      LINE2
          ADVANCE     150,50       100 TO 200 MINUTES ELAPSE.
SUB2    MATCH       SUB3         MUST CHECK DIMENSIONS WITH SUB-3.
          ADVANCE     30,10        20 TO 40 MORE MINUTES IN LINE 2.
          RELEASE     LINE2
          TRANSFER    ,UNITE

ASSY3   QUEUE       LINE3        SUB-3 WAITS FOR LINE 3.
          SEIZE       LINE3
          DEPART      LINE3
          ADVANCE     75,20        55 TO 95 MINUTES ELAPSE.
SUB3    MATCH       SUB2         MUST CHECK DIMENSIONS WITH SUB-2.
          ADVANCE     45,10        35 TO 55 MORE MINUTES IN LINE 3.
          RELEASE     LINE3

* SECTION 4    (TEMPORARILY MATE 3 SUBASSEMBLIES.)

UNITE   GATHER      3
          ADVANCE     45
          TEST E      P1,1,COAT    SUB-2 AND SUB-3 GO TO COAT.
```

Fig. 10-7.   Sections 2 to 4 of program 6.

successive intervals of 45 minutes. But as it is, all three xacts enter the AD-
VANCE block at the same clock instant, and they all emerge 45 clock units later.

The TEST block sends the parent xact to the next sequential block since it has
P1 = 1. The two copy xacts are sent to COAT since they do not have P1 = 1.
Actually, it does not matter at this point which of the three xacts represents
which subassembly. We could just as well have coded "P1,2" or "P1,3" in the
TEST block variable field.

Section 5

For convenience, section 5 of program 6 has been reproduced below. Sub-1
moves from the TEST block in section 4, through the first three blocks in section
5, and into the ASSEMBLE block in section 6. Its movement through these
blocks requires no explanation. (See Figure 10-8.)

Sub-2 and sub-3 are sent by the TEST block in section 4 to the TRANSFER
BOTH block in section 5. The operation of this block was explained in
Chapter 4, but to refresh your memory, here is how it works in this situation:
The TRANSFER   BOTH block attempts to send an entering xact to OXIDE.
If the xact is able to enter the SEIZE block, it does so and seizes the facility
named OXIDE. If this facility is already being seized, the xact is sent by the
TRANSFER block to PAINT where it will never be refused entry.

This arrangement ensures that the two copy xacts, which arrive at the
TRANSFER block at the same clock time, will be properly dispersed, that is, one
will go to OXIDE, and the other will go to PAINT. It should be evident that the
SEIZE block labelled OXIDE is what prevents both xacts from being sent to the
ADVANCE   100,30 block.

When a xact enters the GATE block, a check is made to see if another member
of its assembly set is in the ASSEMBLE block. If none are, the gate stays shut, so
to speak. Thus the sub-2 and sub-3 xacts cannot enter the ASSEMBLE block
before the sub-1 xact. Since the sub-1 xact is always the first member of its assembly set to be assembled, it is always the xact which subsequently leaves the AS-
SEMBLE block.

```
* SECTION 5    (3 SUBASSEMBLIES SEPARATED FOR FINISHING OPERATIONS)

          ADVANCE    100,20      SUB-1 FINISHED IN 80 TO 120 MINUTES.
          MARK       2           PUT CURRENT CLOCK TIME INTO P2.
          TRANSFER   ,FINAL

   COAT   TRANSFER   BOTH,OXIDE,PAINT

   OXIDE SEIZE       OXIDE
          ADVANCE    100,30      SUB-2 FINISHED IN 70 TO 130 MINUTES.
          RELEASE    OXIDE
          TRANSFER   ,HOLD

   PAINT ADVANCE     130,50      SUB-3 FINISHED IN 80 TO 180 MINUTES.

   HOLD   GATE M     FINAL       HOLD SUB-2 AND SUB-3 UNTIL SUB-1 HAS
     *                           ARRIVED AT BLOCK LABELED "FINAL".
```

Fig. 10-8.   Section 5 of program 6.

```
* SECTION 6    (FINAL ASSEMBLY AND INSPECTION)

  FINAL ASSEMBLE    3           SUB-1 XACT WILL ALWAYS ARRIVE BEFORE
*                               SUB-2 AND SUB-3 XACTS, SO LAST 2 XACTS
*                               WILL ALWAYS BE DESTROYED HERE.
        TABULATE    WAIT        TALLY TIME SPENT BY SUB-1 WAITING IN
*                               ASSEMBLE BLOCK.
        ADVANCE     V1
        TABULATE    TIME        TALLY TRANSIT TIMES, FROM BEGINNING TO
*                               END.
        TERMINATE   1

  WAIT  TABLE       MP2,0,10,10
  TIME  TABLE       M1,400,50,15

  1     VARIABLE    20*FN$NORML+120   V1 CONVERTS A RANDOM NO. FROM
*                                     THE STANDARD NORMAL DISTRIBU-
*                                     TION TO ONE FROM THE NORMAL DISTRIBU-
*                                     TION WHOSE MEAN IS 120 AND WHOSE STD.
*                                     DEVIATION IS 20.

        START       50
        END
```

Fig. 10-9. Section 6 of program 6.

Section 6

Section 6 of program 6 is reproduced in Figure 10-9. The sub-1 xact represents a whatsit during the final assembly and inspection phase. Just before this phase begins, the time spent by sub-1 waiting for both sub-2 and sub-3 to join it is tabulated in the table called WAIT.

The length of time spent in the final assembly and inspection phase is a random variable. It is denoted by V1 and its values are normally distributed with a mean of 2 hours and a standard deviation of 20 minutes. V1 is related to FN$NORML as follows:

$$V1 = (\sigma)(FN\$NORML) + \mu$$
$$= (20)(FN\$NORML) + 120$$

The following computations take place every time a xact enters the **AD-VANCE** **V1** block:

1. A value of RN1 is computed.
2. With RN1 as the argument, a value of FN$NORML is computed.
3. This value is used to compute variable 1.[1]

After a whatsit has been completely assembled and inspected, it is removed from the model. Just before that happens, its transit time is tabulated. The table called TIME will indicate how many minutes elapse from the time whatsits are scheduled to begin production until they roll off the assembly line.

The simulation will end when the fiftieth whatsit has been produced. Since

---

[1] GPS K offers a built-in normal distribution which can be referenced in the B-field of a GENERATE or ADVANCE block by using the SNA, NF(σ). So in program 6, both the NORML function and variable 1 could be omitted, and an **ADVANCE** **120,NF(20)** block would "do the trick."

they are presumably produced at the rate of one every 5 hours, the simulation should cover a period of roughly 250 hours, or about 10.5 days.

10.4   RESULTS OF JOB SHOP SIMULATION

We first survey the contents of the printout, and then we analyze their meaning.

Output from Program 6

The symbolic and input listings (not shown) tell us that this model consists of 42 blocks. The cross-reference dictionary (not shown) lists 20 symbolic addresses — 10 for blocks, 4 for facilities, 3 for queues, 2 for tables, and 1 for a function.

The pertinent statistics are summarized in Table 10-2. Note that the clock time of 15,858 corresponds to a simulated period of about 11 days. The block counts (not included in Table 10-2) indicate that 50 whatsits were manufactured during the run, and one was in process when the run ended.

The facility and savevalue data in Table 10-2 are complete, except for the number of the xact seizing facility OXIDE when the run ended. The average contents, per cent zeroes, and average time/xact excluding zero entries have been omitted from the queue statistics.

The two tables have also been omitted, but the number of entries and mean arguments are given in Table 10-2.

Analysis of Output Statistics

The three assembly lines which operate in parallel in the first phase of the process have utilizations of roughly .6 to .7. Thus it would seem that better use can be made of them; that is, they could accommodate a higher volume of work.

The savevalues contain the mean and modifier used for the interarrival times of new jobs. In view of the low utilization of lines 1, 2, and 3, we might very well want to rerun the simulation with $X1 = 200$, or some such value.

The queue statistics confirm our previous observation about assembly lines 1, 2, and 3. At no time was there more than one subassembly waiting to seize its line, and the vast majority of subassemblies did not have to wait at all.

The WAIT table tells us that the main subassembly had to wait an average of 42 minutes to be finally assembled with the other two subassemblies. The table frequencies (not shown in Table 10-2) reveal that about 30% of the main subassemblies had to wait for over 1 hour. This may not be acceptable, but we will let the foreman worry about that.

The TIME table tells us that the average whatsit was completed about 10.5 hours after it was begun. Note that this does not conflict with the fact that whatsits were begun on an average of every 5 hours. After all, the job shop can accommodate several whatsits simultaneously in various stages of manufacture.

TABLE 10-2. SUMMARY OF PROGRAM 6 OUTPUT

Absolute and relative clock times: 15858

Facility statistics

Facility	Average Utilization	Number of Entries	Average Time/Transaction
LINE1	.706	51	219.529
LINE2	.597	51	185.725
LINE3	.641	51	199.352
OXIDE	.322	51	100.392

Contents of fullword savevalues
X1 = 300
X2 = 100

Queue statistics

Queue	Maximum Contents	Total Entries	Zero Entries	Average Time/Transaction
LINE1	1	51	44	5.980
LINE2	1	51	49	.588
LINE3	1	51	49	.901

Table statistics

Table	Number of Entries	Mean Argument
WAIT	50	41.959
TIME	50	628.719

10.5 SUMMARY

It is sometimes advisable to simulate a short period of system operation before configuring the model to perform a full-scale run or sequence of runs. Obvious flaws in the system definition as well as other clear trends in its behavior — sometimes unexpected — will usually show up. This was exemplified by program 4 and again by program 6. In the latter, for instance, the foreman's concern over the 200-minute variation in the starting interval was secondary to the revelation that whatsits could be produced at a significantly higher rate than one every 5 hours.

When a series of consecutive runs are desired for the same basic model, it is possible to suppress the printout of unwanted intermediate statistics by using the NP option in the START card. It is also possible to define savevalues and variables that will present the user with sums and/or averages of key statistics for all of the runs.

GPSS is extremely well suited to the modeling of manufacturing processes. Machines can be represented as facilities and parts as transactions. Related parts can be represented as members of the same assembly set, and their progress through various shop operations can be synchronized via MATCH, AS-SEMBLE, and GATHER blocks.

The concept of *a task seizing a machine* can be expanded to allow its seizure on a priority basis. If tasks of varying importance are represented by xacts with different priorities, and if these xacts are allowed to queue up in front of a facility that represents a machine, then the higher-priority xacts will seize it before the lower-priority xacts. *This is ensured by the order of xacts on the current events chain.*

To carry this further, it is possible to represent *machine failures* as transactions that have the power to *preempt* the facility that represents the machine. The preempting of a facility supercedes xact priorities. It will be explained in the next chapter.

No job shop—or any other—simulation would be valid if realistic constants were not entered into the model. For example, the time spent performing various operations must be correct. This requires the collection of empirical data, usually by direct observation.

CHAPTER 11

Preempting and Interrupt Chains

The main purpose of this chapter is to explain the operation of the PREEMPT and RETURN blocks. In the process, you will become acquainted with the *interrupt chain*, and you will acquire additional insight into the inner workings of GPSS. Illustrative program 7 is also presented.

11.1 GENERAL COMMENTS

Preempting

The ability to award a facility to xacts on a preferential basis is extremely useful in certain modeling situations. For example, we can simulate the operation of a data processing system where certain jobs may "seize" the CPU (or part of it) on a priority basis. Or we might want to simulate a situation where a job is being performed on a machine, and a more important job comes along and preempts it. Or we could simulate breakdowns of a machine by having a failure preempt any jobs that are on, or waiting for, the machine.

Why can we not accomplish these things by simply assigning priorities to xacts so that those with higher priorities will seize the facility before those with lower priorities? The reason is that the PREEMPT/RETURN blocks enable a xact to obtain a facility *while it is occupied by another xact*. Without these blocks, a newly arrived xact, no matter how high its priority, would have to *wait* for the facility to be released by the xact presently seizing it.

PREEMPT and RETURN Blocks

The PREEMPT/RETURN blocks are analogous to the SEIZE/RELEASE blocks inasmuch as they pertain to the capture and freeing of a facility by a xact. The PREEMPT/RETURN blocks enable a xact to preempt a facility that is being *seized*. If the "PR" option is used, the PREEMPT/RETURN blocks also enable a xact to preempt a facility that is being *preempted by a lower priority xact*.

The coding of the PREEMPT/RETURN blocks is summarized below:

PREEMPT   A   Facility address
                B   PR or blank
                C   Block address or blank

                  D   Parameter number or blank
                  E   RE or blank

RETURN   A   Facility address

Subfields B through E of the PREEMPT block are associated with *multilevel preempting* options. Some of these options will be explained later in this chapter.

It is more proper to speak of a facility being preempted than of a transaction being preempted. However, it is usually more convenient to use the latter phraseology. Since there is no ambiguity, we will sometimes take this liberty.

Interrupt Chains

Interrupt chains contain xacts which have been preempted from a facility and are awaiting an opportunity to regain possession of it. So if a program does not contain any PREEMPT/RETURN blocks, no interrupt chains will exist during the run. If a program does contain one or more PREEMPT/RETURN block pairs, interrupt chains may or may not exist, depending on various circumstances. Some of these circumstances are discussed in this chapter.

11.2 SIMPLE PREEMPTING

The most straightforward and common mode of usage of the PREEMPT block is illustrated in Figure 11-1. Only field A is used; this is referred to as *simple preempting*.

Three cases are discussed in this section. Each of them is presented as a situation that could occur in connection *with the above program segment*.

Case 1

T = 5. Transaction 1 enters the PREEMPT block, having been sent there by the TRANSFER block. Since facility 10 is not in use, xact 1 seizes it and

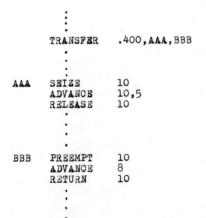

Fig. 11-1. Excerpts from a GPSS program that uses PREEMPT/RETURN blocks.

proceeds to the **ADVANCE**   8 block. It is removed from the current events chain and merged into the future events chain with a BDT of 13.

T = 6 to 12.   Other xacts arrive at the SEIZE and PREEMPT blocks. They are put into delay chains, that is, inactive status in the current events chain.

T = 13.   Xact 1 is removed from the future events chain and put on the current events chain. It is picked up by the current events chain scan and moved into the RETURN block. This causes the status of facility 10 to change from "preempted" to "not preempted." After this operation and several others are performed by the RETURN block subroutine, xact 1 proceeds to the next sequential block.

We have just seen that the PREEMPT/RETURN blocks behave like SEIZE/RELEASE blocks when an arriving xact (xact 1, in our example) finds the facility not to be in use. What about the xacts that arrived while xact 1 was preempting facility 10? We consider them in case 2.

Case 2

In case 1, we said that several transactions arrived at the SEIZE and PREEMPT blocks during the interval 6 to 12 clock units, while xact 1 was preempting facility 10. Let us suppose that three xacts arrived at the SEIZE block, and two arrived at the PREEMPT block.

T = 7.   Xact 2 arrives at the SEIZE block, and xact 3 arrives at the PREEMPT block. Since facility 10 is not available, xact 2 is blocked by the SEIZE block and is put into an NU (facility not in use) delay chain in the current events chain. Similarly, xact 3 is blocked by the PREEMPT block. It is put into an NI (facility not being preempted) delay chain. The status of the model at this point is shown in Figure 11-2a. Note that (incipient) xacts 4 and 5 are due to enter the system at T = 9.

T = 9.   Xact 4 arrives at the PREEMPT block where it receives the same treatment as xact 3. Xact 5 arrives at the SEIZE block where it receives the same treatment as xact 2. Nothing else happens at T = 9. The status of the model at this point is shown in Figure 11-2b. Note that xact 6 is due to enter the system at T = 13.

T = 13.   Xacts 1 and 6 are unlinked from the future events chain and placed at the rear of the current events chain. It happens that xact 1 precedes xact 6 in the current events chain, but this has no bearing upon the outcome. The current events chain scan moves xact 1 to the RETURN block. This causes the RE-TURN block to perform its prescribed operations including the following:

1. Change the status of facility 10 from "being preempted" to "not being preempted."
2. Activate the xacts in the NI delay chain but not those in the NU delay chain.
3. Set the current events chain status change flag.
4. Update various facility 10 and block count statistics.

	External status	Internal status
a At end of T = 7	[2] SEIZE [3] PREEMPT [1] ADVANCE	F.E.C. [1][4][5] 　　　　13　9　9 ←BDT C.E.C. [2][3] 　　　　1　1 ←SSI 　　　NU NI ←Delay chain
b At end of T = 9	[5][2] SEIZE [4][3] PREEMPT [1] ADVANCE	F.E.C. [1][6] 　　　　13　13 ←BDT C.E.C. [2][3][4][5] 　　　　1　1　1　1 ←SSI 　　　NU NI NI NU ←Delay chain
c During T = 13	[5][2] SEIZE [4][3] PREEMPT ADVANCE	F.E.C. C.E.C. [2][3][4][5][6] 　　　　1　0　0　1　0 ←SSI 　　　NU　　　　NU ←Delay chain
d At end of T = 13	[6][5][2] SEIZE [4] PREEMPT [3] ADVANCE	F.E.C. [7][3] 　　　　18　21 ←BDT C.E.C. [2][4][5][6] 　　　　1　1　1　1 ←SSI 　　　NU NI NU NU ←Delay chain

Fig. 11-2. Status of Figure 11-1 model at various times – case 2. F.E.C. = future events chain; C.E.C. = current events chain; BDT = block departure time; SSI = scan status indicator.

The scan continues to move xact 1 as far as it can go at T = 13. It then checks the status change flag and, finding it set, reverts to the beginning of the current events chain. The situation at this point is shown in Figure 11-2c. Note that xact 1 does not appear in the current or future events chain. It may have been destroyed, or it may be in another type of chain. Note also that xact 6 has not yet arrived at the SEIZE or PREEMPT block.

Now, back to the action. The scan sets the status change flag to off and picks up xact 3. Xact 3 enters the PREEMPT block and thus captures facility 10. The status change flag is set, xact 4 is put into an NI delay chain, and its scan status indicator is set to 1.

Xact 3 then enters the ADVANCE 8 block, whereupon it is merged into the future events chain with BDT = 21. The current events chain scan reverts to the beginning of the chain, and it finds all of the xacts to be inactive except for xact 6. So it moves xact 6 to the TRANSFER block (Refer to Figure 11-1.) and then to the SEIZE block.[1]   It is put into the NU delay chain with xacts 2 and 5. The situation at this point is shown in Figure 11-2d.

It is evident that preempting xacts will continue to get into (or capture) facility 10 in preference to seizing xacts.   The reason is simply that xacts in an NU delay chain remain inactive until there are no more xacts in an NI chain.   It is also clear that preempting xacts, regardless of their priorities, must wait their turn behind other preempting xacts as long as only field A of the PREEMPT block has an argument.

Case 3

In cases 1 and 2, only preempting xacts occupied facility 10, and no interrupt chains were involved.   However, the most interesting and significant case is when a preempting xact arrives while a facility is being occupied by a seizing xact.   We now consider such a situation, referring still to Figure 11-1

T = 99.   Facility 10 is empty and no xacts are waiting to use it.

T = 100.   Xact 35 enters the SEIZE block and thus seizes facility 10.   Upon entering the **ADVANCE**   10, 5 block, xact 35 has a delay time of 12 clock units computed for it.   So it is merged into the future events chain with BDT = 112.

T = 103.   Xact 36 arrives at the SEIZE block.   It is blocked at that point since facility 10 is in use.   It is put into an NU delay chain and will remain inactive until facility 10 is not in use.

T = 105.   Xact 37 arrives at the PREEMPT block.   Since facility 10 is not being preempted, xact 37 is allowed to enter the PREEMPT block and take possession of the facility.   Xact 35 is entitled to 7 more clock units in facility 10.   So the BDT of xact 35 is set equal to 7.   Its *preempt count* is incremented from 0 to 1 to signify that it is now being preempted on one facility.   And it is unlinked from the future events chain and put on the interrupt chain.   Since it is the sole member of the interrupt chain, it is perhaps more appropriate to say that xact 1 is placed on interrupt status.

Note that the placing of xact 35 on interrupt status, the assignment of facility 10 to xact 37, and so on, are accomplished by the PREEMPT block.   Note also that xact 37 spends zero clock time in the PREEMPT block.   After these operations (plus some others that were not mentioned) are carried out, xact 37 passes from the PREEMPT block into the ADVANCE block.   At this point it is merged into the future events chain with BDT = 113.

The situation at this time is shown in Figure 11-3a.   Note that the internal status diagram is devoid of other xacts which are elsewhere in the model.   We are only concerned with xacts which are in the portion of the block diagram shown in Figure 11-1 or which are due to enter it.

---

[1] As soon as xact 6 leaves the GENERATE block, a successor incipient xact is created.   It appears in the F.E.C. in Figure 11-2d as xact 7 with BDT = 18.

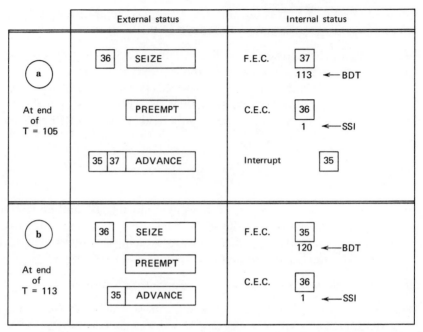

Fig. 11-3. Status of Figure 11-1 model at various times—case 3. F.E.C. = future events chain; C.E.C. = current events chain; BDT = block departure time; SSI = scan status indicator.

T = 113. Xact 37 enters the RETURN block which promptly returns facility 10 to the seizing xact. (Only the xact which preempted a facility is allowed to return it; otherwise an error results.) Xact 35 is removed from the interrupt chain and is merged into the future events chain with BDT = 120.

The current events chain scan then attempts to move xact 37 into the next sequential block. After xact 37 has been moved as far as possible, the scan can do no more. The status at this point is shown in Figure 11-3b.

Xact 36 is a seizing xact. As such, it remains in an NU delay chain until xacts 35 and 37 have both completed their tenures in facility 10. Had xact 36 been a preempting xact, it would have preempted xact 35. Then it would have been immediately followed by xact 37 in facility 10. And then xact 35 would have at last regained the facility.

In case 3, a seizing xact was put into interrupt status when it was preempted. It had been in the future events chain and in an ADVANCE block. Not all seizing xacts are in this situation when preempted, and so they are not always put into interrupt chains. Some of these other possibilities are discussed in the next section.

11.3 NOT-SO-SIMPLE SIMPLE PREEMPTING

It was pointed out in Chapter 7 that a transaction can possess several facilities simultaneously. It may seize or preempt them at the same clock instant or at different clock times. It may release or return them in the order in which it captured them or in some other sequence.   It may also be preempted on several facilities at the same time.   In short, a given xact may be simultaneously seizing, preempting, and preempted on any number of facilities.

It was also pointed out that the concept of *seizing* a facility is broader than the simplistic notion of a xact being *in* a facility.   The correct way to look at it is this: A xact seizes a facility when it enters a SEIZE block, and it releases the facility when it enters the corresponding RELEASE block.   What it does in between need not suggest that the xact is *in* the facility it has seized.

The foregoing comments are relevant to cases 4 to 6 which are presented next.

Case 4

Figure 11-4 depicts a situation that is similar to that in Figure 11-1 except that xacts seize facility 10 while also in possession of facilities 8 and 9.

Imagine that xact 100 has seized all three facilities and is currently in the AD-VANCE   10, 5 block.   Now assume that xact 101 enters the PREEMPT block, thus preempting xact 100 on facility 10.   Xact 100 is placed on the interrupt chain as you know from case 3.

Now imagine that another xact elsewhere in the model preempts facility 9. Xact 100, which is still preempted on facility 10, is now also preempted on facility

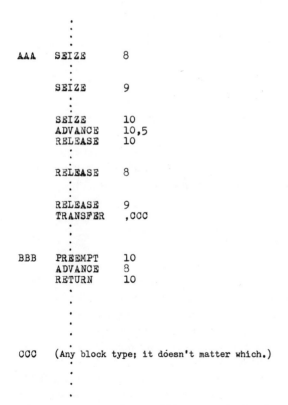

```
        .
        .
        .
AAA   SEIZE      8
        .
        .
      SEIZE      9
        .
        .
      SEIZE      10
      ADVANCE    10,5
      RELEASE    10
        .
        .
      RELEASE    8
        .
        .
      RELEASE    9
      TRANSFER   ,CCC
        .
        .
        .
BBB   PREEMPT    10
      ADVANCE    8
      RETURN     10
        .
        .
        .
        .

CCC   (Any block type; it doesn't matter which.)
        .
        .
        .
```

Fig. 11-4.   Excerpts from a GPSS program that involves multiple seizing of facilities.

9.   It remains on the interrupt chain but has its preempt count increased to 2.   It will remain on the interrupt chain (internally speaking) and in the ADVANCE block (externally speaking) until its preempt count has been reduced to zero. Let us look at this eventuality more closely.

After awhile, facilities 9 and 10 will both have been returned.   At that time, the preempt count of xact 100 is reduced to zero.   If no other xacts are waiting to preempt either of those facilities, xact 100 is unlinked from the interrupt chain and is merged into the future events chain.   Its BDT is made equal to the present clock time plus the number of clock units it had remaining in the AD-VANCE block.

Note that in cases 3 and 4, a seizing xact was in the future events chain at the time it was preempted.   This is only possible if it is residing in an ADVANCE block at the time.   But a seizing xact may be on a matching chain or the current events chain when it is preempted.   Cases 5 and 6, respectively, deal with these possibilities.

Case 5

A xact which has seized a facility may later enter a MATCH, ASSEMBLE, or GATHER block and be placed on the matching chain.   While it is in matching status, its *matching indicator* is set to 1.   During this time, the xact may be preempted on the facility which it had seized, in which case the following things are done to it:

1. Its *preempt flag* is set to one.   The preempt flag is simply one of the bits in one of the words which comprise a transaction in the computer's core.
2. The *preempt count* is incremented to one, assuming that the xact was not also preempted on any other facilities at the time.

The xact under discussion is simultaneously on the matching and interrupt chains, since both its matching indicator and its preempt count are not zero.   It will be returned to the current events chain only when *both of these are decremented to zero*.   Until that time, it remains in the MATCH, ASSEMBLE, or GATHER block.   This holds true regardless of whether it is removed from matching status before being removed from interrupt status or vice versa.

Case 6

A xact that has seized a facility may arrive at a point in the block diagram where its progress is blocked.   For example, it may come up against a SEIZE, GATE, TEST, or TRANSFER block which refuses entry.   Such xacts remain in the current events chain for as many clock updatings as necessary until the blocking condition is removed.   Let us look at this a bit more closely.

There are *two types of blocking conditions—unique* and *nonunique*.   Unique blocking is associated with SEIZE, PREEMPT, ENTER, and GATE blocks other than M and NM modes.   It results in the blocked xact being put into a delay chain; that is, inactive status in the current events chain.   Nonunique blocking is associated with GATE M and NM, TRANSFER BOTH and ALL, and TEST blocks. It results in the blocked xact being left in active status in the current events chain. The significance of inactive versus active status on the current events chain was explained in Chapter 8.

From the preceding paragraph, it is easy to see how a xact may be preempted on a (previously seized) facility *while it is in the current events chain.* Indeed, it may be preempted on several facilities while in this condition. At the time it is preempted, a xact in the current events chain may be in active or inactive status. In either case, the following rule applies:

Current events chain xacts which are preempted on one or more facilities will not be immediately placed on interrupt status. They will be removed from the current events chain only when they enter:

1. An ADVANCE block (as in cases 3 and 4).
2. A MATCH, ASSEMBLE, or GATHER block in which they are put into a matching condition (as in case 5).

Consequently, these xacts can move through an unlimited number of other block types, and they can be delayed (blocked) an unlimited number of times on the way.

Another consequence of the preceding rule is that xacts that are preempted while on the current events chain might never be put on interrupt status. For example, a xact which seized a facility, encountered a blocking condition, and then was preempted could release the facility it had seized by entering a RELEASE block. Alternately, the preempting xact may return the facility before the preempted xact enters an ADVANCE, MATCH, ASSEMBLE, or GATHER block.

Why are preempted current events chain xacts allowed to go "uninterrupted" in the manner that we have just described? Perhaps the best answer is that there is no point in "locking" them in a facility as long as they are not supposed to spend a specified number of clock units in possession of it.

11.4 MULTILEVEL PREEMPTING

Subfields B, C, D, and E of the PREEMPT block are associated with multilevel preempting. These subfields are defined in GPSS/360, GPS K, and Flow Simulator, but not in GPSS III.

Since multilevel preempting is not one of the essential features of GPSS, it will be covered in a more cursory fashion than simple preempting. We shall not consider every possible situation that may arise, nor will we examine the internal operations associated with subfields B to E of the PREEMPT block. But we will see how these arguments are used and how they affect the external behavior of the model.

The arguments used in subfields B, C, D, and E of the PREEMPT block are as follows:

B: The mnemonic "PR" is used if multilevel preempting is desired. If field B is blank, fields C, D, and E are ignored by the GPSS simulator.

C: A block address to which preempted xacts will be sent can be specified if desired. If field C is blank, fields D and E are ignored by the GPSS simulator.

D: A parameter number associated with the preempted xact may be specified. If it is, then the remaining time the xact is scheduled to remain in the future events chain (that is, the ADVANCE block) is placed in this parameter.

E: The mnemonic "RE" may be used to specify that the preempted xact should be completely removed from the NI chain for the facility. The effect is that it forfeits its claim on the facility.

The field C, D, and E options are ignored if the xact is not on the future events chain at the time it is preempted! To illustrate this statement, imagine that xact 50, with a priority of 5, arrives at a PREEMPT block which has arguments in fields A, B, and C. (It may or may not have its field D and/or E arguments specified.) Imagine also that xact 40, with a priority of 4, is presently preempting the field A facility. Xact 40 will be preempted by xact 50, but the operations performed upon the former depend on its status at the moment when it is preempted.

If xact 40 is in an ADVANCE block when xact 50 enters the PREEMPT block, the field C, D, E options will be invoked. But if xact 40 is in matching or interrupt status or is on the current events chain, the PREEMPT block will behave as if only fields A and B contained arguments. End of illustration.

The fundamental nature of multilevel preempting can be summarized as follows:

If a xact attempts to enter the PREEMPT block while the field A facility is being either seized or preempted, the newly arrived xact will succeed in capturing the facility if its own priority is greater than that of the xact it is trying to preempt. Otherwise it will be refused entry into the PREEMPT block.

This rule applies to the *arriving* xact, and it is quite straightforward. It applies whenever PR is coded in field B, irrespective of fields C, D, and E.

The *preempted* xact, on the other hand, may have a variety of things happen to it, depending on which subfields have entries as well as its status at the time it is preempted. The ensuing sections cover some of the more common circumstances that may arise.

Case 1

The most straightforward case of multilevel preempting is when fields A and B of the PREEMPT block have entries while the other three subfields are blank. This case is illustrated in Figure 11-5.

Imagine that xact 100 is preempting facility 1 when xact 105 arrives at the PREEMPT block. If the latter has a priority that is less than or equal to that of xact 100, it will not be allowed to enter the PREEMPT block. It will have to wait until facility 1 is returned by xact 100.

```
PREEMPT     1,PR

RETURN      1
```

Fig. 11-5. Excerpts from a GPSS program that uses multilevel preempting—case 1.

If xact 105 has a higher priority than xact 100, it will succeed in entering the PREEMPT block, and thus it will capture facility 1. The preempted xact will reacquire the facility after xact 105 has returned it. The precise status of xact 100 in the interim depends upon whether it was in the current events, future events, interrupt, or matching chain when preempted. As mentioned earlier, we will not delve into these detailed alternatives.

Case 2

In case 2, fields A, B, and C of the PREEMPT block have entries, while the other two are blank. This case is illustrated in Figure 11-6.

Imagine that xact 100 is preempting facility 1 when xact 105, with a higher priority, arrives at the PREEMPT block. The latter will, of course, enter the PREEMPT block and capture the facility. It will then proceed into the AD-VANCE block where it will remain for 120 clock units (unless it is preempted by a still higher priority xact).

When xact 105 entered the PREEMPT block, xact 100 was put on a list to reclaim facility 1 at the earliest opportunity, that is, when there are no higher priority xacts with a claim on it. Since xact 100 was on the future events chain when preempted, it was switched to the current events chain, scheduled to move

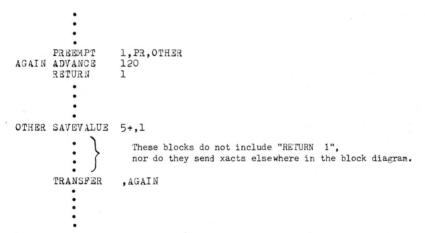

```
            PREEMPT      1,PR,OTHER
      AGAIN ADVANCE      120
            RETURN       1


      OTHER SAVEVALUE    5+,1
                    }    These blocks do not include "RETURN 1",
                    }    nor do they send xacts elsewhere in the block diagram.
            TRANSFER     ,AGAIN
```

Fig. 11-6. Excerpts from a GPSS program that uses multilevel preempting—case 2.

to the block specified in field C of the PREEMPT block. The preempt flag of xact 100 was also set, and its preempt count was incremented by 1.

So after xact 105 comes to rest in the ADVANCE block, xact 100 is moved directly into the SAVEVALUE block where savevalue 5 has its value incremented by 1. Xact 100 moves through several other blocks, indicated by dots with accompanying proviso in Figure 11-6. Depending on what effects these blocks have on it, xact 105 may or may not enter the TRANSFER ,AGAIN and ADVANCE 120 blocks at the present clock instant.

If it arrives at the ADVANCE block while xact 105 is in possession of facility 1, it is not allowed to enter that block and, at the same time, be merged into the future events chain; this is because its preempt flag is set. Instead, it is put on interrupt status where it remains until it can regain facility 1. Then it enters the ADVANCE block and again attempts to remain there for 120 uninterrupted clock units. Sooner or later, it will succeed in doing this, and then it will return facility no. 1.

Several aspects of case 2 deserve special emphasis. When xact 100 was preempted, it was put on a list to regain possession of facility 1. So regardless of where it might be in the block diagram, it would eventually become the possessor of facility 1 as far as the GPSS simulator was concerned. Therefore, the block diagram must be constructed to ensure that xact 100, as well as other xacts which are sent to the field C block address, will subsequently enter a RETURN 1 block. Incidentally, a preempted xact may return a facility before the preempting xact does so by the simple expedient of entering a RETURN block before it regains possession of the facility.

In Figure 11-6, xact 100 cannot return facility 1 until 120 clock units after it has been returned by xact 105. But if we were to replace the TRANSFER ,AGAIN block with a RETURN 1 block, xact 100 would return facility 1 before xact 105.

Looking at Figure 11-6, we notice that savevalue 5 serves as a counter which tells how many times xacts are preempted from facility 1. We also notice that regardless of how long a xact stays in the ADVANCE 120 block, it must start all over again if it is preempted. Thus we are simulating a situation where an interrupted xact must execute a complete recycle.

Case 3

In case 3, fields A, B, C, and D of the PREEMPT block have entries, while field E is blank. This case is illustrated in Figure 11-7, and it bears a fairly close resemblance to the case 2 illustration.

Imagine that xact 100 is preempting facility 1 when xact 105, with a higher priority, arrives at the PREEMPT block. As in case 2, xact 105 preempts facility 1 and enters the ADVANCE block. Xact 100 is put on the list for facility 1 and is merged into the current events chain just as before. But in this case, the remaining time in the ADVANCE block is put into parameter 3.

Xact 100 is sent to the block whose address is OTHER, just as before. But this time we tabulate P3 to obtain a tally of the time remaining when xacts are preempted. Otherwise case 3 is identical to case 2.

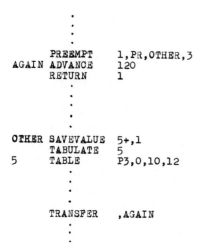

```
            .
            .
            .
       PREEMPT      1,PR,OTHER,3
AGAIN  ADVANCE      120
       RETURN       1
            .
            .
            .
OTHER  SAVEVALUE    5+,1
       TABULATE     5
5      TABLE        P3,0,10,12
            .
            .
            .
       TRANSFER     ,AGAIN
            .
            .
```

Fig. 11-7. Excerpts from a GPSS program that uses multilevel preempting—case 3.

Case 4

In case 4, all of the fields of the PREEMPT block have entries. This case is illustrated in Figure 11-8, and it bears some resemblance to case 3.

Imagine that xact 100 is preempting facility 1 when xact 105, with a higher priority arrives at the PREEMPT block. Xact 105 preempts facility 1, but since field E contains RE, xact 100 is not put on a list for the facility.

Xact 100 is sent to the block whose address is OTHER, and it increments savevalue 5. Then it waits its turn to seize facility 2. The amount of time spent in this facility is twice the remaining time in facility 1. After xact 100 releases this facility, its total time in both facilities is tabulated in table 5. In case it is not

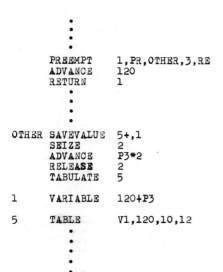

```
            .
            .
            .
       PREEMPT      1,PR,OTHER,3,RE
       ADVANCE      120
       RETURN       1
            .
            .
            .
OTHER  SAVEVALUE    5+,1
       SEIZE        2
       ADVANCE      P3*2
       RELEASE      2
       TABULATE     5
1      VARIABLE     120+P3
5      TABLE        V1,120,10,12
            .
            .
            .
```

Fig. 11-8. Excerpts from a GPSS program that uses multilevel preempting—case 4.

obvious, the definition statement for variable 1 was arrived at as follows:

Time spent in facility 1: $120 - P3$.

Time spent in facility 2: $2 \times P3$.

Total time spent in these facilities: $120 - P3 + 2 \times P3 = 120 + P3$.

Because xact 100 was not put on a list for facility 1, the program has no reason to award it this facility when it is returned by xact 105. Moreover, xact 100 should not attempt to return facility 1 at this point or an error will result.

The situation depicted in Figure 11-8 can be thought of as follows. Machine 1, represented by facility 1, is twice as fast as machine 2, represented by facility 2. If a job is preempted from machine 1, it is completed on machine 2. If it had time P3 remaining on machine 1, it would spend twice that amount of time on machine 2.

11.5   THE SMART SUPPLY DEPOT PROBLEM

The operation of a simple and not very efficient supply depot was simulated in illustrative program 5. It was mentioned that a more sophisticated supply depot would be simulated in illustrative program 7. For convenience, the previous model will be referred to as the "dumb depot" and the improved model as the "smart depot."

Illustrative program 7 is presented in this chapter because it utilizes PREEMPT/RETURN blocks. However, these blocks are used in a very elementary way, as you will see, and they are only of minor interest as far as program 7 is concerned. Our primary interest is in the overall model, especially the ways in which its results differ from those obtained with the dumb depot model.

Operation of the Smart Supply Depot

The smart depot has orders arriving at the same frequency as the dumb depot, and it is also staffed by a clerk and a stock handler. However, orders arrive in duplicate so that the clerk and stock handler can begin their respective tasks whenever they are ready rather than at the same time.

It is assumed that 80% of incoming orders can be filled and that 20% are for items that are out of stock. These figures are probabilities since the status of any given item is a matter of chance.

After picking up his copy of a newly arrived order at the front desk, the stock handler takes from 0.5 to 3.5 minutes to determine whether the specified item is in stock. If it is out of stock, he takes 0.5 minute to return to the front desk with the unfilled order form. He places it on the desk and picks up a copy of the next order if any have arrived. Otherwise, he waits until the next order arrives.

If the item is found to be in stock, the stock handler phones the clerk via the interline. This conversation typically takes 0.5 minute. The stock handler then takes 2 to 4 minutes to pack the item and bring it to the front desk. He places it on the desk and picks up a copy of the next order as soon as one arrives, and then he returns to the stock room.

When a new order arrives, the clerk begins the initial paperwork as soon as he is free to do so. He takes 0.5 to 2.5 minutes to make various entries that apply for all incoming orders, regardless of whether they are in stock. Then he waits until the stock handler either calls to tell him that the item is in stock or appears at the desk with nothing but an order form. While the clerk is waiting, he may begin to process the next order if one has arrived.

When a telephone call comes, the clerk always responds to it, and then he returns to whatever he had been doing. If he is told that a certain item is in stock, he will subsequently spend 0.5 to 4.5 minutes completing its paperwork. If the stock handler returns empty-handed, the clerk spends only 1 minute completing the paperwork.

The processing of an in-stock order is completed at the moment that the invoice (prepared by the clerk) is attached to the package (brought up by the stock handler). The processing of an out-of-stock order is completed when the duplicate copies of the order are both clipped to a reorder form. Thus the total amount of time required to process an order is measured from the time it arrives at the depot until the order forms and/or the item ordered are joined together. As with the dumb depot, we will assume that these final operations consume zero time.

The GPSS Model

A flow diagram of the smart supply depot model is shown in Figure 11-9. It is similar to—but not quite—a GPSS block diagram. The names in parentheses correspond to block addresses in program 7.

It is evident from Figure 11-9 that each parent xact represents the order form that is taken by the stock handler. To be more exact, a parent xact seizes the stock handler (denoted by the facility called STOCK) and does not release him until the order form has found its way back to the front desk. The path of parent transactions is shown by the heavy-line boxes in Figure 11-9. Note that a parent xact may follow either of two paths, depending on whether the item is in stock.

A copy xact is created by each arriving order xact; this copy represents the initial paperwork. After seizing the clerk (denoted by the facility called CLERK), this xact is destroyed, and the clerk is free to be seized again. A second copy xact is created by each parent xact after the status of the ordered item has been conveyed to the clerk. This copy xact represents the final paperwork, and it attempts to seize the clerk. Of course, the clerk may be interrupted at any time by a half-minute telephone call.

Illustrative Program 7

Program 7 is shown in Figure 11-10. As mentioned, the block addresses are keyed to those shown in Figure 11-9. This, coupled with the plentiful comments in the program listing, should obviate the need to explain the program. Instead, we mention a couple of pertinent aspects.

When an order can be filled, the stock handler spends a total of 5 to 15 clock

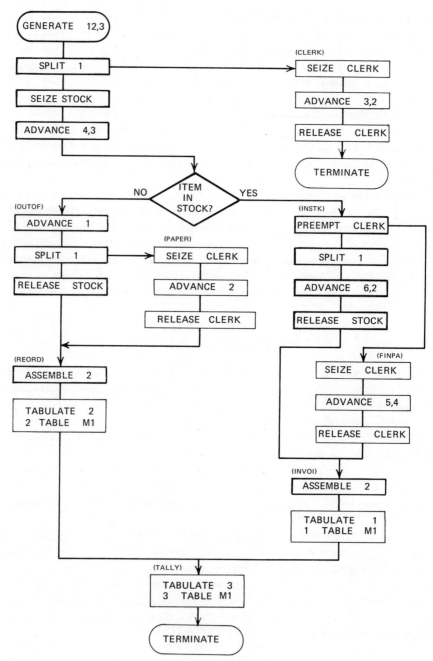

Fig. 11-9. Schematic diagram of smart supply depot model. 1 clock unit = 0.5 minute.

units processing it, not counting the telephone call. This is precisely how much time he spent on orders in the dumb depot. The clerk spends a total of 2 to 14 clock units on an in-stock order, not counting the telephone call. Again, this is exactly how much time he spent in the dumb depot.

This program yields 2 runs which simulate 2 consecutive days. Each day con-

```
* SMART SUPPLY DEPOT

        SIMULATE
        GENERATE    12,3        ORDERS ARRIVE EVERY 4.5 - 7.5 MIN.
        SPLIT       1,CLERK     DUPLICATE COPIES OF EACH ORDER
        SEIZE       STOCK       STOCK HANDLER TAKES ORDER FORM.
        ADVANCE     4,3         .5 - 3.5 MINUTES TO DETERMINE IF
*                              ITEM IS IN STOCK OR NOT.
        TRANSFER    .8,OUTOF,INSTK    ITEMS IN STOCK FOR 80% OF ORDERS

CLERK   SEIZE       CLERK       CLERK TAKES ORDER FORM.
        ADVANCE     3,2         .5 - 2.5 MIN. FOR PRELIM. PAPERWORK
        RELEASE     CLERK       CLERK CAN NOW DO WHATEVER IS WAITING
*                              TO BE DONE, INCLUDING JUST WAITING.
        TERMINATE               COPY XACT IS DESTROYED.

INSTK   PREEMPT     CLERK       STOCK HANDLER PHONES CLERK, AND CLERK
*                              TALKS TO HIM REGARDLESS OF WHAT ELSE
*                              HE WAS DOING AT THE TIME.
        ADVANCE     1           CONVERSATION TAKES .5 MINUTE.
        RETURN      CLERK       PHONE IS HUNG UP.  CLERK RETURNS TO
*                              WHATEVER HE WAS DOING, IF ANYTHING.
        SPLIT       1,FINPA     COPY XACT FOR PAPERWORK TO BE FINISHED
*                              IF ITEM IS IN STOCK.
        ADVANCE     6,2         STOCK HANDLER BRINGS PACKAGED ITEM TO
*                              FRONT DESK IN 2 - 4 MINUTES.
        RELEASE     STOCK       STOCK HANDLER READY FOR NEXT ORDER.
        TRANSFER    ,INVOI      ITEM NOT SHIPPED UNTIL INVOICE AFFIXED

FINPA   SEIZE       CLERK       CLERK FINISHES APPROPRIATE PAPERWORK
*                              IF ITEM IS IN STOCK.
        ADVANCE     5,4         THIS TAKES .5 - 4.5 MINUTES.
        RELEASE     CLERK       CLERK READY FOR NEXT ORDER.
INVOI   ASSEMBLE    2           ITEM WAITS FOR INVOICE OR VICE VERSA.
        TABULATE    1           TALLY TRANSIT TIMES FOR IN-STOCK ORDERS.
        TRANSFER    ,TALLY

OUTOF   ADVANCE     1           STOCK HANDLER RETURNS TO FRONT DESK .5
*                              MINUTE AFTER FINDING ITEM OUT OF STOCK.
        SPLIT       1,PAPER     COPY XACT FOR PAPERWORK TO BE FINISHED
*                              IF ITEM IS OUT OF STOCK
        RELEASE     STOCK       STOCK HANDLER READY FOR NEXT ORDER
        TRANSFER    ,REORD      REJOIN 2 COPIES OF UNFILLED ORDER.

PAPER   SEIZE       CLERK       CLERK FINISHES APPROPRIATE PAPERWORK IF
*                              ITEM IS OUT OF STOCK.
        ADVANCE     2           THIS TAKES 1 MINUTE.
        RELEASE     CLERK       CLERK READY FOR NEXT ORDER

REORD   ASSEMBLE    2           DUPLICATE COPIES OF ORDER REJOINED AND
*                              THROWN INTO "REORDER" BOX

        TABULATE    2           TALLY TRANSIT TIMES FOR OUT-OF-STOCK
                                ORDERS.

TALLY   TABULATE    3           TALLY TRANSIT TIMES FOR ALL ORDERS.
        TERMINATE

      1 TABLE       M1,2,2,20
      2 TABLE       M1,2,2,20
      3 TABLE       M1,2,2,20

        GENERATE    960         CREATE A TIMER XACT AFTER 480 MINUTES
*                              TO SIMULATE AN 8 HOUR DAY.
        TERMINATE   1           DESTROY TIMER XACT.
        START       1

        RESET                   RESET ALL SYSTEM STATISTICS, BUT DO
*                              NOT REMOVE ALL XACTS FROM MODEL.
*                              HAVING DONE THIS, REPEAT THE RUN FOR
*                              ANOTHER 8 HOUR SIMULATED PERIOD.
        START       1
        END
```

Fig. 11-10.   Illustrative program 7.

sists of 960 clock units which are equated to 480 minutes or 8 hours. The
RESET card does not clear the model of xacts. Hence any unfinished orders at
the end of the first day remain to be completed on the second day.

11.6 SIMULATION RESULTS

Analysis of Statistical Output

The output from program 7 is summarized in Table 11-1. For purposes of
comparison, the key statistics from program 5 are summarized in Table 11-2.

In comparing the smart and dumb depots, we first observe that the number of
orders to arrive is not the same for both depots on corresponding days. Why is
this so, considering that both programs use **GENERATE**   **12,3**? The reason
is explained in a while.

For the smart depot, 78% of the items ordered on the first day were in stock, as
were 83% of those ordered on the second day. No such distinction was made
with the dumb depot.

The utilization of the dumb depot was over 90% on both days, but the individual utilizations of the clerk and stock handler were not revealed. The problem
here is that the one who finishes first must wait for the other to finish. He is considered not to be busy only when his partner is not busy, that is, when both are
waiting for the next order to arrive.

The facility statistics for the smart depot are extremely significant because they
reveal that the clerk has a substantial amount of idle time each day. His respon-
sibilities might well be broadened, and the operation could thus be further optimized.

Offhand, we might expect the average time to process orders to be shorter in
the smart depot because out-of-stock orders are dispensed with in less time.
However, the statistical results do not support this expectation. For convenience, the average times to process orders are reproduced below:

	First Day	Second Day
Dumb depot	7.97 minutes	6.64 minutes
Smart depot	6.44 minutes	7.06 minutes

There are two reasons why the smart depot does not show a clear advantage
over the dumb depot. The first is that the smart depot permits the clerk to
begin a new order before he has finished the paperwork for the previous order.
Thus the processing time for some orders, as tabulated by the GPSS program,
includes time spent on another order.

The second reason why the statistics do not show a clear trend is that a 2-day
sample is not adequate to draw conclusions. The advisability and method of
simulating a longer period of time were discussed in Chapter 10 in connection
with illustrative program 5.

TABLE 11-1. SUMMARY OF RESULTS OF SMART SUPPLY DEPOT MODEL (INTERPRETED FROM PROGRAM 7 OUTPUT)

	First Day	Second Day
Total number of orders to arrive	78	77
Number of items in stock	60	64
Average number of minutes to process orders		
If item is in stock	6.78	7.46
It item is out of stock	5.33	5.07
All orders	6.44	7.06
Average utilization of facilities:		
Stock handler	0.806	0.841
Clerk	0.635	0.687

TABLE 11-2. SUMMARY OF RESULTS OF DUMB SUPPLY DEPOT MODEL (INTERPRETED FROM PROGRAM 5 OUTPUT)

	First Day	Second Day
Total number of orders to arrive	79	78
Average number of minutes to process orders	7.97	6.64
Average utilization of facility (depot)	0.949	0.903

It is interesting to note that the question of how fast orders are processed has turned out to be relatively unimportant. It is much more pertinent to ask how many orders the depot can handle in an average day. The dumb depot is obviously close to its limit since it is busy more than 90% of the time. But the smart depot could handle a substantial increase in the incoming order rate without falling behind.

This point can be easily verified by rerunning the two models with shorter interarrival times. This is not done here, but one point is reiterated: it is usually very easy to modify GPSS models by merely changing some of the constants.

Role of Random Numbers in Supply Depot Models

The role of random numbers is quite significant in program 7. Looking at Figure 11-10, we see that a random number is generated every time a xact enters the following blocks:

```
ADVANCE      4,3
TRANSFER     .8,OUTOF,INSTK
ADVANCE      3,2
ADVANCE      6,2
ADVANCE      5,4
```

Of course a random number is also generated every time the GENERATE block creates a transaction.

Since a random number seed is not specified anywhere in the program, the GPSS simulator automatically uses *RN1* to obtain the first random number in the run. The next time a random number is required, it is taken from the sequence of numbers that stem from RN1. Thus the four ADVANCE blocks as well as the TRANSFER and GENERATE blocks draw random numbers from this sequence, so to speak. For instance, the first GENERATE block may use the first, second, fifth, tenth, twelfth, and fifteenth numbers in this sequence.

You may recall that program 5 had the same randomly functioning GENER-ATE block as program 7. But it only had two ADVANCE blocks and no TRANSFER blocks that used random numbers. Thus the first GENERATE block would, in general, draw different members of the random number sequence which derives from RN1. This is why the number of xacts to arrive over a period of 960 clock units was not the same in both programs.

If it were desired to have an identical sequence of interarrival times in two programs, a function could be defined as shown in Figure 11-11.

The function called ARRIV produces uniformly distributed random numbers in the range 9 to 15. As long as RN5 is not specified elsewhere in the program, we can be assured of obtaining the same sequence of interarrival times whenever we use the cards shown in Figure 11-11.

11.7 DIFFERENCES BETWEEN GPSS/360 AND OTHER VERSIONS

From an external standpoint, the PREEMPT and RELEASE blocks are the same in GPS K and Flow Simulator as in GPSS/360. In GPSS III, however, fields B to E of the PREEMPT block are not defined, so of course there is no multilevel preempting.

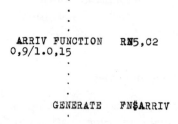

```
·
·
·
·
ARRIV FUNCTION    RN5,C2
0,9/1.0,15
·
·
·
·
GENERATE    FN$ARRIV
·
```

Fig. 11-11. Technique for making intercreation intervals independent of other random events in a GPSS model.

From an internal standpoint, there are some small differences in the way preempting is handled by the GPSS simulator. In GPS K, for example, the list of preempted xacts that were preempted by higher-priority xacts is referred to as an *atom chain*. This concept is used only in GPS K, and is not discussed here.

Except for the few differences just indicated, this chapter entails no other dissimilarities that have not been previously discussed.

11.8   SUMMARY

Program 7 contained nothing new except for the fact that it utilized preempting in a very simple way. The results of the simulation demonstrated, once again, that unexpected trends may be discovered which turn out to be of greater interest than the specific answers being sought.

Facilities have been discussed quite extensively in this book, at least on the upper and middle levels. So after making some comments about preempting, we take the opportunity to summarize the key aspects of facilities.

Preempting of Facilities

Two types of preempting are defined in GPSS. *Simple* (or *basic*) *preempting* is connoted by a blank B-field in the PREEMPT block. In this mode, xacts arriving at a PREEMPT block are awarded the facility on a first come, first served basis regardless of their priorities; and they all have the power to displace seizing xacts.

Multilevel (or *extended*) *preempting* is specified by placing PR in the B-field of the PREEMPT block. In this mode, an xact arriving at a PREEMPT block immediately captures the facility if its priority is higher than that of the currently preempting xact. The fate of the displaced xact depends on the arguments in fields C, D, and E of the PREEMPT block and also on its status in the model at the time it was preempted.

Under certain conditions, xacts that are preempted from a facility are put on an *interrupt* chain. While on this chain, they are ignored by the GPSS simulator and, of course, do not change their position in the block diagram.

Summary of Facilities

A facility is, above all, *an entity that can belong to only one transaction at a time*. The presence of a facility in a model is implied by the inclusion of SEIZE/RELEASE and/or PREEMPT/RETURN blocks; no definition cards are involved. Facility statistics are automatically maintained by the GPSS program, and they are updated wherever a transaction enters one of the four facility-oriented block types.

The GATE block can be used to control the flow of xacts through a model on the basis of whether a facility is in use, not in use, preempted, or not preempted. The COUNT and PREEMPT blocks can also directly affect xacts on the basis of the status of facilities.

Four standard numerical attributes are associated with facilities:

F_j Equals 1 if facility j is in use; equals 0 if facility j is not in use.

FR_j Utilization of facility j in parts per thousand.

FC_j Number of xacts that have entered facility j.

FT_j Average time/xact in facility j.

Four standard logical attributes are associated with facilities:

U_j True if facility j is in use.

NU_j True if facility j is not in use.

I_j True if facility j is being preempted.

NI_j True if facility j is not being preempted.

CHAPTER 12
Macros and User Chains

Macros and **user chains** are two features of GPSS that are entirely unrelated and dissimilar except for the fact that they can be useful to the programmer. They have been put into the same chapter only because the discussion of macros is much too short to stand as a chapter and, yet, had to go somewhere.

A macro is a string of blocks defined by the user which he may later represent with only one card. Thus a frequently used sequence of blocks may be defined as a macro, and a single card can thereafter be used in place of that block sequence. Macros are used to make a source program more compact; they are generally simple to use; and they have no effect on the model. This feature is available in GPSS/360 and GPS K but not in Flow Simulator and GPSS III.

User chains are one of the two types of *chain entities* in GPSS. (**Groups** are the other.) They allow the programmer to temporarily place transactions on inactive status and thus circumvent the operation of the control algorithm. User chains can improve the efficiency of a GPSS model (i.e., shorten the running time), and they also afford the user an additional means for controlling the flow of xacts.

12.1 MACROS

In some GPSS programs it happens that a particular string of blocks appears several times. In such cases it is convenient to define a macro which stands for that string of blocks so that a single MACRO card may thereafter be used instead of repeatedly writing out the individual blocks. The use of macros can shorten a program externally; that is the input deck will contain fewer cards. But the internal deployment and operation of the model are just as they would be if macros were not used.

Three cards are associated with macros: STARTMACRO, ENDMACRO, and MACRO. The first two precede and follow the string of blocks that is to be defined as a macro. A program can contain up to 50 macros, and they must be defined at the very beginning of the input program. The MACRO card is inserted wherever the corresponding string of blocks is supposed to appear in the model.

Coding Rules for Macros

The location field of the STARTMACRO card contains the name of the macro; it is a symbolic label invented by the user. The variable field of this card is always blank. Both the location and variable fields of the ENDMACRO card are always blank.

The location field of the MACRO card contains the name of the macro, exactly as it appears in the STARTMACRO card location field. The variable field of the MACRO card is coded as follows:

Subfield A: the argument to be used in place of #A.

Subfield B: the argument to be used in place of #B.

Subfield C: the argument to be used in place of #C.

    ·

    ·

    ·

Subfield J: the arguments to be used in place of #J.[1]

The coding of the MACRO card's variable field is undoubtedly a mystery to the reader at this point. It is best explained by showing an example. As a matter of fact, the *use* of macros is also best explained with the aid of an example. So let us by all means bring forth an example at this point.

Illustrative Program 8

Program 8 is shown in Figure 12-1. It is equivalent to illustrative program 3 (Figure 5-2) except that a macro is used rather than indirect addressing with AS-SIGN and LOOP blocks.

Looking at Figure 12-1, you can see that a macro has been defined to represent a string of six blocks. The name of the macro is USUAL, but it could be any symbolic address. The string of blocks which comprise the macro has symbols such as #A and #B in place of the usual arguments. The significance of these dummy arguments will soon become apparent.

Following the definition of the macro called USUAL, the SIMULATE, FUNC-TION, and GENERATE cards are identical to those in program 3. After entering the system, transactions proceed through a series of three queues and facilities, just as in program 3. These are represented by using our macro three times in succession. Let us see how this works.

The first MACRO card in program 8 is equivalent to the following string of blocks:

```
QUEUE       1
SEIZE       1
DEPART      1
ADVANCE     10,FN1
RELEASE     1
TABULATE    1
```

---

[1] The MACRO card permits entries in an unusually large number of subfields — 10, as compared to seven for the GENERATE card.

```
*  IDENTICAL TO ILLUSTRATIVE PROGRAM NO. 3, EXCEPT THAT IT USES
*  MACROS INSTEAD OF INDIRECT ADDRESSING.

USUAL STARTMACRO
          QUEUE       #A
          SEIZE       #A
          DEPART      #A
          ADVANCE     #B,#C
          RELEASE     #A
          TABULATE    #A
          ENDMACRO

          SIMULATE
      1 FUNCTION    RN5,C24
0,0/.1,.104/.2,.222/.3,.355/.4,.509/.5,.69/.6,.915/.7,1.2/.75,1.38/
.8,1.6/.84,1.83/.88,2.12/.9,2.3/.92,2.52/.94,2.81/.95,2.99/.96,3.2/
.97,3.5/.98,3.9/.99,4.6/.995,5.3/.998,6.2/.999,7/.9997,8

          GENERATE    15,FN1
USUAL MACRO         1,10,FN1
USUAL MACRO         2,10,FN1
USUAL MACRO         3,10,FN1
          TERMINATE   1

      1 TABLE       M1,10,10,10
      2 TABLE       M1,10,10,10
      3 TABLE       M1,10,10,10

          START       200
          END
```

Fig. 12-1. Illustrative program 8.

Thus #A = 1, #B = 10, and #C = FN1. Incidentally, this string of blocks appears in the symbolic listing (in the printout) immediately following the first MACRO card. This is one of the only instances when the symbolic listing is not an exact replica of the input deck.

The second MACRO card in program 8 specifies #A = 2, #B = 10, and #C = FN1. And the third MACRO card specifies #A = 3, #B = 10, and #C = FN1. It should be clear that #A denotes the A-field of the MACRO card; that is, it takes on the value of the A operand of the MACRO card. Similarly, #B denotes the B-field of the MACRO card, #C denotes the C-field, and so forth. Thus the strings of blocks represented by the second and third MACRO cards in program 8 are as shown below.

MACRO	2,10,FN1		MACRO	3,10,FN1
QUEUE	2		QUEUE	3
SEIZE	2		SEIZE	3
DEPART	2		DEPART	3
ADVANCE	10,FN1		ADVANCE	10,FN1
RELEASE	2		RELEASE	3
TABULATE	2		TABULATE	3

As mentioned earlier, program 8 is equivalent to program 3, and so the same output is obtained. Thus we take leave of illustrative program 8.

Fancier Usage of Macros

We have just seen a rather simple application of macros. However, their use can be extended to more complex situations. We shall not go into them in detail, but two of them will be mentioned.

Macros can be *nested* up to two levels. This means that a macro can be called within a macro that lies within another macro. To illustrate the concept of nested macros, Figure 12-2 shows a GPSS program in which a macro called AAA is nested within a macro called BBB. The coding and interpretation of nested macros are fairly straightforward and are not discussed here.

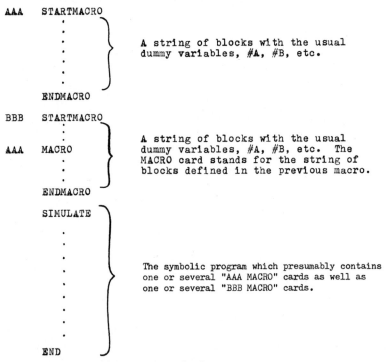

```
AAA    STARTMACRO
         .
         .                    A string of blocks with the usual
         .              ⎫     dummy variables, #A, #B, etc.
         .
         .
       ENDMACRO

BBB    STARTMACRO
         .
         .                    A string of blocks with the usual
AAA    MACRO                  dummy variables, #A, #B, etc.  The
         .                    MACRO card stands for the string of
         .                    blocks defined in the previous macro.
       ENDMACRO

       SIMULATE
         .
         .
         .
         .                    The symbolic program which presumably contains
         .                    one or several "AAA MACRO" cards as well as
         .                    one or several "BBB MACRO" cards.
         .
         .
         .
       END
```

Fig. 12-2.   Nesting of macros to one level.

From what has been said about macros thus far, it may seem that the string of objects sandwiched between the STARTMACRO and ENDMACRO cards always consists of user-specified blocks with dummy arguments in their variable fields. However, it is also permissible to use dummy arguments in place of some of the block names, that is, in the operation field. Thus we could define a macro such as

```
CCC    STARTMACRO
       QUEUE          #A
       #B             #A
       DEPART         #A
       ADVANCE        #C,#D
       #E             #A
       ENDMACRO
```

In this case, the B-field and E-field of the MACRO card would specify block types. This obviously affords greater flexibility in the use of macros, since a macro can stand for several different strings of blocks. The use of macros in this way is explained in reference 2.

12.2   USER CHAINS

Thus far we have encountered the current events, future events, delay, matching, and interrupt chains. These are not classified as entities, except in Flow Simulator. The two remaining chains—*user chains* and *groups*—are regarded as entities. They have block types and SNAs associated with them, and they are established and manipulated at the user's discretion. Groups are not covered in this book; user chains are discussed now.

User chains are associated with the LINK/UNLINK blocks. They enable a programmer to place xacts on inactive status on a user chain and to later restore them to active status. To put it another way, xacts can be removed from the current events chain and linked to a user chain until they are later returned to the former. Xacts which enter a LINK block are (not always) placed on a user chain. Xacts which enter the UNLINK block cause *other* (inactive) xacts to be unlinked from a user chain and merged into the current events chain.

What good are user chains? They allow the user to partially circumvent the normal operation of the GPSS simulator. This extends his ability to manipulate xacts, and it also permits more efficient running simulations in some cases. In addition, the LINK/UNLINK blocks have a number of options for sending xacts to various places or stalling them, depending on the status of user chains.   And the user chain-oriented SNAs can be used to relate the behavior of the model to the status of user chains. Some of these things are brought out in the ensuing discussion.

Coding Rules for LINK/UNLINK Blocks

The variable field of the LINK block contains the following arguments:

A: Address of the user chain to which entering xacts will be linked.
B: A symbol (FIFO or LIFO) or a parameter number that defines the ordering of the chain, that is, the way in which newly arrived xacts are merged into it.
C: Address of block to which xacts proceed if they are not put on the field A chain.

If field C is blank, every xact that enters the LINK block is merged into a user chain. If field C is not blank, entering xacts may either be put on a user chain or sent to the field C block, depending on the status of the *link indicator*. This will be explained soon.

The variable field of the UNLINK block contains the following arguments:

A: Number of the user chain from which xacts will be unlinked.
B: Address of the next block to which unlinked xacts are sent.

C: *Unlink count:* either a number (a SNA) or the word "ALL" specifies how many xacts should be unlinked from the user chain, subject to the field D argument, when a xact enters the UNLINK block.

D: A symbol (BVj or BACK) or a parameter number that defines the way in which xacts are to be unlinked from the user chain.

E: An argument whose value is matched with the value of Pj (specified in field D) of xacts on the user chain.

F: Address of next block for entering xacts under certain circumstances; for example, if no xacts are unlinked from user chain.

The use of subfields D, E, and F is optional. Any or all of them may be used with one restriction: Field E can be used only if field D contains a parameter number; it must be blank if field D contains BACK or BVj.

The foregoing rules will make more sense when we look at some examples of how various combinations of LINK/UNLINK block arguments work. In the process of discussing these examples, most of the variable field options are explained.

Case 1

Case 1 deals with the simplest possible usage of the LINK/UNLINK blocks. Field C of the LINK block is blank as are fields D, E, F of the UNLINK block. An example is given in Figure 12-3.

The presence of LINK/UNLINK blocks in the input program causes user chains to be established. Each user chain has a link indicator associated with it, and this indicator may either be *on* or *off*. If field C of the LINK block is blank, the indicator is always on. If it is not blank, the indicator is initially off.

For the program segment depicted in Figure 12-3, user chain 5 would be established, and its link indicator would always be on. When a xact enters the

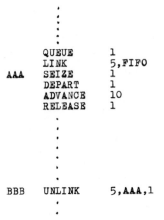

Fig. 12-3. Excerpts from a GPSS program that uses LINK/ UNLINK blocks — case 1.

LINK block, here is what happens:

1. The field A argument is evaluated and it is ascertained that user chain 5 is the one to which the entering xact will be linked.
2. The field B argument is evaluated to determine whether the xact will be placed at the rear of user chain 5 (which it will in this case), or at the front (LIFO), or according to the value of a parameter.

A xact that enters the LINK block in Figure 12-3 remains dormant in that block until it is finally removed from user chain 5.   At that time, it is merged into the current events chain so that the scan can move it to the next sequential block.

Now let us see what happens when a xact enters the UNLINK block in Figure 12-3:

1. The field A argument is evaluated to determine the user chain address.
2. The user chain is tested to determine whether there are any xacts on it. If there are no xacts in user chain 5, the xact that entered the UNLINK block proceeds directly to the next sequential block.
3. If there are any xacts in chain 5, the field C argument is evaluated, and it is determined that one xact should be removed from the chain.   This xact is unlinked from the beginning of the chain.
4. The xact that was removed from the user chain will be placed on the current events chain scheduled to enter the (SEIZE) block specified in field B of the UNLINK block.
5. The xact that entered the UNLINK block proceeds to the next sequential block.

Note that xacts that enter the LINK block in Figure 12-3 would never leave it if no xacts entered the UNLINK block at BBB.   Note also that xacts that enter the UNLINK block need not be "related" in any way to the xacts that are unlinked from the user chain.   A single xact can cause one or more xacts to be removed from the user chain, depending on the unlink count in field C of the UNLINK block.

Case 2

Case 2 is illustrated in Figure 12-4.   It is outwardly similar to case 1 except that (1) field C of the LINK block is used and (2) the UNLINK block immediately follows the RELEASE block. As you will see, these small changes make a big difference in the behavior of the model.

The first xact to enter the LINK block finds the link indicator off, so it is not placed on user chain 5.   Instead, it turns on the link indicator and takes the field C exit to the SEIZE block.   Having seized facility 1, it proceeds to the ADVANCE block whereupon it is merged into the future events chain.

Assume that the second xact arrives while the first xact is in facility 1.   Upon entering the LINK block, xact 2 finds the link indicator on and is therefore merged into user chain 5.   It is alone on the user chain at this point.

```
                .
                .
                .
                .
                .
        QUEUE       1
        LINK        5,FIFO,AAA
AAA     SEIZE       1
        DEPART      1
        ADVANCE     10
        RELEASE     1
        UNLINK      5,AAA,1
                .
                .
                .
                .
                .
```

Fig. 12-4. Excerpts from a GPSS program that uses LINK/UNLINK blocks — case 2.

Xact 1 releases the facility and enters the UNLINK block, whereupon the following operations are carried out:

1. The first xact on the user chain (xact 2) is unlinked since there is a "1" in the UNLINK block's C-field, and it is merged into the current events chain scheduled to enter the SEIZE block specified in field B of the UNLINK block.

2. The status change flag is set to ensure that the current events chain scan will latch onto xact 2 at the present clock time.

3. The link indicator is not turned off because a xact was able to be unlinked from the user chain.

After the UNLINK block subroutine has been executed, xact 1 leaves the UNLINK block and is moved as far as possible by the current events chain scan. Then xact 2 seizes facility 1, enters the ADVANCE block, and is merged into the future events chain.

Assume that no other xacts arrive at the LINK block while xact 2 is in the AD-VANCE block. When xact 2 enters the UNLINK block, the following things happen:

1. User chain 5 is tested and is found to contain no xacts.

2. Since user chain 5 contains no xacts, its link indicator is turned off.

Transaction 2 then proceeds to the next sequential block, and so on.

Now let us summarize the behavior of the LINK block when all three fields have entries. When a transaction enters, it may find the link indicator for the field A user chain either on or off. If it is *on*, the xact is linked into the user chain in the manner prescribed in field B, and it remains in the LINK block until it is eventually unlinked from the user chain. If the link indicator is *off*, it is turned on, and the entering xact is not merged into the user chain but is sent to the field C block.

Before we leave Figure 12-4 and case 2, it should be pointed out that the use of LINK/UNLINK blocks can reduce the running time of this program. To see this, imagine that the LINK/UNLINK blocks are deleted from Figure 12-4. Now imagine that 20 xacts queue up at the SEIZE block while xact 1 is in facility 1. When xact 1 releases the facility, all 20 of these xacts are switched from inactive status (in a delay chain) to active status on the current events chain. As soon as one of them seizes facility 1, the remaining 19 xacts are restored to inactive status. It is obviously inefficient to switch the status of so many xacts that do not have a chance to enter the facility anyway.

Now let us consider the Figure 12-4 model, as is. If 20 xacts arrive at the LINK block while facility 1 is being seized by xact 1, they will all be put into user chain 5. When xact 1 releases facility 1, nothing is done to those 20 xacts because they are not in the current events chain. When xact 1 enters the UNLINK block, the first xact in user chain 5 will be unlinked and will now be able to seize facility 1. The remaining 19 xacts will not even be looked at. Clearly this is more efficient than it would be without the LINK/UNLINK blocks.

Case 3

Case 3 is illustrated in Figure 12-5. It is outwardly identical to case 2 except that we now use field F of the UNLINK block. As stated in the coding rules, this argument specifies the address of the next block for xacts that enter the UNLINK block and find no xacts able to be unlinked from the field A user chain.

When a transaction enters the UNLINK block, a test is made to determine if there are any xacts in user chain 5. If there are, the one at the front is unlinked and sent to block AAA, and the link indicator remains on. Then the entering xact proceeds to the next sequential block. This is no different than in case 2.

If, when a transaction enters the UNLINK block, no xacts are found to be on user chain 5, the link indicator is turned off, and the entering xact is sent to the block at address BBB.

Thus case 3 is identical to case 2 except when a xact enters the UNLINK block and finds the user chain empty. In this circumstance, the entering xact is sent to the field F address rather than to the next sequential block. To put it in more concrete terms: If a xact that causes facility 1 to be released finds that there are

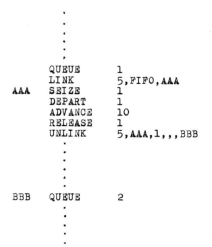

```
            QUEUE       1
            LINK        5,FIFO,AAA
      AAA   SEIZE       1
            DEPART      1
            ADVANCE     10
            RELEASE     1
            UNLINK      5,AAA,1,,,BBB
              .
              .
              .
              .
      BBB   QUEUE       2
              .
              .
```

Fig. 12-5. Excerpts from a GPSS program that uses LINK/UNLINK blocks—case 3.

no xacts waiting to seize it, the xact proceeds to the field F block address rather than to the next sequential block after UNLINK.

Case 4

Case 4, shown in Figure 12-6, is outwardly identical to case 2 except that field D of the UNLINK block is used. The behavior of case 4 is also identical to that of case 2 except for one aspect: When a xact enters the UNLINK block, the GPSS program examines its parameter 3. Then it checks the P3 values of the xacts in user chain 5, starting at the front of the chain. As soon as it finds a xact with P3 equal to P3 of the xact in the UNLINK block, it unlinks that xact from chain 5.

This feature allows the programmer to remove specific xacts from the user chain. For example, it may be desired to keep a certain xact out of circulation until a certain event takes place in the model. We could assign a number such as *641* to P3 (for example) of both the "out of circulation" xact and the "certain event" xact. We would organize the block diagram so that the latter xact would enter an UNLINK block immediately after the event occurred, thus reactivating the other xact.

In Figure 12-6, we could have specified BACK rather than a parameter number in field D of the UNLINK block. In this case, one xact would be unlinked from the rear of user chain 5 each time an xact entered the UNLINK block.

We could also specify a boolean variable BVj in field D. If this is done, here is what happens. The value of BVj is computed whenever a xact enters the UNLINK block. If Bvj = 0, no xacts are unlinked from the user chain. If BVj = 1, the number of xacts specified in field C of the UNLINK block are unlinked from the front of the user chain.

It is evident that fields C and D of the UNLINK block work in conjunction with each other. If field D is blank, the number of xacts specified in field C is removed from the *front* of the user chain. If field D contains BACK, the number of xacts specified in field C is removed from the *rear* of the user chain. If field D specifies Pj, the number of xacts specified in field C which have their *j*th

```
        .
        .
        .
        .
        QUEUE       1
        LINK        5,FIFO,AAA
AAA     SEIZE       1
        DEPART      1
        ADVANCE     10
        RELEASE     1
        UNLINK      5,AAA,1,3
        .
        .
        .
        .
```

Fig. 12-6. Excerpts from a GPSS program that uses LINK/UNLINK blocks—case 4.

parameter equal to Pj of the current xact are unlinked from the user chain, starting from its front end.

Case 5

Case 5, shown in Figure 12-7, is outwardly identical to case 4 except that field E of the UNLINK block is used. The behavior of case 5 is also identical to that of case 4 except for one aspect: the first xact whose P3 is found to be equal to the value of X8 (i.e., the SNA in field E of the UNLINK block) is unlinked from user chain 5.

```
              .
              .
              .
              .
       QUEUE      1
       LINK       5,FIFO,AAA
AAA    SEIZE      1
       DEPART     1
       ADVANCE    10
       RELEASE    1
       UNLINK     5,AAA,1,3,X8
              .
              .
              .
              .
```

Fig. 12-7. Excerpts from a GPSS program that uses LINK/UNLINK blocks—case 5.

Case 6

Case 6, shown in Figure 12-8, utilizes all fields of the LINK and UNLINK blocks. The outward appearance as well as the behavior of this case differ from the previous case in only one respect: If, when a xact enters the UNLINK block, no xact can be unlinked from user chain 5, the xact will be sent to the block whose address is BBB rather than to the next sequential block. There are two circumstances in which no xact is unlinked from user chain 5:

1. If there are no xacts in user chain 5.

2. If none of the xacts in user chain 5 have their values of P3 equal to X8.

```
              .
              .
              .
              .
       QUEUE      1
       LINK       5,FIFO,AAA
AAA    SEIZE      1
       DEPART     1
       ADVANCE    10
       RELEASE    1
       UNLINK     5,AAA,1,3,X8,BBB
              .
              .
              .
              .
```

Fig. 12-8. Excerpts from a GPSS program that uses LINK/UNLINK blocks—case 6.

To recapitulate the operation of the LINK and UNLINK blocks, let us briefly run through a representative sequence of events in case 6.

Assume that xact 1 enters the LINK block and finds user chain 5 empty and the link indicator off. The link indicator is turned on, and xact 1 proceeds to the block whose address is in field C, namely, the SEIZE block. Xact 1 seizes facility 1 and comes to rest in the ADVANCE block.

Assume that xact 2 arrives at the LINK block several clock units later. Since the link indicator is on, it is immediately merged into user chain 5.

Assume that xact 3 arrives at the LINK block in the next clock instant. It also finds the link indicator to be on, and it is merged into user chain 5 behind xact 2 since FIFO is specified in field B.

Ten clock units after it seized facility 1, xact 1 releases it and enters the UNLINK block. User chain 5 is tested and is found to contain transactions. P3 of xact 2 is examined. If it is equal to the current value of savevalue 8, xact 2 will be unlinked. Otherwise, P3 of xact 3 will be examined. Let us assume that xact 2 meets the test and is unlinked from user chain 5. It will be scheduled to attempt to enter block AAA.

Xact 1 now proceeds to the next sequential block. It does not go to BBB because a xact was able to be unlinked from user chain 5. Xact 2 now seizes facility 1. And so it goes.

User Chain Standard Numerical Attributes

There are five standard numerical attributes associated with user chains.

CAj is the average number of xacts on user chain j. It is equal to the *cumulative time integral* divided by the relative clock time. The cumulative time integral is the sum of all of the clock units spent by all of the xacts on user chain j up to the moment when CAj is requested. To clarify the meaning of CAj, let us imagine that CA7 is used as a block argument somewhere in a GPSS model and that a transaction happens to enter that block when C1 = 100. Assume that four xacts have spent time in user chain 7 up to this point:

Xact 2: 23 clock units.

Xact 6: 42 clock units.

Xact 7: 37 clock units.

Xact 9 (presently in user chain 7): 28 clock units.

The cumulative time integral is simply the sum of 23, 42, 37, and 28. So CA7 = 130/100 = 1.3.

CHj is the current number of xacts on user chain j. If CH7 in the example above were referenced at C1 = 100, it would have a value of 1.

CMj is the maximum number of xacts simultaneously on user chain j thus far.

CCj is the total number of xacts that have been on user chain j thus far.

CTj is the average time each xact was on user chain j. It is equal to the cumulative time integral for user chain j, divided by the number of xacts that have been on user chain j, that is, CCj.

12.3 DIFFERENCES BETWEEN GPSS/360 AND OTHER VERSIONS

The LINK/UNLINK blocks, user chains, and user chain SNAs are the same in all four versions of GPSS with the following exceptions:

1. BVj is not permitted in the UNLINK block D-field in Flow Simulator and GPSS III, since these versions do not include boolean variables.

2. CHj is the only SNA provided for user chains in GPSS III.

As mentioned at the beginning of this chapter, Flow Simulator and GPSS III do not provide the macro feature. GPS K includes macros, but there are a number of differences between GPS K and GPSS/360 macros. The remainder of this section deals with macros in GPS K.

There is no limit to the number of macro calls a user may define in his model, so long as the computer can accommodate all of the cards and entities they represent. There is also no limit to how many macros can be nested, one within the other.

The STARTMACRO and ENDMACRO cards are coded as in GPSS/360, but the macro name must appear in field A of both cards rather than just the former.

Instead of a MACRO card, GPS K uses the following card to call a macro:

Column 1: the letter M.

Columns 8 to 13: the user-defined macro name.

Columns 19 and on: parameters that replace the arguments in the macro definition.

The dummy arguments in the macro definition are denoted by $\#j$, where j can be either a number or a letter. The $\#1$ is the same as $\#A$; $\#2$ is the same as $\#B$; and so forth.

12.4 SUMMARY

Macros can be used in GPSS/360 and GPS K to streamline a GPSS program. A macro is a string of blocks that is defined at the very beginning of a model and is thereafter inserted by the GPSS program wherever it is called by a MACRO card (M card in GPS K). The use of macros does not conserve core space since every block and entity implied by calling a macro must be individually represented inside the computer.

User chains are established and manipulated by LINK and UNLINK blocks. Fields A and B of the LINK block and fields A, B, and C of the UNLINK block must have entries. The use of LINK block field C and UNLINK block fields D, E, and F is optional.

Xacts that enter a LINK block are put on a user chain if the chain's link indicator is on. They remain on this chain in an inactive status until the entry of some other xact into an UNLINK block causes them to be unlinked. Inactive xacts on a user chain reside in the LINK block in the block diagram.

Xacts may be linked to a user chain in various ways, depending on the field B argument of the LINK block. They may be placed at the front, the rear, or in a position corresponding to the value of a specified parameter.

When a xact enters an UNLINK block, the first step is to unlink one or more xacts from the user chain, if possible. The unlinking can be done from the front, the rear, or according to values of a specified parameter. The second step is to send the xact that entered the UNLINK block to the appropriate next block.

CHAPTER 13

Output Options

We have seen that a GPSS simulation run automatically yields a properly formatted printout of the relevant system statistics. No special cards need be included to request this output or specify its format. This is the *standard output option*. It can be thought of as a super default option that is built into all four versions of GPSS and can be characterized as follows:

1. You get it without having to ask for it.
2. It affords virtually no control over the output *format*, but it does allow you to exercise several options with regard to *what* is output and *when*.

All of the standard output options are exercised via the following four cards: START, PRINT, TRACE, and UNTRACE. The first is a control card, and the other three are block types. These cards are discussed in Section 13.1.

In addition to the standard output, GPSS/360, GPS K, and Flow Simulator offer an *output editor*, or *report generator* feature that allows the programmer to dictate the *contents and format* of the output. The output editor includes two options. One pertains to the selection of output statistics as well as their spacing, titling, and layout. The other pertains to the representation of SNA values and tables in the form of bar graphs.

The report generator does not allow the user to have any statistics displayed other than those that would appear in the standard output. It merely allows him to delete unwanted statistics and to customize the arrangement and wording of the printout.

The output editor is invoked by inserting a series of special cards (described in Sections 13.2 and 13.3) after the last START card in the input deck. The rules for coding these cards are relatively tedious, and they are somewhat cumbersome to use at first. For this reason—and because the report generator does not enable the user to obtain any data not obtainable from the standard output—the following approach has been taken:

1. The portion of the output editor pertaining to the selection and formatting of output statistics is fully covered in Section 13.2 for GPSS/360. But the differences between GPSS/360 and GPS K and Flow Simulator—which are in some cases significant—are not spelled out in detail in the section describing differences (Section 13.4).
2. The portion of the output editor pertaining to the graphic output is covered in Section 13.3 for GPSS/360, but not in complete detail. The dif-

217

ferences between GPSS/360 and the other two versions—which are relatively minor—are again not fully spelled out in Section 13.4.

The reader can skim or skip Sections 13.2 and 13.3 until such time as he wishes to become more familiar with the output editor option. But the material having to do with the standard output (in Section 13.1 and parts of Sections 13.4 and 13.5) should *not* be browsed over too casually.

13.1 STANDARD OUTPUT

We can define the *normal standard output* as consisting of the portion of the printout that is produced by the GPSS simulator at the end of a run following the input listing. If we were to run a model that contained at least one of every entity type, the normal output would consist of the following:

Clock times.

Block counts.

Savevalue contents.

Matrix savevalue contents.

Facility statistics.

Storage statistics.

Queue statistics.

Frequency tables.

These figures and statistics are collected and computed continuously as the run proceeds. Thus the run could be suddenly halted at any time, and the statistics up to that instant could be displayed. (In addition, it is possible to display the current status of logic switches as well as the status and composition of transaction chains.) This suggests that a GPSS simulation run can be momentarily frozen at any time to have a snapshot taken, and then it could resume as though nothing had happened. From this point of view, the normal output can be characterized as giving a picture of the model at the instant when the run termination count is reduced to zero.

The foregoing comments imply a couple of facts about the GPSS standard output:

1. It is possible to have transaction chain and logic switch data printed out, although these are not included in the normal output.
2. It is possible to have various data printed out while the run is in progress—not only when it ends.

These options can be invoked by using one or more of the following:

1. Fields C and D of the START card.
2. PRINT block.
3. TRACE/UNTRACE blocks.

The four card types are now described.

START Card

The START card has three main functions:

1. It tells the simulator that the input cards have all been received so that the run can start.
2. It specifies the *run termination count* which, in combination with one or more TERMINATE blocks, determines the simulation run length.
3. It provides several options which pertain to the standard output.

As you know, field A of the START card contains the run termination count. When this count has been decremented to zero or less, the run ceases, and the final accumulated statistics for the system are printed out.

If the mnemonic "NP" is entered in field B of the START card, no printout of output statistics will occur at the end of the run. This option does not affect the normal accumulation of system statistics; it merely prevents their being printed. This feature is useful for priming a model so that a steady state condition can be reached before statistics are accumulated which will be printed out.

Field C of the START card can be used to specify a *snap interval count* which is decremented in the same way as the field A termination count. When the snap interval count has been reduced to zero or less, a normal statistical output occurs. The snap interval count is reinitialized to its original value, and the decrementing process begins again. This process is repeated until the field A termination count is decremented to zero. This feature allows the user to obtain statistics during a simulation run as well as at the end of it. Consider the following example:

```
START     500,,150
```

In this example, the snap interval count will be decremented to zero three times during the run — when the run termination count is 350, 200, and 50. The first snap interval printout would be entitled "SNAP 1 OF 3," and it would show the status of the model after 150 terminations. The second snap interval printout would show the status of the model after 300 terminations. It would show the statistics accumulated *since the beginning* of the run, not since the previous snap interval. SNAP 3 OF 3 would show the statistics after 450 terminations. The final statistics would, of course, be printed after 500 terminations.

Field D of the START card may be used to indicate that the statistical output (at snap intervals as well as at the end of the run) should also include a listing of transactions in the current events chain, future events chain, user chains, interrupt status, and matching status. This option is invoked by entering the numeric character "1" in field D.

PRINT Block

The PRINT block is used to obtain a specified statistical output whenever it is entered by a transaction. The operation of the PRINT block can best be explained by means of an example:

```
PRINT     1,4,F
```

Every time a xact enters this block, the statistics for facilities 1 through 4 will be printed out.   They will be current statistics; that is, what we would get if the run were to end at that point.   They will have the standard format for facility statistics.

Fields A and B of the PRINT block contain the lower and upper index numbers, respectively, of the range of entities we want to have printed out.   If these fields are blank (commas in columns 19 and 20), then statistics will be printed for *all* of the field C entities that are in the model.   Note that a PRINT block can be used to specify only one type of entity; thus facilities and queues (for instance) cannot be specified on the same PRINT card.

Table 13-1 contains a list of the mnemonics that can be used in field C.   Note that fields A and B should be blank if field C contains MOV, FUT, I, MAT, or C. If the other mnemonics are used, fields A and B may both have entries, or they may both be blank.   The field A and B entries can be SNAs or indirect addresses.   Two examples will now be given:

PRINT   ,,S   The statistics for every storage in the model will be printed
                     whenever a transaction enters this block.

PRINT   *5,*5,T   The table whose index number is given by parameter 5 of
                     the entering xact will be printed.

Field D of the PRINT card can be used for a *paging indicator*.   If field D is left blank, a page will be skipped before each print operation.   But if field D contains any alphameric character, a page will not be skipped before each print operation.

TABLE 13-1. FIELD C MNEMONICS FOR PRINT BLOCK

MOV	Current events chain	
FUT	Future events chain	
I	Interrupt chain	Fields A and B should
MAT	Matching chain	be blank
C	Relative and absolute clock times	
B or N or W	Block counts	
F	Facility statistics	
S	Storage statistics	
Q	QUEUE statistics	
T	Table statistics	
U	User chain statistics	
CHA	User chain listing	Fields A and B may or
LG	Status of logic switches	may not have entries
G	Current members of group	
X or blank	Contents of fullword savevalue(s)	
XH	Contents of halfword savevalue(s)	
MX	Contents of fullword matrix savevalue(s)	
MH	Contents of halfword matrix savevalue(s)	

PRINT blocks should be used with discretion because something is printed every time a transaction enters one. It is usually wise to make sure that only a limited number of transactions will enter the PRINT blocks in your program when you use them.

TRACE and UNTRACE Blocks

The TRACE and UNTRACE blocks are used to verify that xacts are following the desired paths through the block diagram. The coding of these blocks is utterly simple: the location and variable fields are always blank.

When a xact enters a TRACE block, its *tracing indicator* (flag) is set. It remains set until the xact enters an UNTRACE block. If a xact whose tracing indicator is set enters a TRACE block, nothing happens. It simply passes directly to the next sequential block. By the same token, the UNTRACE block has no effect on xacts whose tracing indicator is *not* set. Thus a xact may pass through several TRACE blocks with no intervening UNTRACE blocks. Also, a xact that was never flagged may pass through one or more UNTRACE blocks with no effect.

So far we have said that a xact has its tracing indicator set by a TRACE block and turned off by an UNTRACE block. Every time a flagged xact enters a block, a line of output is produced which says the following, in an abbreviated form:

Transaction number _____ moved from block _____ to _____ at clock time _____, and the present value of the run termination count is _____.

This is followed by a second line of output which contains information pertaining to the xact such as its priority, assembly set number, and parameter contents.

The progress of a flagged xact will be printed out as it moves through the block diagram. This will cease to occur only when it enters an UNTRACE or TERMINATE block.

The TRACE/UNTRACE blocks should be used with caution, since a flagged xact causes a printout every time it enters a block. A useful technique is shown in Figure 13-1.

A single xact is created by the second GENERATE block, and it immediately has its tracing indicator set. The progress of this xact through the model is

```
        GENERATE   100,FN3,200
        TRANSFER   ,AAA
        GENERATE   100,,,1
        TRACE
AAA       .
          .
          .
          .
          .
          .

        UNTRACE
          .
          .
          .
```

Fig. 13-1. Efficient technique for tracing the progress of transactions through a block diagram.

printed out until it enters the UNTRACE block. All of the other (unflagged) xacts pass through the UNTRACE block with no effect.

13.2   REPORT GENERATOR: STATISTICAL OUTPUT

The output editor includes a total of 15 card types (16 in GPS K and 10 in Flow Simulator). These can be classified as *control, editing* (or *statistic selection*), and *graph* cards. The distinction between control and editing cards is somewhat arbitrary, and both types are covered in this section. The graph cards are covered in Section 13.3. For the sake of perspective, the output editor cards and their classifications are shown in Table 13-2 for GPSS/360.

The services of the output editor are obtained by placing a REPORT card after the last START card. The REPORT card is followed by a series of *output editor request cards* which specify the statistical and/or graphic outputs desired.

The output editor is designed to "press on regardless." If an error is detected in an output editor request card, a message is printed, and the card is not processed. Request cards are processed independently, irrespective of whether other request cards have errors. If any of the output editor request cards are found to be in error, the standard output is automatically listed after the last request card has been serviced.

Before starting our discussion of the control and editing cards, we should mention the following:

1. The material in this section applies fairly faithfully to GPS K.
2. Of the nine cards involved, only four (REPORT, COMMENT, FORMAT, and TEXT) are included in Flow Simulator, but they have a broader range

TABLE 13-2.   OUTPUT EDITOR CARDS

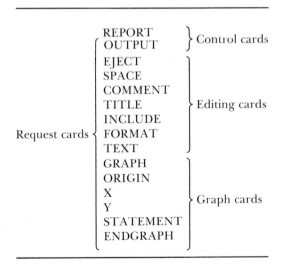

	REPORT OUTPUT	Control cards
Request cards	EJECT SPACE COMMENT TITLE INCLUDE FORMAT TEXT	Editing cards
	GRAPH ORIGIN X Y STATEMENT ENDGRAPH	Graph cards

of functions which enables them to more or less duplicate the capabilities of the nine control and editing cards in GPSS/360.

REPORT Card

The REPORT card always has blank location and variable fields. It is used to call the report generator, and it must precede all of the output editor request cards. If a REPORT card is encountered in the midst of the request cards, an error message will be printed, and the remaining cards will be processed as though nothing were wrong.

The presence of the REPORT card cancels the normal standard output unless the following occur:

1. There is an error among the output editor request cards.
2. An OUTPUT card is included as one of the output editor request cards.
3. There are no output editor request cards.

EJECT and SPACE Cards

The EJECT card is used to ensure that the next item of output requested will start on a new page. It may be desirable to place an EJECT card immediately after the REPORT card so that the output will start on a fresh page rather than under the input listing. The EJECT card has blank location and variable fields.

The SPACE card enables the user to skip 1, 2, or 3 lines between outputs. Its location field is always blank, and its A-field (column 19, actually) is used to specify 1, 2, or 3.

It is important to realize that the sequence of output editor request cards is interpreted quite literally by the GPSS program. Each card is processed and its instructions adhered to; nothing is taken for granted or figured out by the program. There is no page skipping or line spacing between outputs except where an EJECT or SPACE card has been inserted. The two exceptions are the OUTPUT and GRAPH cards, both of which cause their respective outputs to begin on a new page.

COMMENT Card

The COMMENT card is used to insert a comment in the printout. It is similar in coding format to the comment cards used to insert remarks in the symbolic listing. It has an asterisk in column 1, and it is not divided into location, operation, and operand fields. Thus the word "COMMENT" does *not* appear in columns 8 to 14 of this card.

Columns 2 to 71 of the COMMENT card contain the comment. The character in column 2 of the COMMENT card will appear in column 1 on the printout page. A comment may be as long as 132 characters. Comments longer than 70 characters are specified by using two cards as follows:

First card: asterisk in column 1; comment in columns 2 to 71; any nonblank character in column 72.

Second card: comment in columns 1 to 62.

TITLE Card

The TITLE card enables the user to have a portion of the output statistics printed under a title that he composes. The requested statistics appear in the same format as they would in the standard output except for two aspects:

1. They are preceded by a user-defined title which may be up to 124 characters in length.
2. They may pertain to a single entity (if so specified) rather than to all of the queues or all of the facilities or all of the storages, or whatever, in the model.

The operation of the TITLE card will be explained with the aid of some examples, but first the coding rules are given.

The location field is used to specify the type of entity for which statistics are to be printed out. Any of the mnemonics in Table 13-3 may be entered in the location field, left-justified.

If field A is blank (i.e., a comma in column 19), all of the entities of the type specified by the location field mnemonic will have their statistics printed out in the standard output format. Field A may be used to specify the address of a particular entity, in which case only its statistics will appear under the field B title. This option does not apply if block or clock statistics are specified. In other words, field A must be blank if either BLO or CLO appears in the location field.

As mentioned, field B contains the user-specified title. If it is too long to fit on the TITLE card, it can be continued on the next card, starting in column 1, if a

TABLE 13-3. LOCATION FIELD MNEMONICS FOR TITLE AND INCLUDE CARDS

BLO	Block counts[a]
CHA	User chain statistics
CLO	Clock times[a]
FAC	Facility statistics
GRO	Group members
HSAV	Halfword savevalue contents
MHSA	Halfword matrix savevalue contents
MSAV	Fullword matrix savevalue contents
QUE	Queue statistics
SAV	Fullword savevalue contents
STO	Storage statistics
TAB	Table statistics

[a] Cannot be used with INCLUDE card.

nonblank character is entered in column 72 of the TITLE card. The total length of the title may not exceed 124 characters.

The use of the TITLE card is now explained by describing the results obtained with several sample TITLE cards.

FAC   TITLE   BOOTH,TELEPHONE BOOTH STATISTICS

This card would produce the following lines of output:

1. The phrase "TELEPHONE BOOTH STATISTICS."
2. A blank line.
3. Two lines with the usual column headings for facility statistics: "facility," "average utilization," "number entries," and so on.
4. A row of statistics for facility BOOTH, each under its proper heading.

The blank line mentioned in item 2 is built into the TITLE card output, so to speak. But the TITLE card inserts no blank lines ahead of or following the five lines of output described above. The three lines of printing mentioned in items 3 and 4 are identical to what we would obtain in the standard output if we had a model that contained only one facility whose label happened to be "BOOTH."

BLO   TITLE   ,THESE ARE BLOCK STATISTICS.

This card would produce the following lines of output:

1. The sentence "THESE ARE BLOCK STATISTICS."
2. A blank line.
3. The words "BLOCK COUNTS."
4. Block count column headings: "block," "current," "total," and so on.
5. An appropriate number of rows of block statistics.

The lines of output mentioned in items 3, 4, and 5 would be identical to what we would get in the standard output.

TAB   TITLE   3,TRANSIT TIMES FOR LATECOMERS

This card would produce the following lines of output:

1. The phrase "TRANSIT TIMES FOR LATECOMERS."
2. A blank line.
3. The words "TABLE 3."
4. The standard printout for table 3 including all of the usual headings, statistics, and so on.

INCLUDE Card

The INCLUDE card is used to print only those statistics of a given entity type that the user specifies. It differs from the TITLE card in three major respects:

1. No title can be specified; only appropriate column headings are printed out.

2. Statistics can be requested for *any* number of entities (all of the same type) rather than for either *one* or *all* of them.

3. Statistics can be deleted. For example, we could have the facility utilization—but no other facility statistics—printed out.

The operation of the INCLUDE card will be described with some examples. But first the coding rules are summarized.

The location field of the INCLUDE card, like that of the TITLE card, contains an entity mnemonic, left-justified. The allowable mnemonics are the same as those for the TITLE card except for BLO and CLO which cannot be used with the INCLUDE card. (See Table 13-3.)

The variable field may have one of two formats, depending on which entity type is specified in the location field. If the location field contains CHA, FAC, QUE, STO, or TAB, the variable field contains a dual entry consisting of a *range specification separated by a slash from an output columns specification*. If the location field contains SAV, HSAV, MSAV, MHSAV, or GRO, the variable field contains a *comma followed by a range specification*.

Let us take a closer look at how the INCLUDE card is used to specify user chain, facility, queue, storage, or table statistics. The entry to the left of the slash has the form "Ai-Aj," where:

1. "A" is one of the following mnemonics: CH, F, Q, S, or T.
2. "i" is the address of the first entity in the range.
3. "j" is the address of the last entity in the range.

Thus "CH1–CH8" is used to obtain statistics for user chains 1 through 8. Similarly, "T\$WAIT-T\$WAIT" is used to obtain statistics for the table labeled WAIT.

The entry to the right of the slash is a series of numbers, each of which identifies a column of statistics to be printed out. These column request numbers, defined in Table 13-4, must be in ascending order, and they must be valid for the entity involved.

The following example demonstrates the operation of the INCLUDE card when used in the "range/columns" mode:

    STO   INCLUDE   S2–S4/1,2,5,6

This card would produce the following lines of output:

1. Two lines containing the following headings: "storage," "capacity," "entries," and "average time/tran."

2. Three lines of statistics, one for each of the specified storages: index numbers 2, 3, and 4.

3. Four columns of storage statistics, corresponding to the column request numbers, rather than the usual eight columns of storage statistics provided in the standard output.

Savevalues, matrix savevalues, and group outputs do not involve columns of statistics such that each line pertains to one particular entity. So it is appropriate to specify only the *range* of entities for which statistics should be printed. The

TABLE 13-4.   COLUMN REQUEST NUMBERS FOR INCLUDE CARD

Facilities	*User Chains*
1 Facility address	1 User chain address
2 Average utilization	2 Total entries
3 Number of entries	3 Average time/xact
4 Average time/xact	4 Current contents
5 Seizing xact number	5 Average contents
6 Preempting xact number	6 Maximum contents
Storages	*Tables*
1 Storage address	1 Table address
2 Capacity	2 Number of entries
3 Average contents	3 Mean argument
4 Average utilization	4 Standard deviation
5 Number of entries	5 Sum of arguments
6 Average time xact	6 Number of entries, weighted
7 Current contents	7 Mean argument, weighted
8 Maximum contents	8 Standard deviation, weighted
	9 Sum of arguments, weighted
Queues	10 Upper limit
1 Queue address	11 Observed frequency
2 Maximum contents	12 Per cent of total
3 Average contents	13 Cumulative percentage
4 Total entries	14 Cumulative remainder
5 Zero delay entries	15 Multiple of mean
6 Per cent zero entries	16 Deviation from mean
7 Average time/xact	
8 Average time/xact, excluding zero entries	
9 Qtable number	
10 Current contents	

range specification again takes the form "Ai–Aj," but "A" is one of the following: X, XH, MX, MH, or GRO.   The use of the INCLUDE card with these entities can be amply understood by looking at several examples:

```
SAV     INCLUDE   ,X1–X5
HSAV    INCLUDE   ,XH3–XH4
MSAV    INCLUDE   ,MX$AAA–MX$DDD
MHSAV   INCLUDE   ,MH7–MH11
GRO     INCLUDE   ,G2–G4
```

In each case, the standard output statistics will be printed for the type and range of entities specified.

FORMAT Card

The FORMAT card is used to compose a table of statistics which may be drawn from different entity types.   For example, we might have six queues and six facilities in our model, and we might want to have a table printed out such that:

1. Row 1 would pertain to both queue 1 and facility 1. Row 2 would pertain to queue 2 and facility 2. And so on.
2. The first column would contain the queue/facility index numbers.
3. The second, third, and fifth columns would contain queue statistics: maximum contents, total entries, and average time/xact.
4. The fourth and sixth columns would contain facility statistics: number of entries and average time/xact.

This sort of table can be obtained with a FORMAT card. The card that produces the just-described table is shown after we point out the main differences between the FORMAT and INCLUDE cards and summarize the coding rules for the former.

The FORMAT card differs from the INCLUDE card in two basic respects:

1. It allows the mixing of entity types.
2. It produces statistical tables with no column headings of any kind.

The location field of the FORMAT card is used to specify the print position for the first (leftmost) column of statistics. The location field entry must be left-justified. If there is no entry, the first column of statistics will begin in column 1 on the printout page.

The variable field contains a range of entity index numbers, separated by a slash from a sequence of symbols that specify which statistics should be printed for which entity types. These symbols are given in Table 13-5.

To obtain the table described earlier, containing queue/facility statistics for six queues and facilities, the following FORMAT card would be used:

FORMAT   1–6/Q1,Q2,Q4,F3,Q7,F4

This card will cause a table with six rows (one for each queue/facility pair) and six columns (corresponding to Q1, Q2, etc.) to be printed. This table will have no column headings; it will consist only of numbers.

Since the FORMAT card produces tables without headings, a COMMENT card can be inserted ahead of the FORMAT card with appropriate titles. To do this, the user must know in advance how many print columns are occupied by each column of statistics. There is no way to control the lateral spacing, but as a rule of thumb, each column of statistics occupies approximately 15 print columns. This figure should be used as a guide when setting up headings for statistics that are output by means of a FORMAT card.

Some confusion may have been caused by the fact that the word "column" has been used to refer to three different things in our discussion of the FORMAT card:

1. *Print* column (132 of these on a page of output).
2. *Card* column (80 of these on a card).
3. *Statistics* column (up to 8 of these may be specified in a FORMAT card).

TABLE 13-5.   SYMBOLS USED IN FORMAT CARD VARIABLE FIELD TO SPECIFY COLUMNS OF OUTPUT STATISTICS[a]

F1	Facility address	T5	Sum of arguments (X)
F2	Average utilization	T6	Number of entries, weighted
F3	Number of entries	T7	Mean argument, weighted
F4	Average time/xact	T8	Standard deviation, weighted
F5	Seizing xact number (X)	T9	Sum of arguments, weighted (X)
F6	Preempting xact number (X)	T10	Upper limit (X)
		T11	Observed frequency (X)
S1	Storage address	T12	Per cent of total (X)
S2	Capacity (X)	T13	Cumulative percentage (X)
S3	Average contents	T14	Cumulative remainder (X)
S4	Average utilization	T15	Multiple of mean (X)
S5	Number of entries	T16	Deviation from mean (X)
S6	Average time/xact		
S7	Current contents	CH1	User chain address
S8	Maximum contents	CH2	Total entries
		CH3	Average time/xact
Q1	Queue address	CH4	Current contents
Q2	Maximum contents	CH5	Average contents
Q3	Average contents	CH6	Maximum contents
Q4	Total entries		
Q5	Zero entries	X	All savevalue statistics (X)
Q6	Per cent zero entries		
Q7	Average time/xact	X1	Savevalue address (Y)
Q8	Average time/xact except zero entries	X2	Contents of savevalue (Y)
Q9	Qtable number (X)		
Q10	Current contents	XH1	Halfword savevalue address (Y)
		XH2	Contents of halfword savevalue (Y)
T1	Table address		
T2	Number of entries	XH	All halfword savevalue statistics (X)
T3	Mean argument		
T4	Standard deviation	B	All block statistics (X)

[a] (X): not legal in GPSS/360; (Y): not legal in Flow Simulator.

There are 132 print columns on a page of output, and each column of statistics is allotted approximately 15 print columns.   Up to 8 columns of statistics may be specified in a FORMAT card, since there are not enough print columns to accommodate any more.   The term "card column" requires no explanation.

TEXT Card

The TEXT card is altogether different from the TITLE, INCLUDE, and FORMAT cards in what it does.   It allows the user to insert one or several items of numerical output data into a sentence.   For example, a TEXT card could be used to express the maximum contents of a particular queue in the following form:

THE LARGEST NUMBER OF MESSAGES WAITING
TO BE PROCESSED WAS 27.

The TEXT card can also be used to alter the form of numerical output data. For example, a facility utilization of .538 could be printed out as 53.8%.

The location field is used to specify the starting print position (column) for the sentence on the output page. The specified column number, if any, must begin in column 2 of the TEXT card. If the location field is blank, print column 1 will be assumed by the program.

The alphameric sentence with embedded data specification(s) may extend to column 71 of the TEXT card and, if necessary, may be continued on another card by entering a nonblank character in column 72 of the TEXT card. It may occupy columns 1 through 71 of the second card. At first glance, these rules appear to permit comments of up to 134 characters in length, but as you will see, several of the characters do not appear in the printout.

The operation of the TEXT card will now be demonstrated by means of an example:

TEXT   THERE WERE #S1,7/X# BOOTHS IN USE WHEN THE RUN ENDED.

Except for "#S1,7/X#," the specified sentence will be printed exactly as it appears above, starting in column 1 of the printout page. The symbols that are set off by #'s specify which data item is to be inserted into the sentence, and they also specify its format. The entry to the left of the slash is interpreted as "data item 7 for storage 1." The entry to the right of the slash specifies the number of spaces that will be occupied by the aforementioned data item when it appears in the specified sentence.

A complete list of entries which may appear to the left of the slash in a TEXT card is given in Table 13-6. Bear in mind that all of these quantities represent numbers which are either integers or decimals.

In general, the format specification (to the right of the slash) consists of the following:

1. An instruction to move the decimal point to the left or right.
2. One or more X's, each representing one digit in the output.
3. A decimal point that is located among the X's in exactly the same position that the decimal point should be placed among the digits in the printout.

Items 1 and 3 obviously do not apply if the data item happens to be an integer. The leftmost portion of the format specification governs the shifting of the decimal point relative to where it would appear in the standard output. "3R" would move the decimal point three places to the right, and "1L" would move it one place to the left. The decimal shift specification takes the form "pS," where.

$$p (= 1 \text{ to } 5) = \text{number of positions to shift decimal point}$$
$$S = L \text{ (left) or } R \text{ (right)}$$

If the data item is an integer, or if no decimal point shift is desired, the "pS" portion of the format specification is simply omitted. (Do not leave a blank or insert a comma in its place.)

TABLE 13-6.   DATA SPECIFICATION SYMBOLS FOR TEXT CARD[a]

For Facility n		Qn,8 Average time/xact, excluding zero entries
Fn,2	Average utilization	Qn,10 Current contents
Fn,3	Number of entries	
Fn,4	Average time/xact	*For Table n*
		Tn,2 Entries in table
For Storage n		Tn,3 Mean argument
Sn,3	Average contents	Tn,4 Standard deviation
Sn,4	Average utilization	Tn,6 Entries in table, weighted
Sn,5	Number of entries	Tn,7 Mean argument, weighted
Sn,6	Average time/xact	Tn,8 Standard deviation, weighted
Sn,7	Current contents	
Sn,8	Maximum contents	*For Savevalue n*
		Xn,2 Contents of savevalue
For Queue n		XHn,2 Contents of halfword savevalue
Qn,2	Maximum contents	
Qn,3	Average contents	*For User Chain n*
Qn,4	Total entries	CHn,2 Total entries
Qn,5	Zero entries	CHn,3 Average time/xact
Qn,6	Per cent zero entries	CHn,4 Current contents
Qn,7	Average time/xact	CHn,5 Average contents
		CHn,6 Maximum contents

[a] If "n" is a symbolic address, it must be prefixed with a dollar sign ($).

The remainder of the format specification consists of X's and, if appropriate, a decimal point.   There should be one X for every digit desired in the output. The format specification will now be illustrated by several examples.

Data as They Would Appear in Standard Output	Format Specification to Right of Slash	Data as They Will Now Appear
37	XXXX	37
37	XX	37
.492	2RXX.X	49.2
21	3L.XXX	.021

It is evident that the user ought to have a good idea of what his data look like before using the TEXT command.   If any significant digits are lost in the process of converting data to the specified format, the data will be printed unaltered, along with an error message.

It is permissible to embed several data items in a sentence specified by a TEXT card.   It is also permissible to use a data specification alone without a sentence.

OUTPUT Card

The OUTPUT card is used to obtain the standard output in addition to the report generator output.   The former output starts on a new page—an exception to the rule about always using an EJECT card to jump to a new page.   The location and variable fields of the OUTPUT card are always blank.

13.3   REPORT GENERATOR: GRAPHIC OUTPUT

The *graphic request cards* are not all described in detail as were the editing request cards. Instead, their functions are discussed in general terms so that you will know what the graphic output option does and, approximately, how it is used.

The following sequence of request cards is used to define a single graph:

GRAPH

ORIGIN

X

Y

STATEMENT (Optional.   None, one, or several may be used.)

ENDGRAPH

No other cards may be inserted into this group; it must be uninterrupted and in the order shown. A group of graphic request cards may be inserted anywhere after the REPORT card, and any number of graphs may be requested.

Physical Appearance of Graphs

A group of graphic request cards always produces a bar graph that has the general appearance of Figure 13-2. It has a horizontal *x*-axis, a vertical *y*-axis, and vertical bars or frequency classes.

The print page should be thought of as a grid or matrix consisting of 60 rows and 132 columns. The origin of the graph will be the intersection of a specified row and column. The *x*-axis will occupy part of a row, and the *y*-axis will occupy

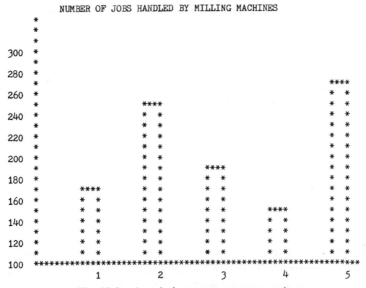

Fig. 13-2.   A typical report generator graph.

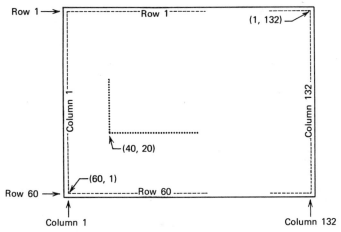

Fig. 13-3.   Printout page as a 60×132 matrix.

part of a column.   Unless specified otherwise, all of the lines on a graph are formed with asterisks.

The number of bars and their width and spacing are specified by the user. But their heights represent end-of-run statistical results.   There are provisions for labeling the axes and for incorporating titles, headings, and comments on the graph.

GRAPH Card

The GRAPH card will be fully described because it designates the quantity to be plotted.   In particular, it is used to specify which SNA is to be plotted, the range of the entity to be plotted, and the character to be used in plotting the graph.   Its location field is always blank.

The A-field may contain any of the SNAs in Table 13-7.   Note that four of them pertain to columns of numbers from a *single table* whereas all the others may involve a *range of entities*.   This is significant because the coding rules for some of the graph cards (including the GRAPH card itself) depend on which type of SNA is specified in field A of the GRAPH card.

If field A contains a symbol other than TF, TP, TD, or TR, fields B and C contain the lower and upper limits, respectively, of the range of entities to be plotted.   If field A contains TF, TP, TD, or TR, field B specifies the table address, and field C is blank.

Field D can be used to specify a character that will be used to plot the graph. For example, a period may be specified.   If field D is blank, asterisks are used as in Figure 13-2.

The function of the GRAPH card can be better appreciated by looking at some examples:

(a) GRAPH   FT,7,15

(b) GRAPH   CM,6,10,X

(c) GRAPH   TF,WAIT,,.

TABLE 13-7. FIELD A MNEMONICS FOR GRAPH CARD

Facilities		*User Chains*	
FR	Utilization	CA	Average contents
FC	Entry count	CH	Current contents
FT	Average time/xact	CM	Maximum contents
		CC	Entry count
		CT	Average time/xact
Storages			
SR	Utilization		
SA	Average contents	*Tables*	
S	Current contents	TC	Entry count
SM	Maximum contents	TB	Mean
SC	Entry count	TS	Standard deviation
ST	Average time/xact	TF	Observed frequencies[a]
		TP	Per cent of total[a]
Queues		TD	Cumulative percentage[a]
QA	Average contents	TR	Cumulative remainder[a]
Q	Current contents		
QM	Maximum contents	*Blocks*	
QC	Entry count	N	Block counts
QZ	Number of zero entries		
QT	Average time/xact	*Fullword Savevalues*	
QX	Average time/xact, excluding zero entries	X	Contents
		Halfword Savevalues	
Groups		XH	Contents
G	Current contents		

[a] GRAPH card must specify a single entity and not a range of entities. Hence C-field must be blank.

Card (a) requests a graph which will have nine bars that correspond to facilities 7 through 15. The heights of these bars will represent the average time/xact for the respective facilities, and the y-axis will be graduated appropriately.

Card (b) requests a graph which will have five bars representing the end-of-run contents of user chains 6 through 10. The axes and bars will be made up of X's.

Card (c) requests a graph whose vertical bars correspond to frequency classes in the table labeled WAIT. (The number of frequency classes is specified on the X card.) The heights of these bars represent the number of observations in the respective frequency classes. The axes and bars will be made up of periods. Incidentally, this particular graph will depict table WAIT as a histogram.

Other Graphic Request Cards

The ORIGIN card specifies the row and column of the origin. Field A contains the row number and field B contains the column number. The position of rows and columns on a printout page was shown in Figure 13-3.

The X card is used to specify the labeling of the x-axis and the width and spacing of the bars. The X card has one format that is associated with all the

Table 13-7 SNAs not marked with a superscript. It has another format when TF, TP, TD, or TR appears in field A of the GRAPH card.

The Y card is used to specify the lower limit for Y values, the number of increments, and the number of rows per increment. The y-axis is automatically labeled on the basis of this information.

The STATEMENT card is used to specify a comment or heading on the graph. The row and starting column for the statement are specified along with the number of characters in it and, of course, the statement itself. If the entire statement cannot be specified on a single STATEMENT card, it can be continued on another card. Any number of STATEMENT cards may be used for a given graph.

The ENDGRAPH card signifies the end of the graph definition. It follows the last STATEMENT card for the graph.

13.4   DIFFERENCES BETWEEN GPSS/360 AND OTHER VERSIONS

The differences between GPSS/360 and the other versions are summarized in Table 13-8 in a gross but handy way. The standard output options are substantially alike for all four versions. The few differences that exist are spelled out in this section for each version.

The GPS K report generator is quite similar to that of GPSS/360 in all major respects, but most of the request cards differ in various details. These detailed differences are not expounded in this section, since a sufficiently accurate picture of the GPS K report generator was conveyed by Sections 13.2 and 13.3. The detailed rules for its usage can be found in reference 3 when the need arises.

The Flow Simulator report generator is quite similar to that of GPSS/360 as far as the graphic request cards are concerned. But its statistical selection and control cards differ substantially from their GPSS/360 counterparts. These differences will only be mentioned in general terms in this section. Detailed rules for using the Flow Simulator output editor can be found in reference 4.

GPS K

The GPS K START card is identical to the GPSS/360 START card, but has two additional aspects:

1. If the START card has a blank variable field, the model will be assembled, but no simulation run will ensue.

2. In addition to "NP" or blank, field B may contain the entry "PZ." This entry causes the printout to include statistics for facilities, storages, queues, and user chains that had zero entries and also for savevalues and matrix savevalues with zero contents.

The GPS K PRINT block is identical to the one in GPSS/360 except for the following details:

1. The field C mnemonics are the same as those in Table 13-1 except that GPS K lacks MAT, C, XH, and MH. Also, GPS K uses "GRO" rather than "G."

TABLE 13-8. COMPARISON OF OTHER VERSIONS TO GPSS/360 WITH REGARD TO OUTPUT OPTIONS

Card Type	GPS K	Flow Simulator	GPSS III
Standard Output			
START	1	1	1
PRINT	1	1	2
TRACE/UNTRACE	1	1	1
		3	
Output Editor or Report Generator			Not included
REPORT	1	1	
OUTPUT	1	4	
EJECT	1	4	
SPACE	1	4	
COMMENT	1	5	
TITLE	1	4	
INCLUDE	1	4	
FORMAT	1	5	
TEXT	1	1	
GRAPH	1	1	
ORIGIN	1	1	
X	1	1	
Y	1	1	
STATEMENT	1	1	
ENDGRAPH	1	1	
	6		

Notes
1. Essentially identical to GPSS/360; may differ in a few minor details.
2. More limited than in GPSS/360.
3. Includes SNAP block.
4. Not included in Flow Simulator.
5. Substantially broader functions than in GPSS/360.
6. Includes ENDREPORT card.

2. There are some minor differences concerning the field A and B entries as a function of which field C mnemonic is used.

The TRACE/UNTRACE blocks are the same in GPS K as in GPSS/360. However, the output that occurs whenever a flagged xact enters a block consists of one line; the transaction data are not printed.

The GPS K report generator always starts with a REPORT card and ends with an ENDREPORT card. (The latter is not used in GPSS/360.) The COMMENT, EJECT, and SPACE cards have the same functions as in GPSS/360.

The TITLE, INCLUDE, FORMAT, and TEXT cards are basically very much like those in GPSS/360. However, there are some minor differences. For example, the TITLE card location field may not contain CLO, HSAV, or MHSA.

The graphic output is generally similar to that of GPSS/360, but again, it differs in certain details. For example, a graph is defined on a 56×122 grid, and its bars may be printed with a different character than its axes.   As in GPSS/360, a graph is defined by a set of GRAPH, ORIGIN, X, Y, STATE-MENT, and ENDGRAPH cards.

Flow Simulator

The START card is identical to the one in GPSS/360 except for one thing: if it is omitted from the input deck, the model will be assembled, but no run will occur.   (Its omission in GPSS/360 causes an error.)

The PRINT block is identical to the one in GPSS/360 except that neither group nor matrix savevalues can be requested since these entities do not exist in Flow Simulator.

The TRACE/UNTRACE blocks operate like those in GPSS/360, but only the first line of output is produced each time a flagged xact enters a block.

Flow Simulator provides a SNAP block which permits the user to obtain "snapshots" of the state of the system.   Thus SNAP cards, like PRINT cards, may appear any place in the input deck, and as frequently as desired.

If field A of the SNAP card is blank, a standard printout of the following statistics will occur whenever a xact enters the SNAP block: relative and absolute clock times, blocks, facilities, queues, storages, and tables.

If field A of the SNAP block contains a 1, the printout will be accompanied by a printout of the transaction chains.   As you have probably recognized, the functions of a SNAP card could be performed by an appropriate string of PRINT cards.   Like the PRINT, TRACE, and UNTRACE blocks, the SNAP block should be used with discretion so as not to escalate the running time.

The output editor is roughly equivalent to the GPSS/360 version in its overall capabilities.   But it utilizes fewer cards, some of which do more things than their GPSS/360 counterparts.

The Flow Simulator REPORT card serves the same purpose as the REPORT and OUTPUT cards in GPSS/360, depending on whether it is used alone or with a set of output editor request cards.

The Flow Simulator COMMENT card is used for spacing and page skipping as well as comments.   It contains the word "COMMENT," and it has no asterisk in column 1.   It does the job of the COMMENT, EJECT, and SPACE cards in GPSS/360.

The FORMAT card is the key editing card in Flow Simulator.   It duplicates the functions of the GPSS/360 FORMAT card, and it has an option for requesting column headings.   It also does some of the things done by the GPSS/360 INCLUDE and TITLE cards.

The graphic option utilizes the same six cards as GPSS/360, but their coding rules differ in various details.   Flow Simulator uses a different convention for numbering rows: row 1 is at the bottom of the page rather than the top.

GPSS III

The START card is identical to that of GPSS/360.   The TRACE and UN-TRACE blocks are also the same except for the fact that only the first line is printed every time a flagged xact enters a block.

The GPSS III PRINT block works like the one in GPSS/360, but it is more limited. The field A and B arguments must be constants; other SNAs are not allowed. The C-field may contain only the following mnemonics:

MOV, FUT, CHA, I, N, or W   (A-field and B-field always blank.)

F, S, Q, T, X, or blank   (A-field and B-field need not be blank.)

As mentioned, GPSS III does not include a report generator.

13.5   SUMMARY

The standard output, in its simplest form, consists of the normal unasked-for end-of-run statistical output such as we have obtained in connection with all of the illustrative programs thus far. This set of statistics pertains to all of the entities in the model for which statistics are inherently accumulated. The normal standard output occurs when the run termination count is reduced to zero.

The standard output options are embodied in the START, PRINT, TRACE, UNTRACE, and SNAP (Flow Simulator only) cards. These options enable the programmer to control what is output and when — up to a point. But they give him negligible control over the format of the output.

The end-of-run output can be expanded to include transaction chain data in addition to the normal standard output. Or it can be suppressed completely. Full or partial sets of statistics can be obtained during a run by specifying a snap interval or using PRINT, TRACE/UNTRACE, or SNAP blocks.

The aforementioned blocks are used primarily as debugging and diagnostic aids. Since they cause print operations to occur during a run, they should be used sparingly.

The report generator output can appear in place of, or in addition to, the standard output. It allows the user to dictate the contents and format of the output. To use this feature effectively, he must have a good idea of what the standard output would include — not the actual numbers, of course, but the kinds of statistics, their formats, and approximate magnitudes. The output editor feature is especially advantageous for a large model which (1) would produce many unwanted statistics in the standard output mode and (2) is utilized often (rather than on a "one-shot" basis).

The output editor takes the form of a series of cards at the very end of the model. The first of the cards must always be REPORT. All of the others are output editor request cards, and they can be classified as editing, graphic, or control cards. There are six graphic cards, and their order is rigid. There are seven editing cards (in GPSS/360 and GPS K), and they may appear in any order. There is one control card (two in GPS K) besides the REPORT card.

CHAPTER 14
Illustrative Program 9

Program 9 is the last illustrative program to be presented here. Its main purpose is to provide a further demonstration of GPSS model building and program writing. In addition, it incorporates *matrix savevalues,* the *report generator,* and several block types not previously used in the context of a program.

We simulate the operation of a toll plaza which has two regular and two exact-change booths. The interarrival times of vehicles are exponentially distributed about an average which, unlike previous cases, *varies during the simulated time period.* A certain percentage of drivers have exact change, and they choose what they believe will be the fastest of the four lanes. Drivers not having exact change are, of course, limited to one of the two regular booths.

The presentation of the toll plaza model and program 9 is preceded by a discussion of the (hypothetical) events that led to their formulation. This discussion takes the form of a scenario that serves as a review of how a practical problem may give rise to a GPSS simulation.

14.1 GROUNDWORK FOR TOLL PLAZA MODEL

The events leading to the definition of the toll plaza model are now described. The process of deciding what should be simulated is recounted, and the system is defined.

The Scenario

There was a well-traveled highway whose maintenance costs consistently exceeded the available highway department budget allotment. So it was decided to install tollbooths to help defray the cost of maintaining the road. A location for the proposed tollbooth plaza was shrewdly chosen to ensure that no reasonable bypass route would be available to motorists. For this reason, and because the toll charge would only be 10 cents, the level of traffic was expected to stay the same after the toll plaza went into operation.

The cost-conscious personnel responsible for the project wanted to install the smallest possible number of booths so as to minimize construction costs. They also wanted as many of these as practical to be exact-change booths so as to minimize the number of toll collectors.

In attempting to arrive at the optimum arrangement, they found that there were many questions to be answered before they could even begin to evaluate various alternatives. For instance, what percentage of drivers could be expected to have exact change? How long does it take for a car to pass through a toll-booth if the driver has exact change? How long if he does not have exact change? What is the traffic pattern at the proposed tollbooth site during rush hours and at other times? Is the traffic rate in the northbound lanes reciprocal to that in the southbound lanes, or does the traffic tend to run simultaneously heavy in both lanes?

To obtain the required data, observers were stationed at the proposed toll-booth site to record the rates of traffic in both directions at various times. Experienced tollbooth designers were consulted, and the results of pertinent studies were obtained. A special effort was made to obtain data regarding the operation of tollbooths charging 10 cents per vehicle.

Analysis of Empirical Data

The empirical data were assimilated, and the following parameters were settled upon for study purposes:

1. Percentage of automobiles with exact change: 72.
2. Time in booth for cars with exact change: 2 to 7 seconds.
3. Time in booth for cars without exact change: 5 to 16.5 seconds.

It was agreed that the effects of varying the percentage of automobiles with exact change would be examined later. The peak traffic in the northbound and southbound lanes would of course dictate the number of tollbooths needed. Once this was decided, it would be fairly easy to determine how many regular booths could be closed during sparse traffic periods. (Exact-change booths would presumably operate full time.) After arriving at the optimum numbers and types of tollbooths for northbound and southbound lanes alone, the possible advantages of using some of the middle booths both ways (at different times of day!) could be investigated.

To keep the discussion within reasonable limits, we hereafter confine our attention to the *peak traffic in the northbound lanes*. Observers found that cars arrived in Poisson fashion every 1.2 seconds, on the average, during the heaviest traffic period. To put it another way, the interarrival times of cars were exponentially distributed about a mean value of 1.2 seconds.

It was easy to calculate the number of booths needed to accommodate this traffic rate, using average values. With a frequency of 50 cars per minute, there would be 36 with exact change and 14 without. (This assumes 72% with exact change.) Those with exact change would consume a total of $4.5 \times 36 = 162$ "booth-seconds." Those without exact change would consume a total of $10.75 \times 14 = 150.5$ booth-seconds. Dividing these figures by 60 reveals that drivers with exact change could be accommodated by 2.7 (exact change or regular) booths while those without exact change could be handled by 2.5 (regular) booths.

It was suggested that three regular and two exact-change booths might be a good solution. However, it was pointed out that the peak rate of 50 cars per minute is relatively short-lived, and that perhaps only a temporary bottleneck would occur if two regular and two exact-change booths were used. This idea seemed worth investigating since the planners wanted to get by with the smallest possible number of regular booths.

In an effort to evaluate the adequacy of four booths, additional calculations were performed assuming various average rates of arrivals, times in booths, and so on. But these did not provide a satisfactory indication of the lengths of waiting lines under various combinations of circumstances because the parameters are random variables.

Thus it was decided to develop a simulation model to determine whether four tollbooths would be adequate. This model would have to permit the easy substitution of various automobile arrival patterns. It should also allow the percentage of drivers with exact change to be varied. If four tollbooths were deemed adequate, this model could then be used to decide when one of the regular booths could be closed to traffic. If four tollbooths were deemed inadequate, the model could be modified to include an additional regular and/or exact-change booth.

System Definition

The system to be simulated was fairly well described in the preceding section. Now we define it in a more formal and detailed manner. The physical system is very much like the one depicted in Figure 1-2, except that it contains two regular and two exact-change booths. The key elements and parameters in this problem are shown in Figure 14-1.

Vehicles arrive at random intervals which are exponentially distributed about a mean value denoted by X1. Unlike in previous models, this value does not remain fixed throughout the simulated time period. As shown by the graph in Figure 14-1, the frequency of arrivals (inverse of X1) increases to a maximum of 50 cars per minute—a car every 1.2 seconds—and then decreases.

It is assumed that 72% of arriving drivers have exact change. These drivers first look at the exact-change lanes. If neither is empty, they check the regular lanes as well. If none of the four lanes is empty, a driver with exact change makes a choice between the shortest exact change lane and the shortest regular lane. It is assumed that he will tend to choose the exact-change lane even if it has more cars because he expects it to move faster. Of course, this is only true up to a certain point, and this threshold is treated as one of the variables in the model.

A driver with exact change is assumed to spend from 2 to 7 seconds in the tollbooth. This includes the time it takes for him to drive in, stop (or slow down), toss in his coin, and vacate the booth. A driver with exact change is assumed to spend the stated amount of time in a booth regardless of whether it is an exact-change or regular booth. No provision is made in the model to account for the aberrant drivers who aim badly and miss the basket or those who discover, too late, that they do not have exact change.

A driver without exact change always chooses one of the two regular lanes, presumably the one with the shortest queue. These drivers are assumed to spend 5 to 16.5 seconds in a booth.

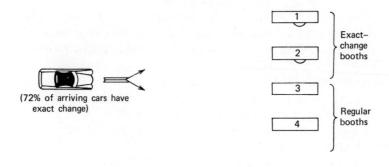

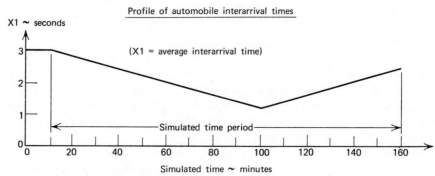

Fig. 14-1.   Major elements in toll plaza model.

The graph in Figure 14-1 shows that a 2.5-hour period will be simulated, since it brackets the peak traffic condition.   However, there is no reason why a 24-hour period could not be simulated by using an X1 profile for a typical day.

14.2   TOLL PLAZA MODEL

The GPSS model will be described with the aid of the flow diagram in Figure 14-2.   The format of this diagram is, once again, a hybrid block diagram/flow chart, and the names in parentheses more or less correspond to block addresses in program 9.

Before we start working our way through the model, these basic aspects should be noted:

1. Lanes 1 and 2 are used only by cars with exact change.

2. Lanes 3 and 4 may be selected by cars with or without exact change.

3. The unit of system (clock) time is one tenth of a second.

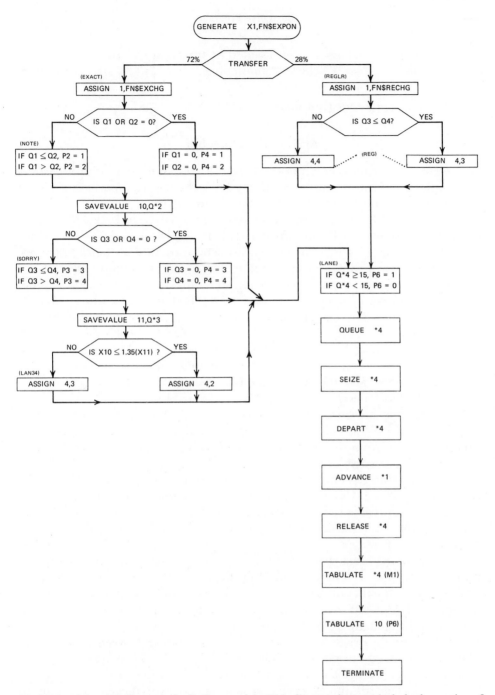

Fig. 14-2. Schematic diagram of toll plaza model. This diagram does not include the portion of the model that assigns values to X1, controls the simulation run length, and periodically records selected statistics in a matrix savevalue. (See back pocket for a duplicate of this illustration which can be kept in view while reading the chapter.)

4. Arriving automobiles are represented by transactions. In fact, the words "transaction," "car," "vehicle," "automobile," and "driver" are here used interchangeably.

5. The average interarrival time is given by X1.

Arrival of Automobiles

The entry of a transaction into the system corresponds to a car approaching the toll plaza. The mechanism for varying X1 as the simulation progresses is not shown in Figure 14-2, and it is not discussed until later.

The TRANSFER block sends 72% of arriving xacts to have a value of 20 to 70 clock units assigned to P1 by function EXCHG. These are cars with exact change. The other 28% of arriving xacts are sent to an ASSIGN block which references function RECHG to assign a value of 50 to 165 clock units to P1.

From a logical standpoint, it may seem preferable to initially decide whether or not a car has exact change and to compute its booth time *later,* when it actually enters the booth. The model could certainly have been so structured, but the approach taken in Figure 14-2 is entirely equivalent and probably more efficient.

The xacts that have P1 computed by function RECHG select either lane 3 or lane 4, whichever has the fewest cars. The number of the selected lane is put into parameter 4, and the car proceeds to that lane. This corresponds to reaching the block designated as "LANE" in Figure 14-2.

It can be seen that cars with exact change go through a much more complicated selection process before they get to the LANE block. Let us follow this process, starting from the point where the booth time (computed by function EXCHG) has been assigned to P1.

If lane 1 or lane 2 is empty, the selected lane number is put into P4, and the transaction goes to LANE without further ado. In other words, if a driver with exact change finds an empty exact-change lane, he will go to it. The booth itself may be occupied, but the driver figures that the booth will be vacated by the time he pulls up to it.

If neither of the exact-change lanes is empty, the number of the shorter queue is put into P2, and its length is stored in savevalue 10. The xact next looks at lanes 3 and 4. If either of these lanes is empty, its number is put into P4, and the xact goes to LANE. If neither is empty, the number of the shorter queue is put into P3, and its length is stored in savevalue 11.

At this point, the driver with exact change must choose between the two lanes whose queue lengths are in savevalues 10 and 11. The following rule is used: choose the exact-change lane unless it is more than 35% longer than the regular lane. In other words, the exact-change lane will be favored even if it has up to 35% more cars than the regular lane. The number of the chosen lane is put into P4, and the car goes to that lane.

It is important to recognize that the entire selection process for cars with or without exact change occurs in zero clock time. However, an ADVANCE block could be inserted, if desired, to allow for the fact that drivers who carry the exact versus regular lane decision process to its bitter end may lose a couple of seconds as they slow down to survey the situation and decide on a lane.

At this point, we have covered all parts of the Figure 14-2 flow chart that feed into the LANE block. Keep in mind that every xact, upon reaching this point, has its booth time in P1 and its lane number in P4.

Operations at Queues and Booths

Just before a transaction enters its chosen lane, a test is made to determine what percentage of motorists, after selecting the best available lane, must still wait behind 15 or more cars. If the length of the tested queue (given by $Q*4$) is 15 or more, P6 of the entering xact is set to one; otherwise, it remains equal to zero. The frequency of xacts with $P6 = 1$ can be easily tabulated to determine what percentage of cars found themselves entering unacceptably long waiting lines.

The assumption that 15 cars constitute an unacceptably long line is arbitrary. The main point here is that some sort of threshold queue length has been postulated, and a test is provided for determining how often it is exceeded. The GPSS mechanism for making this test is shown later in this chapter.

After the test has been made, all xacts proceed to enter the queue and booth specified in parameter 4. The amount of time spent in the booth is specified in parameter 1. After leaving its tollbooth, every xact has its transit time and also the value of P6 tabulated before being destroyed, that is, leaving the system.

14.3   ILLUSTRATIVE PROGRAM 9

The GPSS program that was written to carry out the toll plaza simulation is divided into eight sections by means of asterisk cards. Section 1 includes the loading of constants and the definition of functions. The next four sections comprise the basic model as diagrammed in Figure 14-2. Section 6 includes the mechanisms for varying X1 and for recording queue lengths as functions of time. Section 7 contains variable and table definition cards as well as the START cards. Section 8 contains output editor cards.

We have taken advantage of this division of program 9 into sections to spread the symbolic listing over five figures as follows:

Figure 14-3: Sections 1 and 2.

Figure 14-4: Sections 3 and 4.

Figure 14-5: Sections 5 and 6.

Figure 14-7: Section 7.

Figure 14-8: Section 8.

The source program, as it appears in these figures, is generously endowed with explanatory comments. For this reason—and because the logical structure of the model was explained in the preceding section—the ensuing discussion focuses on noteworthy aspects of program 9 rather than taking it step by step.

Matrix Savevalues

Since five of the first six noncomment cards in section 1 pertain to a *matrix savevalue*, we take this opportunity to explain formally how they are used. You may recall that a few things have already been said about matrix savevalue entities:

1. They are analogous to savevalues except that they store an *array of constants* rather than a single value.
2. There are both fullword and halfword matrix savevalues, and there is a special SNA for each type, namely, MXj(m,n) and MHj(m,n). These SNAs denote the current value in row m, column n of the matrix savevalue whose address (numeric or symbolic) is j.
3. The INITIAL card can be used to load constants into matrix savevalues.

Aside from the INITIAL card, there are two card types associated with matrix savevalues. The MATRIX definition card specifies the number of rows and columns and also the type of matrix, that is, fullword or halfword. The MSAVE-VALUE block is used to enter constants into specified cells of specified matrix savevalues.

Every matrix savevalue used in a model must be defined by a MATRIX card which is placed among the very first cards in the deck. The MATRIX card must precede any other card that refers to the matrix savevalue it defines. The MA-TRIX card is coded as follows:

Location field: Address of matrix savevalue entity.

Field A: X or H to denote fullword or halfword.

Field B: Number of rows.

Field C: Number of columns.

The MSAVEVALUE block is used to enter values into a matrix savevalue much as a SAVEVALUE block is used to enter values into a savevalue. Both are zero-delay blocks that never refuse entry to xacts. The MSAVEVALUE card is coded as follows:

Field A: Address of matrix savevalue.

Field B: Row number.

Field C: Column number.

Field D: Quantity to be stored in the cell whose row and column are in fields B and C, respectively.

Field E: Blank if fullword savevalue; H is halfword savevalue.

The MSAVEVALUE block may operate in the replacement, addition, or subtraction modes in the same manner as the SAVEVALUE block. These modes are specified by appending nothing, a plus sign, or a minus sign, respectively, to the field A argument. The operation of the MSAVEVALUE block is illustrated by the following examples:

(a) MSAVEVALUE   FNB,3,X10,FN3

(b) MSAVEVALUE   5-,XH1,2,Q*4,H

When a transaction enters block (a), function 3 computes a value that is entered into a cell of the fullword matrix savevalue labeled FNB. This cell is in row 3 and has its column specified by savevalue 10.

When a transaction enters block (b), the length of the queue whose index number is specified in parameter 4 of the entering xact is subtracted from the current contents of a cell in halfword matrix savevalue 5. This cell is in the row specified by savevalue 1 and in column 2.

Section 1

Section 1 of program 9 is shown in Figure 14-3. The MATRIX card defines halfword matrix savevalue 1 as having 6 rows and 16 columns. The first INITIAL card puts positive constants into four fullword savevalues although, as it happens, halfword savevalues would be adequate. In this connection, a word of caution is offered: when specifying halfword savevalues, you should be confident that they will not be required to store too large a number during the run. For example, the initial value of a halfword savevalue might be 4700, which is all right. But if a value such as 35,000 is subsequently computed to be stored in that savevalue, an error will result.

Returning to section 1, the next four INITIAL cards are used to enter 16 constants into row 1 of halfword matrix savevalue 1. Note that each INITIAL card is independent of the others; that is, they are not continuations of one another as are the function follower cards in function EXPON.

```
*           TOLL  PLAZA  SIMULATION  WITH  FOUR  TOLL  BOOTHS

* SECTION 1:  LOAD CONSTANTS AND DEFINE FUNCTIONS.

1     MATRIX     H,6,16
      INITIAL    X1,30/X3,720/X4,35/X6,15

      INITIAL    MH1(1,1),30/MH1(1,2),28/MH1(1,3),26/MH1(1,4),24
      INITIAL    MH1(1,5),22/MH1(1,6),20/MH1(1,7),18/MH1(1,8),16
      INITIAL    MH1(1,9),14/MH1(1,10),12/MH1(1,11),14/MH1(1,12),16
      IBITIAL    MH1(1,13),18/MH1(1,14),20/MH1(1,15),22/MH1(1,16),24

EXPON FUNCTION   RN7,C24       EXPONENTIAL PROBABILITY DISTRIBUTION
0,0/.1,.104/.2,.222/.3,.355/.4,.509/.5,.69/.6,.915/.7,1.2/.75,1.38/
.8,1.6/.84,1.83/.88,2.12/.9,2.3/.92,2.52/.94,2.81/.95,2.99/.96,3.2/
.97,3.5/.98,3.9/.99,4.6/.995,5.3/.998,6.2/.999,7/.9997,8

EXCHG FUNCTION   RN3,C2        BOOTH TIME, WITH EXACT CHANGE
0,20/1,70

RECHG FUNCTION   RN3,C2        BOOTH TIME, WITHOUT EXACT CHANGE
0,50/1,165


* SECTION 2:  ARRIVAL OF AUTOS AND DETERMINATION OF BOOTH TIMES

      SIMULATE
      GENERATE   X1,FN$EXPON
      TRANSFER   .X3,REGLR,EXACT   PROB. OF EXACT IS X3/1000
REGLR ASSIGN     1,FN$RECHG        P1 = BOOTH TIME FOR REG. AUTOS.
      TRANSFER   ,REG
EXACT ASSIGN     1,FN$EXCHG        P1 = BOOTH TIME FOR EXACT AUTOS.
```

Fig. 14-3. Sections 1 and 2 of program 9.

The 16 constants in row 1 of the matrix savevalue will be recognized as the X1 distribution shown in Figure 14-1 except that they are in tenths of a second. They will be used during the run as the mean interarrival times in a way that will be explained when we get to section 6.

Section 2

Section 2 is shown in Figure 14-3. Xacts representing cars enter the system at random intervals of time that are exponentially distributed about the current value of savevalue 1. This value is 30 when the run begins by virtue of the first INITIAL card, but X1 later takes on the values in row 1 of matrix savevalue 1.

When using the fractional selection mode, it is permissible to specify an SNA or to use indirect addressing in the A-field of a TRANSFER block. If this is done, the numerical value of the field A argument is interpreted as the number of *parts per thousand*. The operation of the TRANSFER block in this mode can be summarized by means of an example:

TRANSFER   .X30,AAA,BBB

1. If X30 ≤ 0, the entering xact goes to AAA and never to BBB.
2. If X30 = 45, the entering xact has a .045 probability of going to BBB.
3. If X30 = 450, the entering xact has a .450 probability of going to BBB.
4. If X30 ≥ 1000, the entering xact goes to BBB and never to AAA.

On the basis of this example, it should be clear that the second block in section 2 will send 72% of arriving xacts to "EXACT" and the rest to "REGLR." The percentage of cars having exact change can be easily varied by reinitializing savevalue 3.

While we are talking about *this* TRANSFER block, it should be noted that its field B entry is superfluous. This is because a blank entry in field B of a fractional selection TRANSFER block is interpreted as the address of the next sequential block.

Sections 3 and 4

Sections 3 and 4 pertain to the selection of the best available lane by newly arrived vehicles, and they are shown in Figure 14-4.

The first SELECT block in section 3 works as follows. When a xact enters it, Q1 is tested. If it is equal to zero, the number 1 is put into P4, and the xact proceeds to the next sequential block. If it is not equal to zero, Q2 is tested. If it is equal to zero, the number 2 is put into P4, and the xact proceeds to the next sequential block. If Q2 is also not zero, the xact proceeds to the block whose address is NOTE.

So if either Q1 or Q2 is zero, the queue number is put into P4, and the xact proceeds to the block whose address is LANE. If neither Q1 nor Q2 is zero, the xact proceeds to the SELECT block whose address is NOTE. This block puts the number 1 or 2 into P2 of the entering xact. The length of the queue whose index number is in P2 is then stored in savevalue 10. Having noted which of the two exact change queues is shorter, the xact is now ready to check the regular lanes.

```
* SECTION 3:  SELECTION OF A LANE BY AUTOS WITH EXACT CHANGE

        SELECTE    4,1,2,K0,Q,NOTE    IS EITHER EXACT CHG. LANE EMPTY?
        TRANSFER   ,LANE              IF SO, GO TO THE SELECTED LANE.
  NOTE  SELECTMIN  2,1,2,,Q           IF NOT, PUT NO. OF SHORTER LANE
*                                     INTO P2.  THEN LOOK AT REG. LANES.
        SAVEVALUE  10,Q*2             PUT LENGTH OF SHORTER EXACT CHANGE
*                                     LANE INTO X10.

        SELECTE    4,3,4,K0,Q,SORRY    IS ONE OF REG. LANES EMPTY?
        TRANSFER   ,LANE              IF SO, GO TO SELECTED LANE.
 SORRY  SELECTMIN  3,3,4,,Q           IF NOT, PUT NO. OF SHORTER LANE
*                                     INTO P3.
        SAVEVALUE  11,Q*3             PUT LENGTH OF SHORTER REGULAR LANE
*                                     INTO X11.

        TEST LE    X10,V$LNGTH,LAN34
  LNGTH FVARIABLE  (1+X4/100)X11

        ASSIGN     4,P2               PUT NO. OF SHORTER EXACT LANE IN P4.
        TRANSFER   ,LANE              GO TO SELECTED LANE.

 LAN34  ASSIGN     4,P3               PUT NO. OF SHORTER REG. LANE IN P4.
        TRANSFER   ,LANE              GO TO SELECTED LANE.


* SECTION 4:  SELECTION OF A LANE BY AUTOS WITHOUT EXACT CHANGE

  REG   SELECTMIN  4,3,4,,Q
```

Fig. 14-4. Sections 3 and 4 of program 9.

The third SELECT block in section 3 is similar to the first SELECT block, except that it involves lanes 3 and 4 rather than 1 and 2. If neither of the regular lanes is empty, the index number of the one with the shorter queue is put into P3, and the queue length is stored in savevalue 11. The xact must now choose between the better exact-change lane (length in X10) and the better regular lane (length in X11).

The variable LNGTH has been defined to compute a value equal to 1.35 times the length of the shorter *regular* queue. (Note that the fractional part of the multiplier is easily altered by specifying a different constant in savevalue 4.) The value computed for V$LNGTH is the maximum length that the *exact* change queue could be and still be chosen in preference to the regular lane.

The TEST block is where the xact chooses between the lanes whose numbers are stored in P2 and P3. If X10 is less than or equal to V$LNGTH, the (exact-change) lane in P2 is chosen. If X10 is greater than V$LNGTH, the (regular) lane in P3 is chosen.

It is instructive to note that the SELECT blocks used in section 3 could have been replaced by an arrangement of TEST, ASSIGN, and TRANSFER blocks. For example, the first two blocks in section 3 are equivalent to the following sequence:

```
        TEST E      Q1,K0,LANE2
        ASSIGN      4,1
        TRANSFER    ,LANE
 LANE2  TEST E      Q2,K0,NOTE
        ASSIGN      4,2
        TRANSFER    ,LANE
```

The SELECT blocks are obviously more concise in this situation.   Moreover, they reduce the execution time of the model when used in place of the relatively awkward sequence shown above.

Section 5

The first block in section 5, shown in Figure 14-5, puts the number 1 into parameter 6 of xacts which enter a queue having 15 or more cars in it.   The operation of this block will now be described to serve as a review of how the COUNT block works.

This COUNT block counts how many of the items defined by fields B, C, and E are greater than or equal to the item in field D.   The field D SNA is X6 which was initialized as 15.   The field E SNA denotes the current contents of the queues whose lower and upper index numbers are specified in fields B and C, respectively.   Since fields B and C specify the same queue address, the COUNT block tests only one queue length, namely, the one whose index number is stored in parameter 4 of the current xact.   Thus the count (placed in parameter 6 of the current xact) can be at most 1 if $Q*4 \geq 15$.   It is zero if $Q*4 < 15$.

The **TABULATE**   *4 block will produce four tables, one corresponding to each lane.   These tables will contain automobile transit times in seconds.   They are further discussed in section 7.   The **TABULATE**   10 block will produce one table in which the value of P6 is tabulated.   This too is discussed in section 7.

```
* SECTION 5:  AUTOS GO TO APPROPRIATE LANES AND BOOTHS AFTER
*             CHECKING IF QUEUE EXCEEDS REASONABLE THRESHOLD.

LANE  COUNT GE    6,*4,*4,X6,Q      P6 = 1 IF Q*4 GE X6.

      QUEUE       *4                CARS ENTER QUEUE GIVEN BY P4.
      SEIZE       *4                CARS SEIZE BOOTH GIVEN BY P4.
      DEPART      *4                CARS DEPART QUEUE GIVEN BY P4.
      ADVANCE     P1                TIME IN BOOTH GIVEN BY P1.
      RELEASE     *4                CARS RELEASE BOOTH GIVEN BY P4.
      TABULATE    *4                TABULATE TRANSIT TIMES IN TABLE
*                                   WHOSE NUMBER IS GIVEN BY P4.
      TABULATE    10                TABULATE P6 VALUES IN TABLE 10.
      TERMINATE                     DESTROY XACTS DENOTING AUTOS.


* SECTION 6:  CONTROL XACTS PASS THROUGH EVERY 10 MINUTES.   THEY
*             ASSIGN A NEW VALUE TO X1 EACH TIME.   THEY ALSO PUT
*             THE CURRENT QUEUE LENGTHS AND CLOCK TIME INTO MH1.

      GENERATE    6000              6000 CLOCK UNITS = 10 MINUTES.
      SAVEVALUE   2+,1              ADD 1 TO SAVEVALUE NO. 2.
      SAVEVALUE   1,MH1(1,X2)       SET SAVEVALUE NO. 1 = MH1(1,X2).

      MSAVEVALUE  1,2,X2,Q1,H       SET MH1(2,X2) = Q1.
      MSAVEVALUE  1,3,X2,Q2,H       SET MH1(3,X2) = Q2.
      MSAVEVALUE  1,4,X2,Q3,H       SET MH1(4,X2) = Q3.
      MSAVEVALUE  1,5,X2,Q4,H       SET MH1(5,X2) = Q4.

      MSAVEVALUE  1,6,X2,V$TIME,H   SET MH1(6,X2) = TIME IN MINUTES.

      TERMINATE   1                 DESTROY CONTROL XACT.
```

Fig. 14-5. Sections 5 and 6 of program 9.

Section 6

This section, shown in Figure 14-5, can be regarded as the control and book-keeping portion of program 9. A total of 16 *control xacts* are generated during the run, and they are created at intervals of 6000 clock units, that is, 10 minutes of system time. These xacts trigger certain events that are important to the functioning of our model. Let us see what is involved here.

When the run starts, X1 = 30 because it was so initialized. When 10 minutes have elapsed, the first control xact is created. It immediately increments savevalue 2 from 0 to 1. It then causes the value of MH1(1,X2) to be put into X1. Since X2 = 1 at this point, MH1(1,X2) is 30. So the first control xact does not alter the value of X1 since MH1(1,1) happens to be equal to 30.

The first control xact causes the current contents of queue 1 to be entered into column 1 of row 2 of matrix savevalue 1. It then causes Q2 to be entered into column 1 of row 3 of matrix savevalue 1. Similarly, Q3 is put into MH1(4,1) and Q4 is put into MH1(5,1).

The control xact next causes the current clock time, in minutes, to be placed into column 1 of row 6 of MH1. Then it is terminated. The contents of halfword matrix savevalue 1 at this point are shown in Figure 14-6. The circled zeroes indicate that all four queues were empty at the 10-minute mark. All the other zeroes are simply initial values of the MH1 cells that have not yet been changed.

The second control xact is created at the 20-minute mark. It increments X2 to 2, and then it sets X1 to MH1(1,2), which is 28. It then causes the current queue lengths to be put into column 2 of rows 2 through 5 of the matrix savevalue. Lastly, it causes the current time to be put into MH1(6,2).

The sixteenth control xact is created at the 160-minute mark, that is, when C1 = 96000. It sets X1 to MH1(1,16), and it causes appropriate values to be put into MH1(2,16), MH1(3,16), MH1(4,16), MH1(5,16), and MH1(6,16). Then it is destroyed.

Columns	1	2	3	4 15	16
Rows					
1	30	28	26	24 22	24
2	⓪	0	0	0	0
3	0	0	0	0	0
4	0	0	0	0	0
5	0	0	0	0	0
6	10	0	0	0 0	0

Fig. 14-6. Contents of matrix savevalue 1 after termination of first control transaction.

Each control xact passes through the section 6 blocks in zero clock time. Since the run termination count is 16 (as is seen in section 7), the termination of the sixteenth control xact signals the end of the run. Thus the setting of X1 to 24 at C1 = 96000 is incidental, since the run ends at that point.

Section 7

This section (shown in Figure 14-7) contains all of the variable and table definition cards except for the variable LNGTH which was included in section 3 as a matter of convenience. The variable TIME is referenced whenever a value is to be entered in row 6 of matrix savevalue 1. This variable computes the current clock time in minutes, based on the fact that 600 tenths of a second equals 1 minute. The variable DIVID computes the transit time of xacts in seconds every time it is referenced.

Table 10 tabulates the values of P6 which are always either 0 or 1. Thus a certain percentage of the entries in table 10 will have an upper limit of zero, and all the rest will have an upper limit of one. The mean argument of table 10 will give the proportion of xacts with P6 = 1. To see why this is so, assume that 35 of 100 xacts have P6 = 1 while the rest have P6 = 0. The sum of arguments will be 35. The mean argument is this sum divided by the number of entries, that is, 35/100 = .350.

The combined run termination count of the two START cards is 16, and so the run ends upon the termination of the sixteenth control transaction. The first START card provides a 10-minute interval to prime the system by establishing a flow of traffic. The end-of-run statistics will not include this initialization period. For example, facility utilizations will reflect the behavior of the system between 6000 and 96,000 clock units, that is, an interval of 2.5 hours.

Section 8

Section 8, shown in Figure 14-8, contains the output specifications and the END card, since program 7 involves just one run. The REPORT card tells the program that the *output editor* option is being utilized, and the ensuing *request cards* specify the desired output. Notice that no blank cards have been included

```
* SECTION 7:  DEFINE VARIABLES AND TABLES.  CONTROL RUN LENGTH.

TIME   VARIABLE    C1/600              GIVES CLOCK TIME IN MINUTES
DIVID  VARIABLE    M1/10               GIVES TRANSIT TIME IN SECONDS

     1 TABLE        V$DIVID,10,10,30
     2 TABLE        V$DIVID,10,10,30
     3 TABLE        V$DIVID,10,10,30
     4 TABLE        V$DIVID,10,10,30
    10 TABLE        P6,0,1,3

       START        1,NP
       START        15
```

Fig. 14-7.   Section 7 of program 9.

* SECTION 8:   SPECIFY DESIRED OUTPUT.

```
      REPORT _____ - _____ _____ - _____ - - _____ ⎫
      EJECT                                                    ⎪
      SPACE       2                                            ⎪
                  RESULTS OF TOLL PLAZA SIMULATION WITH FOUR BOOTHS ⎪
      SPACE       3                                            ⎪
* ROW 1 OF MATRIX CONTAINS AVERAGE INTERARRIVAL TIMES IN TENTHS OF A SEC ⎪
COND.  ROWS 2 THROUGH 5 CONTAIN CURRENT QUEUE CONTENTS.        ⎪
* ROW 6 GIVES THE TIME IN MINUTES FOR EACH COLUMN OF THE MATRIX. ⎪
      SPACE       3                                            ⎪
MHSA  TITLE       1,THIS MATRIX CONTAINS BOTH INPUT DATA AND RESULTS.  ⎬ Editing cards
      SPACE       3                                            ⎪
      TEXT        #T10,3/2RXX.X#% OF CARS ENTERED A QUEUE WITH #X6,2/XXC ⎪
# CARS ALREADY IN IT.                                          ⎪
      SPACE       3                                            ⎪
* THE TABLE BELOW CONTAINS FACILITY AND QUEUE STATISTICS.  FACILITIES 1U ⎪
 AND 2 REPRESENT EXACT CHANGE BOOTHS, AND FACILITIES 3 AND 4  ⎪
* REPRESENT REGULAR CHANGE BOOTHS.  TIMES ARE IN TENTHS OF A SECOND. ⎪
      SPACE       2                                            ⎪
*           NO. OF      AVG. UTIL.     NO. OF AUTOS    AVG. TIME  AVG. NOO ⎪
. OF AVG. TIME                                                 ⎪
*           BOOTH        OF BOOTH      DURING RUN     IN BOOTH   CARS INN ⎪
 LINE  IN QUEUE                                                ⎪
      SPACE       1                                            ⎭
8     FORMAT      1-4/F1,F2,F3,F4,Q3,Q7 _____ - _____ - _____ ⎫
      GRAPH       QM,1,4                                        ⎪
      ORIGIN      50,10                                         ⎪
      X           ,5,10                                         ⎬ Graph cards
      Y           30,5,10,4                                     ⎪
1     STATEMENT   2,76,THIS GRAPH SHOWS THE MAXIMUM LENGTHS OF THE 4 QU1 ⎪
EUES DURING THE SIMULATION.                                   ⎪
      ENDGRAPH _____ - _____ - _____ - - _____ ⎭
      OUTPUT
      END
```

Fig. 14-8.   Section 8 of program 9.

among the request cards because the output editor only recognizes those cards that are listed in Table 13-2. You will also notice that program 9 utilizes all of the Table 13-2 card types except the INCLUDE card.

The *editing cards* produce a single page of output containing the indicated output data. The *graph cards* produce a printout page which contains a bar graph giving maximum queue lengths. The OUTPUT card causes the two user-designed output pages to be followed by the normal standard output that would have occurred if the output editor had not been used.

14.4   RESULTS OF SIMULATION

The printout from program 9 consists of the following:

1. Symbolic listing, cross-reference dictionary, and input listing.
2. Report generator output—one page of edited statistics and one page containing a graph.
3. Standard end-of-run statistics including clock times, block counts, facility and queue statistics, savevalue and matrix savevalue contents, and frequency tables.

RESULTS OF TOLL PLAZA SIMULATION WITH FOUR BOOTHS

ROW 1 OF MATRIX CONTAINS AVERAGE INTERARRIVAL TIMES IN TENTHS OF A SECOND. ROWS 2 THROUGH 5 CONTAIN CURRENT QUEUE CONTENTS. ROW 6 GIVES THE TIME IN MINUTES FOR EACH COLUMN OF THE MATRIX.

THIS MATRIX CONTAINS BOTH INPUT DATA AND RESULTS.

MATRIX HALFWORD SAVEVALUE 1

COL.	1	2	3	4	5	6	7	8	9	10	11	12	13	14	15	16
ROW 1	30	28	26	24	22	20	18	16	14	12	14	16	18	20	22	24
2	0	0	1	0	1	0	0	2	1	21	33	57	46	41	6	0
3	0	0	1	0	1	0	0	3	0	21	33	57	45	41	7	0
4	0	0	0	0	3	1	0	4	4	16	29	44	45	33	22	13
5	0	0	0	0	2	0	0	3	4	15	28	44	45	33	20	12
6	10	20	30	40	50	60	70	80	90	100	110	120	130	140	150	160

39.5% OF CARS ENTERED A QUEUE WITH 15 CARS ALREADY IN IT.

THE TABLE BELOW CONTAINS FACILITY AND QUEUE STATISTICS. FACILITIES 1 AND 2 REPRESENT EXACT CHANGE BOOTHS, AND FACILITIES 3 AND 4 REPRESENT REGULAR CHANGE BOOTHS. TIMES ARE IN TENTHS OF A SECOND.

NO. OF BOOTH	AVG. UTIL. OF BOOTH	NO. OF AUTOS DURING RUN	AVG. TIME IN BOOTH	AVG. NO. OF CARS IN LINE	AVG. TIME IN QUEUE
1	.906	1944	44.757	12.758	630.031
2	.689	1471	45.027	12.405	809.601
3	.906	876	99.295	13.042	1408.368
4	.735	744	94.889	12.651	1606.565

Fig. 14-9. Report generator statistical output for program 9. Note: This is a type-set facsimile of the computer printout. Therefore the spacing and positioning of various sentences and columns of numbers is not identical to the printout. For example, the sentence beginning with "the table below..." occupies 2 lines on the printout but 3 lines in this representation.

Output from Program 9

The editing cards in Figure 14-8 produced the page of output shown in Figure 14-9. The matrix provides a history of the queue lengths with respect to the mean interarrival time (row 1) and clock time (row 6). It is interesting to note that the queues tended to peak around 10 to 20 minutes *after* the interval of minimum average interarrival time had occurred.

The queue lengths in the last few columns indicate that the exact-change lanes recovered more rapidly from their swamped state than the regular lanes. In practice, we would expect some cars in the regular lanes to notice this and switch over to an exact-change lane. Only drivers having exact change could do this of course, and it is not possible to say how many drivers would qualify, since the model was not designed to keep track of exact-change cars going to regular booths. The desirability of incorporating this effect into the model is questionable, but it could be done if desired.

The 39.5% figure is the mean argument of table 10 with the decimal point shifted. From the table at the bottom of Figure 14-9 we see that cars in exact-change lanes waited in line for more than 1 minute, on the average. Cars in regular lanes waited for about 2.5 minutes.

The graph cards in Figure 14-8 produced the graph shown in Figure 14-10. This graph is self-explanatory, although the bar heights are not perfectly readable. From left to right, they are 59, 59, 49, and 48.

The statistics of interest that were not included in the report generator output have been summarized in Table 14-1. They are self-explanatory.

Analysis of Output

From the standpoint of the toll plaza planners, the results of program 9 are probably borderline. On the negative side, the following was found:

1. The average time spent by cars at the toll plaza ranged from 67 seconds for lane 1 vehicles to 171 seconds for lane 4 vehicles.

2. The percentage of cars spending 1 minute or less at the toll plaza ranged from 65% for lane 1 vehicles to 43% for lane 4 vehicles.

3. Around 40% of arriving automobiles found themselves entering queues that already contained 15 or more cars—and they were choosing the best lane available!

4. During a half-hour period the four lanes were all backed up quite badly, with queues containing roughly 40 to 60 vehicles apiece.

The foregoing results apply to a 2.5-hour simulated time period. But the flow of automobile traffic was relatively light during the first hour, and the situation only became bad during the last hour or so. Therefore, the average transit times and percentages are diluted by the fact that almost half of the simulated time period involved a relatively mild rate of traffic.

This suggests the advisability of taking a closer look at what happens during the "bad hour." For example, consider the following. If 49 cars are waiting in line for a regular booth, and if the average booth time is 11 seconds, the last car

THIS GRAPH SHOWS THE MAXIMUM LENGTHS OF THE 4 QUEUES
DURING THE SIMULATION.

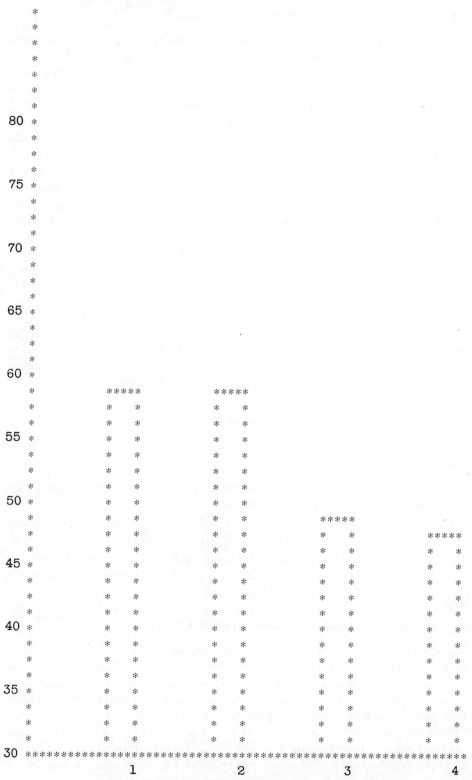

Fig. 14-10. Report generator graphic output for program 9.

TABLE 14-1. PROGRAM 9 RESULTS – SELECTED STANDARD OUTPUT STATISTICS

Absolute and relative clock times: 96000

Block counts, interpreted
  Number of vehicle xacts to enter system: 5060
  Number of vehicle xacts to leave system: 5032
  Number of control xacts to enter and leave system: 16

Queue statistics

	1	2	3	4
Number of zero entries	267	245	104	87
Percent of zero entries	13.7	16.6	11.6	11.5

Table statistics

	1	2	3	4
Mean argument[a]	67.064	85.014	150.993	170.598
Cumulative percent for class with upper limit = 60[b]	64.9	54.0	52.9	43.0

[a] Average transit time in seconds.

[b] Percentage of cars with transit times $\leq$ 60 seconds.

must wait for about 9 minutes to finally enter the booth. So if the average transit time was 67 to 171 seconds over the entire 2.5-hour period, it must have been far higher during the bad hour. Similarly, the other statistics would look substantially worse if confined to the bad hour.

Do these findings rule out the use of only two exact-change and two regular booths? It would seem so. However, there are some other avenues to be explored before going to five booths in the northbound lanes. For example, it might be advisable to narrow the simulated time period to the bad hour and make several runs using different random number sequences. It may be that program 9 happened to give the worst possible results. If the southbound lanes have light traffic during the northbound traffic peak, it may be feasible to temporarily designate a southbound booth as a fifth northbound booth.

In any event, it would appear that further simulations should be performed. The basic model can be modified easily to provide them. Eventually the toll plaza planners will obtain enough results to permit a sound decision on the matter.

14.5 DIFFERENCES BETWEEN GPSS/360 AND OTHER VERSIONS

Program 9 introduced no differences that have not previously been discussed except for matrix savevalues.

Since GPS K does not use halfwords, the A-field of the MATRIX card always contains X, and the D-field of the MSAVEVALUE block is not used.

Flow Simulator and GPSS III do not include matrix savevalues. To vary X1 in program 9, a list numerical-valued function could have been used. To store the queue lengths, 64 savevalue locations could have been used.

14.6 SUMMARY

We saw how a realistic problem was solved — well, not quite *solved* — by constructing a GPSS model and using simulation results as the basis for making a decision. In particular, the process of collecting empirical data and defining the system was illustrated. The formulation and operation of the model were described. And the simulation results were presented and interpreted.

Matrix savevalues provide a powerful means for loading constants into a model and for storing time series data. A generalized model can be structured to simulate a variety of different situations simply by specifying different arrays of constants.

The usefulness of the SELECT blocks was demonstrated. These blocks often do the job of several other blocks, and they are more efficient in running time as well as in reducing the number of cards needed. This would be more dramatically demonstrated if program 9 were modified to include more than two exact-change and regular booths.

Program 9 provides a good example of the occasional disparity between *simulation* time and *simulated* time. The process of lane selection takes more simulation time than the process of passing through a booth. But the former occurs in zero simulated time whereas the booth times span quite a few clock units.

In view of the long queues that formed in the toll plaza model, we could have significantly reduced the running time by inserting user chains as explained in Section 12.2.

CHAPTER 15
Summary and Review

The purpose of this chapter is to review what has been covered in the *GPSS Primer*. We take inventory of what you should know and what remains to be learned if you wish to pursue GPSS further. This chapter generally applies to all four versions of GPSS; the reader is expected to recognize which items do not pertain to the particular version in which he is interested.

15.1 GENERAL REVIEW

Background

Digital computer simulation is rapidly growing in importance. It is being applied in a wide variety of fields ranging from production schedules to hospital designs. The use of computer simulation techniques permits a system to be evaluated, manipulated, tested, or optimized without any direct action on the real system. A simulation run shows how a system will behave, given a certain set of ground rules and assumptions. It will not generally solve for unknowns or find true optimum solutions. The approach taken is to "try something and see what happens."

GPSS has become the most widely used *discrete-change* simulation language. It is a very high level language which has most of its organizational structure and logic built in. As a result, its external appearance is relatively uncluttered, and it is easy to use.

Bird's-Eye View of GPSS

GPSS is more than a language. It is a *system* that involves the expression of a *model* as a *block diagram* through which *units of traffic* flow. Virtually any system that can be idealized in this fashion can be well represented as a GPSS model. By its nature, GPSS is the best language available for *queuing* problems.

GPSS processes events *one at a time* and in sequence although they may occur either simultaneously *or* sequentially in the (real) system being simulated. To accomplish this, the underlying program logic is embodied in a *control algorithm* that involves a *clock, scan, transaction chains,* and *indicators.*

GPSS can be viewed by the student as having three *levels.* The *upper level* is concerned with model building, program writing, cards, entities, output, and so on. In short, it consists of the visible aspects of GPSS and those with which a beginner first becomes familiar.

The *middle level* is associated with the control algorithm and the underlying logical structure of GPSS. In other words, it pertains to the logical operation of the GPSS simulator. A fairly good understanding of this level can be attained without difficulty, and it is well worth having because it (1) enhances your ability to work with the upper level of GPSS and (2) provides valuable insight into how GPSS works.

The *lower level* pertains to the physical or electronic deployment of a model in the core. It also pertains to the makeup of the built-in GPSS programs and subroutines that reside in a core during a run and breathe life into an input deck. The lower level has been discussed superficially in this book to provide a general idea of what is involved. An intimate knowledge of the lower level is unnecessary, except to the advanced GPSS programmer.

Role of Randomness

Most GPSS models involve events that occur at *random intervals* of time. Indeed, the usefulness of GPSS would be greatly diminished if everything happened at regular intervals!

The element of randomness takes many different forms in a model. Units of traffic may enter the system at various times. They may be delayed in the system for random lengths of time. They may be randomly classified as having different characteristics. And so forth. But in every case, the desired type of random behavior emanates from the built-in *random number generator*.

Whenever a random event is supposed to occur, the *GPSS simulator* obtains a random number and uses it in an appropriate manner. It may be used *implicitly,* or its use may be *explicitly* specified by the programmer.

Writing a GPSS Program

Writing a GPSS program is more or less equivalent to constructing a GPSS model or block diagram. To convert a real (or postulated) system into a GPSS model/block diagram/program, you must analyze and define it and obtain appropriate empirical data. The model can often be viewed as a *generalized logical structure* whose specific makeup and behavior are determined by the input data.

At any rate, the block diagram finally takes the form of a *symbolic program* (also called a *source or input deck*). This program consists of *block, control, definition, and comment cards*. In many cases, it is possible to write a symbolic program without the intervening steps of formally defining the system, constructing a flow chart, and drawing a block diagram.

Block cards must, of course, be arranged in a very definite order since they represent the block diagram through which *transactions* move. Most of the definition cards may be placed almost anywhere in the input deck. Most control cards go near the end of the deck. Comment cards may be interspersed throughout the deck.

We have been discussing GPSS in terms of *cards* since they are easy to visualize and are most commonly used. This does not cause any loss of generality because a card is synonymous with a line of coding. As a matter of fact, it is usual to refer to each line in a GPSS program as a "card" even when magnetic tape is being used.

It is worth reiterating that GPSS offers a repertoire of predefined card types (approximately 100 in GPSS/360). The user selects block, definition, and control cards from this repertoire and, in most cases, customizes them to suit his purposes.

Blocks and Transactions

Blocks and **transactions** are the *basic entities* in GPSS. The ordered assemblage of blocks is known as the block diagram, and the units of traffic that flow through it are called transactions. Transactions are the driving force in a GPSS model because the status of the system does not change unless xacts move through it. Xacts progress from block to block, moving down the program listing so to speak, unless they are diverted to a nonsequential block.

Whenever a xact enters a block, it causes that block to execute its particular *block-type subroutine*. Roughly half of all GPSS blocks are designed to do something *to the xacts* which enter them. They may do one or more of the following things:

Pass them to the next sequential block.

Pass them to a block other than the next sequential block.

Pass them without any delay, that is, in the same clock instant that they entered.

Delay them for a specified length of time (ADVANCE block only).

Block them until a specified condition is met or a particular situation exists.

Modify transaction parameters or other attributes, such as priority and mark time.

Destroy entering transactions.

Every xact created by a GENERATE block represents an *assembly set* of one. If it enters a SPLIT block, all of the *copy xacts* become members of its assembly set as do all subsequent copies which can be related back to the original *parent transaction*. Again, "original" parent xacts are always created by GENERATE blocks.

A transaction can be thought of as having three simultaneous images, one on each level. On the upper level it is a unit of traffic whose progress through the block diagram is monitored by the program. On the middle level it is manipulated by the GPSS scan and is linked to various chains. On the lower level it is a collection of computer words at a location designated by its number.

The *current events chain scan* attempts to service only one transaction at a time. It normally moves this xact—the *current transaction*—through as many blocks as possible before it lets go and latches onto another xact. The current xact is the only "live" xact in the model at any time, and the four SNAs associated with xacts always pertain to it.

Other Entities

Facilities, storages, and **logic switches** are classified as *equipment entities.* A facility may be either *seized* or *preempted* by only *one* xact at a time. A storage is very much like several facilities in parallel. Facilities and storages are always empty at the beginning of a run.

Logic switches may be either *reset* or *set.* Their status can be used to control the flow of xacts via GATE blocks. (This statement is also true of facilities, storages, and assembly sets.) Logic switches are initially reset unless specified otherwise.

Queues and **frequency tables** are classified as *statistical entities* because their only function in a model is to collect statistics. However, these statistics can be referenced during the run and used to affect the behavior of the model. The formation of waiting lines in a GPSS model occurs irrespective of the presence or absence of queue entities. The latter are included by the user when he wants to obtain queue statistics.

Functions and **variables** are classified as *computational entities.* No block types are associated with these entities—just definition cards. They compute values whenever they are referenced by appropriate SNAs.

There are three types of *numerical-valued* functions: D, C, and L. There are two types of *attribute-valued* functions: E and M. All functions are referenced by the *standard numerical attribute* FNj.

There are two types of variables. *Arithmetic variables* are subcategorized as *arithmetic* and *floating-point,* and they are referenced by Vj. *Boolean variables* always compute a value of 0 or 1, and they are referenced by BVj.

Savevalues and **matrix savevalues** are classified as *reference entities* because they store numerical values that can be referenced by appropriate SNAs. A savevalue stores a *single value* while a matrix savevalue stores an *array of numbers.* These entities are used in many ways. For example, there is no way to obtain a parameter value from a transaction other than the current xact unless it is stored in a savevalue.

A very important use of matrix savevalues is to load constants into a model. This allows a generalized model to simulate a large number of variations which can be specified by simply plugging in a different array of constants.

User chains and **groups** are classified as *chain entities.* User chains are created and manipulated by means of LINK/UNLINK blocks. They are used to temporarily place xacts on inactive status so that they will be ignored until the time has come to bring them back under the control of the GPSS scan. A transaction on a user chain can only be removed from it when *another xact* enters an UNLINK block.

There are five block types which can be used to establish, manipulate, and dismantle groups. (See Table A-1.) A group consists of a collection of transactions or numbers. A *group of xacts* may represent the items in a model which have a common characteristic, such as a certain color. If these items belong to a group, they can all be referenced at the same time regardless of their position and status in the model. A *group of numbers* may, for example, represent all the logic switches that are set or all of the queues whose contents exceed a certain limit.

Entity Addresses

There are two ways of looking at *entity addresses*. From the user's point of view, they are *tags* or *labels* which he assigns to entities so they can be referred to elsewhere in his model. From the simulator's point of view, they denote the *locations* of entities in the computer.

The user can directly or indirectly specify the addresses of the entities in his model, except for transactions. *Direct specification* is accomplished by assigning *symbolic tags* or *index numbers*. *Indirect specification* pertains to the use of *SNAs* and *indirect addressing;* it can be thought of as *dynamic* addressing.

Before a *simulation run* can proceed, all of the entities directly specified in the source program are assigned *core locations* by the *assembly program*. These locations are denoted by numerical addresses, and they remain unchanged throughout the run. Entities that are dynamically specified are also assigned core locations which they also retain for the duration of the run.

The preceding three paragraphs pertain to entities *other than transactions*. Xacts are created and destroyed during a run, and they are never labeled by the user. When a xact is created, the GPSS program assigns it an address which is the lowest numbered location available. It occupies that location for the duration of its existence in the model.

Entity Statistics

As a simulation run proceeds, the GPSS program automatically maintains appropriate *statistics* for all of the entities in the model except logic switches, functions, and variables. Most of these statistics are frequently updated and recomputed as the run proceeds.

Since entity statistics are continually kept current, it is possible to interrupt a run at any time and display meaningful statistics. This "principle" is applied in several ways:

1. To *obtain* a set of *final statistics* at the end of a run, whenever the end happens to occur.
2. To *obtain intermediate statistics* during a run.
3. To *use individual statistics* to affect the behavior of the model via SNAs.

The kinds of statistics maintained by the GPSS simulator can be surmised from Appendices D and F which summarize the standard numerical attributes and the standard GPSS output, respectively.

Entity Attributes

In general, entities have two kinds of addressable attributes—*standard numerical attributes* and *standard logical attributes*. SNAs and SLAs afford the user a means for making the operation of one part of his system dependent on the status or behavior of other parts of the model. They represent properties or states of the simulated system, and they provide dynamic access to the results of the simulation as it proceeds.

There are 45 SNAs in the four versions of GPSS. Three are *systemwide attributes,* and all the others are associated with specific entities. Every entity except logic switches has at least one SNA associated with it. SNAs, when referenced, assume numerical values that are almost always integers. The standard numerical attributes are listed and defined in Table D-1.

There are 12 SLAs in all four versions of GPSS. Ten are associated with equipment entities and two with transactions. An SLA expresses a possible status of the entity to which it pertains. If the entity is in that status, the SLA is true; otherwise it is false. The standard logical attributes are listed and defined in Table E-1.

The nonaddressable, as well as addressable attributes of the various entity types can be discerned by looking at the core words for each entity type. In this way, you can learn which data items (i.e., attributes) comprise each entity.

Output

One of the biggest attractions of GPSS is the fact that it automatically provides a complete output of system statistics without the need for instructions pertaining to the accumulation or formatting of these statistics. The normal end-of-run output, referred to as the *standard output,* includes statistical data pertaining to the simulator clock and most of the entities in the model. (See Appendix F.) From it, the user can deduce the behavior of his model and its final status. The standard output occurs in the absence of serious error conditions, the no-print option, and the output editor option.

The *output editor* (*report generator*) may either supersede or augment the standard output. It is used to produce a user-designed output which includes only those statistics of interest. Selected statistics may also be displayed in the form of bar graphs or histograms.

In addition to the end-of-run output, there are various intermediate outputs that can be obtained during a run. The *snap interval* option causes the complete set of statistics to be printed out at various times during the run. There are also several block types, used mainly for diagnostic purposes, that cause selected data to be printed out during a run.

15.2   WHAT HAS—AND HAS NOT—BEEN COVERED

Being an introductory book, the *GPSS Primer* has not attempted to cover all phases of GPSS. In particular, some of the more advanced features and internal aspects have been treated sketchily, and some have not been discussed at all. However, most of the external and internal aspects—especially the former—have been covered. From this broad foundation, it is only a short step to learning the remaining aspects of GPSS.

The purpose of this section is to take stock of what you should know at this point. While we are taking inventory of what has been covered, we also take note of what has not been covered.

Entities

The two *basic entities* were discussed in some detail, especially transactions. However, we did not describe the transaction data that can be printed out by various means, such as the PRINT block and field D of the START card. Although we covered most of the block types, we did not pay very much attention to the fact that blocks are entities for which two block types, CHANGE and EXECUTE, exist.   In addition, there are several control cards which enable the user to override the normal assignment of block addresses by the assembly program.   (See Appendix C.)

The three *equipment entities* and two *reference entities* were covered fairly thoroughly.   Facilities, logic switches, and savevalues are defined implicitly in a model by the presence of certain block types.   But storages and matrix savevalues require definition cards.

The two *statistical entities* were discussed at some length, but frequency tables were only partially covered.   For example, we did not talk about the *weighting option,* and we did not discuss the various *modes* in which tables can be used.   These will be brought out soon, but for now the point is made that the usefulness of table entities extends far beyond the tabulation of SNAs such as M1.

Most aspects of the three *computational entities* were covered.   Both arithmetic (ordinary as well as floating-point) and boolean variables were explained.   Numerical-valued functions were discussed in some detail, especially C-type functions used to obtain random values from probability distributions.   (See Appendix G.)   Attribute-valued functions, however, were not covered.

One of the two *chain entities* — user chains — was covered in some detail.   But groups were not discussed at all except for a brief description in the preceding section.

Blocks—The Box Score

You should now be familiar with 35 of the 44 block types in GPSS/360.   All of the blocks in all four versions of GPSS are listed in Appendix A along with an indication of what goes in their respective subfields.

You should know quite well how to use and code 33 of the aforementioned 35 blocks.   The other two blocks, TRANSFER and TABULATE, were only partially covered.   The TRANSFER block can be used in any of nine different modes of which only three were described: unconditional, fractional, and BOTH.   The ALL, PICK, function (FN), parameter (P), subroutine (SBR), and simultaneous (SIM) modes were not discussed.

As far as the TABULATE block is concerned, the significance of field B was not shown.   It can be used to specify a weighting factor which has the effect of making more than one entry in the table for each xact to enter the TABULATE block.

The ALTER, EXAMINE, JOIN, REMOVE, and SCAN blocks were not mentioned.   They are associated with group entities.   They are used to create and operate upon groups.

The CHANGE and EXECUTE blocks were also not mentioned. The CHANGE block is used to change a block in a model by causing a specified block to be substituted for it. The EXECUTE block can temporarily "act" like some other specified block in the model.

The HELP block is used to call in non-GPSS program segments during the execution of a GPSS model. For example, it may be desired to perform a FORTRAN or PL/I computation in order to obtain needed results efficiently.

The WRITE block, when entered by a transaction, collects certain information concerning that xact and causes it to be written on a tape. This information includes the number of clock units since the entry of the previous xact and the parameters values of the current xact, among other things. In this way, a sequence of xacts is recorded on a tape for future reference.

Definition Cards — The Box Score

You should know how to use and code all ten definition cards, although several were not covered in all their aspects. The definition cards for all four versions of GPSS are listed in Appendix B along with their coding rules and pertinent remarks. The only cards we will mention here are those that have not been described fully.

The FUNCTION and function follower cards were not described for attribute-valued functions. The E-type function is analogous to the D-type function except that the Y arguments are SNAs rather than constants. The M-type function differs from the L-type function in the same way.

The TABLE card has been used with SNAs such as M1 and Pj in its A-field. However, three other types of arguments can be used: (1) an SNA followed by a minus sign, (2) the mnemonic "RT," and (3) the mnemonic "IA." These correspond to the *difference, arrival rate, and interarrival time modes,* respectively.

Control Cards — The Box Score

Of the 54 control cards listed in Table C-1 for the four versions of GPSS, approximately half have been discussed. This may seem unimpressive, but it is not bad at all when you consider that only three are essential: SIMULATE, START, and END.

The GPSS control cards serve a variety of purposes. The so-called *basic control cards* have all been covered as have the *output editor and macro cards.* In addition, several miscellaneous control cards have been mentioned. We will not attempt to take inventory of the control cards here since there are so many of them, and most are not essential in the same sense as the block and definition cards. However, a handy summary of the control cards and their general functions is provided in Appendix C.

SNA's, SLA's, and Mnemonic Operators

We have said that GPSS offers a predefined repertoire of card types that are used to construct models. Similarly, it includes a repertoire of *mnemonic symbols* which are used as card *arguments* and *auxiliary operators.* These symbols comprise standard numerical attributes, standard logical attributes, conditional operators, and various other symbols that do not fit into these three categories.

Most of the 45 standard numerical attributes in GPSS were not individually discussed. However, they are all defined in Table D-1, and beyond that, no explanation is really necessary. The 12 standard logical attributes and the 6 conditional operators have been discussed in connection with the block types which utilize them as auxiliary operators. They are listed in Table E-1.

Among the "various other symbols" are the auxiliary operators MAX and MIN, TRANSFER block mode designators, TABLE card mode designators, and so on. In addition, there is a long list of SNA-like mnemonics that are used in the E-fields of the COUNT and SELECT blocks and in various output editor request cards. The great majority of these symbols have been listed at appropriate places in this book and can easily be looked up when needed.

Output

Both the standard and the report generator outputs were covered quite thoroughly except for the fact that not all of the output editor cards were explained in detail. The various methods of obtaining output during a run were also well covered.

Two modes of output were not described. First, we did not describe the transaction information that is printed out under certain circumstances, for example, a "1" in field D of the START card. Second, we did not talk about the outputs that occur under various error conditions.

As far as the nonoutput part of the printout—namely the *program listing*—is concerned, we did not discuss the LIST and UNLIST cards. These two control cards can be inserted in the deck to suppress the listing of all the cards sandwiched between them.

Internal Aspects

You should have a good basic understanding of how the control algorithm works. The roles and operation of the various transaction chains and scans should be fairly clear. It remains for you to become familiar with all the indicators and flags and which ones are set under which circumstances—if you want to fill in all the missing details.

It should be mentioned that GPS K, unlike the other three versions, uses the *atom chain* concept. This concept is associated with groups, multilevel preempting, and multiple queue membership by xacts. GPS K also departs from GPSS/360 in not distinguishing between *interrupt and matching chains.* In both cases, xacts are treated as being on *interrupt status.*

The built-in GPSS programs were not identified and described except for references to portions of the package such as the assembly program, GPSS simulator, random number generator, block-type subroutines, and so on. A familiarity with these programs is useful only to an advanced practitioner of GPSS.

The *partitioning of the core* into *entities sections* and a *common area* and the *alloca-*

tion of entities within these sections were discussed. However, we did not look at the detailed makeup (i.e., the words, bytes, and bits) of each entity type. To do so would be to identify every attribute (addressable and nonaddressable) of each entity type.

Errors and Diagnostics

Errors and *diagnostics* have not been discussed at all except for scattered remarks about illegal entries and some potentially error-causing practices. GPSS features an elaborate system of error detection that is designed (1) to provide the user with a clear indication of the source of the problem (within reason), (2) to minimize the number of runs needed to eliminate the errors in a model, and (3) to distinguish between fatal and lesser errors so that a run will occur if at all possible.

There are two classes of errors—*assembly errors,* which are detected during the assembly phase, and *execution* (or *running*) errors, which occur during the simulation run. The detection of an error condition during the assembly phase does not cause the assembly program to quit. It continues to look for additional errors in order to minimize the number of runs required to remove such conditions. Appropriate messages are inserted into the symbolic listing beneath any cards that are found to have an error. If no significant errors are found, the simulation will be initiated. If there are any significant (fatal) assembly errors, the run will be deleted. Incidentally, the majority of assembly errors are fatal.

Once the simulation is under way, an execution (or input or running or simulation) error may occur. As a rule, the run is immediately terminated, and an error message is printed, followed by a "dump" of the transaction chain contents along with the standard statistical output up to that point. There are a few special situations where a suspected execution error condition will be stated in the printout as a warning although the run is allowed to proceed.

Most of the GPSS manuals (see the list of references) contain lists of error messages. The longest list is provided by GPSS/360 which defines assembly, input, execution, and output errors as well as execution warning messages. It may be worthwhile to peruse the list of error messages in your manual since it will give you an indication of some things you should not do or should at least be aware of.

Miscellaneous Features

Numeric, symbolic, and indirect addressing of entities have been fully explained, but *relative addressing* has not. The latter, available in all four versions, enables the programmer to specify a block address relative to some other block address. A block address can be specified in a variable subfield as the (symbolic) address of some other block, plus-or-minus *n* blocks. For example, TRANSFER   ,AAA+3 sends entering transactions to the third block after the block labeled AAA.

Macros, offered in GPSS/360 and GPS K, were covered, but not in complete detail. The *reallocate* feature, offered in all four versions, was explained in general terms, but the rules for its usage were not given.   The HELP block, included in all versions except Flow Simulator, was mentioned but not explained.   It is a feature that can be invaluable in certain situations but is not ordinarily used in the "average" GPSS model.

A number of other features were not discussed, all of them associated with various control cards.   For example, we did not explain how to alter the *random number seed*, although we indicated that there are provisions to do so.   We did not discuss the building and *updating* of models on *tape*, nor did we discuss the role of tape or disk storage in connection with GPSS.   You can get a general idea of what can be done by perusing Appendix C.

15.3 WHAT NEXT?

Before we talk about where to go from here, let us take note of where "here" is.   You should now be in a position to construct reasonably sophisticated GPSS models.   (However, before the cards are punched, it would be advisable to check some of the details in the manual for the particular version of GPSS you are using, especially if it is not GPSS/360.)   You should be able to follow the logic of relatively complex GPSS models.   And you should have an appreciation of discrete-event simulation systems and modeling that extends beyond the specific structure of GPSS.

Where you go from here depends on your own particular purposes and inclinations.   If you wanted to equip yourself with the ability to build a GPSS model, or if you just wanted to learn GPSS, you are now there.   But if you want to learn the "rest" of GPSS and become proficient in its application, then:

1. Consult your manual to become familiar with its contents and also the items not covered in this book.
2. Examine GPSS programs that have been written by others in order to acquire more of a feel for the composition of GPSS models and for programming techniques.
3. Construct and run GPSS models; *there is no substitute for this type of experience.*

While we are talking about what lies ahead, we should reiterate two points:

1. If you will be using GPSS V, you should have been reading Chapters 1 to 15 and Appendices A to G through the eyes of a GPSS/360 user.   Now, you should read Appendix H to bridge the gap between GPSS/360 and GPSS V.
2. By and large, a knowledge of GPSS/360, not to mention GPSS V, will stand you in good stead for future versions of GPSS.

APPENDIX A
GPSS Blocks

There are 44 block types in GPSS/360. This figure includes the HELP block which, due to its specialized nature, is sometimes omitted from lists of GPSS blocks. The HELP block is used by experienced programmers to incorporate non-GPSS program segments into a GPSS model. It should be mentioned that the 44 block types listed in Table A-1 comprise the "standard" GPSS/360 set; modified versions at certain installations may contain a few additional block types.

As was just stated, Table A-1 applies to GPSS/360 without qualification. But it should be used in conjunction with Table A-2 for the other three versions.

GPS K offers the same inventory of 44 blocks as GPSS/360. There are a few differences in the subfields associated with several of them, and these are noted in Table A-2. However, GPS K has been designed to accept any block card, except HELP, that is legal in GPSS/360.

Flow Simulator lacks eight of the blocks found in GPSS/360 and includes two that are not, namely, RANDOM and SNAP. The variable field arguments for the 36 blocks common to GPSS/360 and Flow Simulator are the same for both versions in virtually every instance. Table A-2 indicates which blocks are included in Flow Simulator.

GPSS III is a "proper subset" of GPSS/360 as far as its blocks and their legal entries are concerned. Thus all 36 of the GPSS III blocks are also found in GPSS/360, and all of the variable field entries allowed in GPSS III are legal in GPSS/360. Table A-2 shows which block types are included in GPSS III, and it notes the main differences between GPSS III and GPSS/360 with respect to allowable subfield entries.

TABLE A-1. GPSS/360 BLOCKS

Block Type (Entity With Which It Is Associated)		Variable Field Arguments			Remarks
		Subfield and Description	Legal Entries	①	
ADVANCE (xacts)	A	Mean	②	O	
	B	Modifier or spread	②	O	
ALTER (groups)	A	Group address	②	M	Not covered in this book
	B	Count	② or ALL	M	
	C	Attribute	Pn or PR	M	
	D	Argument	②	M	
	E	Attribute	Pn or PR	M	
	F	Argument	②	O	
	G	Next block	Block address	O	
ASSEMBLE (xacts)	A	Number of xacts to be assembled	②	M	
ASSIGN (xacts)	A	Parameter number	②	M	Field A entry may be followed by + or −
	B	Value assigned to param.	②	M	
	C	Function modifier	FNj	O	
BUFFER (xacts)		*none*			
CHANGE (blocks)	A	"From" block number	②	M	Not covered in this book
	B	"To" block number	②	M	
COUNT ③ (xacts)	A	Parameter number	②	M	Modifies a xact parameter but counts other entities
	B	Lower limit	②	M	
	C	Upper limit	②	M	
	D	Matching argument	②	O	
	E	SNA mnemonic to be counted	Mnemonic	M	
DEPART (facilities)	A	Queue address	②	M	
	B	Number of units	②	O	
ENTER (storages)	A	Storage address	②	M	
	B	Number of units	②	O	
EXAMINE (groups)	A	Group address	②	M	Not covered in this book
	B	Numeric quantity	②	O	
	C	Alternate exit	Block address	M	
EXECUTE (blocks)	A	Block to execute	Block address	M	Not covered in this book
GATE ③ (equipment)	A	Equipment or block address	②	M	Also pertains to xacts (if auxiliary operator is M or NM)
	B	Next block if condition is false	Block address	O	

Block Type (Entity With Which It Is Associated)	Variable Field Arguments			Remarks
	Subfield and Description	Legal Entries	①	
GATHER (xacts)	A Number of xacts to be gathered	②	M	
GENERATE (xacts)	A Mean intercreation interval B Modifier or spread C Offset interval D Creation limit E Priority F Number of parameters G Parameter type	Kn, FNj, Vj, Xj, or XHj F or H	O O O O O O O	
HELP (not applicable)	A Label of routine B . . Displacements . G	Symbolic label ② 	M . M .	Not covered in this book. Used to call non-GPSS subroutines during run
INDEX (xacts)	A Parameter number B Number to be added	② ②	M M	
JOIN (groups)	A Group address B Numeric quantity	② ②	M O	Not covered in this book
LEAVE (storages)	A Storage address B Number of units	② ②	M O	
LINK (user chains)	A User chain address B Ordering of chain C Alternate exit	② LIFO, FIFO, Pj Block address	M M O	
LOGIC③ (logic switches)	A Logic switch address	②	M	Auxiliary operator is R, S, or I.
LOOP (xacts)	A Parameter number B Next block	② Block address	M M	
MARK (xacts)	A Parameter number	②	O	
MATCH (xacts)	A Conjugate MATCH block	Block address	M	
MSAVEVALUE (matrix savevalues)	A Matrix address B Row number C Column number D Value E Word type	② ② ② ② H	M M M M O	Field A entry may be followed by + or −

TABLE A-1 continued

Block Type (Entity With Which It Is Associated)	Variable Field Arguments				Remarks
	Subfield and Description		Legal Entries	(1)	
PREEMPT (*facilities*)	A	Facility address	(2)	M	
	B	Priority mode specification	PR	O	
	C	Block for preempted xact	Block address	O	
	D	Parameter number	(2)	O	
	E	Removal indicator	RE	O	
PRINT (*not applicable*)	A	Lower limit	(2)	O	
	B	Upper limit	(2)	O	
	C	Entity type	Entity mnemonic	M	
	D	Paging indicator	Alphameric character	O	
PRIORITY (*xacts*)	A	Priority	(2)	M	
	B	Buffer option	BUFFER	O	
QUEUE (*queues*)	A	Queue address	(2)	M	
	B	Number of units	(2)	O	
RELEASE (*facilities*)	A	Facility address	(2)	M	
REMOVE (*groups*)	A	Group address	(2)	M	Not covered in this book
	B	Count	(2), ALL	O	
	C	Numeric quantity	(2)	O	
	D	Xact attribute	Pj, PR	O	
	E	Matching value	(2)	O	
	F	Alternate exit	Block address	O	
RETURN (*facilities*)	A	Facility address	(2)	M	
SAVEVALUE (*savevalues*)	A	Savevalue address	(2)	M	Field A entry may be followed by + or −
	B	Numeric quantity	(2)	M	
	C	Savevalue type	H	O	
SCAN (*groups*)	A	Group address	(2)	M	Not covered in this book
	B	Xact attribute	Pj, PR	M	
	C	Match argument	(2)	M	
	D	Desired attribute	Pj, PR	M	
	E	Parameter number	(2)	M	
	F	Alternate exit	Block address	O	
SEIZE (*facilities*)	A	Facility address	(2)	M	
SELECT (3) (*xacts*)	A	Parameter number	(2)	M	Modifies a xact parameter but
	B	Lower limit	(2)	M	

274

Block Type (Entity With Which It Is Associated)	Variable Field Arguments			Remarks
	Subfield and Description	Legal Entries	(1)	
SELECT, cont'd	C Upper limit	(2)	M	examines other entities
	D Matching argument	(2)	M	
	E SNA mnemonic to examine	Mnemonic	M	
	F Alternate exit	Block address	O	
SPLIT (xacts)	A Number of copies	(2)	M	
	B Next block for copies	Block address	M	
	C Parameter for serial numbering	(2)	O	
	D Number of parameters	(2)	O	
TABULATE (tables)	A Table address	(2)	M	
	B Number of units	(2)	O	
TERMINATE (xacts)	A Number of units	(2)	O	
TEST (3) (xacts)	A Argument 1	(2)	M	
	B Argument 2	(2)	M	
	C Next block if condition is false	Block address	O	
TRACE (xacts)	none			
TRANSFER (xacts)	A Selection mode	SNAs, mnemonics	M	3 of 9 selection modes covered in this book
	B Next block	(2)	O	
	C Next block	(2)	O	
	D Indexing factor	Kn	O	
UNLINK (user chains)	A User chain address	(2)	M	
	B Next block for unlinked xacts	Block address	M	
	C Unlink count	(2) ALL	O	
	D Unlinking mode	Pj, BVj, BACK	O	
	E Match argument	(2)	O	
	F Next block for entering xacts	Block address	O	
UNTRACE (xacts)	none			
WRITE (not applicable)	A Jobtape number	Mnemonic	M	Field A mnemonics, JOBTA1, JOBTA2, or JOBTA3

Notes

(1) M = mandatory entry; O = optional entry.
(2) Legal entries include: constant, n; any SNA; *n; SNA*n.
(3) An auxiliary operator must appear in the operation field.

TABLE A-2. GPS K, FLOW SIMULATOR, AND GPSS III BLOCKS IN RELATION TO GPSS/360 BLOCKS

Block Type	GPS K	Flow Simulator	GPSS III
ADVANCE	①	①	①
ALTER	①	Not included	Not included
ASSEMBLE	①	①	①
ASSIGN	①	①	①
BUFFER	①	①	①
CHANGE	①	①	①
COUNT	①	Not included	Not included
DEPART	①	①	①
ENTER	①	①	①
EXAMINE	①	Not included	Not included
EXECUTE	①	①	①
GATE	①	①	①
GATHER	①	①	①
GENERATE	①, except fields F and G not defined; see ②	①, except see ②	①, except field G not defined
HELP	Arguments unlike those in GPSS/360	Not included	Similar to GPSS/360
INDEX	①	①	①
JOIN	①	Not included	Not included
LEAVE	①	①	①
LINK	①	①	①
LOGIC	①	①	①
LOOP	①	①	①
MARK	①	①	①
MATCH	①	①	①
MSAVEVALUE	①, except field E not defined	Not included	Not included
PREEMPT	①	①	Only field A is defined
PRINT	①	①	1 , except field C not defined
PRIORITY	①	①	①
QUEUE	①	①	①
RANDOM	Not included	Unique to Flow Simulator	Not included
RELEASE	①	①	①
REMOVE	①	Not included	Not included

276

TABLE A-2 continued

Block Type	GPS K	Flow Simulator	GPSS III
RETURN	①	①	①
SAVEVALUE	①, except field C not defined	①	①, except field C not defined
SCAN	①	Not included	Not included
SEIZE	①	①	①
SELECT	①	①	Not included
SNAP	Not included	Unique to Flow Simulator	Not included
SPLIT	①, except field D not defined	①	①
TABULATE	①	①	①
TERMINATE	①	①	①
TEST	①	①	①
TRACE	①	①	①
TRANSFER	①	①	①
UNLINK	①	①	①
UNTRACE	①	①	①
WRITE	①	①	①

Notes

① Same as GPSS/360 in the respect that it has the same subfields defined. However, legal entries in a given subfield may differ in some cases as may auxiliary operators, where they are used.

② Unlike GPSS/360 and GPSS III, field C interval is added to fields A and B interval.

APPENDIX B
Entity Definition Cards

Six of the 14 GPSS entities require definition cards whenever they are included in a model:

Functions: FUNCTION, function follower.

Matrix savevalues: MATRIX.

Arithmetic variables: VARIABLE, FVARIABLE.

Boolean variables: BVARIABLE.

Storages: STORAGE.

Tables: TABLE, QTABLE.

The INITIAL card is also a definition card; it may be used if the model includes savevalues, matrix savevalues, or logic switches.

Queues, logic switches, facilities, groups, savevalues, transactions, user chains, and blocks do not require definition cards. They are implicitly defined by various block types. However, it should be noted that blocks can be regarded as being denoted by block definition cards; that is, each block card *defines* a particular block entity.

Table B-1 lists the ten GPSS definition cards in alphabetical order. Each card type is accompanied by a description of the proper location and operand field arguments as well as pertinent remarks. The latter include an indication of which versions of GPSS contain the particular definition card.

TABLE B-1. ENTITY DEFINITION CARDS

Card type	Location Field	Operand Field	Remarks
BVARIABLE	Boolean variable address	Variable definition statement	(YYNN)
FUNCTION	Function address	A Function argument B Function type designation and number of points	(YYYY)
Function Follower	*none*	*none*	(YYYY) Not divided into fields. Contains a string of coordinated pairs. See note 5.
FVARIABLE	Arithmetic variable address	Variable definition statement	(YYNN)
INITIAL	Blank	Series of savevalues, matrix savevalues, and/or logic switch reset specifications	(YYYY) No matrix savevalues in Flow Simulator. Can initialize only savevalues in GPSS III
MATRIX	Matrix savevalue address	A X or H B Number or rows C Number of columns	(YYNN) Field A always contains X in GPS K
QTABLE	Qtable address	A Queue address B Upper limit of lowest interval C Width of intervals D Number of intervals	(YYYY) Field F defined in GPS K. See note 4.
STORAGE	Storage address *or* *none*	A Storage capacity *or* Series of storage addresses and capacities	(YYYY) First mode is used to define one storage with definition card. Second mode allows multiple storage definitions on one card; it is not permitted in GPSS III
TABLE	Table address	A Table argument B Upper limit of lowest interval C Interval width D Number of intervals E Arrival rate time interval	(YYYY) Field A may contain any SNA except Kn. The SNA may be followed by a minus (−) sign. Field A may alternately contain RT or IA. See note 4.
VARIABLE	Arithmetic variable address	Variable definition statement	(YYYY)

Notes

1. The versions of GPSS in which the various definition cards are used are indicated by the parenthesized Y's and N's in the Remarks column. Y = yes and N = no. From left to right, these symbols stand for GPSS/360, GPS K, Flow Simulator, and GPSS III. Example:

   (YNYN) means "yes" for GPSS/360 and Flow Simulator, and "no" for GPS K and GPSS III.

Table B-1 *Notes* **continued**

2. The card type name appears in the operation field in every case, except for the function follower cards which have no identifying name or fields.
3. The MATRIX and INITIAL cards should be placed at the beginning of the input deck. For the most part, the other definition cards may be placed just about anywhere ahead of the START card.
4. Field F of the TABLE card is defined in GPS K. Like the F-field of the QTABLE card, it may contain a table heading. Incidentally, field E of the QTABLE card is always blank in GPS K.
5. Fixed-format function follower cards are accepted by all four versions of GPSS. Free-format cards are accepted by all versions except GPSS III.

APPENDIX C
Control Cards

A total of 53 control cards are listed in Table C-1 for the four versions of GPSS. Each card type is followed by a string of four letters in parentheses that indicate the versions in which it is used. From left to right, these letters refer to GPSS/360, GPS K, Flow Simulator, and GPSS III. For example:

REPORT (YYYN) *Yes*, the REPORT card is included in GPSS/360, GPS K, and Flow Simulator. *No*, it is not in GPSS III.

MODEL (NYNN) *No* for GPSS/360, Flow Simulator, and GPSS III. *Yes* for GPS K.

The GPSS control cards have been divided into seven categories in Table C-1. All of the cards in the first three categories (namely, *basic, output editor,* and *macros*) have been discussed in the body of this book; several of the cards in the miscellaneous category have also been covered. To provide at least a rough idea of what the remaining cards are used for, their functions are now briefly summarized.

Block Addressing

The five cards in this category afford the user a degree of control over the allocation of block addresses. The ICT (increment) card is used to add a specified number to the block number that would otherwise be assigned by the assembly program. The ORG (origin) card specifies the next block number to be assigned by the assembly program. The SYN (synonymous) card equates one block symbol with another. The ABS and ENDABS cards are used to sandwich a string of cards that incorporate only absolute (rather than symbolic) addresses.

Tape Operations

The JOBTAPE card serves two purposes, both relating to sequences of transaction data that have previously been established on tape, for example, by a WRITE block. It can be used to skip transaction files, or it can be used to ready a transaction tape for input to a specified block during a subsequent run.

The REWIND card causes a specified tape to be rewound. It is used in conjunction with the WRITE block and JOBTAPE card. The SAVE card causes a model and all of its accumulated statistics to be written onto a specified external storage device. The READ card is used to retrieve a previously saved model.

TABLE C-1.　GPSS CONTROL CARDS

Basic Control Cards		Block Addressing	
SIMULATE	(YYNY)	ICT	(YYYY)
START	(YYYY)	ORG	(YYYY)
RESET	(YYYY)	SYN	(YYYY)
CLEAR	(YYYY)	ABS	(YNNY)
JOB	(YNYY)	ENDABS	(YNNY)
MODEL	(NYNN)		
END	(YYYY)	Tape Operations	
		JOBTAPE	(YYYY)
Output Editor		REWIND	(YYYY)
REPORT	(YYYN)	SAVE	(YYYY)
OUTPUT	(YYNN)	READ	(YYYY)
EJECT	(YYNN)		
SPACE	(YYNN)	Updating of Files	
COMMENT	(YYYN)	UPDATE	(YNNN)
TITLE	(YYNN)	CREATE	(YNNN)
INCLUDE	(YYNN)	ADD	(YNNN)
FORMAT	(YYYN)	DELETE	(YNNN)
TEXT	(YYYN)	REPLACE	(YNNN)
GRAPH	(YYYN)	ENDUPDATE	(YNNN)
ORIGIN	(YYYN)	PROG	(NYNN)
X	(YYYN)		
Y	(YYYN)	Miscellaneous	
STATEMENT	(YYYN)	LIST	(YYYY)
ENDGRAPH	(YYYN)	UNLIST	(YYYY)
ENDREPORT	(NYNN)	EQU	(YNNN)
		EQUATE	(NNYN)
Macros		REALLOCATE	(YNYN)
MACRO	(YNNN)	CONTROL	(NYNY)
M	(NYNN)	HEADING	(NYNN)
STARTMACRO	(YYNN)	HELPBLOCK	(NYNN)
ENDMACRO	(YYNN)	RMULT	(YNNN)
		SEED	(NYNN)

Note

The versions of GPSS in which the various control cards are used are indicated by the Y's and N's in parentheses next to each card type. Y = yes and N = no. From left to right, these symbols stand for GPSS/360, GPS K, Flow Simulator, and GPSS III. Example:

(NYNY) means "yes" for GPS K and GPSS III, and "no" for GPSS/360 and Flow Simulator.

Updating of Files

The first six cards in this category in Table C-1 are used to implement the GPSS/360 update feature. This feature allows the user to create and update a master tape or disk and to make punched cards from it. Thus it frees him from having to handle and store large symbolic decks.

The CREATE card is placed in front of a symbolic deck that is to be written on a master tape. The other five cards types are used to modify the tape in various ways or to obtain a card image of its contents.

GPS K provides a similar update system, but it involves a different set of cards, all of which have PROG in the operation field. Each card type is denoted by a special *action director* designation in columns 1 to 4. These designations are: $INS (insert), $COR (correct), $SEL (select), $POS (position), and $DEL (delete).

Miscellaneous

Half of the cards in this category have been briefly discussed at various places in this book, but all of them are summarized here for your convenience.

If an UNLIST card is inserted into the source deck, the cards that follow it will not be reproduced in the symbolic listing. The LIST card is inserted at the point where the listing should resume. In other words, any part of the deck that is sandwiched between the UNLIST and LIST cards will not show up in the symbolic listing. The UNLIST/LIST cards have no effect on the model or the statistical output.

Both the EQU and EQUATE cards are used to equate numerical and symbolic addresses of entities. They allow the analyst to choose a numerical address for a symbolically labeled entity rather than allowing the assembly program to do so.

The REALLOCATE and CONTROL cards are used to allocate the entities section of the core among various entity types in a nonstandard way. For example, the analyst may wish to trade off some facilities and storages for extra variables in a particular model.

The HEADING card is used to specify a heading that will appear atop every page of the output for the model in which this card is included.

A HELPBLOCK card must be inserted at the beginning of any GPS K model which utilizes one or more HELP blocks. The HELPBLOCK card identifies the program segment that will be requested by the HELP block during the simulation run.

The RMULT card enables the user to alter the initial seeds for the random number sequences that correspond to RN1, RN2, . . ., RN8. It also enables him to reset or change the random number sequence at certain times during a simulation run. The SEED card is analogous to the RMULT card, but it is more limited in its functions. It allows the analyst to alter the initial seed for RN1 at the beginning of a run.

APPENDIX D
Standard Numerical Attributes

Standard numerical attributes, by definition, take on numerical values when referenced. These values are nearly always integers. The most notable exception is FNj when it appears in field B of the ADVANCE or GENERATE block or field C of the ASSIGN block.

There are a total of 45 SNAs. Forty-two of them are associated with specific entities, and the other three are system-wide attributes. Two of the 42 — namely EF and NF (a) — are unusual in that they are built in and can be specified any time with no such function having been defined (included) by the user. Incidentally, logic switches are the only one of the 14 GPSS entities that have no SNAs associated with them.

Table D-1 lists and describes all of the SNAs for all four versions of GPSS. To indicate which versions of GPSS contain each SNA, the following scheme has been used. Every SNA is followed by a string of four Y's and/or N's in parentheses. From left to right, these letters tell whether the SNA is included in GPSS/360, GPS K, Flow Simulator, and GPSS III, respectively. For example:

(YYYY) → *Yes*, the SNA is in all 4 versions of GPSS.

(YYNN) → *Yes* for GPSS/360 and GPS K.
        No for Flow Simulator and GPSS III.

TABLE D-1. STANDARD NUMERICAL ATTRIBUTES

Systemwide Attributes

Kn	(YYYY)	An integer constant. Constants may also be specified without the "K." For example, K473 = 473.
RNx	(YYYY)	Specifies initial random number seed and thereafter takes on values computed by random number generator. In GPSS/360 and Flow Simulator, x can be 1 to 8. In GPS K and GPSS III, x must be 1.
C1	(YYYY)	Relative clock time, measured from last RESET or CLEAR card.

Transaction Attributes

Pj	(YYYY)	Contents (value) of parameter j of the current xact.
PR	(YYYN)	Priority of the current xact.
M1	(YYYY)	Transit time of current xact = current clock time − mark time.
MPj	(YYYY)	Parameter transit time of current xact = current clock time − Pj.

Block Attributes

Nj	(YYYY)	Number of xacts to have entered block j during run.
Wj	(YYYY)	Wait count; that is, number of xacts currently waiting at block j.

Facility Attributes

Fj	(YYYY)	Status of facility j. Fj = 0 if facility is available; that is, not in use. Fj = 1 if facility is in use.
FRj	(YYYN)	Utilization of facility in parts per thousand. For example, if utilization is .807, then FRj = 807.
FCj	(YYYN)	Number of xacts to have "entered" facility j during run.
FTj	(YYYN)	Average time (number of clock units) each xact has "used" facility j. Fractional part is truncated.

Storage Attributes

Sj	(YYYY)	Current contents of storage j.
Rj	(YYYY)	Remaining contents of storage j; that is, number of units of space presently available, or unoccupied.
SRj	(YYYN)	Utilization of storage j in parts per thousand. For example, if utilization is .095, then SRj = 95.
SAj	(YYYN)	Average contents of storage j. Fractional part is truncated.
SMj	(YYYN)	Maximum contents of storage j at any one time.
SCj	(YYYN)	Number of xacts to have entered storage j during run.
STj	(YYYN)	Average time each xact used storage j. Fractional part is truncated.

Queue Attributes

Qj	(YYYY)	Current contents (length) of queue j.
QAj	(YYYN)	Average contents of queue j. Fractional part is truncated.
QMj	(YYYN)	Maximum contents of queue j at any one time.
QCj	(YYYN)	Number of xacts to have entered queue j during run.
QZj	(YYYN)	Number of zero entries (xacts spending zero clock time) in queue j during run.
QTj	(YYYN)	Average time each xact has spent in queue j; includes all xacts to have entered queue j. Fractional part is truncated.
QXj	(YYYN)	Average time each xact has spent in queue j, excluding zero entries. Fractional part is truncated.

Table D-1 continued

User Chain Attributes

CHj	(YYYY)	Number of xacts currently on user chain *j*.
CAj	(YYYN)	Average number of xacts on user chain *j*. Fractional part is truncated.
CMj	(YYYN)	Maximum number of xacts on user chain *j* at any one time.
CCj	(YYYN)	Number of xacts that have been linked to user chain *j* thus far.
CTj	(YYYN)	Average time each xact was on user chain *j*. Fractional part is truncated.

Group Attribute

Gj	(YYNN)	Current number of members of group *j*.

Savevalue Attributes

Xj	(YYYY)	Contents (value) of fullword savevalue *j*.
XHj	(YNYN)	Contents (value) of halfword savevalue *j*.
MXj(m,n)	(YYNN)	Contents (value) of row m, column n of fullword matrix savevalue *j*.
MHj(m,n)	(YNNN)	Contents (value) of row m, column n of halfword matrix savevalue *j*.

Computational Attributes

FNj	(YYYY)	Computed value of function *j*. Fractional part is truncated except when in B-field of GENERATE or ADVANCE block or C-field of ASSIGN block.
EF	(NYNN)	Computed random value from exponential distribution whose mean is 1.
NF(a)	(NYNN)	Computed random value from normal distribution whose standard deviation is "a."
Vj	(YYYY)	Computed value of arithmetic variable *j*. Fractional part is truncated.
BVj	(YYNN)	Computed value (either 1 or 0) of boolean variable *j*.

Table Attributes

TBj	(YYYY)	Mean value (argument) of table *j*.
TCj	(YYYN)	Number of entries in table *j*.
TDj	(YYYN)	Standard deviation of table *j*.

Note

The versions of GPSS in which the various standard numerical attributes are used are indicated by the Y's and N's in parentheses accompanying each SNA. Y = yes and N = no. From left to right, these symbols stand for GPSS/360, GPS K, Flow Simulator, and GPSS III. Example:

(YYYN) means "yes" for GPSS/360, GPS K, and Flow Simulator, and "no" for GPSS III.

APPENDIX E

Standard Logical Attributes and Other Auxiliary Operators

Five of the GPSS block types require an *auxiliary operator* in their operation fields following the block type designation. These blocks are COUNT, GATE, LOGIC, SELECT, and TEST.

A total of 23 different operators are involved of which 12 are classified as *standard logical attributes* (SLAs); six are classified as *conditional operators;* and the remaining five are not specially classified. The 23 auxiliary operators are listed in Table E-1, and the blocks with which they are used are indicated for all four versions of GPSS.

Standard logical attributes pertain to the status of specific equipment entities or assembly set members. If the entity in question is found to exhibit the status expressed by the SLA being tested, the SLA is true; otherwise, it is false.

Conditional operators express algebraic relationships, and they take the form of mnemonics consisting of one or two letters. The three LOGIC block operators and the two special SELECT block operators are also mnemonics whose meaning is obvious.

It should be pointed out that the ten equipment-oriented SLAs are also used as boolean variable operators, but in a slightly different form than is shown in Table E-1. As boolean variable operators they are:

FUj or Fj   FIj   SFj   SEj   LRj
FNUj   FNIj   SNFj   SNEj   LSj

TABLE E-1. STANDARD LOGICAL ATTRIBUTES AND OTHER AUXILIARY OPERATORS[a]

Mnemonic	Type of Operator	Blocks Used With	Meaning
U	SLA	COUNT, GATE, SELECT	Facility in use
NU	SLA	COUNT, GATE, SELECT	Facility not in use
I	SLA	COUNT, GATE, SELECT	Facility interrupted
NI	SLA	COUNT, GATE, SELECT	Facility not interrupted
SE	SLA	COUNT, GATE, SELECT	Storage empty
SNE	SLA	COUNT, GATE, SELECT	Storage not empty
SF	SLA	COUNT, GATE, SELECT	Storage full
SNF	SLA	COUNT, GATE, SELECT	Storage not full
LR	SLA	COUNT, GATE, SELECT	Logic switch reset
LS	SLA	COUNT, GATE, SELECT	Logic switch set
M	SLA	GATE	Match condition exists
NM	SLA	GATE	No match condition exists
L	Conditional	COUNT, SELECT, TEST	Less than
LE	Conditional	COUNT, SELECT, TEST	Less than or equal to
E	Conditional	COUNT, SELECT, TEST	Equal to
NE	Conditional	COUNT, SELECT, TEST	Not equal to
G	Conditional	COUNT, SELECT, TEST	Greater than
GE	Conditional	COUNT, SELECT, TEST	Greater than or equal to
S	Not applicable	LOGIC	Set logic switch
R	Not applicable	LOGIC	Reset logic switch
I	Not applicable	LOGIC	Invert logic switch
MAX	Not applicable	SELECT	Maximum
MIN	Not applicable	SELECT	Minimum

[a] The GATE, LOGIC, and TEST blocks are included in GPSS/360, GPS K, Flow Simulator, and GPSS III. The COUNT block is included in GPSS/360 and GPS K but not the other two versions. The SELECT block is not inluded in GPSS III, but it is in the other three versions.

Content of Standard GPSS Output

The *standard output* following a GPSS simulation run includes statistics for all of the entities in the model except transactions, logic switches, groups, functions, and variables. Thus end-of-run statistics are normally printed for the following eight entity types insofar as they are used in the model: blocks, facilities, storages, queues, user chains, savevalues, matrix savevalues, and frequency tables.

The purpose of this section is to delineate all of the statistics that appear in the standard output for each of the eight entities listed above. This section applies specifically to GPSS/360; it also applies to the other three versions, but with the following qualifications:

1. Flow Simulator and GPSS III do not provide a matrix savevalue output, since they lack this particular entity type.
2. GPS K and GPSS III do not distinguish between halfword and fullword savevalues. Also, GPS K does not distinguish between halfword and fullword matrix savevalues.
3. The array of statistics displayed for any given entity type is not always identical for all four versions. Those which are printed in GPSS/360 will be described in this section.

Before the individual outputs are described, the concept of the *cumulative time integral* will be explained since it plays such an important part in the accumulation of statistics for various entities.

Cumulative Time Integral

The cumulative time integral for a facility is easy to visualize because a facility can belong to only one transaction at a time. So the cumulative time integral is simply the total number of clock units during which the facility has been seized or preempted (i.e., occupied) during the run. These clock units are accumulated serially, and so the cumulative time integral for a facility cannot exceed the relative clock time.

The cumulative time integral for a storage *can* exceed the relative clock time since several "compartments" of the storage can be contributing simultaneously. For example, consider a storage with a capacity of three:

1. Compartment 1 is occupied during 80 out of 100 clock units.
2. Compartment 2 is occupied during 75 out of 100 clock units.
3. Compartment 3 is occupied during 60 out of 100 clock units.

The cumulative time integral would be equal to 215 when the relative clock was reading 100.

The cumulative time integral for a queue has an essentially analogous interpretation. It is the sum total of all of the clock units spent by all of the xacts in the queue. Similarly, the cumulative time integral for a user chain is the sum total of clock units amassed by all of the xacts that have been on the chain.

Statistics Included in Standard Output

The absolute and relative clock times are given first. Then come the entity statistics which will now be delineated.

Blocks

1. Block number.
2. Current count: number of xacts at block when run ends.
3. Total count: number of xacts entering block since beginning of run or since last RESET or CLEAR card.

Facilities

1. Facility address.
2. Average utilization: cumulative time integral divided by relative clock time.
3. Number of entries during run.
4. Average time per transaction; cumulative time integral divided by number of entries.
5. Number (address) of xact which is seizing facility at end of run.
6. Number (address) of xact which is preempting facility at end of run.

Storages

1. Storage address.
2. Capacity of storage.
3. Average contents: cumulative time integral divided by relative clock time.
4. Average utilization: cumulative time integral divided by product of relative clock and capacity.
5. Number of entries during run.
6. Average time per transaction: cumulative time integral divided by number of entries.
7. Current contents: number of xacts in storage when run ends.
8. Maximum contents: maximum number of xacts in storage at any time during run.

Queues

1. Queue address.
2. Maximum contents: maximum number of xacts in queue at any time during run.
3. Average contents: cumulative time integral divided by relative clock time.
4. Total entries into queue during run.
5. Zero entries: number of xacts spending zero time in queue, that is, passing through QUEUE and DEPART blocks in same clock instant.
6. Per cent zeroes: number of zero entries divided by total entries.
7. Average time per transaction: cumulative time integral divided by total entries.
8. Average time per transaction excluding zero entries: cumulative time integral divided by number of non-zero entries.
9. Number of associated Qtable, if any.
10. Current contents: number of xacts in queue when run ends.

User Chains

1. User chain address.
2. Maximum number of xacts on user chain.
3. Average contents: cumulative time integral divided by relative clock time.
4. Total entries: number of xacts placed on user chain during run.
5. Average time per transaction: cumulative time integral divided by total entries.

Savevalues

1. Savevalue location.
2. Value stored there at end of run.

Matrix Savevalues

1. Matrix savevalue address.
2. Matrix, in the form of an array with rows and columns.

Note: Fullword and halfword savevalues are listed separately; that is, all of the fullword savevalues, followed by all of the halfword savevalues. Similarly, fullword matrix savevalues are listed ahead of halfword matrix savevalues. Savevalues and matrix savevalues with zero contents do not appear in the printout.

Frequency Tables

1. Table address.
2. Number of entries during run.
3. Mean argument: sum of arguments divided by number of entries.
4. Standard deviation.
5. Sum of arguments.

6. One line for each frequency interval, with the following items appearing on each line and, themselves, forming columns:
   a. Upper limit of frequency class.
   b. Number of times the table argument fell into that frequency class.
   c. Percentage of total entries that fell into that frequency class.
   d. Cumulative percentage of total entries that fell into that frequency class or lower classes.
   e. Difference between 100% and item *d*.
   f. Multiple of mean: upper limit of frequency class divided by mean argument.
   g. Deviation from mean: upper limit of frequency class expressed as a multiple of the standard deviation from the mean argument.

Mathematical Basis for Probabilistic GPSS Functions

As explained in Section 2.3, GPSS incorporates a random number generator that produces values of RN that are uniformly distributed in the range zero to 1. To translate values of RN into random values that are distributed differently, the analyst defines an appropriate continuous numerical-valued function that has RNx as its argument. The values computed for this function may be used directly, or they may be adjusted by multiplication and/or addition to obtain the desired random numbers.

The purpose of this appendix is to explain how the three most commonly used random GPSS functions are obtained, that is, where the coordinates on the function follower cards come from. The three functions and what they do are as follows:

1. Uniform: converts values of RN to uniformly distributed values which lie in the range A to B.
2. Exponential: converts values of RN to exponentially distributed values whose mean is 1.
3. Normal: converts values of RN to normally distributed values whose mean is zero and whose standard deviation is 1.

In all three cases the user defines a *cumulative probability distribution* in order to obtain a single-valued functional relationship between RN (the independent variable) and FN (the dependent variable). Before the three cases are discussed, the significance of cumulative distributions are considered.

Cumulative Probability Distributions

A simple discrete probability distribution is shown in Figure G-1a. There is a 20% probability that $y = 2$, 70% that $y = 3$, and 10% that $y = 6$.

The distribution is shown in cumulative form in Figure G-1b. Note that 20% of the F-scale corresponds to $y = 2$, 70% to $y = 3$, and 10% to $y = 6$. The cumulative representation of the original probability distribution has two important properties that we shall make use of:

1. The curve is monotone, so that it is possible to reverse the roles of the variables, that is, let y be dependent and let F be independent.
2. The independent variable F covers the same range as RN, namely, 0 to 1.

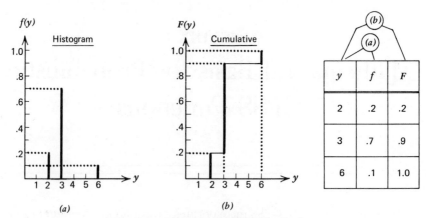

Fig. G-1. Discrete probability distribution.

The next step is to equate $F(y)$ with RN, equate y with FN, and switch the axes to obtain the Figure G-2 graph. The horizontal axis represents the independent variable and the vertical axis, the dependent variable. It is clear that, if values of RN are generated in the usual way by the GPSS random number generator, 20% of them will fall in the interval 0 to .199999, 70% of them will fall in the interval .2 to .899999, and 10% of them will fall in the interval .9 to .999999. Thus the probabilities of having FN ($= y$) equal to 2, 3, and 6 are exactly as they should be.

This example involved a *discrete* distribution, but the principle applies to *continuous* distributions also, since any probability function can be plotted as a cumulative distribution. The conversion of a probability function to a cumulative distribution was accomplished *graphically* in our simple example, but it can be done *analytically*. The analytical approach is best suited to continuous functions, and it is now briefly described.

The *probability function* is generally referred to as the *probability density function* or the *probability function of the distribution,* and it is defined as follows:

$$\int_{-\infty}^{+\infty} f(y)\ dy = 1 \tag{1}$$

This says simply that the area under a probability curve is 1. The *cumulative probability* is referred to as the *distribution function of $f(y)$* or, simply, the *distribution.*

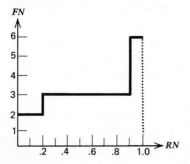

Fig. G-2. Random probability distribution.

It is obtained from $f(y)$ as follows:

$$F(y) = \int^y f(y)\ dy \tag{2}$$

Now we are ready to take the uniform, exponential, and normal probability functions and obtain cumulative distributions.

Uniform Distribution

If integers are picked at random from the range A to B, inclusive, the probability of any particular one being picked is given by the density function:

$$f(y) = \frac{1}{B - A}, \qquad \text{where} \quad A \le y \le B \tag{3}$$

The cumulative probability F is obtained by substituting the expression for the probability density into equation 2:

$$F(y) = \int_A^y \frac{1}{B - A}\ dy = \frac{y - A}{B - A} \tag{4}$$

Solving for y, we obtain

$$y = A + (B - A)F \tag{5}$$

From (4) we see that F varies between 0 and 1 since y varies from A to B. So we can substitute RN for F in equation 5 and thus make y a random variable which is a function of RN.

$$y = A + (B - A)RN \tag{6}$$

If we change the name of the dependent variable from y to FN, we obtain the desired cumulative plot of the uniform probability distribution. The end points of the cumulative curve are specified on a function follower card, and the GPSS program interpolates between them with a straight line. (It always interpolates linearly between any two adjacent points specified on function follower cards.) Let us look at an example.

Assume that we want uniformly distributed random numbers in the range 20 to 40. In this case $A = 20$ and $B = 40$. From equation 6 we have $y = 20 + (20)RN$. This is the equation of a straight line which is the distribution

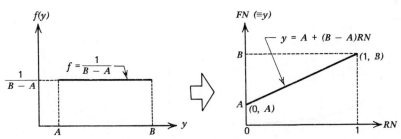

Fig. G-3. Uniform probability distribution.

for this example. In terms of (RN, y) coordinates — or (RN, FN) coordinates, if you prefer — the end points of this line are $(0, 20)$ and $(1, 40)$. These are the coordinates that would be entered on the function follower card to specify this particular distribution.

Exponential Distribution

The exponential probability density is given by

$$f(y) = \lambda e^{-\lambda y} \tag{7}$$

The cumulative probability is obtained by plugging (7) into (2) which yields

$$F(y) = \int_0^y \lambda e^{-\lambda y}\, dy = 1 - e^{-\lambda y} \tag{8}$$

Since y ranges from 0 to ∞, F varies from 0 to 1. So we can substitute RN for F and then solve equation 8 for y to obtain

$$y = -\frac{1}{\lambda}\ln(1 - RN) \tag{9}$$

It can be shown that the exponential distribution whose probability density is that given by equation 7 has a mean of $1/\lambda$. If we denote this mean by m, and if we rename y as FN, equation 9 becomes:

$$FN = -m \times \ln(1 - RN) \tag{10}$$

This is the cumulative exponential distribution, and it is plotted in Figure G-4 along with the original density function for $m = 1$.

From equation 10 it is clear that the value of FN can be obtained by finding the value of $\ln(1 - RN)$ and then multiplying it by the mean m. In other words, we can pluck values from the exponential distribution whose mean is 1, and then we can multiply by m to obtain a corresponding value from the exponential distribution whose mean is m.

The coordinates given in the function follower cards for an exponential distribution are simply the coordinates of points on the FN versus RN curve in Figure G-4. We have used 24 points to define the cumulative exponential curve in

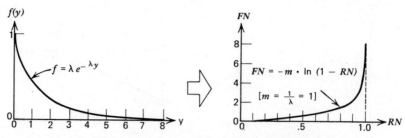

Fig. G-4. Exponential probability distribution.

several of the illustrative programs, but we could have taken any number, depending on how accurately we wished to approximate the curve.

Normal Distribution

The use of a normal distribution in a GPSS model can be described as follows. The user wants to obtain random values V from a distribution with mean μ and

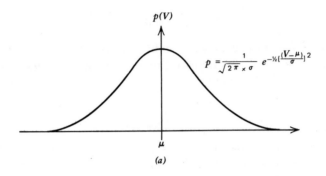

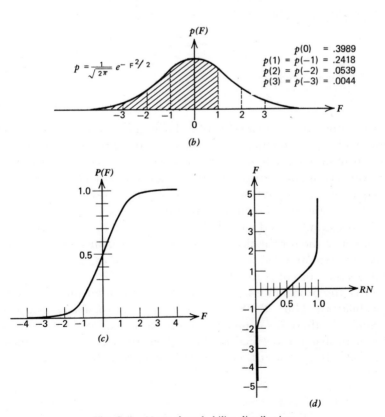

Fig. G-5. Normal probability distribution.

standard deviation σ. To do this, he defines a cumulative *standard normal distribution* from which random values F are obtained. These values of F are translated into values of V by means of a simple equation. This procedure is carried out in illustrative program 6.

Having outlined the method, let us examine the reasoning behind it. To begin with, recall that a normal distribution is completely defined if its mean and standard deviation are given. A normal probability curve is shown in Figure G-5a, and its equation (i.e., probability density) is

$$p(V) = \frac{1}{\sqrt{2\pi} \times \sigma} \times e^{-[(V-\mu)/\sigma]^2/2} \tag{11}$$

A standard normal distribution is defined as one with a mean of zero and a standard deviation of 1. Its density function is obtained by substituting these values into equation 11 to obtain

$$p(F) = \frac{1}{\sqrt{2\pi}} e^{-F^2/2} \tag{12}$$

The standard normal distribution is shown in Figure G-5b along with some values of p. (The shading will be explained soon.) Note that each unit of F is equal to 1 standard deviation since $\sigma = 1$.

Any normally distributed variable V can be translated into a value of F by using the definition of the standard normal deviate:

$$F = \frac{V - \mu}{\sigma} \tag{13}$$

Equation 13 can be rewritten as follows:

$$V = \sigma F + \mu \tag{14}$$

If we can somehow obtain a value of F (belonging to the standard normal distribution), we can use equation 14 to convert it to a value of V (belonging to the normal distribution defined by μ and σ.) Our next step then, is to translate Figure G-5b into a cumulative distribution. We shall not do it by plugging equation 12 into equation 2, although we could. Instead, we use a combination of the graphic method and some keen observations.

The total area under the Figure G-5b curve is equal to 1. The area to the left of any ordinate is the probability that F will take on a value up to the value of that ordinate. For example, the shaded area is .8438, and this is the probability that F will be less than or equal to +1.

Notice that the probabilities associated with areas under the curve are *cumulative* probabilities. Thus .8438 is the cumulative probability associated with $F = 1$. Similarly, there is a cumulative probability associated with every value of F, and that probability is equal to the area to the left of the ordinate corresponding to F. If we denote the cumulative probability by $P(F)$, some representative values are:

F	-3	-2	-1	0	1	2	3
$P(F)$	.0014	.0228	.1587	.5000	.8438	.9772	.9987

A plot of $P(F)$ is shown in Figure G-5c.

Figure G-5d is obtained by switching the axes in Figure G-5c and using RN instead of P. The F will assume values ranging from approximately -4 to $+4$ as RN varies from 0 to 1. The variable F is what we referred to as FN$NORML in program 6, and it is the dependent variable. The function follower cards for a normal distribution contain the coordinates of points on the Figure G-5d curve.

Let us recapitulate the process depicted in Figure G-5. We started off by showing that the values from a *standard* normal distribution can be converted into values belonging to *any* normal distribution by means of equation 14. Then we converted the standard normal curve into *cumulative* form to obtain a monotone increasing function. Then we reversed the dependency of the variables. At that point, the element of randomness had *not yet* been introduced. But as soon as we designated the independent variable as being random, the dependent variable *FN* followed suit.

APPENDIX H

GPSS V

The purpose of Appendix H is to describe the main differences between GPSS V and GPSS/360 consistent with the level of detail in this book. Since the material to be covered is so much broader in scope than in any of the other appendices, this one is organized along the same lines as the chapters in this book. Incidentally, the material in this section should provide a better perspective on certain aspects of GPSS/360.

GPSS V is essentially a refinement and extension of GPSS/360. It incorporates a number of new features that increase its power and flexibility but also make it more intricate in several respects. It is important to note that *GPSS V has been designed to be compatible with GPSS/360*. Almost any GPSS/360 model will run on a GPSS V system, as is.

H.1 CODING FORMAT

GPSS V allows the use of a free-form coding format that is somewhat similar to that of Flow Simulator. Of course it also accepts the fixed format of GPSS/360. The rules for the free format are as follows:

1. If there is a location field entry, it must begin in column 1. The absence of an alphameric character in column 1 indicates the absence of a location field entry.

2. The location field entry, if any, must be separated from the operation field entry by at least one blank space. If there is no location field entry, the operation field entry should begin in or to the right of column 2; it cannot begin in column 1.

3. The operation field entry must be separated from the operand field entries, if any, by at least one blank space. And the operand field entries must be separated by at least one blank space from any comment that may follow.

4. If the operation field entry includes an auxiliary operator, it may be separated from the block "name" by one blank space, or else it may immediately follow the name with no intervening blank. The auxiliary operator must be followed by at least one blank space.

5. The operand field arguments are separated by commas and include no embedded blanks, exactly as in GPSS/360.

6. There are some cards (e.g., CLEAR, TERMINATE, and MARK) which may or may not have operands specified. To enable the assembly program to distinguish between operands and comments, the following special rule applies to such cards:

   a. If no operands are specified, a comment cannot begin to the left of column 21 unless it has @ as its leftmost character.

   b. If any operands are specified, they must begin to the left of column 21.

   To avoid confusion, it may be wise to always begin operands to the left of column 21 and to never start comments to the left of column 21.

7. Comments may extend to column 72, exactly as in GPSS/360.

The free format can be used for almost all block, definition, and control cards that have location, operation, operand, and comments fields. The exception is the output editor cards which must adhere to the fixed-field format of GPSS/360.

The free format allows the programmer to utilize the coding sheet more efficiently and to improve the appearance of the source program. However, care must be taken that this greater freedom does not result in cluttered, unevenly spaced symbolic programs. Some examples of the free format are given in Figure H-1.

H.2 SAVEVALUES AND MATRIX SAVEVALUES

In addition to *halfword* and *fullword* savevalues and msavevalues (matrix savevalues), GPSS V includes *byte* and single precision *floating-point* savevalues and msavevalues. The magnitudes of numbers that can be accommodated by the four types of savevalues and msavevalues are as follows:

Byte: 127.

Halfword (2 bytes): 32,767.

Fullword (4 bytes): 2.15 billion, approximately.

Floating-point (4 bytes): 16.8 million, approximately, without loss of accuracy.

Byte, halfword, and fullword savevalues and msavevalues store integer constants. Floating-point savevalues and msavevalues store floating-point constants, to be discussed later.

The existence of four types of savevalues and msavevalues necessitates additional SNAs plus some changes in the SAVEVALUE and MSAVEVALUE blocks and also in the MATRIX and INITIAL cards. These are now described.

Standard Numerical Attributes

The following SNAs are associated with savevalues:

XBj: contents of byte savevalue j.

XHj: contents of halfword savevalue j.

Xj or XFj: contents of fullword savevalue j.

XLj: contents of floating-point savevalue j.

```
AAA6   ADVANCE  70,12  WAIT FOR 58 TO 82 SECONDS.
AAA6   ADVANCE  70,12
       ADVANCE  70,12  WAIT FOR 58 TO 82 SECONDS.
       ADVANCE  70,12
       ADVANCE  WAIT FOR ZERO TIME.
       ADVANCE  @ WAIT FOR ZERO TIME.
GATELS FN3,FALSE  @GO TO FALSE IF LOGIC SWITCH GIVEN BY FN3 IS RESET.
TRY    GATE LS  FN3,FALSE  GO TO FALSE IF LOGIC SW. GIVEN BY FN3 IS RESET.
```

Fig. H-1.   Examples of GPSS V free-form coding format.

The following SNAs are associated with msavevalues:

MBj(a,b): contents of row a, column b of byte msavevalue j.

MHj(a,b): contents of row a, column b of halfword msavevalue j.

MXj(a,b): contents of row a, column b of fullword msavevalue j.

MLj(a,b): contents of row a, column b of floating-point msavevalue j.

Savevalue Block

Field A can specify a *range of savevalue index numbers* or a *single savevalue address.* The field A entry may be followed with a minus or plus sign to denote subtraction or addition, respectively. Field B specifies the SNA to be saved, added, or subtracted. Field C specifies the savevalue type via one of the following symbols: XB, XH, X, XF, or XL. If field C is blank, the field A savevalues are assumed to be fullword. Some sample SAVEVALUE blocks will now be shown:

(a) SAVEVALUE   2−X1+,XH1

(b) SAVEVALUE   PB3,20,XH

(c) SAVEVALUE   MB10(1,1)−,MH3(X2,2),XH

When a xact enters block (a), the contents of halfword savevalue 1 are added to fullword (since field C is blank) savevalue 2 and to all of the consecutive fullword savevalues up to and including the one whose index number is equal to the contents of fullword savevalue 1.

When a xact enters block (b), the constant *20* is put into the halfword savevalue whose index number is contained in byte parameter 3 of the entering xact.[1]

When a xact enters block (c), the B-field value is subtracted from the halfword savevalue whose index number is in row 1, column 1 of byte msavevalue 10. The B-field value is the integer in a cell of halfword msavevalue 3, that cell being located in column 2 and in the row given by fullword savevalue 2.

Msavevalue Block

Fields A to E are defined for the MSAVEVALUE block, and their functions are basically the same in GPSS V as in GPSS/360. However, field A can now specify a *range of msavevalues*, field B can specify a *range of rows*, and field C can specify a *range of columns*. Field E may contain one of the following symbols: MB, MH, MX, or ML. If field E is blank, fullword msavevalues are assumed. Some sample MSAVEVALUE blocks will now be shown:

(a) MSAVEVALUE   AAA+,5,2−4,8,MB

(b) MSAVEVALUE   MH6(1,1),3,XB2,V$SAVE,MX

(c) MSAVEVALUE   3−6,1−4,1−4,MB1(X1,X2),MH

When a xact enters block (a), 8 is added to cells 2, 3, and 4 in row 5 of the byte msavevalue labeled AAA.

---

[1] GPSS V includes four types of transaction parameters—byte, halfword, fullword, and floating-point—and they are discussed in Section H.3.

When a xact enters block (b), variable SAVE is computed, and the result is put into a cell of the fullword matrix savevalue whose index number is given by the A operand. The cell is in row 3 and in the column whose number is contained in byte savevalue 2. The fullword msavevalue's index number is contained in row 1, column 1 of halfword matrix savevalue 6.

When a xact enters block (c), the value of the specified cell in byte msavevalue 1 is placed into cells 1 to 4 in rows 1 to 4 of halfword msavevalues 3, 4, 5, and 6. The specified cell in byte msavevalue 1 has its row given by fullword savevalue 1 and its column given by fullword savevalue 2.

Matrix and Initial Cards

These definition cards are the same in GPSS V as in GPSS/360 except that:

1. The legal A-field operands for the MATRIX card are MB, MH, MF, and ML rather than H and F.
2. The new SNAs (given earlier) must be used to denote savevalues and msavevalues on the INITIAL card.

H.3   TRANSACTION PARAMETERS

In GPSS/360, a transaction may have 0 to 100 halfword parameters or 0 to 100 fullword parameters. Its parameters are *all of the same type*, that is, it can never have some halfword and some fullword parameters. So if you specify a parameter number, there is no ambiguity with regard to type.

The situation is not so simple in GPSS V because four types of parameters (byte, halfword, fullword, and floating-point) are defined, and a given transaction may possess up to 255 of each. The four parameter types have the same capacities as given earlier for the corresponding savevalue types.

The availability of four types of parameters enables the analyst to utilize the core capacity more efficiently by specifying parameters whose sizes more closely approximate those of the constants being stored. The ability to utilize as many as 1020 parameters per xact can be quite useful in certain situations. And the provisions for storing floating-point numbers can improve the accuracy of certain computations.

The fact that a given transaction may have more than one type of parameter associated with it introduces a number of minor complications not found in GPSS/360. It is not enough to specify "parameter j"; you must specify the *type* as well as the *number*. The major ramifications of the expanded parameter provisions are now discussed.

Standard Numerical Attributes

There are four transaction-oriented SNAs in GPSS/360: M1, PR, Pj, and MPj. The first two are unchanged in GPSS V, but Pj and MPj are replaced by SNAs that denote the type of parameter in addition to its number. Pj is replaced by:

PBj: contents of byte parameter j.

PHj: contents of halfword parameter j.

PFj: contents of fullword parameter j.

PLj: contents of floating-point parameter j.

The mark time can be stored in a halfword or fullword parameter but not in a byte or floating-point parameter. Thus the suffix "PH" or "PF" is appended to MPj in GPSS V; that is, MPjPH and MPjPF are used instead of MPj.

The GPSS V simulator will accept MPj and Pj since it is designed to execute GPSS/360 as well as GPSS V models. Since a GPSS/360 xact always has all of its parameters of the same type, there can be no question of which one is meant by MPj or Pj.

GENERATE Block

Fields A to E are the same in GPSS V as in GPSS/360. But fields F to I are devoted to the specification of parameters in GPSS V whereas fields F and G serve this purpose in GPSS/360. The following rules apply to subfields F to I in GPSS V:

1. If all four fields are blank, the GPSS program assigns 12 halfword parameters to each xact created by that GENERATE block.
2. If a zero is entered in field F, the GPSS program assigns no parameters to the xacts created by that GENERATE block.
3. The parameter types can be specified in any order by coding the following symbols in fields F to I:

   nPB: n byte parameters.

   nPH: n halfword parameters.

   nPF: n fullword parameters.

   nPL: n floating-point parameters.

   The number of parameters, n, may range from 0 to 255.
4. The first blank entry encountered in fields F to I terminates the search for parameter operands. For example, if field G is blank, the field H and I entries (if any) are ignored.

The use of the GENERATE block to assign parameters to newly created transactions can be better appreciated with the aid of some examples:

(a) GENERATE   20,,,,,,50PF,25PL

(b) GENERATE   X4,,,,,10PB,255PF,120PH

(c) GENERATE   418,FN1,,,,30PL,,100PH

In example (a), 12 halfword parameters will be allocated to each xact because field F is blank which causes the field G and H entries to be ignored.

In example (b), 10 byte, 255 fullword, and 120 halfword parameters will be allocated to each transaction.

In example (c), 30 floating-point parameters will be allocated to each xact. The field H entry is ignored.

ASSIGN Block

Since a transaction may have up to four types of parameters and up to 255 of each, the procedure for assigning values to them is a bit more involved than in GPSS/360. The ASSIGN block D-field is used to specify the type of parameter, and the A-field may be used to specify a range of parameter numbers. (In GPSS/360, the D-field is not defined for the ASSIGN block, and the A operand may pertain to only one parameter.)

To specify a range of parameters, an entry of the form "i–j" is used, where i and j are the numbers of parameters, and j is greater than i. Thus the argument "6–8" would denote parameters 6, 7, and 8.

The field B and C entries are the same in GPSS V as in GPSS/360. Field B specifies the value to replace, be added to, or be subtracted from the field A parameters. Field C can be used to specify the address of a function modifier.

Field D is used to specify the parameter type that is associated with the field A entry. PB, PH, PF, and PL are the legal field D entries. If field C is not used to specify a function address, it can be used (instead of field D) to specify the parameter type. No parameter type need be specified as long as every xact to enter the ASSIGN block has only byte parameters, only halfword parameters, or only fullword parameters.

The use of the ASSIGN block can be clarified with some examples:

(a) ASSIGN   X1–,X2,,PH
(b) ASSIGN   X1–,X2,PH
(c) ASSIGN   PB2–XB1+,20,1,PH
(d) ASSIGN   10,V$CONVT

ASSIGN block (a) will subtract the value of fullword savevalue 2 from a halfword parameter of the entering xact. The number of this halfword parameter is contained in fullword savevalue 1. ASSIGN block (b) operates in exactly the same way as block (a).

ASSIGN block (c) will add the field B/C value to the range of halfword parameters specified in field A. The lower limit is given by the contents of byte parameter 2 of the entering xact, and the upper limit is given by the contents of byte savevalue 1. (If XB1 is not bigger than PB2, an error results.) The product of 20 and a value of function 1 is added to the halfword parameters in the specified range.

Every xact that enters ASSIGN block (d) must have all of its parameters of the same type—byte, halfword, or fullword. The variable labeled CONVT computes a value that is stored in parameter 10 of the entering xact.

Suffixes

In addition to the A-field operand of the ASSIGN block, there are 24 other block subfields which denote parameter numbers or numbers of parameters:

ALTER	C and E	MARK	A
COUNT	A	PREEMPT	D
FUNAVAIL	C	REMOVE	D
GENERATE	F, G, H, and I	SCAN	B, D, and E
INDEX	A	SELECT	A
LINK	B	SPLIT	C, D, E, F, and G
LOOP	A	UNLINK	D

You will note that the FUNAVAIL block is new; it is discussed later.

With the ASSIGN block, the parameter *number* is entered in field A and the parameter *type* in field D (or C). But for the cases listed above, the parameter number and type are *both indicated in the same subfield.* This is accomplished by specifying the parameter number and appending to it a suffix that denotes its type. Let us consider an example to see how this works.

The entry in field A of the LOOP block specifies a particular parameter associated with the entering xact. Since the entering xact may possess several types of parameters, it is necessary to specify both the type and the number of the parameter. To specify byte parameter 20, we would code 20PB in field A. Halfword parameter 100 would be denoted by 100PH. These entries are quite straightforward; they are constants with suffixes. But what if we wished to specify the halfword parameter whose number is given by fullword parameter 4? This would be denoted by PF4PH. Similarly, X1PB stands for the byte parameter whose number is contained in fullword savevalue 1.

The use of suffixes is not really difficult, though it may lead to some tricky looking expressions. You will have no difficulty if you keep in mind that the suffix tells which *type* of parameter is involved, and the symbols to its left give the *number of the parameter* or the *number of parameters.* (More about this soon.)

We know what X1PB (or XF1PB) stands for, if used in the LOOP block A-field. But what if the parameter number were stored in the fullword savevalue labeled "STORE" instead of the savevalue labeled "1"? Then the field A entry would be XF$STORE$PB. This denotes the byte parameter whose number is given by fullword savevalue STORE. Note that the suffix must be preceded by a dollar sign ($) if the SNA index is symbolic.

The use of suffixes is further illustrated in the next section. You will see that field C of the SPLIT block specifies the number of a parameter while fields D to G each specify a number of parameters.

SPLIT Block

The SPLIT block, like the GENERATE block, has provisions for specifying how many parameters of each type will be associated with newly created transactions. These provisions involve subfields D to G, and they involve the use of suffixes. Field C also involves the use of suffixes.

Field A specifies the number of copy xacts to be made, and field B contains the block address to which the copies are sent. Field C may be used to specify a parameter that is used for serial numbering. In GPSS V, the C-field operand consists of a parameter number with a suffix that denotes its type. PB, PH, and PF are legal suffixes; floating-point parameters cannot be used for serial numbering. The user should be certain that both the parent and copy xacts possess the parameter specified in field C.

Fields D to G are used to specify the types and quantities of parameters for copy xacts. All parameters for which the parent xact has a counterpart are assigned the same values (by the GPSS simulator) as the corresponding parent xact parameters. All other copy xact parameters contain zeroes.

Parameter types can be specified in any order in fields D to G. If none are specified, the copy xacts have the same complement of parameters as their parents. As soon as a blank subfield is encountered, the remaining ones are disregarded. Some examples are now given:

(a) SPLIT   XB7,NEXT,5PB,,50PL
(b) SPLIT   3,AAA5,PB5PH,X1PB,XH8PH,100PF
(c) SPLIT   Q23,BCD,XH$GOVRN$PB

When a xact enters block (a), the number of copy xacts created is given by byte savevalue 7. Copy xacts are sent to block NEXT. Byte parameter 5 of the parent and offspring xacts is numbered serially. Since field D is blank, field E is ignored, and all copy xacts have the same sets of parameters as their parent xacts.

When a xact enters block (b), three copy xacts are created and sent to block AAA5. The halfword parameter whose number is in byte parameter 5 is used for serial numbering. Copy xacts are allocated (1) the number of byte parameters given by fullword savevalue 1, (2) the number of halfword parameters given by halfword savevalue 8, and (3) 100 fullword parameters.

When a xact enters block (c), the number of copy xacts created is equal to the current length of queue 23. Copy xacts are sent to block BCD. The byte parameter whose number is given by halfword savevalue GOVRN is used for serial numbering. Copy xacts have the same sets of parameters as their parent xacts.

H.4 INDIRECT ADDRESSING

Indirect addressing in GPSS V differs from indirect addressing in GPSS/360 in two main respects:

1. It reflects the fact that xact parameters may be byte, halfword, fullword, or floating-point.
2. It has been expanded to include expressions of the form $SNA*SNAj$.

Before we discuss indirect addressing in GPSS V, we briefly review it in GPSS/360.

GPSS/360

Indirect addressing can be used to specify the entity index number in a block subfield. For this purpose, the following expressions are equivalent: *n, K*n, and Pn. All of them denote the (integer) value stored in parameter n of the current xact. For example, the A-field entries in the following blocks all stand for the facility whose index number is in parameter 9:

```
SEIZE     *9
SEIZE     K*9
SEIZE     P9
```

Indirect addressing can also be used to supply an entity index number for a SNA. This mode of usage is signified by SNA*n. The meaning of this representation is best explained with some examples:

FN*6   The value of the function whose index number is given by parameter 6 of the current xact.

P*5   The value stored in the parameter whose number is stored in parameter 5, both parameters pertaining to the current xact.

GPSS/360 does not allow the number following the asterisk to be expressed as a SNA; it must be an integer constant which denotes a parameter number. Thus an expression such as Q*X1 (the length of the queue whose index number is stored in savevalue 1) is illegal in GPSS/360.

GPSS V

GPSS V does not utilize block arguments of the form *n or K*n; only the form Pn has been retained—that is, the GPSS V *equivalent* of Pn is used. In other words, *PBn, PHn,* or *PFn* should be used in GPSS V in those instances where *n, K*n, or Pn would be used in GPSS/360. This is illustrated by the following examples:

	GPSS V	GPSS/360 Equivalent
SEIZE	PH3	P3, *3, or K*3
ADVANCE	PF10	P10, *10, or K*10
QUEUE	PH15	P15, *15, or K*15

As stated earlier, GPSS/360 allows you to obtain the entity index number for a SNA from parameter n, this form of indirect addressing being signified by SNA*n. GPSS V offers an extended capability: you may specify an SNA index number via any SNA, not just a parameter. This mode of indirect addressing is signified by SNA*SNAj, and it is now illustrated with some examples:

X*PH10   Contents of the fullword savevalue whose index number is in halfword parameter 10. Nearest GPSS/360 equivalent is X*10.

TB*PB25   Mean value of the table whose index number is in byte parameter 25. Nearest GPSS/360 equivalent is TB*25.

SA*XB$HOLD   Average contents of the storage whose index number is in byte savevalue HOLD.   No equivalent in GPSS/360.

V*MX1(1,2)   Value of the variable whose index number is in row 1, column 2 of fullword msavevalue 1.   No equivalent in GPSS/360.

There are some restrictions on which SNAs may be "asterisked" together under certain circumstances.   These restrictions are not detailed here.

H.5   FLOATING-POINT CONSTANTS

To appreciate the significance of floating-point constants in GPSS, you should first be familiar with (1) the role of constants in GPSS and (2) what is meant by a "floating-point" number.   The ensuing discussion is organized on this basis.

GPSS Constants

A constant in a GPSS model may be "visible" in the sense that it appears in the symbolic program as a block or definition card operand.   Or else it may be computed during the run and stored in a parameter, savevalue, or msavevalue.

Positive or negative constants may be stored, but only positive constants may appear as block arguments.   Negative constants can be introduced indirectly via INITIAL or VARIABLE cards.   For example, we could place −50 into byte savevalue 5 in the following ways:

```
INITIAL          XB5,−50
```

or

```
SAVEVALUE        5,V1,XB
1 VARIABLE       (−1)(50)
```

Only integer constants can be stored in parameters, savevalues, and msavevalues in GPSS/360.   Thus the user may not assign decimal numbers to these entities, and the noninteger results of floating-point variables and functions are truncated before being stored.

Floating-Point Numbers

In computing language jargon, a *fixed-point* number is an ordinary decimal number which is called an *integer* if it contains no decimal point and *real* if it does contain a decimal point.   For example:

Integer: 3,   1063,   −423   ⎫
                                              ⎬   Fixed-point
Real: 3.,   −.216,   2799.01 ⎭

A floating-point number is expressed as xEy where (1) x is a fixed-point number, (2) E is simply the uppercase letter E, and (3) y is an integer which denotes the power of 10 by which x is multiplied.   Here are some examples:

$$6.42E2 = 642$$
$$6.42E-2 = .0642$$
$$-6.42E2 = -642$$
$$13E5 = 1300000$$
$$13.E5 = 1300000$$
$$-1432.681E-1 = -143.2681$$

Thus a floating-point number is one that is expressed as some number times a power of 10. This notation is more practical than the fixed-point form for numbers such as .0000003, 76200000000, and so on.

Role of Floating-Point Numbers in GPSS V

Decimal constants (fixed-point or floating-point) can be assigned directly to floating-point parameters via the ASSIGN block; for example:

```
ASSIGN     1,7.22,PL
ASSIGN     1,72.2E-1,PL
```

Incidentally, the INDEX block cannot be used to specify decimal constants because it applies to byte, halfword, and fullword—but not floating-point—parameters.

Floating-point constants can be assigned directly to floating-point savevalues and msavevalues via the INITIAL, SAVEVALUE, and MSAVEVALUE cards; for example:

```
INITIAL            XL2,-43E4/ML6(1,4-6),233.16E-2
SAVEVALUE          10,4E8,XL
MSAVEVALUE         2,1,1-3,2.103E-5,ML
```

In GPSS V, the final result computed for an fvariable is not truncated if it is entered into a floating-point parameter, savevalue, or msavevalue; for example:

```
        ASSIGN      10,V$AMNT,PL
AMNT    FVARIABLE   Q4*800/TG1
```

H.6 UNAVAILABILITY OF FACILITIES AND STORAGES

In certain modeling situations it is desirable to make a facility or storage unavailable for a period of time. For example, we may be simulating a 1 week period during which a particular facility should only be available 8 hours a day. An obvious way to make it unavailable for 16 hours each day is to have a control transaction preempt it for that amount of time, release it, preempt it 8 hours later, and so on. This approach has the drawback that facility statistics are accumulated for all of the time it is utilized. The GPSS simulator does not distinguish between the time it is possessed by the control xact and the time it is possessed by other xacts. To convey a better appreciation of this, we carry our example further.

Suppose we have a facility that is utilized an average of 6 hours a day by noncontrol xacts and for 16 hours by a control xact. The GPSS simulator would consider this facility to be in use during 22 out of 24 hours which is a utilization of .916. In actuality, the facility is used during 6 of the 8 hours that it is available which is a .75 utilization.

To allow the user to make facilities unavailable without contributing to their utilization time, two new blocks have been incorporated into GPSS V: FAVAIL and FUNAVAIL. The SAVAIL and SUNAVAIL blocks have also been included so that storages can be made unavailable.

FUNAVAIL/FAVAIL Blocks

The FUNAVAIL (pronounced *eff-unavail*) block causes a single facility or range of facilities to become unavailable until such time as they are again made available by an FAVAIL (pronounced *eff-avail*) block. Although fields A to H are defined for the FUNAVAIL block, only field A need be used. The A-field operand specifies the facility or range of facilities to be made unavailable. For example:

(a) FUNAVAIL   BOOTH
(b) FUNAVAIL   6-XH14

When a xact enters block (a), the facility labeled BOOTH is made unavailable. If it were already unavailable, this block would have no effect.

When a xact enters block (b), facility 6 becomes unavailable as do all consecutively numbered facilities up to and including the one whose number is in halfword savevalue 14. If any of these facilities were already unavailable, they would be unaffected.

What happens to xacts that are seizing, preempting, or waiting for a facility at the time it becomes unavailable? The xact that is currently using the facility is temporarily interrupted. When the unavailable period is over, it resumes its hold on the facility. Xacts which had been preempted or are awaiting their turn to seize or preempt the facility are not allowed access to it. Xacts which attempt to seize or preempt the facility while it is unavailable are put on a delay chain to await its availability.

The B to H operands provide the analyst with a variety of options concerning:

1. The xact controlling the facility at the moment it became unavailable.
2. Xacts which were previously preempted and were awaiting their chance to regain the facility.
3. Xacts that had not yet captured the facility but were waiting to seize or preempt it.

These options are not described here.

The FAVAIL block has only field A defined. The A operand specifies the facility or range of facilities to be made available. When a xact enters an FAVAIL block, the specified facilities become available, and all effects previously invoked by an FUNAVAIL block are canceled.

SUNAVAIL/SAVAIL Blocks

Both the SUNAVAIL (pronounced *ess-unavail*) and SAVAIL (pronounced *ess-avail*) blocks have only field A defined. Field A specifies the address of a single storage or a range of storages.

When a xact enters an SUNAVAIL block, the specified storages are made unavailable. No xacts are allowed to enter these storages during the unavailable period. Waiting xacts and those which arrive during the unavailable period are queued up on a delay chain. If any xacts are in a storage when it becomes unavailable, they are unaffected. They may enter a LEAVE block during the unavailable period.

The unavailability of storages affects only xacts that are waiting to enter it, not those already in it. Thus a storage is used during unavailable periods by those xacts that were in it at the moment it became unavailable. The storage statistics have been expanded to show average utilization during available and unavailable periods.

When a xact enters an SAVAIL block, the specified storages are made available. Delayed xacts are permitted to enter the storages to the extent that the latter have capacity available.

GATE Block

In addition to the 12 standard logical attributes indicated in Table E-1, the GPSS V GATE block may have the following SLAs as auxiliary operators: FV, FNV, SV, and SNV. Their meanings can be amply explained by means of some examples:

(a) GATE FV   DESK
(b) GATE FNV   PB1,ALT
(c) GATE SV   XH*PH5,TRY7
(d) GATE SNV   PB10

If facility DESK is available, a xact is allowed to enter block (a) and pass to the next sequential block. If the facility is unavailable, this GATE block cannot be entered.

When a xact enters block (b), the status of the facility whose index number is given by byte parameter 1 is tested. If that facility is unavailable, the xact proceeds to the next sequential block. If the facility is available, the xact is sent to the block labeled ALT.

When a xact enters block (c), the status of the storage whose index number is in the halfword savevalue given by halfword parameter 5 is tested. If that storage is available, the xact passes to the next sequential block. If the storage is unavailable, the xact is sent to block TRY7.

If the storage whose index number is in byte parameter 10 is unavailable, a xact is allowed to enter block (d) and pass to the next sequential block. If the storage is available, the xact is blocked.

H.7   CORE ALLOCATION

GPSS V provides convenient means for specifying which entities, HELP routines, and GPSS program modules[2] should reside in core[3] during a run and which ones should reside on an auxiliary storage device.   This capability is extremely useful in several respects.   (1) It enables the analyst to construct extremely large models, that is, ones whose sizes exceed the core capacity.   (2) It allows him to reduce execution time by storing the most frequently referenced items in core while relegating lesser used portions to an auxiliary storage device.

These options are embodied in two new control cards — LOAD and AUXILIARY — and in the REALLOCATE card.   These cards are not explained in detail here, but their functions are described.

The REALLOCATE card has the same role in GPSS V as in GPSS/360 although the details of its use are not identical in the two versions.   This card is used to specify a nonstandard mix of entities within the core.   Incidentally, there are three standard configurations for GPSS V which are not described here except to mention their overall sizes: 62K, 96K, and 170K.

The LOAD card is used to specify which GPSS modules and/or user-written HELP routines (in FORTRAN or PL/I) should reside in core for the duration of the run.   This feature enables the user to reduce the execution time by keeping frequently called program segments in core rather than having to retrieve them from an auxiliary storage device (where they would normally reside) each time they are needed.   For example, a given model might contain PRINT blocks, or it may have frequent snap intervals.   In such cases, it would be worthwhile to retain the primary GPSS output module in core rather than recalling it every time a printout occurred.

GPSS is a relatively slow computational language.   In cases where a simulation model consists largely of mathematical portions, pure GPSS can be quite inefficient.   To circumvent this deficiency, the HELP block can be used to call non-GPSS routines during the execution of a model.   This capability has been enhanced in two ways in GPSS V:

1. The interface between the GPSS block diagram and user-written routines (in FORTRAN or PL/I) has been improved, that is, the HELP block works better.

2. Key HELP routines can be stored in the core along with the GPSS model by virtue of the LOAD card.

It now becomes conceivable to use a GPSS model as the framework for a simulation that consists mainly of, say, PL/I portions.   At any rate, the flexibility and applicability of GPSS are substantially enhanced.

The AUXILIARY card enables the user to specify how many of a given entity

---

[2] The entities are implicit in the user's model; the HELP routines are written by the user; the (thirteen) GPSS program modules are components of the GPSS software package.

[3] We use the term "core" to connote the primary storage (memory) of the computer's CPU although we acknowledge the fact that some computers utilize non-core type primary storage units.

should reside in core and how many on an auxiliary storage device. This feature allows him to deploy a very large model in such a way as to minimize execution time. Obviously, the most frequently referenced entities would reside in core, and the less used entities would be assigned to auxiliary storage.

H.8 SUMMARY

This section contains more than a straightforward digest of the material in Sections H.1 through H.7. It incorporates the aforesaid material into a broader summary of the differences between GPSS V and GPSS/360.

Compatibility of GPSS V and GPSS/360

First and foremost, GPSS V has been designed to be compatible with GPSS/360 models. To be specific, the GPSS V-OS software package will accept symbolic programs written in GPSS/360, versions 1 and 2.

Blocks

GPSS V includes the FAVAIL, FUNAVAIL, SAVAIL, and SUNAVAIL blocks in addition to the 44 blocks in GPSS/360. Some of those 44 blocks have additional subfields defined to allow for the new parameter and savevalue types. For instance, the GENERATE, SPLIT, and ASSIGN blocks have their rightmost operands redefined to reflect the possibility of transactions having up to four parameter types. And the SAVEVALUE and MSAVEVALUE blocks have their rightmost operands redefined in accordance with the fact that there are four types of savevalues and msavevalues.

The ASSIGN, SAVEVALUE, and MSAVEVALUE blocks have had various subfields expanded to permit a range of items to be specified rather than just a single item. Block arguments of the form $SNA*n$ have given way to the more powerful form, $SNA*SNAj$. And two dozen block arguments involve the use of suffixes to specify the parameter type.

Non-Block Cards

Remarks (asterisk) cards are the same in GPSS V as in GPSS/360. Definition cards are also basically the same except that the INITIAL card is referred to as a control card in GPSS V whereas it is counted as a definition card in GPSS/360 — a minor point.

GPSS V utilizes the 44 control cards that are listed in Table C-1 for GPSS/360. However, there are a number of differences in the operand field entries for various cards. These are not mentioned here except to note that the SIMU-LATE card can now be used to specify the maximum allowable run time in minutes. In addition to the aforementioned 44 control cards, GPSS V incorporates two new control cards: LOAD and AUXILIARY.

Entities and Chains

GPSS V introduces no new entity types. Except for having additional delay chains pertaining to facility and storage availability, GPSS V incorporates no new chains.

Attributes

GPSS V incorporates the same twelve standard logical attributes as GPSS/360. It also incorporates four new ones having to do with facility and storage availability: FV, FNV, SV, and SNV.

The majority of the standard numerical attributes in GPSS/360 are found in GPSS V. Most of the differences stem from the existence of byte and floating-point parameters, savevalues, and msavevalues in GPSS V. For the record, GPSS/360 has 43 SNAs, while GPSS V has 53.

The SNAs associated with facility, storage, queue, user chain, table, group, function, and variable entities in GPSS V are identical to those in GPSS/360. But there are some differences in the systemwide, transaction, savevalue, and msavevalue SNAs.

Kn has been deleted from GPSS V. Constants should be specified without prefixing the letter "K." Two new system numerical attributes have been added. AC1 gives the current absolute clock time, and TG1 gives the number of terminations to go.

Pj has been superceded by PBj, PHj, PFj, and PLj. MPj has been replaced by MPjPH and MPjPF.

To Xj and XHj have been added XBj, XFj, and XLj. To MHj(m,n) and MXj(m,n) have been added MBj(m,n) and MLj(m,n).

Facilities and Storages

Facilities and storages can be made unavailable during user-specified intervals of time. This feature allows the analyst to more faithfully emulate the behavior of certain entities as reflected in the output statistics.

The operation of the PREEMPT block has been altered slightly with respect to the preempted xact when the priority option is in effect. This modification is not described here, but it usually yields a more realistic representation of what happens when a facility's usage is based on priority.

Constants

GPSS V has provisions for specifying single precision floating-point constants and storing them in parameters, savevalues, and msavevalues. Integer constants can be stored in byte, halfword, or fullword parameters, savevalues, and msavevalues.

Coding Rules

GPSS V permits free-form coding of all card types that have location, operation, and variable fields except for output editor cards. It is worth noting that

IBM's GPSS V manuals (refs. 10 and 11) refer to definition and control cards as *statements* rather than cards. For example, the INITIAL and QTABLE cards are referred to as the *INITIAL* and *QTABLE statements.* The term "statement" does not conjure up as concrete an image as "card," but it is less restrictive in its connotation.

The GPSS V manuals refer to the variable subfields or arguments as *operands.* For example, we might speak of the "A operand." This is merely a matter of semantics, but it is probably best to settle upon a standard term.

Core Allocation

GPSS V has provisions that allow the user to construct huge models and to fully dictate their deployment in the core and on an auxiliary storage device. These provisions also make it possible to retain key HELP routines and GPSS program modules in core, thus reducing execution time. The improved interface between the block diagram and PL/I or FORTRAN routines greatly enhances the power and usefulness of GPSS.

References

Manuals

1. *General Purpose Simulation System/360 Introductory User's Manual,* IBM publication No. H20-0304-1, 1967.
2. *General Purpose Simulation System/360 User's Manual,* IBM publication No. H20-0326-2, 1968.
3. *General Purpose Simulator K,* Honeywell publication, File No. 123.8405.001 K, April 1969.
4. *Flow Simulator Reference Manual,* RCA publication No. 70-00-617, April 1969.
5. *Flow Simulator Information Manual,* RCA publication No. 70-35-503, October 1967.
6. *Flow Simulator,* RCA publication No. 70-05-008, October 1967.
7. *General Purpose Systems Simulator III Introduction,* IBM publication No. B20-0001-0, 1965.
8. *General Purpose Systems Simulator III User's Manual,* IBM publication No. H20-0163-1.
9. Gordon, Geoffrey, *Preliminary Manual for GPS—A General Purpose Systems Simulator,* January 1962.
10. *General Purpose Simulation System V Introductory User's Manual,* IBM publication No. SH20-0866-0, October 1971.
11. *General Purpose Simulation System V User's Manual,* IBM publication No. SH20-0851-0, October 1970.

Books, Articles, Other

1. Freeman, D. E., "Discrete Systems Simulation. A Survey and Introduction," *Simulation,* September 1966, pp. 142–148.
2. Gordon, G., *System Simulation,* Prentice-Hall, Inc., 1969.
3. Greenberger, M., "A New Methodology for Computer Simulation," *M.I.T. Preprint No. 9c-465,* October 1964.
4. Hollingdale, S. H., *Digital Simulation in Operational Research,* American Elsevier Publishing Co., Inc., 1967.
5. Kiviat, P. J., "Computer Simulation Programming Languages: Perspective and Prognosis," A technical paper, September 1967.
6. Naylor, T. H., Balintfy, J. C., Burdick, D. S., and Chu, K., *Computer Simulation Techniques,* John Wiley & Sons, Inc., 1966.
7. Punga, V., "Computer Simulation Techniques," Lecture notes from course given at Rensselaer Polytechnic Institute's Hartford Graduate Center, Fall semester, 1968–69.
8. Reitman, J., "GPSS/360-Norden, The Unbounded and Displayed Version of GPSS," Report No. 4212 R 0001, Norden Division of United Aircraft Corporation, November 1967.
9. Reitman, J., "The User of Simulation Languages—the Forgotten Man," *Proceedings of the 22nd National Conference of the ACM,* Thompson Book Co., pp. 573–579.
10. Sackman, H., *Computers, System Science, and Evolving Society,* John Wiley & Sons, Inc., 1967.
11. Teichroew and Lubin, "Computer Simulation—Discussion of the Technique and Comparison of Languages," *Communications of the ACM,* Vol. 9, No. 10, October 1966, pp. 723–741.

Index